Built to Last

BUILT
TO
LAST

Successful Habits of Visionary Companies

James C. Collins
Jerry I. Porras

HarperBusiness

A Division of HarperCollins*Publishers*

HarperCollins books may be purchased for educational, business, or sales promotional use. For information, please write: Special Markets Department, HarperCollins Publishers, Inc., 10 East 53rd Street, New York, NY 10022.

Designed by Alison Lew
Illustrations by Irving Perkins Associates, Inc.

Library of Congress Cataloging-in-Publication Data

Collins, James C. (James Charles)
    Built to last : successful habits of visionary companies / James C. Collins and Jerry I. Porras.
      p. cm.
    Includes index.
    ISBN 0-88730-671-3
    1. Success in business—United States. 2. Industrial management—United States. 3. Entrepreneurship—United States. I. Porras, Jerry I. II. Title
HF5386.C735   1994
658—dc20   94-20571

96 97 98 HC 20

To Joanne and Charlene

CONTENTS

ACKNOWLEDGMENTS

Winston Churchill once said that writing a book goes through five phases. In phase one, it is a novelty or a toy. But by phase five, it becomes a tyrant ruling your life. And just when you are about to be reconciled to your servitude, you kill the monster and fling it to the public. Well, without all the wonderful people who helped us to make this book a reality, the monster would have won—hands down.

Our friend and colleague Morten Hansen deserves special mention for his contributions to the project. Morten took a leave from his job at Boston Consulting Group to join our Stanford research team for six months as a Fulbright Scholar, during which time he played a key role in selecting and analyzing the comparison companies. After he left the project, he remained in close touch with our work—pushing us continually to unshackle ourselves from our preconceptions and pay attention to the hard evidence, even if it didn't fit with our previous views of the world. Morten is one of the most intellectually honest people we know and he never let us slide easily into the trap of seeing only what we wanted to see. As we developed our final ideas, we always asked ourselves, "Will this pass the 'Morten Standard'?"

Darryl Roberts and Jose Vamos worked as research assistants on the project for multiple years while doing their graduate studies at Stanford. Darryl did the background coding on a number of very important companies in our project, including Merck, J&J, 3M, and Philip Morris. He also played a key role in the original CEO survey to select the visionary companies and served as an excellent sounding board for testing our ideas. Jose performed a large chunk of the financial analyses that underpin many of our findings. One piece of his work involved doing income statement and balance sheet financial ratio analysis for our companies going back to the year 1915—a *huge* project that in itself lasted a full year. Both Darryl and Jose did a superb job.

We were also blessed with a number of other dedicated research assistants—mostly MBA and Ph.D. students at Stanford—who joined our team for up to a year. In particular, we wish to thank: Tom Bennett, Chidam Chidambaram, Richard Crabb, Murali Dharan, Yolanda Alindor, Kim Graf, Debra Isserlis, Debbie Knox, Arnold Lee, Kent Major, Diane Miller, Anne Robinson, Robert Silvers, Kevin Waddell, Vincent Yan, and Bill Youstra.

We received immense help from the staff at Stanford's Jackson Library, including Betty Burton, Sandra Leone, Janna Leffingwell, and Suzanne Sweeney. We are particularly thankful to research librarian Paul Reist for tracking down any number of obscure references on our companies from decades past. Carolyn Billheimer of Dialog Information Services, Inc., generously contributed her expertise and time to help us locate articles on the visionary companies. Linda Bethel, Peggy Crosby, Ellen DiNucci, Betty Gerhardt, Ellen Kitamura, Sylvia Lorton, Mark Shields, Karen Stock, and Linda Taoka all contributed their administrative talents at various points in the project. Ellen Kitamura organized the thousands of documents into nice, neat files and boxes—an effort that saved us hundreds of hours and frustration over the course of the project. Linda Taoka performed the nearly impossible task of managing our schedules so we could work on the project.

We are indebted to nearly all of the companies in our study—both visionary and comparison companies—for sending us current and archival materials on their company. Two individuals stand out for their invaluable help. Karen Lewis, of the Hewlett-Packard Company archives, spent days working with one of our research assistants to identify and explain literally hundreds of documents on the early days of HP. Without her help, we could not have possibly gained the depth of understanding about HP that proved so pivotal in our thinking. Jeff Sturchio, corporate archivist at Merck during our project, delivered historical materials by the boxload. He even managed to get original copies—on faded brittle parchment—of George Merck's first speeches that outlined the vision for Merck. To both Karen and Jeff, we cannot thank you enough.

We benefited greatly from a number of thoughtful and incisive individuals who commented on early drafts of our work. In particular, we wish to thank: Jim Adams of Stanford, Les Denend of Network General, Steve Denning of General Atlantic, Bob Haas of Levi Strauss, Bill Hannemann of Giro Sport Design, Dave Heenan of Theo Davies, Gary Hessenauer of General Electric, Bob Joss of Westpac Banking Corporation, Tom Kosnik of Stanford, Edward Leland of Stanford, Arjay Miller of Stanford, Mads Øvlisen of Novo Nordisk, Don Petersen of Ford, Peter Robertson of USC, T. J. Rodgers of Cypress Semiconductor, Jim Rosse of Freedom Communications, Ed Schein of MIT, Harold Wagner of Air Products, Dave Witherow of PC Express, Bruce Woolpert of Granite Rock, and John Young of Hewlett-Packard. Our most trusted advisers—our spouses Joanne Ernst and Charlene Porras—proofread and commented on chapters as they emerged from the laser printer. They lived with the book, helped us write it, *and* stayed married to us as we struggled through the long months of writing. Lucky we are.

Virginia Smith, our editor at HarperBusiness, worked closely with us from day one, editing and commenting on each chapter as we went along.

She gave us many helpful tips and excellent overall guidance to improve the manuscript. Just as important, she believed in the project and gave us much-needed encouragement each step along the way. We did not want to let her down.

Finally, we could not have found a better adviser, ally, and friend than our agent Peter Ginsberg of Curtis Brown, Ltd. Peter, you saw the value of our work long before we had a proposal. You fought for us. You gave us momentum. Truly, without you, it would never have turned out this well. We are eternally grateful.

PREFACE

We believe every CEO, manager, and entrepreneur in the world should read this book. So should every board member, consultant, investor, journalist, business student, and anyone else interested in the distinguishing characteristics of the world's most enduring and successful corporations. We make this bold claim not because we wrote this book, but because of what these companies have to teach.

We did something in researching and writing this book that, to our knowledge, has never been done before. We took a set of truly exceptional companies that have stood the test of the time—the average founding date being 1897—and studied them from their very beginnings, through all phases of their development to the present day; and we studied them *in comparison* to another set of good companies that had the same shot in life, but didn't attain quite the same stature. We looked at them as start-ups. We looked at them as midsize companies. We looked at them as large companies. We looked at them as they negotiated dramatic changes in the world around them—world wars, depressions, revolutionary technologies, cultural upheavals. And throughout we kept asking, "What makes the truly exceptional companies *different* from the other companies?"

We wanted to go beyond the incessant barrage of management buzzwords and fads of the day. We set out to discover the *timeless* management principles that have consistently distinguished outstanding companies. Along the way, we found that many of today's "new" or "innovative" management methods really aren't new at all. Many of today's buzzwords—employee ownership, empowerment, continuous improvement, TQM, common vision, shared values, and others—are repackaged and updated versions of practices that date back, in some cases, to the 1800s.

Yet, much of what we found surprised us—even shocked us at times. Widely held myths fell by the dozen. Traditional frameworks buckled and cracked. Midway through the project, we found ourselves disoriented, as evidence flew in the face of many of our own preconceptions and prior "knowledge." We had to unlearn before we could learn. We had to toss out old frameworks and build new ones, sometimes from the ground up. It took six years. But it was worth every minute.

As we look back on our findings, one giant realization towers above all the others: Just about *anyone* can be a key protagonist in building an extraordinary business institution. The lessons of these companies can be learned and applied by the vast majority of managers at all levels. Gone forever—at least in our eyes—is the debilitating perspective that the trajectory of a company depends on whether it is led by people ordained with rare and mysterious qualities that cannot be learned by others.

We hope you take many things from this book. We hope the hundreds of specific examples will stimulate you to immediately take action in your own organization. We hope the concepts and frameworks will embed themselves in your mind and help guide your thinking. We hope you take away pearls of wisdom that you can pass along to others. But, above all, we hope you take away confidence and inspiration that the lessons herein do not just apply to "other people." You can learn them. You can apply them. You can build a visionary company.

JCC and JIP
Stanford, California
March 1994

chapter 1 | THE BEST OF THE BEST

> As I look back on my life's work, I'm probably most proud of having helped to create a company that by virtue of its values, practices, and success has had a tremendous impact on the way companies are managed around the world. And I'm particularly proud that I'm leaving behind an ongoing organization that can live on as a role model long after I'm gone.
>
> WILLIAM R. HEWLETT, COFOUNDER, HEWLETT-PACKARD COMPANY, 1990[1]

> Our commitment must be to continue the vitality of this company—its growth in physical terms and also its growth as an institution—so that this company, this institution, will last through another 150 years. Indeed, so it will last through the ages.
>
> JOHN G. SMALE, FORMER CEO, PROCTER & GAMBLE, CELEBRATING P&G'S 150TH BIRTHDAY, 1986[2]

This is not a book about charismatic visionary leaders. It is not about visionary product concepts or visionary market insights. Nor even is it about just having a corporate vision.

This is a book about something far more important, enduring, and substantial. This is a book about **visionary companies**.

What is a visionary company? Visionary companies are premier institutions—the crown jewels—in their industries, widely admired by their peers and having a long track record of making a significant impact on the world around them. The key point is that a visionary company is an *organization*—an institution. *All* individual leaders, no matter how charismatic or visionary, eventually die; and all visionary products and services—all "great ideas"—eventually become obsolete. Indeed, entire markets can become obsolete and disappear. Yet visionary *companies* prosper over long periods of time, through multiple product life cycles and multiple generations of active leaders.

Pause for a moment and compose your own mental list of visionary companies; try to think of five to ten organizations that meet the following criteria:

- Premier institution in its industry
- Widely admired by knowledgeable businesspeople
- Made an indelible imprint on the world in which we live
- Had multiple generations of chief executives
- Been through multiple product (or service) life cycles
- Founded before 1950*

Examine your list of companies. What about them particularly impresses you? Notice any common themes? What might explain their enduring quality and prosperity? How might they be different from other companies that had the same opportunities in life, but didn't attain the same stature?

In a six-year research project, we set out to identify and systematically research the historical development of a set of visionary companies, to examine how they differed from a carefully selected control set of comparison companies, and to thereby discover the underlying factors that account for their extraordinary long-term position. This book presents the findings of our research project and their practical implications.

We wish to be clear right up front: The "comparison companies" in our study are not dog companies, nor are they entirely *un*visionary. Indeed, they are good companies, having survived in most cases as long as the visionary companies and, as you'll see, having outperformed the general stock market. But they don't quite match up to the overall stature of the visionary companies in our study. In most cases, you can think of the visionary company as the gold medalist and the comparison company as the silver or bronze medalist.

We chose the term "visionary" companies, rather than just "successful" or "enduring" companies, to reflect the fact that they have distinguished themselves as a very special and elite breed of institutions. They are *more*

---

* We used 1950 as the cutoff date in the study. You could also use a fifty-year minimum age cutoff.

than successful. They are *more* than enduring. In most cases, they are the best of the best in their industries, and have been that way for decades. Many of them have served as role models—icons, really—for the practice of management around the world. (Table 1.1 shows the companies in our study. We wish to be clear that the companies in our study are not the *only* visionary companies in existence. We will explain in a few pages how we came up with these particular companies.)

Yet as extraordinary as they are, the visionary companies do not have perfect, unblemished records. (Examine your own list of visionary companies. We suspect that most if not all of them have taken a serious tumble at least once during their history, probably multiple times.) Walt Disney faced a serious cash flow crisis in 1939 which forced it to go public; later, in the early 1980s, the company nearly ceased to exist as an independent entity as corporate raiders eyed its depressed stock price. Boeing had serious difficulties in the mid-1930s, the late 1940s, and again in the early 1970s when it laid off over sixty thousand employees. 3M began life as a failed mine and almost went out of business in the early 1900s. Hewlett-Packard faced severe

Table 1.1

The Companies in our Research Study

Visionary Company	Comparison Company
3M	Norton
American Express	Wells Fargo
Boeing	McDonnell Douglas
Citicorp	Chase Manhattan
Ford	GM
General Electric	Westinghouse
Hewlett-Packard	Texas Instruments
IBM	Burroughs
Johnson & Johnson	Bristol-Myers Squibb
Marriott	Howard Johnson
Merck	Pfizer
Motorola	Zenith
Nordstrom	Melville
Philip Morris	RJR Nabisco
Procter & Gamble	Colgate
Sony	Kenwood
Wal-Mart	Ames
Walt Disney	Columbia

cutbacks in 1945; in 1990, it watched its stock drop to a price below book value. Sony had repeated product failures during its first five years of life (1945–1950), and in the 1970s saw its Beta format lose to VHS in the battle for market dominance in VCRs. Ford posted one of the largest annual losses in American business history ($3.3 billion in three years) in the early 1980s before it began an impressive turnaround and long-needed revitalization. Citicorp (founded in 1812, the same year Napoleon marched to Moscow) languished in the late 1800s, during the 1930s Depression, and again in the late 1980s when it struggled with its global loan portfolio. IBM was nearly bankrupt in 1914, then again in 1921, and is having trouble again in the early 1990s.

Indeed, all of the visionary companies in our study faced setbacks and made mistakes at some point during their lives, and some are experiencing difficulty as we write this book. Yet—and this is a key point—visionary companies display a remarkable *resiliency*, an ability to bounce back from adversity.

As a result, visionary companies attain extraordinary *long-term* performance. Suppose you made equal $1 investments in a general-market stock fund, a comparison company stock fund, and a visionary company stock fund on January 1, 1926.[3] If you reinvested all dividends and made appropriate adjustments for when the companies became available on the Stock Exchange (we held companies at general market rates until they appeared on the market), your $1 in the general market fund would have grown to $415 on December 31, 1990—not bad. Your $1 invested in the group of comparison companies would have grown to $955—more than twice the general market. But your $1 in the visionary companies stock fund would have grown to $6,356—over six times the comparison fund and over fifteen times the general market. (Chart 1.A shows cumulative stock returns from 1926 to 1990; Chart 1.B shows the ratio of the visionary companies and comparison companies to the general market over the same period.)

But the visionary companies have done more than just generate long-term financial returns; they have woven themselves into the very fabric of society. Imagine how different the world would have looked and felt without Scotch tape or 3M Post-it notepads, the Ford Model T and Mustang, the Boeing 707 and 747, Tide detergent and Ivory soap, American Express cards and travelers checks, ATM machines pioneered on a wide scale by Citicorp, Johnson & Johnson Band-Aids and Tylenol, General Electric light bulbs and appliances, Hewlett-Packard calculators and laser printers, IBM 360 computers and Selectric typewriters, Marriott Hotels, anticholesterol Mevacor from Merck, Motorola cellular phones and paging devices, Nordstrom's impact on customer service standards, and Sony Trinitron TVs and portable Walkmans. Think of how many kids (and adults) grew up with

Chart 1.A

Cumulative Stock Returns of $1 Invested
January 1, 1926 — December 31, 1990

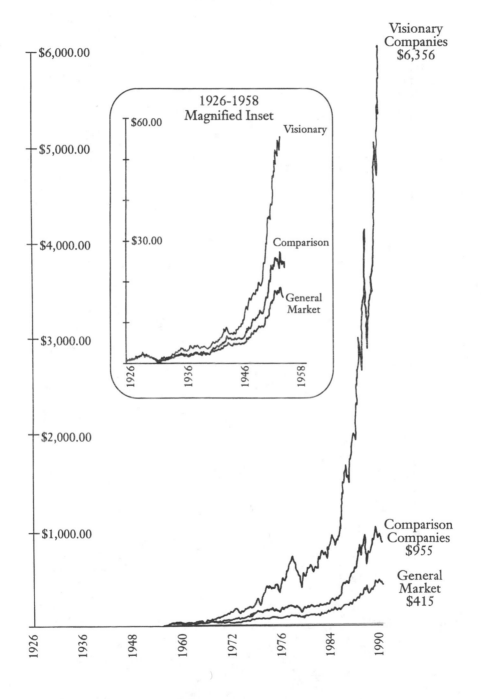

Chart 1.B

**Ratio of Cumulative Stock
Returns to General Market
1926—1990**

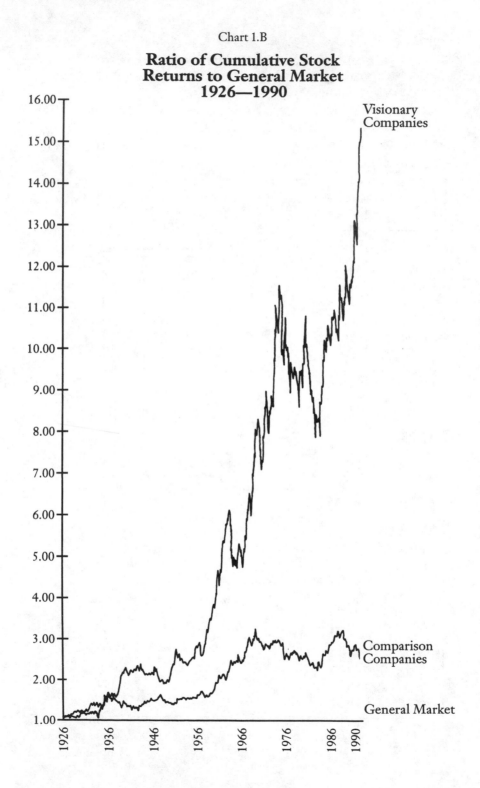

Disneyland, Mickey Mouse, Donald Duck, and Snow White. Picture an urban freeway without Marlboro cowboy billboards or rural America without Wal-Mart stores. For better or worse, these companies have made an indelible imprint on the world around them.

The exciting thing, however, is to figure out *why* these companies have separated themselves into the special category that we consider highly visionary. How did they begin? How did they manage the various difficult stages of corporate evolution from tiny start-ups to global institutions? And, once they became large, what characteristics did they share in common that distinguished them from other large companies? What can we learn from their development that might prove useful to people who would like to create, build, and maintain such companies? We invite you on a journey through the rest of this book to discover answers to these questions.

We dedicate the second half of this chapter to describing our research process. Then, beginning in Chapter 2, we present our findings, which include a number of surprising and counterintuitive discoveries. As a preview of our findings, we present here a dozen common myths that were shattered during the course of our research.

TWELVE SHATTERED MYTHS

Myth 1: It takes a great idea to start a great company.

Reality: Starting a company with a "great idea" might be a bad idea. Few of the visionary companies began life with a great idea. In fact, some began life without *any* specific idea and a few even began with outright failures. Furthermore, regardless of the founding concept, the visionary companies were significantly *less* likely to have early entrepreneurial success than the comparison companies in our study. Like the parable of the tortoise and the hare, visionary companies often get off to a slow start, but win the long race.

Myth 2: Visionary companies require great and charismatic visionary leaders.

Reality: A charismatic visionary leader is absolutely *not required* for a visionary company and, in fact, can be detrimental to a company's long-term prospects. Some of the most significant CEOs in the history of visionary companies did not fit the model of the high-profile, charismatic leader—indeed, some explicitly shied away from that model. Like the founders of the United States at the Constitutional Convention, they

concentrated more on architecting an enduring institution
than on being a great individual leader. They sought to be
clock builders, not time tellers. And they have been more
this way than CEOs at the comparison companies.

Myth 3: The most successful companies exist first and foremost to
maximize profits.

Reality: Contrary to business school doctrine, "maximizing shareholder wealth" or "profit maximization" has not been the
dominant driving force or primary objective through the
history of the visionary companies. Visionary companies
pursue a cluster of objectives, of which making money is
only one—and not necessarily the primary one. Yes, they
seek profits, but they're equally guided by a core
ideology—core values and sense of purpose beyond just
making money. Yet, paradoxically, the visionary companies
make more money than the more purely profit-driven
comparison companies.

Myth 4: Visionary companies share a common subset of "correct"
core values.

Reality: There is no "right" set of core values for being a visionary
company. Indeed, two companies can have radically different ideologies, yet both be visionary. Core values in a
visionary company don't even have to be "enlightened" or
"humanistic," although they often are. The crucial variable
is not the content of a company's ideology, but how deeply
it *believes* its ideology and how consistently it lives,
breathes, and expresses it in all that it does. Visionary
companies do not ask, "What should we value?" They ask,
"What do we *actually* value deep down to our toes?"

Myth 5: The only constant is change.

Reality: A visionary company almost religiously preserves its core
ideology—changing it seldom, if ever. Core values in a
visionary company form a rock-solid foundation and do
not drift with the trends and fashions of the day; in some
cases, the core values have remained intact for well over
one hundred years. And the basic purpose of a visionary
company—its reason for being—can serve as a guiding
beacon for centuries, like an enduring star on the horizon.

Yet, while keeping their core ideologies tightly fixed, visionary companies display a powerful drive for progress that enables them to change and adapt without compromising their cherished core ideals.

Myth 6:   Blue-chip companies play it safe.

Reality: Visionary companies may appear straitlaced and conservative to outsiders, but they're not afraid to make bold commitments to "Big Hairy Audacious Goals" (BHAGs). Like climbing a big mountain or going to the moon, a BHAG may be daunting and perhaps risky, but the adventure, excitement, and challenge of it grabs people in the gut, gets their juices flowing, and creates immense forward momentum. Visionary companies have judiciously used BHAGs to stimulate progress and blast past the comparison companies at crucial points in history.

Myth 7.   Visionary companies are great places to work, for everyone.

Reality: Only those who "fit" extremely well with the core ideology and demanding standards of a visionary company will find it a great place to work. If you go to work at a visionary company, you will either fit and flourish—probably couldn't be happier—or you will likely be expunged like a virus. It's binary. There's no middle ground. It's almost cult-like. Visionary companies are so clear about what they stand for and what they're trying to achieve that they simply don't have room for those unwilling or unable to fit their exacting standards.

Myth 8:   Highly successful companies make their best moves by brilliant and complex strategic planning.

Reality: Visionary companies make some of their best moves by experimentation, trial and error, opportunism, and—quite literally—accident. What looks *in retrospect* like brilliant foresight and preplanning was often the result of "Let's just try a lot of stuff and keep what works." In this sense, visionary companies mimic the biological evolution of species. We found the concepts in Charles Darwin's *Origin of Species* to be more helpful for replicating the success of certain visionary companies than any textbook on corporate strategic planning.

Myth 9:   Companies should hire outside CEOs to stimulate funda-
            mental change.

Reality: In seventeen *hundred* years of combined life spans across the
            visionary companies, we found only *four* individual inci-
            dents of going outside for a CEO—and those in only two
            companies. Home-grown management rules at the vision-
            ary companies to a far greater degree than at the compari-
            son companies (by a factor of six). Time and again, they
            have dashed to bits the conventional wisdom that signifi-
            cant change and fresh ideas cannot come from insiders.

Myth 10:   The most successful companies focus primarily on beating
            the competition.

Reality: Visionary companies <u>focus primarily on beating them-
            selves.</u> Success and beating competitors comes to the vi-
            sionary companies not so much as the end goal, but as a
            residual *result* of relentlessly asking the question "How can
            we improve ourselves to do better tomorrow than we did
            today?" And they have asked this question day in and day
            out—as a disciplined way of life—in some cases for over
            150 years. No matter how much they achieve—no matter
            how far in front of their competitors they pull—they never
            think they've done "good enough."

Myth 11:   You can't have your cake and eat it too.

Reality: Visionary companies do not brutalize themselves with the
            "Tyranny of the OR"—the purely rational view that says
            you can have either A *OR* B, but not both. They reject
            having to make a choice between stability OR progress;
            cult-like cultures OR individual autonomy; home-grown
            managers OR fundamental change; conservative practices
            OR Big Hairy Audacious Goals; making money OR living
            according to values and purpose. Instead, they embrace the
            "Genius of the AND"—the paradoxical view that allows
            them to pursue both A *AND* B at the same time.

Myth 12:   Companies become visionary primarily <u>through "vision
            statements."</u>

Reality: The visionary companies attained their stature not so
            much because they made visionary pronouncements (al-
            though they often did make such pronouncements). Nor

did they rise to greatness because they wrote one of the vision, values, purpose, mission, or aspiration statements that have become popular in management today (although they wrote such statements more frequently than the comparison companies and decades before it became fashionable). Creating a statement can be a helpful *step* in building a visionary company, but it is only one of thousands of steps in a never-ending process of expressing the fundamental characteristics we identified across the visionary companies.

THE RESEARCH PROJECT

Origins: Who Is the Visionary Leader at 3M?

In 1988, we began to wrestle with the question of corporate "vision": Does it actually exist? If so, what exactly is it? Where does it come from? How do organizations end up doing visionary things? Vision had received much attention in the popular press and among management thinkers, yet we felt highly unsatisfied by what we read.

For one thing, the term "vision" had been tossed around by so many people and used in so many different ways that it created more confusion than clarification. Some viewed vision as about having a crystal-ball picture of the future marketplace. Others thought in terms of a technology or product vision, such as the Macintosh computer. Still others emphasized a vision of the organization—values, purpose, mission, goals, images of an idealized workplace. Talk about a muddled mess! No wonder so many hard-nosed practical businesspeople were highly skeptical of the whole notion of vision; it just seemed so—well—fuzzy, unclear, and impractical.

Furthermore—and what bothered us most—the image of something called a "visionary leader" (often charismatic and high-profile) lurked in the background of nearly all discussions and writings about vision. But, we asked ourselves, if "visionary leadership" is so critical to the development of extraordinary organizations, *then who is the charismatic visionary leader of 3M?* We didn't know. Do you? 3M has been a widely admired—almost revered—company for decades, yet few people can even name its current chief executive, or his predecessor, or even his predecessor, and so on.

3M is a company that many would describe as visionary, yet doesn't seem to have (or have had in its past) an archetypal, high-profile, charismatic visionary leader. We checked into the history of 3M and learned that it had been founded in 1902. So, even if it had a visionary leader in its past, that person would almost certainly have died a long time ago. (In fact, as of 1994, 3M had ten generations of chief executives.) It also became clear that 3M could not possibly trace its success primarily to a visionary product concept, market insight, or lucky break; no such product or lucky break could create nearly one hundred years of corporate performance.

It occurred to us that 3M represented something beyond visionary leadership, visionary products, visionary market insights, or inspiring vision statements. 3M, we decided, could best be described as a visionary *company*.

And thus we began the extensive research project on which this book is based. In a nutshell, we had two primary objectives for the research project:

1. To identify the underlying characteristics and dynamics common to highly visionary companies (and that distinguish them from other companies) and to translate these findings into a useful conceptual framework.
2. To effectively communicate these findings and concepts so that they influence the practice of management and prove beneficial to people who want to help create, build, and maintain visionary companies.

Step 1: What Companies Should We Study?

Stop and think for a minute. Suppose you wanted to create a list of visionary companies to study. No prior list exists in any literature; the concept of a "visionary company" is new and untested. How might you go about creating a list of companies?

We wrestled with this question and concluded that we, as individuals, should not construct the list. We might have biases that would excessively favor one company over another. We might not know the corporate landscape well enough. We might be partial to California-based or technology-based companies because we're more familiar with them.

To minimize individual bias, therefore, we elected to survey chief executive officers at leading corporations from a wide range of sizes, industries, types, and geographical locations and ask them to help us create the list of visionary companies to study. We believed that CEOs, given their unique vantage point as practitioners atop leading corporations, would have the most discerning and seasoned judgment in selecting companies. We trusted CEO input more than input from academics because CEOs are in constant touch with the practical challenges and realities of building and managing companies. Leading CEOs, we reasoned, would have excellent working knowledge of the companies in their industry and related industries. We also reasoned that the effective chief executive keeps close tabs on the companies that his or her company works with and competes against.

In August 1989, we surveyed a carefully selected representative sample of seven hundred CEOs from the following populations:

- *Fortune* 500 industrial companies
- *Fortune* 500 service companies
- *Inc.* 500 private companies
- *Inc.* 100 public companies.

To ensure a representative sample across industries, we selected CEOs from every industry classification in the *Fortune* 500 listings, both service and industrial (250 from each). The *Inc.* listings ensured adequate representation from smaller companies, both public and private (we surveyed a representative sample of 200 companies across these two populations). We asked each CEO to nominate up to five companies that he or she perceived to be "highly visionary." We specifically asked that the CEOs *personally* respond and to not delegate the response to someone else in their organization.

We received a 23.5 percent response rate from the CEOs (165 cards) with an average of 3.2 companies listed per card. We performed a series of statistical analyses to confirm that we received a representative sample from all target populations.[4] In other words, no one group of CEOs dominated the final survey data; we had statistically representative input from all parts of the country and from all types and sizes of companies.[5]

Using the survey data, we created a list of visionary companies to study by identifying the twenty organizations most frequently mentioned by the CEOs. We then eliminated from the list companies founded after 1950; we reasoned that any company founded before 1950 had proven itself to be more than the beneficiary of a single leader or a single great idea. By rigorously applying the pre-1950 criteria, we culled the final list to eighteen visionary companies to study. The youngest companies in our study were founded in 1945 and the oldest was founded in 1812. At the time of our survey, the companies in our study averaged ninety-two years of age, with an average founding date of 1897 and a median founding date of 1902. (See Table 1.2 for founding dates.)

Step 2: Avoiding the "Discover Buildings" Trap (A Comparison Group)

We could have simply put the visionary companies off in a corral by themselves, studied them, and asked the question "What common characteristics do we see across these companies?" But there is a fundamental flaw in merely pursuing a "common characteristic" analysis.

What would we find if we just looked for common characteristics? Just to use an extreme example, we would discover that all eighteen of the

Table 1.2

Founding Dates

	1812	Citicorp
	1837	Procter & Gamble
	1847	Philip Morris
	1850	American Express
	1886	Johnson & Johnson
	1891	Merck
	1892	General Electric
	1901	Nordstrom
Median:	1902	3M
	1903	Ford
	1911	IBM
	1915	Boeing
	1923	Walt Disney
	1927	Marriott
	1928	Motorola
	1938	Hewlett-Packard
	1945	Sony
	1945	Wal-Mart

companies have buildings! That's right; we would find a perfect 100 percent correlation between being a visionary company and having buildings. We would also find a perfect 100 percent correlation between being a visionary company and having desks, and pay systems, and boards of directors, and accounting systems, and—well, you get the idea. We agree that it would be absurd to then conclude that a key factor in being a visionary company is to have buildings. Indeed, *all* companies have buildings; so discovering that 100 percent of the visionary companies have buildings tells us nothing valuable.

Please don't take our harping on this point the wrong way. We're not trying to belabor an obvious concept that's as clear and straightforward to you as it is to us. We're harping on it because the sad fact is that much business research and writing falls into the "discover buildings" trap. Suppose you study a group of successful companies and you find that they emphasize customer focus, or quality improvement, or empowerment; how do you know that you haven't merely discovered the management practice equivalent of having buildings? How do you know that you've discovered something that *distinguishes* the successful companies from other companies? You don't know. You *can't* know—not unless you have a control set, a comparison group.

The critical question is not "What's common across a group of companies?" Rather, the critical issues are: "What's essentially *different* about these companies? What *distinguishes* one set of companies from another?" We therefore concluded that we could only reach our research objectives by studying our visionary companies in contrast to other companies that had a similar start in life.

We systematically and painstakingly selected a comparison company for each visionary company (see Table 1.1 earlier in this chapter for the comparison pairs). We selected the comparison companies using the following criteria:

choosing comparison companies

- *Same founding era.* In each case, we looked for a comparison company founded in the same era as the visionary company. The comparison companies in our study had an average founding date of 1892 versus 1897 for the visionary companies.

- *Similar founding products and markets.* In each case, we looked for a comparison company that pursued similar products, services, and markets in its early days. However, the comparison company need not be in precisely the same industry later in its history; we wanted companies that *started* in the same place, but didn't necessarily end up in the same place. For example, Motorola (a visionary company) expanded far beyond consumer electronics, whereas Zenith (Motorola's comparison company) did not; we wanted to see what guided these widely divergent outcomes, even though they had very similar beginnings.

- *Fewer mentions in the CEO survey.* In each case, we looked for a comparison company that garnered substantially fewer mentions than the visionary company in the CEO survey. Since we relied heavily on the CEOs in our selection of visionary companies, we wanted to rely on the same input in selecting our comparison set.

- *Not a dog company.* We didn't want to compare the visionary companies to total failures or poor performers. We believed that a conservative comparison (that is, comparing to other good companies) would give our ultimate findings much more credibility and value. If we compared the visionary companies to a bunch of abysmal failures, we'd certainly find differences, but not helpful differences. If you compare Olympic championship teams to high school teams, you'd certainly see some differences, but would those differences be meaningful? Would they tell you anything valuable? Of course not. But if you compare Olympic gold medal teams with silver or bronze medal teams and find systematic differences, then you've got something credible and useful. *We wanted to compare gold medal teams to silver and bronze medal teams whenever possible to give real meaning to our findings.*

Gold to Bronze Comparison

Step 3: History and Evolution

We decided to undertake the daunting task of examining the companies throughout their entire histories. We didn't just ask "What attributes do these companies have *today*?" We primarily asked such questions as "How did these companies get started? How did they evolve? How did they negotiate the pitfalls of being small, cash-strapped enterprises? How did they manage the transition from start-up to established corporation? How did they handle transitions from founder to second-generation management? How did they deal with historical events such as wars and depressions? How did they handle the invention of revolutionary new technologies?"

We pursued this historical analysis for three reasons. First, we wanted to glean insights that would be valuable not only to readers in large corporations, but also to people in small to midsize companies. We have practical experience and academic knowledge across the continuum—from entrepreneurship and building small companies to planned organizational change in large corporations—and we wanted to create knowledge and tools that would prove useful from both of these perspectives.

Second, and even more important, we believed that only an evolutionary perspective could lead to understanding the fundamental dynamics behind visionary companies. To use an analogy, you can't fully understand the United States without understanding its history—the Revolutionary War, the ideals and compromises of the Constitutional Convention, the Civil War, the expansion westward, the cataclysmic national Depression of the 1930s, the influence of Jefferson, Lincoln, and Roosevelt, and many other historical factors. In our view, corporations resemble nations in that they reflect the accumulation of past events and the shaping force of underlying genetics that have roots in prior generations.

How could we possibly understand Merck today without examining the origins of its underlying philosophy laid down by George Merck in the 1920s ("Medicine is for the patient; not for the profits. The profits follow")? How could we possibly understand 3M today without examining the fact that it began life nearly bankrupt as a failed mine? How could we possibly understand General Electric under the stewardship of Jack Welch without examining GE's systematic leadership development and selection processes that trace back to the early 1900s? How could we possibly understand Johnson & Johnson's response to the Tylenol poisoning crisis in the 1980s without examining the historical roots of the J&J Credo (penned in 1943) that guided the company's response to the crisis? We couldn't.

Third, we believed our comparison analysis would be much more powerful from a historical perspective. Just looking at the visionary versus comparison companies in current time would be like merely watching the last thirty seconds of a marathon footrace. Sure, you could see who won the gold medal, but you wouldn't understand *why he* or she had won. To fully understand the outcome of a race, you have to see the entire race and the events that led up to it—to look at the various runners during their training, during their prerace preparations, during mile one, mile two, mile three, and so on. Similarly, we wanted to look back in time to find answers to such intriguing questions as:

- How did Motorola successfully move from a humble battery repair business into car radios, television, semiconductors, integrated circuits, and cellular communications, while Zenith—started at the same time with similar resources—never became a major player in anything other than TVs?
- How did Procter & Gamble continue to thrive 150 years after its founding, while most companies are lucky to survive even 15 years? And how did P&G, which began life substantially behind rival Colgate, eventually prevail as the premier institution in its industry?
- How did Hewlett-Packard Company remain healthy and vibrant after Bill Hewlett and Dave Packard stepped aside, while Texas Instruments—once a high-flying darling of Wall Street—nearly self-destructed after Pat Haggarty stepped aside?
- Why did Walt Disney Company become an American icon, surviving and prospering through hostile takeover attempts, while Columbia Pictures slowly lost ground, never became an icon, and eventually sold out to a Japanese company?
- How did Boeing emerge from obscurity in the commercial aircraft industry and unseat McDonnell Douglas as the premier commercial aircraft company in the world; what did Boeing have in the 1950s that McDonnell Douglas lacked?

UNCOVERING TIMELESS PRINCIPLES Can we legitimately draw conclusions by looking at history? Can we learn anything useful from looking at what companies did ten, thirty, fifty, or one hundred years ago? Certainly the world has changed dramatically—and will continue to change. The specific methods used by these companies in the past may not directly apply to the future. We acknowledge this. But throughout our research we kept looking for underlying, timeless, *fundamental principles* and patterns that might apply across eras. For example, the specific methods visionary companies use to "preserve the core and stimulate progress" (a key principle discussed throughout the book) will continue to evolve, but the underlying principle itself is timeless—equally valid and essential in 1850 as 1900,

1950, and 2050. Our goal has been to use the long range of corporate history to gain understanding and develop concepts and tools that will be useful in preparing organizations to be visionary in the twenty-first century and beyond.

INDEED, if we had to identify one aspect of this book that most separates it from all previous management books, we would point to the fact that we looked at companies throughout their entire life spans and in direct comparison to other companies. This proved to be the key method for calling into question powerfully entrenched myths and discerning fundamental principles that apply over long stretches of time and across a wide range of industries.

Step 4: Crates of Data, Months of Coding, and "Tortoise Hunting"

Once we'd selected our companies and decided on the historical and comparison method, we faced another difficult problem: Precisely *what* should we examine over the history of the companies? Should we examine corporate strategy? Organization structure? Management? Culture? Values? Systems? Product lines? Industry conditions? Since we didn't know ahead of time what factors would explain the enduring stature of the visionary companies, we couldn't pursue a narrow research focus; we had to gather evidence across a wide range of dimensions.

Throughout our research, we kept in mind the image of Charles Darwin taking his five-year voyage on the H.M.S. *Beagle*, exploring the Galapagos Islands, and stumbling across huge tortoises (among other species) that varied from island to island. These unexpected observations planted a seed that provoked his thinking during his ride home on the *Beagle* and during his subsequent work in England. Darwin had the opportunity to gain new insights in part because he had the good fortune of unexpected observations. He wasn't looking specifically for variations in tortoises, yet there they were—these big, waddling, weird-looking tortoises wandering around the islands and not fitting neatly into prior assumptions about species.[6] We, too, wanted to stumble into a few unexpected, weird-looking tortoises that might provoke our thinking.

Of course, we wanted to be much more systematic than just wandering around aimlessly, hoping to randomly bump into a tortoise or two. To ensure systematic and comprehensive data collection, we employed a framework based on a technique called "Organization Stream Analysis" for collecting and sorting information.[7] Using this framework, our research team gathered and tracked nine categories of information over the entire history of each company. (See Table A.1 in Appendix 3.) These categories encompassed virtually all aspects of a corporation, including organization, business strategy, products and services, technology, management, ownership structure, culture, values, policies, and the external environment. As part of this effort, we systematically analyzed annual financial statements back to the year 1915 and monthly stock returns back to the year 1926. In addition, we did an overview of general and business history in the United States from 1800 to 1990, and an overview of each industry represented by the companies in our study.

To gather information for thirty-six separate companies over an average life span of ninety-plus years, we sourced nearly a hundred books and over three thousand individual documents (articles, case studies, archive materials, corporate publications, video footage). As a conservative estimate, we reviewed over sixty thousand pages of material (the actual number is probably closer to a hundred thousand pages). The documents for this project filled three shoulder-height file cabinets, four bookshelves, and twenty megabytes of computer storage space for financial data and analyses. (Table A.2 in Appendix 3 outlines our sources.)

Step 5: Harvesting the Fruits of our Labor

Next came the most difficult task of the entire project. We distilled the nearly overwhelming amount of information (much of it qualitative) down to a few key concepts linked together in a framework—a set of conceptual hooks on which to hang and organize the rich detail and supporting evidence from our research. We looked for repeating patterns and sought to identify underlying trends and forces; we aimed to identify those concepts that would explain the historical trajectory of the visionary companies *and* would provide practical guidance to managers building their companies for the twenty-first century.

The underlying backbone of our findings comes from comparison analyses. Throughout our work, we kept coming back to the primary question "What *separates* the visionary companies from the comparison companies over the long course of history?" As you read the book, you'll find reference to tables in Appendix 3 where we methodically compared the visionary companies to the comparison companies on a given dimension.

We also combined this analytic comparison process with creative processes. We wanted to break as free as possible from the constraining dogmas of business schools and the popular management press. In particular, we sought to stimulate our thinking with ideas that had nothing, on the surface, to do with business and merged these with observations from our research. We therefore read extensively from *non*business disciplines: biology (especially evolutionary theory), genetics, psychology, social psychology, sociology, philosophy, political science, history, and cultural anthropology.

Step 6: Field Testing and Application in the Real World

Throughout the entire research project, we continually tested our findings and concepts by throwing them into the teeth of hard reality via consulting engagements and board of directors responsibilities. At the time of this writing, we have personally applied frameworks and tools based on our research at over thirty separate organizations, ranging from young companies with less than $10 million in revenue to multibillion-dollar *Fortune* 500 corporations across a wide range of industries, including those in computers, health care, pharmaceuticals, biotechnology, construction, retailing, mail order, sporting goods, electronic instruments, semiconductors, computer software, movie theater chains, environmental engineering, chemicals, and commercial banking. Working with senior management, usually at the direct request of the CEO, we were able to expose our ideas to some of the most incisive, practical, demanding, and hard-nosed people in business.

This "trial by fire" provided a valuable feedback loop that helped us to continually improve our concepts as we moved through the research. For example, during a working session at a pharmaceutical firm, an executive asked, "Are there 'right' and 'wrong' core values? In other words, does the *content* of core values count the most, or does the *authenticity and consistency* of core values—whatever the content—count the most? Is there any particular subset of core values that show up across all visionary companies?" We then returned to our research data and systematically answered these questions (see Chapter 3), thus completing the loop from research to practice and back again (see Figure 1.A). This looping process occurred many times across a wide range of issues during the five-year period of the research project and contributed greatly to this book.

LET THE EVIDENCE SPEAK

All research projects in the social sciences suffer from inherent limitations and difficulties, and ours is no exception. For one thing, we cannot perform controlled, repeatable experiments where we hold all but one critical variable constant and assess various outcomes from tweaking that variable. We would love to make petri dishes of corporations, but we can't; we have to

Figure 1.A

Feedback Loop

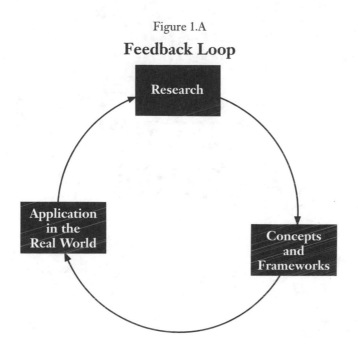

take what history gives us and make the best of it. In Appendix 1 at the end of this book, we've described a variety of concerns—and our responses to those concerns—that a critical reader might raise about our research methodology.

Nonetheless, even taking full account of those concerns, the sheer volume of information we examined combined with the continual looping process from research to theory to practice gives us confidence that our conclusions are reasonable and—perhaps most important—*helpful* to the development of outstanding organizations. We do not claim to have found Truth with a capital *T*. No one in the social sciences can claim that. But we do claim that this research has given us better understanding of organizations and better conceptual tools for building outstanding companies than we had before.

We now turn to share the findings of our work. We hope you drink deeply from this book, for the history of these companies can teach us much. But, at the same time, we hope you think critically and objectively as you read; we would rather that you thoughtfully consider and ultimately reject our findings than that you blindly and unquestioningly accept them. Let the evidence speak for itself. You're the judge and jury.

CLOCK BUILDING, NOT TIME TELLING

chapter **2**

Above all, there was the ability to build and build and build—never stopping, never looking back, never finishing—the institution. . . . In the last analysis, Walt Disney's greatest creation was Walt Disney [the company].

RICHARD SCHICKEL, *THE DISNEY VERSION*[1]

I have concentrated all along on building the finest retailing company that we possibly could. Period. Creating a huge personal fortune was never particularly a goal of mine.

SAM WALTON, FOUNDER, WAL-MART[2]

Imagine you met a remarkable person who could look at the sun or stars at any time of day or night and state the exact time and date: "It's April 23, 1401, 2:36 A.M., and 12 seconds." This person would be an amazing time teller, and we'd probably revere that person for the ability to tell time. But wouldn't that person be even more amazing if, instead of telling the time, he or she *built a clock* that could tell the time forever, even after he or she was dead and gone?[3]

Having a great idea or being a charismatic visionary leader is "time telling"; building a company that can prosper far beyond the presence of any single leader and through multiple product life cycles is "clock building." In the first pillar of our findings—and the subject of this chapter—we demonstrate how the builders of visionary companies tend to be clock builders, not time tellers. They concentrate primarily on building an organization— building a ticking clock—rather than on hitting a market just right with a visionary product idea and riding the growth curve of an attractive product life cycle. And instead of concentrating on acquiring the individual personality traits of visionary leadership, they take an architectural approach and concentrate on building the organizational traits of visionary companies. The primary output of their efforts is not the tangible implementation of a great idea, the expression of a charismatic personality, the gratification of their ego, or the accumulation of personal wealth. Their greatest creation is *the company itself* and what it stands for.

We came upon this finding when the evidence from our research punched holes in two widely held and deeply cherished myths that have dominated popular thinking and business school education for years: the myth of the great idea and the myth of the great and charismatic leader. In one of the most fascinating and important conclusions from our research, we found that creating and building a visionary company absolutely does not require *either* a great idea or a great and charismatic leader. In fact, we found evidence that great ideas brought forth by charismatic leaders might be *negatively correlated* with building a visionary company. These surprising findings forced us to look at corporate success from an entirely new angle and through a different lens than we had used before. They also have implications that are profoundly liberating for corporate managers and entrepreneurs alike.

THE MYTH OF THE "GREAT IDEA"

On August 23, 1937, two recently graduated engineers in their early twenties with no substantial business experience met to discuss the founding of a new company. However, they had no clear idea of what the company would make.* They only knew that they wanted to start a company with each other

---

*The organizing meeting took place in 1937; the official founding occurred in early 1938.

in the broadly defined field of electronic engineering. They brainstormed a wide range of initial product and market possibilities, but they had no compelling "great idea" that served as the founding inspiration for the fledgling company.

Bill Hewlett and Dave Packard decided to first start a company and *then* figure out what they would make. They just started moving forward, trying anything that might get them out of the garage and pay the light bills. According to Bill Hewlett:

> When I talk to business schools occasionally, the professor of management is devastated when I say that we didn't have any plans when we started—we were just opportunistic. We did anything that would bring in a nickel. We had a bowling foul-line indicator, a clock drive for a telescope, a thing to make a urinal flush automatically, and a shock machine to make people lose weight. Here we were, with about $500 in capital, trying whatever someone thought we might be able to do.[4]

The bowling foul-line indicator didn't become a market revolution. The automatic urinal flushers and fat-reduction shock machines didn't go anywhere, either. In fact, the company stumbled along for nearly a year before it got its first big sale—eight audio oscilloscopes to Walt Disney for work on the movie *Fantasia*. Even then, Hewlett-Packard continued its unfocused ways, sputtering and tinkering with a variety of products, until it got a boost from war contracts in the early 1940s.

Texas Instruments, in contrast, traces its roots to a highly successful initial concept. TI began life in 1930 as Geophysical Service, Inc., "the first independent company to make reflection seismograph surveys of potential oil fields, and its Texas labs developed and produced instruments for such work."[5] TI's founders, unlike Hewlett and Packard, formed their company to exploit a *specific* technological and market opportunity.[6] TI started with a "great idea." HP did not.

Neither did Sony. When Masaru Ibuka founded his company in August of 1945, he had no specific product idea. In fact, Ibuka and his seven initial employees had a brainstorming session—*after* starting the company—to decide what products to make. According to Akio Morita, who joined the company shortly after its founding, "The small group sat in conference . . . and for weeks they tried to figure out what kind of business this new company could enter in order to make money to operate."[7] They considered a wide range of possibilities, from sweetened bean-paste soup to miniature golf equipment and slide rules.[8] Not only that, Sony's first product attempt (a simple rice cooker) failed to work properly and its first significant product (a tape recorder) failed in the marketplace. The company kept itself alive in the early days by stitching wires on cloth to make crude, but sellable, heating pads.[9] In comparison, Kenwood's founder, unlike Ibuka at Sony, appeared to have a specific category of products in mind. He christened his company with the name "Kasuga Wireless Electric Firm" in 1946 and "since its foundation," according to the *Japan Electronics Almanac*, "Kenwood has always been a specialist pioneer in audio technology."[10]   *Walton*

Like fellow legendaries Ibuka and Hewlett, Sam Walton also started without a great idea. He went into business with nothing other than the desire to work for himself and a little bit of knowledge (and a lot of passion) about retailing. He didn't wake up one day and say, "I have this great idea around which I'm going to start a company." No. Walton started in 1945 with a single Ben Franklin franchise five-and-dime store in the small town of Newport, Arkansas. "I had no vision of the scope of what I would start," Walton commented in a *New York Times* interview, "but I always had confidence that as long as we did our work well and were good to our customers, there would be no limit to us."[11] Walton built incrementally, step by step, from that single store until the "great idea" of rural discount popped out as a natural evolutionary step almost two decades after he started his company. He wrote in *Made in America:*

> Somehow over the years folks have gotten the impression that Wal-Mart was something that I dreamed up out of the blue as a middle aged man, and that it was just this great idea that turned into an over-night success. But [our first Wal-Mart store] was totally an outgrowth of everything we'd been doing since [1945]—another case of me being unable to leave well enough alone, another experiment. And like most over-night successes, it was about twenty years in the making.[12]

In a twist of corporate irony, Ames Stores (Wal-Mart's comparison in our study), had a four-year head start over Sam Walton's company in rural discount retailing. In fact, Milton and Irving Gilman founded Ames in 1958 specifically to pursue the "great idea" of rural discount retailing. They "believed that discount stores would succeed in small towns" and the company achieved $1 million in sales in its first year of operation.[13] (Sam Walton didn't open his first rural discount retail store until 1962; until then, he had simply operated a collection of small, main-street variety stores.)[14] Nor was Ames the only other company that had a head start over Walton. According to Walton biographer Vance Trimble, "Other retailers were out there [in 1962] trying to do just what he was doing. Only he did it better than nearly anyone."[15]

HP, Sony, and Wal-Mart put a large dent in the widely held mythology of corporate origins—a mythology that paints a picture of a far-seeing entrepreneur founding his or her company to capitalize on a visionary product idea or visionary market insight. This mythology holds that those who launch highly successful companies usually begin first and foremost with a brilliant idea (technology, product, market potential) and then ride the growth curve of an attractive product life cycle. Yet this mythology—as compelling and pervasive as it is—does not show up as a general pattern in the founding of the visionary companies.

Indeed, few of the visionary companies in our study can trace their roots to a great idea or a fabulous initial product. J. Willard Marriott had the desire to be in business for himself, but no clear idea of what business to be in. He finally decided to start his company with the only viable idea he could think of: take out a franchise license and open an A&W root beer stand in Washington, D.C.[16] Nordstrom started as a small, single-outlet shoe store in downtown Seattle (when John Nordstrom, just returned from the Alaska Gold Rush, didn't know what else to do with himself).[17] Merck started merely as an importer of chemicals from Germany.[18] Procter & Gamble started as a simple soap and candle maker—one of eighteen such companies in Cincinnati in 1837.[19] Motorola began as a struggling battery eliminator repair business for Sears radios.[20] Philip Morris began as a small tobacco retail shop on Bond Street in London.[21]

Furthermore, some of our visionary companies began life like Sony—with outright failures. 3M started as a failed corundum mine, leaving 3M investors holding stock that fell to the barroom exchange value of "two shares for one shot of cheap whiskey."[22] Not knowing what else to do, the company began making sandpaper. 3M had such a poor start in life that its second president did not draw a salary for the first eleven years of his tenure. In contrast, Norton Corporation, 3M's comparison in the study, began life with innovative products in a rapidly growing market, paid steady annual dividends in all but one of its first fifteen years of operations, and multiplied its capital fifteenfold during the same time.[23]

Bill Boeing's first airplane failed ("a handmade, clumsy seaplane copied from a Martin seaplane" which flunked its Navy trials), and his company faced such difficulty during its first few years of operations that it entered the furniture business to keep itself aloft![24] Douglas Aircraft, in contrast, had superb initial success with its first airplane. Designed to be the first plane in history to make a coast-to-coast nonstop trip and to lift more load than its own weight, Douglas turned the design into a torpedo bomber which he sold in quantity to the Navy.[25] Unlike Boeing, Douglas never needed to enter the furniture business to keep the company alive.[26]

Walt Disney's first cartoon series *Alice in Cartoon Land* (ever heard of it?) languished in the theaters. Disney biographer Richard Schickel wrote that it was "by and large a limp, dull and cliché ridden enterprise. All you could really say for it was that it was a fairly ordinary comic strip set in motion and enlivened by a photographic trick."[27] Columbia Pictures, unlike Disney, attained substantial success with its first theater release. The film, *More to Be Pitied Than Scorned* (1922), cost only $20,000 and realized income of $130,000, thus launching Columbia forward with a sizable cash cushion that funded the making of ten additional profitable movies in less than two years.[28]

WAITING FOR "THE GREAT IDEA" MIGHT BE A BAD IDEA

In all, *only three* of the visionary companies began life with the benefit of a specific, innovative, and highly successful initial product or service—a "great idea": Johnson & Johnson, General Electric, and Ford. And even in the GE and Ford cases, we found some slight dents in the great idea theory. At GE, Edison's great idea turned out to be inferior to Westinghouse's great idea. Edison pursued direct current (DC) system, whereas Westinghouse promoted the vastly superior alternating current (AC) system, which eventually prevailed in the U.S. market.[29] In Ford's case, contrary to popular mythology, Henry Ford didn't come up with the idea of the Model T and *then* decide to start a company around that idea. Just the opposite. Ford was able to take full advantage of the Model T concept because he already had a company in place as a launching pad. He founded the Ford Motor Company in 1903 to capitalize on his automotive engineering talent—his third company in as many years—and introduced five models (Models A, B, C, F, and K) before he launched the famous Model T in October of 1908.[30] In fact, Ford was one of 502 firms founded in the United States between 1900 and 1908 to make automobiles—hardly a novel concept at the time. In contrast to the visionary companies, we traced the founding roots of eleven comparison companies much closer to the great-idea model: Ames, Burroughs, Colgate, Kenwood, McDonnell Douglas, Norton, Pfizer, R.J. Reynolds, Texas Instruments, Westinghouse, and Zenith.

In other words, we found that the visionary companies were much less likely to begin life with a "great idea" than the comparison companies in our study. Furthermore, whatever the initial founding concept, we found that the visionary companies were less likely to have early entrepreneurial success than the comparison companies. In only three of eighteen pairs did the visionary company have greater initial success than the comparison company, whereas in ten cases, the comparison company had greater initial success than the visionary company. Five cases were indistinguishable. *In short, we found a negative correlation between early entrepreneurial success and becoming a highly visionary company.* The long race goes to the tortoise, not the hare.

In Appendix 2, we give a more detailed description of the founding roots of all the visionary and comparison companies. (Even though it's in an appendix—we put it there so as not to break the flow of the text—we encourage you to browse through it.)

If you are a prospective entrepreneur with the desire to start and build a visionary company but have not yet taken the plunge because you don't have a "great idea," we encourage you to lift from your shoulders the burden of the great-idea myth. Indeed, the evidence suggests that it might be better to *not* obsess on finding a great idea before launching a company. Why? Because the great-idea approach shifts your attention away from seeing the company as your ultimate creation.

THE COMPANY ITSELF IS THE ULTIMATE CREATION

In courses on strategic management and entrepreneurship, business schools teach the importance of starting first and foremost with a good idea and well-developed product/market strategy, and *then* jumping through the "window of opportunity" before it closes. But the people who built the visionary companies often didn't behave or think that way. In case after case, their actions flew in the face of the theories being taught at the business schools.

Thus, early in our project, we had to reject the great idea or brilliant strategy explanation of corporate success and consider a new view. We had to put on a different lens and look at the world backward. We had to *shift from seeing the company as a vehicle for the products to seeing the products as a vehicle for the company.* We had to embrace the crucial difference between time telling and clock building.

To quickly grasp the difference between clock building and time telling, compare GE and Westinghouse in their early days. George Westinghouse was a brilliant product visionary and prolific inventor who founded fifty-nine other companies besides Westinghouse.[31] Additionally, he had the insight that the world should favor the superior AC electrical system over Edison's DC system, which it eventually did.[32] But compare George Westinghouse to Charles Coffin, GE's first president. Coffin invented not a single product. But he sponsored an innovation of great significance: the establishment of the General Electric Research Lab, billed as "America's first industrial research laboratory."[33] George Westinghouse told the time;

Charles Coffin built a clock. Westinghouse's greatest creation was the AC power system; Coffin's greatest creation was the General Electric Company.

Luck favors the persistent. This simple truth is a fundamental cornerstone of successful company builders. The builders of visionary companies were highly persistent, living to the motto: Never, never, *never* give up. But what to persist *with*? Their answer: The company. *Be prepared to kill, revise, or evolve an idea* (GE moved away from its original DC system and embraced the AC system), *but never give up on the company.* If you equate the success of your company with success of a specific idea—as many businesspeople do—then you're more likely to give up on the company if that idea fails; and if that idea happens to succeed, you're more likely to have an emotional love affair with that idea and stick with it too long, when the company should be moving vigorously on to other things. But if you see the ultimate creation as the company, not the execution of a specific idea or capitalizing on a timely market opportunity, then you can persist beyond any specific idea—good or bad—and move toward becoming an enduring great institution.

For example, HP learned humility early in its life, due to a string of failed and only moderately successful products. Yet Bill Hewlett and Dave Packard kept tinkering, persisting, trying, and experimenting until they figured out how to build an innovative company that would express their core values and earn a sustained reputation for great products. Trained as engineers, they could have pursued their goal by *being* engineers. But they didn't. Instead, they quickly made the transition from designing products to designing an organization—creating an environment—conducive to the creation of great products. As early as the mid-1950s, Bill Hewlett displayed a clock-building perspective in an internal speech:

> Our engineering staff [has] remained fairly stable. This was by design rather than by accident. Engineers are creative people, so before we hired an engineer we made sure he would be operating in a stable and secure climate. We also made sure that each of our engineers had a long range opportunity with the company and suitable projects on which to work. Another thing, we made certain that we had adequate supervision so that our engineers would be happy and would be productive to the maximum extent. . . . [*The process of*] *engineering is one of our most important products* [emphasis added]. . . . we are going to put on the best engineering program you have ever seen. If you think we have done well so far, just wait until two or three years from now when we get all of our new lab people producing and all of the supervisors rolling. You'll see some real progress then![34]

Dave Packard echoed the clock-building orientation in a 1964 speech: "The problem is, how do you develop an environment in which individuals can be creative? . . . I believe that you have to put a good deal of thought to your organizational structure in order to provide this environment."[35] In 1973, an interviewer asked Packard what specific *product* decisions he considered the most important in the company's growth. Packard's response didn't include one single product decision. He answered entirely in terms of organizational decisions: developing an engineering team, a pay-as-you-go policy to impose fiscal discipline, a profit-sharing program, personnel and management policies, the "HP Way" philosophy of management, and so on. In a fitting twist, the interviewer titled the article, "Hewlett Packard Chairman Built Company by Design, Calculator by Chance."[36]

> **BILL** Hewlett and Dave Packard's ultimate creation wasn't the audio oscilloscope or the pocket calculator. It was the Hewlett-Packard Company and the HP Way.

Similarly, Masaru Ibuka's greatest "product" was not the Walkman or the Trinitron; it was Sony the company and what it stands for. Walt Disney's greatest creation was not *Fantasia*, or *Snow White*, or even Disneyland; it was the Walt Disney Company and its uncanny ability to make people happy. Sam Walton's greatest creation wasn't the Wal-Mart concept; it was the Wal-Mart Corporation—an organization that could implement retailing concepts on a large scale better than any company in the world. Paul Galvin's genius lay not in being an engineer or inventor (he was actually a self-educated but twice-failed businessman with no formal technology training),[37] but in his crafting and shaping of an innovative engineering organization that we've come to call the Motorola Company. William Procter and James Gamble's most significant contribution was not hog fat soap, lamp oils, or candles, for these would eventually become obsolete; their primary contribution was something that can never become obsolete: a highly adaptable organization with a "spiritual inheritance"[38] of deeply ingrained core values transferred to generation after generation of P&G people.

We ask you to consider this crucial shift in thinking—the shift to seeing the company itself as the ultimate creation. If you're involved in building and managing a company, this shift has significant implications for how you spend your time. It means spending less of your time thinking about specific product lines and market strategies, and spending more of your time thinking about organization design. It means spending less of your time thinking like George Westinghouse, and spending more of your time thinking like Charles Coffin, David Packard, and Paul Galvin. It means spending less of your time being a time teller, and spending more of your time being a clock builder.

We don't mean to imply that the visionary companies never had superb products or good ideas. They certainly did. And, as we'll discuss later in the book, most of them view their products and services as making useful and important contributions to customers' lives. Indeed, these companies don't exist just to "be a company"; they exist to do something useful. But we suggest that *the continual stream of great products and services from highly visionary companies stems from them being outstanding organizations, not the other way around.* Keep in mind that all products, services, and great ideas, no matter how visionary, eventually become obsolete. But a visionary company does not necessarily become obsolete, not if it has the organizational ability to continually change and evolve beyond existing product life cycles. (In later chapters, we will describe how the visionary companies achieve this.)

Similarly, all leaders, no matter how charismatic or visionary, eventually die. But a visionary company does not necessarily die, not if it has the organizational strength to transcend any individual leader and remain visionary and vibrant decade after decade and through multiple generations.

This brings us to a second great myth.

THE MYTH OF THE GREAT AND CHARISMATIC LEADER

When we ask executives and business students to speculate about the distinguishing variables—the root causes—in the success of the visionary companies, many mention "great leadership." They point to George W. Merck, Sam Walton, William Procter, James Gamble, William E. Boeing, R. W. Johnson, Paul Galvin, Bill Hewlett, Dave Packard, Charles Coffin, Walt Disney, J. Willard Marriott, Thomas J. Watson, and John Nordstrom. They argue that these chief executives displayed high levels of persistence, overcame significant obstacles, attracted dedicated people to the organization, influenced groups of people toward the achievement of goals, and played key roles in guiding their companies through crucial episodes in their history.

But—and this is the crucial point—so did their counterparts at the comparison companies! Charles Pfizer, the Gilman brothers (Ames), William Colgate, Donald Douglas, William Bristol, John Myers, Commander

[handwritten: grt. leadership doesn't seem to distinguish]

Eugene F. McDonald (Zenith), Pat Haggarty (TI), George Westinghouse, Harry Cohn, Howard Johnson, Frank Melville—these people *also* displayed high levels of persistence. They *also* overcame significant obstacles. They *also* attracted dedicated people to the organization. They *also* influenced groups of people toward the achievement of goals. They *also* played key roles in guiding their companies through crucial episodes in their history. A systematic analysis revealed that the comparison companies were just as likely to have solid "leadership" during the formative years as the visionary companies. (See Table A.3 in Appendix 3.)

In short, we found no evidence to support the hypothesis that great leadership is the distinguishing variable during the critical, formative stages of the visionary companies. Thus, as our study progressed, we had to reject the great-leader theory; it simply did not adequately explain the *differences* between the visionary and comparison companies.

[handwritten: reject grt. leader theory]

Charisma Not Required

Before we describe what we see as the crucial difference between the early shapers of visionary companies versus the comparison companies (for we do think there is a crucial difference), we'd like to share an interesting corollary: *A high-profile, charismatic style is absolutely not required to successfully shape a visionary company.* Indeed, we found that some of the most significant chief executives in the history of the visionary companies did not have the personality traits of the archetypal high-profile, charismatic visionary leader.

Consider William McKnight. Do you know who he is? Does he stand out in your mind as one of the great business leaders of the twentieth century? Can you describe his leadership style? Have you read his biography? If you're like most people, you know little or nothing about William McKnight. As of 1993, he had not made it onto *Fortune* magazine's "National Business Hall of Fame."[39] Few articles have ever been written about him. His name doesn't appear in the *Hoover's Handbook* sketch of the company's history.[40] When we started our research, we're embarrassed to say, we didn't even recognize his name. Yet the company McKnight guided *for fifty-two years* (as general manager from 1914 to 1929, chief executive from 1929 to 1949, and chairman from 1949 to 1966) earned fame and admiration with businesspeople around the world; it carries the revered name Minnesota, Mining, and Manufacturing Company (or 3M for short). 3M is famous; McKnight is not. We suspect he would have wanted it exactly that way.

McKnight began work in 1907 as a simple assistant bookkeeper and rose to cost accountant and sales manager before becoming general manager. We could find no evidence that he had a highly charismatic leadership style. Of

[handwritten bottom margin: McKnight — 3M]

the nearly fifty references to McKnight in the company's self-published history, only one refers to his personality, and that described him as "a soft-spoken, gentle man."[41] His biographer described him as "a good listener," "humble," "modest," "slightly stooped," "unobtrusive and soft-spoken," "quiet, thoughtful, and serious."[42]

McKnight is not the only significant chief executive in the history of the visionary companies who breaks the archetypal model of the charismatic visionary leader. Masaru Ibuka of Sony had a reputation as being reserved, thoughtful, and introspective.[43] Bill Hewlett reminded us of a friendly, no-nonsense, matter-of-fact, down-to-earth farmer from Iowa. Messrs. Procter and Gamble were stiff, prim, proper, and reserved—even deadpan.[44] Bill Allen—the most significant CEO in Boeing's history—was a pragmatic lawyer, "rather benign in appearance with a rather shy and infrequent smile."[45] George W. Merck was "the embodiment of 'Merck restraint.' "[46]

We've worked with quite a few managers who have felt frustrated by all the books and articles on charismatic business leadership and who ask the sensible question, "What if high-profile charismatic leadership is just not my style?" Our response: Trying to develop such a style might be wasted energy. For one thing, psychological evidence indicates that personality traits get set relatively early in life through a combination of genetics and experience, and there is little evidence to suggest that by the time you're in a managerial role you can do much to change your basic personality style.[47] For another—and even more important—our research indicates that you don't need such a style anyway.

IF you're a high-profile charismatic leader, fine. But if you're not, then that's fine, too, for you're in good company right along with those that built companies like 3M, P&G, Sony, Boeing, HP, and Merck. Not a bad crowd.

Please don't misunderstand our point here. We're not claiming that the architects of these visionary companies were poor leaders. We're simply pointing out that a high-profile, charismatic style is clearly not required for building a visionary company. (In fact, we speculate that a highly charismatic style might show a slight negative correlation with building a visionary company, but the data on style are too spotty and soft to make a firm statement.) We're also pointing out—and this is the essential point of this section—that *both* sets of companies have had strong enough leaders at

doesn't explain the Δ

formative stages that great leadership, be it charismatic or otherwise, cannot explain the superior trajectories of the visionary companies over the comparison companies.

We do not deny that the visionary companies have had superb individuals atop the organization at critical stages of their history. They often did. Furthermore, we think it unlikely that a company can remain highly visionary with a continuous string of mediocre people at the top. In fact, as we will discuss in a later chapter, we found that the visionary companies did a better job than the comparison companies at developing and promoting highly competent managerial talent from inside the company, and they thereby attained greater *continuity* of excellence at the top through multiple generations. But, as with great products, perhaps *the continuity of superb individuals atop visionary companies stems from the companies being outstanding organizations, not the other way around.* continuity of grt. co's.

Consider Jack Welch, the high-profile CEO at General Electric in the 1980s and early 1990s. We cannot deny that Welch played a huge role in revitalizing GE or that he brought an immense energy, drive, and a magnetic personality with him to the CEO's office. But obsessing on Welch's leadership style diverts us from a central point: Welch grew up in GE; he was a product of GE as much as the other way around. Somehow GE *the organization* had the ability to attract, retain, develop, groom, and select Welch the leader. GE prospered long before Welch and will probably prosper long after Welch. After all, Welch was not the first excellent CEO in GE's history, and he probably will not be the last. Welch's role was not insignificant, but it was only a small slice of the entire historical story of the General Electric Company. The selection of Welch stemmed from a good corporate architecture—an architecture that traces its roots to people like Charles Coffin, who, in contrast to George Westinghouse, took an architectural approach to building the company. (We will more thoroughly discuss Welch and GE in Chapter 8.)

Jack Welch

A product of GE

AN ARCHITECTURAL APPROACH: CLOCK BUILDERS AT WORK

As in the case of Charles Coffin versus George Westinghouse, we did see in our study differences between the two groups of early shapers, but the differences were more subtle than "great leader" versus "not great leader." The key difference, we believe, is one of orientation—the evidence suggests to us that the key people at formative stages of the visionary companies had a stronger organizational orientation than in the comparison companies, regardless of their personal leadership style. As the study progressed, in fact, we became increasingly uncomfortable with the term "leader" and began to

Strong org. orientation

embrace the term "architect" or "clock builder." (A second key difference relates to the *type* of clock they built—the subject of later chapters.) The following contrasts further illustrate what we mean by an architectural, or clock-building, approach.

Citicorp Versus Chase

Stillman

James Stillman, Citicorp's president from 1891 to 1909 and chairman to 1918, concentrated on organizational development in pursuit of his goal to build a great national bank.[48] He transformed the bank from a narrow parochial firm into "a fully modern corporation."[49] He oversaw the bank as it opened new offices, instituted a decentralized multidivisional structure, constructed a powerful board of directors composed of leading CEOs, and established management training and recruiting programs (instituted three decades earlier than at Chase).[50] *Citibank 1812–1970* describes how Stillman sought to architect an institution that would thrive far beyond his own lifetime:

> Stillman intended National City [precursor to Citicorp] to retain its position [as the largest and strongest bank in the United States] even after his death, and to ensure this he filled the new building with people who shared his own vision and entrepreneurial spirit, people who would build an organization. He would step aside himself and let them run the bank.[51]

Stillman wrote in a letter to his mother about his decision to step aside, to the role of chairman, so that the company could more easily grow beyond him:

An organiz.- builder

> I have been preparing for the past two years to assume an advisory position at the Bank and to decline re-election as its official head. I know this is wise and it not only relieves me of the responsibility of details, but gives my associates an opportunity to make names for themselves [and lays] the foundation for limitless possibilities, greater even for the future than what has been accomplished in the past.[52]

Albert Wiggin, Stillman's counterpart at Chase (president from 1911 to 1929), did not delegate at all. Decisive, humorless, and ambitious, Wiggin's primary concern appeared to be with his own aggrandizement. He sat on the boards of fifty other companies and ran Chase with such a strong, centralized controlling hand that *Business Week* wrote, "The Chase Bank is Wiggin and Wiggin is the Chase Bank."[53]

[handwritten: Walton had flamb. pers.]

Wal-Mart Versus Ames

No doubt Sam Walton had the personality characteristics of a flamboyant, charismatic leader. We cannot help but think of his shimmy-shaking down Wall Street in a grass skirt and flower leis backed by a band of hula dancers (to fulfill a promise to employees for breaking 8 percent profit), or his leaping up on store counters and leading hundreds of screaming employees through a rousing rendition of the Wal-Mart Cheer. Yes, Walton had a unique and powerful personality. *But so did thousands of other people who didn't build a Wal-Mart.*

Indeed, the key difference between Sam Walton and the leaders at Ames is not that he was a more charismatic leader, but that he was much more of a clock builder—an architect. By his early twenties, Walton had pretty much settled upon his personality style; he spent the bulk of his life in a never-ending quest to build and develop the capabilities of the Wal-Mart organization, not in a quest to develop his leadership personality.[54] This was true even in Walton's own eyes, as he wrote in *Made in America*:

> What nobody realized, including a few of my own managers at the time, was that we were really trying from the beginning to become the very best operators—the most professional managers—that we could. There's no question that I have the personality of a promoter. . . . But underneath that personality, I have always had the soul of an operator, somebody who wants to make things work well, then better, then the best they possibly can. . . . I was never in anything for the short haul; I always wanted to build as fine a retailing organization as I could.[55]

For example, Walton valued change, experimentation, and constant improvement. But he didn't just preach these values, he instituted concrete *organizational* mechanisms to stimulate change and improvement. Using a concept called "A Store Within a Store," Walton gave department managers the authority and freedom to run each department as if it were their own business.[56] He created cash awards and public recognition for associates who contribute cost saving and/or service enhancements ideas that could be reproduced at other stores. He created "VPI (Volume Producing Item) Contests" to encourage associates to attempt creative experiments.[57] He instituted merchandise meetings, to discuss experiments that should be selected for use throughout the entire chain, and Saturday morning meetings, which often featured an individual employee who tried something novel that worked really well. Profit sharing and employee stock ownership produced a direct incentive for employees to come up with new ideas, so that

[handwritten: ESOP, ↑ shr.]

the whole company might benefit. Tips and ideas generated by associates got published in the Wal-Mart internal magazine.[58] Wal-Mart even invested in a satellite communications system "to spread all the little details around the company as soon as possible."[59] In 1985, stock analyst A. G. Edwards described the ticking Wal-Mart clock:

> Personnel operate in an environment where change is encouraged. For example, if a . . . store associate makes suggestions regarding [merchandising or cost savings ideas], these ideas are quickly disseminated. Multiply each suggestion by over 750 stores and by over 80,000 employees (who can potentially make suggestions) and this leads to substantial sales gains, cost reductions and improved productivity.[60]

Ames - dictatorial

Whereas Walton concentrated on creating an organization that would evolve and change on its own, Ames leaders dictated all changes from above and detailed in a book the precise steps a store manager should take, leaving no room for initiative.[61] Whereas Walton groomed a capable successor to take over the company after his death (David Glass), the Gilmans had no such person in place, thus leaving the company to outsiders who did not share their philosophy.[62] Whereas Walton passed along his clock-building orientation to his successor, postfounder CEOs at Ames recklessly pursued disastrous acquisitions in an blind, obsessive pursuit of raw growth for growth's sake, gulping down 388 Zayre stores in one bite. In describing Wal-Mart's key ingredient for future success, David Glass said "Wal-Mart associates will find a way" and "Our people are relentless."[63] Ames CEO of the same era said, "The real answer and the only issue is market share."[64]

In a sad note, a 1990 *Forbes* article on Ames noted, "Co-founder Herbert Gilman has seen his creation destroyed."[65] On a happier note, Sam Walton died with his creation intact and the belief that it could prosper long beyond him, stronger than ever. He knew that he would probably not live to the year 2000, yet shortly before he died in 1992, he set audacious goals for the company out to the year 2000, displaying a deep confidence in what the company could achieve independent of his presence.[66]

Motorola Versus Zenith

MOT

Motorola's founder, Paul Galvin, dreamed first and foremost about building a great and lasting company.[67] Galvin, architect of one of the most successful technology companies in history, did not have an engineering background, but he hired excellent engineers. He encouraged dissent, discussion, and disagreement, and gave individuals "the latitude to show what they could do largely on their own."[68] He set challenges and gave people immense responsibility so as to stimulate the organization and its people to grow and learn, often by failures and mistakes.[69] Galvin's biographer summarized, "He was not an inventor, but a builder whose blueprints were people."[70] According to his son, Robert W. Galvin, "My father urged us to reach out ... to people—to all the people—for their leadership contribution, yes their creative leadership contribution. . . . Early on, [he] was obsessed with management succession. *Ironically, he did not fear his own demise. His concern was for the company* [emphasis ours]."[71]

In contrast, Zenith's founder, Commander Eugene F. McDonald, Jr., had no succession plan, thus leaving a void of talent at the top after his unexpected death in 1958.[72] McDonald was a tremendously charismatic leader who moved the company forward primarily through the sheer force of his gigantic personality. Described as "the volatile, opinionated mastermind of Zenith," McDonald had "colossal self-assurance . . . based on a very high opinion of his own judgment."[73] He expected all except his closest friends to address him as "Commander." A brilliant tinkerer and experimenter who pushed many of his own inventions and ideas, he had a rigid attitude that almost caused Zenith to miss out on television.[74] A history of Zenith states:

> McDonald's flamboyant style was echoed in the company's dramatic advertising methods and this style, coupled with innovative genius and an ability to sense changes in public tastes, meant that for more than three decades, in the public perception McDonald *was* Zenith.[75]

Two and an half years after McDonald's death, *Fortune* magazine commented: "[Zenith] is still growing and reaping profits from the drive and imagination of its late founder. McDonald's powerful personality remains a palpable influence in the company. But Zenith's future now depends on its ability and new drive to meet conditions McDonald never anticipated."[76] A competitor commented, "As time goes on, Zenith will miss McDonald more and more."[77]

Galvin and McDonald died within eighteen months of each other.[78] Motorola sailed successfully into new arenas never dreamed of by Galvin; Zenith languished and, as of 1993, it never regained the energy and innovative spark that it had during McDonald's lifetime.

Walt Disney Versus Columbia Pictures

Quick, stop and think: Disney. What comes to mind? Can you create a clear image or set of images that you associate with Disney? Now do the same thing for Columbia Pictures. What comes to mind? Can you put your finger on distinct and clear images? If you're like most people, you can conjure up images of what Disney means, but you probably had trouble with Columbia Pictures.

In the case of Walt Disney, it is clear that Walt brought immense personal imagination and talent to building Disney. He personally originated many of Disney's best creations, including *Snow White* (the world's first-ever full-length animated film), the character of Mickey Mouse, the Mickey Mouse Club, Disneyland, and EPCOT Center. By any measure, he was a superb time teller. But, even so, in comparison to Harry Cohn—Disney's counterpart at Columbia Pictures—Walt was much more of a clock builder. *Cohn — Tyrant*

Cohn "cultivated his image as a tyrant, keeping a riding whip near his desk and occasionally cracking it for emphasis, and Columbia had the greatest creative turnover of any major studio, due largely to Cohn's methods."[79] An observer of his funeral in 1958 commented that the thirteen hundred attendees "had not come to bid farewell, but to make sure he was actually dead."[80] We could find no evidence of any concern for employees by Cohn. Nor could we find any evidence that he took steps to develop the long-term capabilities or distinct self-identity of Columbia Pictures as an institution.

The evidence suggests that Cohn cared first and foremost about becoming a movie mogul and wielding immense personal power in Hollywood (he became the first person in Hollywood to assume the titles of president *and* producer) and cared little or not at all about the qualities and identity of the Columbia Pictures Company that might endure beyond his lifetime.[81] Cohn's personal purpose propelled Columbia Pictures forward for years, but such personal and egocentric ideology could not possibly guide and inspire a company after the founder's death. Upon Cohn's death, the company fell into listless disarray, had to be rescued in 1973, and was eventually sold to Coca-Cola. *Cohn— not a co-builder*

Walt Elias Disney, on the other hand, spent the day before he died in a hospital bed thinking out loud about how to best develop Disney World in Florida.[82] Walt would die, but Disney's ability to make people happy, to bring joy to children, to create laughter and tears would not die. Throughout his life, Walt Disney paid greater attention to developing his company and its capabilities than did Cohn at Columbia. In the late 1920s, he paid his creative staff more than he paid himself.[83] In the early 1930s, he established art classes for all animators, installed a small zoo on location to provide live creatures to help improve their ability to draw animals, invented new animation team processes (such as storyboards), and continually invested in the most advanced animation technologies.[84] In the late 1930s, he installed the first generous bonus system in the cartoon industry to attract and reward good talent.[85] In the 1950s, he instituted employee "You Create Happiness" training programs and, in the 1960s, he established Disney University to orient, train, and indoctrinate Disney employees.[86] Harry Cohn took none of these steps.

Granted, Walt did not clock build as well as some of the other architects in our study, and the Disney film studio languished for nearly fifteen years after his death as Disneyites ran around asking themselves, "What would Walt do?"[87] But the fact remains that Walt, unlike Cohn, created an institution much bigger than himself, an institution that could still deliver the "Disney Magic" to kids at Disneyland decades after his death. During the same time period that Columbia ceased to exist as an independent entity, the Walt Disney Company mounted an epic (and ultimately successful) fight to prevent a hostile takeover. To the Disney executives and family, who could have made a tidy multimillion-dollar profit on their stock had the raiders been successful, Disney had to be preserved as an independent entity *because it was Disney*. In the preface to his book *Storming the Magic Kingdom*, a superb account of the Disney takeover attempt, John Taylor wrote:

> To accept [the takeover offer] was unthinkable. Walt Disney Productions was not just another corporate entity . . . that needed to be rationalized by liquidation of its assets to achieve maximum value for its shareholders. Nor was Disney just another brand name. . . . The company's executives saw Disney as a force shaping the imaginative life of children around the world. It was woven into the very fabric of American culture. Indeed, its mission—and it did, they believed, have a mission as important as making money for its stockholders—was to celebrate American values.[88]

Disney went on in the 1980s and 1990s to rekindle the heritage installed by Walt decades earlier. In contrast, Cohn's company had little to save or rekindle. No one felt Columbia had to be preserved as an independent entity; if the shareholders could get more money by selling out, then so be it.

THE MESSAGE FOR CEOS, MANAGERS, AND ENTREPRENEURS

One of the most important steps you can take in building a visionary company is not an action, but a shift in perspective. There will be plenty of action-oriented findings in the chapters that follow. But to make good use of them requires first and foremost acquiring the right frame of mind. And that's the point of this chapter. We're doing nothing less than asking you to make a shift in thinking as fundamental as those that preceded the Newtonian revolution, the Darwinian revolution, and the founding of the United States.

Prior to the Newtonian revolution, people explained the world around them primarily in terms of a God that made specific decisions. A child would fall and break his arm, and it was an act of God. Crops failed; it was an act of God. People thought of an omnipotent God who made each and every specific event happen. Then in the 1600s people said, "No, that's not it! What God did was to put in place a universe with certain principles, and what we need to do is figure out how those principles work. God doesn't make all the decisions. He set in place processes and principles that would carry on."[89] From that point on, people began to look for basic underlying dynamics and principles of the entire system. That's what the Newtonian revolution was all about.

Similarly, the Darwinian revolution gave us a dramatic shift in thinking about biological species and natural history—a shift in thinking that provides fruitful analogies to what we've seen in the visionary companies. Prior to the Darwinian revolution, people primarily presumed that God created each and every species intact and for a specific role in the natural world: Polar bears are white because God created them that way; cats purr because God created them that way; robins have red breasts because God created them that way. We humans have a great need to explain the world around us by presuming that someone or something must have had it all figured out—something must have said, "We need robins with red breasts to fit here in the ecosystem." But if the biologists are right, it doesn't work that way. Instead of jumping directly to robins with red breasts (time telling), we have instead an *underlying process* of evolution (the genetic code, DNA, genetic variation and mutation, natural selection) which eventually produces robins with red breasts that appear to fit perfectly in the ecosystem.[90] The beauty and functionality of the natural world springs from the success of its underlying processes and intricate mechanisms in a marvelous "ticking clock."

Likewise, we're asking you to see the success of visionary companies—at least in part—as coming from underlying processes and fundamental dynamics embedded in the organization and not primarily the result of a single great idea or some great, all-knowing, godlike visionary who made great decisions, had great charisma, and led with great authority. If you're involved in building and managing a company, we're asking you to think less in terms of being a brilliant product visionary or seeking the personality characteristics of charismatic leadership, and to think more in terms of being an *organizational* visionary and building the characteristics of a visionary company.

Indeed, we're asking you to consider a shift in thinking analogous to the shift required to found the United States in the 1700s. Prior to the dramatic revolutions in political thought of the seventeenth and eighteenth centuries, the prosperity of a European kingdom or country depended in large part on *process · focused*

the quality of the king (or, in the case of England, perhaps the queen). If you had a good king, then you had a good kingdom. If the king was a great and wise leader, then the kingdom might prosper as a result.

Now compare the good-king frame of reference with the approach taken at the founding of the United States. The critical question at the Constitutional Convention in 1787 was not "Who should be president? Who should lead us? Who is the wisest among us? Who would be the best king?" No, the founders of the country concentrated on such questions as "What *processes* can we create that will give us good presidents long after we're dead and gone? What type of enduring country do we want to build? On what principles? How should it operate? What guidelines and mechanisms should we construct that will give us the kind of country we envision?"

Thomas Jefferson, James Madison, and John Adams were not charismatic visionary leaders in the "it all depends on me" mode.[91] No, they were organizational visionaries. They created a constitution to which they and all future leaders would be subservient. They focused on building a country. They rejected the good-king model. They took an architectural approach. They were clock builders!

But notice: In the case of the United States, it's not a cold, mechanistic Newtonian or Darwinian clock. It's a clock based on human ideals and values. It's a clock built on human needs and aspirations. It's a clock with a spirit.

And that brings us to the second pillar of our findings: It's not just building any random clock; it's building *a particular type of clock*. Although the shapes, sizes, mechanisms, styles, ages, and other attributes of the ticking clocks vary across visionary companies, we found that they share an underlying set of fundamental characteristics. In the chapters that follow, we describe these characteristics. For now, the important thing to keep in mind is that once you make the shift from time telling to clock building, most of what's required to build a visionary company *can be learned*. You don't have to sit around waiting until you're lucky enough to have a great idea. You don't have to accept the false view that until your company has a charismatic visionary leader, it cannot become a visionary company. There is no mysterious quality or elusive magic. Indeed, once you learn the essentials, you—and all those around you—can just get down to the hard work of making your company a visionary company.

NO "TYRANNY OF THE OR"
(EMBRACE THE "GENIUS OF THE AND")

You'll notice throughout the rest of this book that we use the yin/yang symbol from Chinese dualistic philosophy. We've consciously selected this symbol to represent a key aspect of highly visionary companies: They do not oppress themselves with what we call the "Tyranny of the OR"—the rational view that cannot easily accept paradox, that cannot live with two seemingly contradictory forces or ideas at the same time. The "Tyranny of the OR" pushes people to believe that things must be either A OR B, but *not both*. It makes such proclamations as:

- "You can have change *OR* stability."
- "You can be conservative *OR* bold."
- "You can have low cost *OR* high quality."
- "You can have creative autonomy *OR* consistency and control."
- "You can invest for the future *OR* do well in the short-term."
- "You can make progress by methodical planning *OR* by opportunistic groping."

No "or" (handwritten annotation)

- "You can create wealth for your shareholders *OR* do good for the world."
- "You can be idealistic (values-driven) *OR* pragmatic (profit-driven)."

Instead of being oppressed by the "Tyranny of the OR," highly visionary companies liberate themselves with the "Genius of the AND"—the ability to embrace both extremes of a number of dimensions at the same time. Instead of choosing between A *OR* B, they figure out a way to have both A *AND* B.

As we move into the rich detail of the next eight chapters, you'll encounter, as we did in our research, a series of these paradoxes—apparent contradictions in many of the visionary companies. For example, you will encounter:

On the one hand:		Yet, on the other hand:
purpose beyond profit	AND	pragmatic pursuit of profit
a relatively fixed core ideology	AND	vigorous change and movement
conservatism around the core	AND	bold, committing, risky moves
clear vision and sense of direction	AND	opportunistic groping and experimentation
Big Hairy Audacious Goals	AND	incremental evolutionary progress
selection of managers steeped in the core	AND	selection of managers that induce change
ideological control	AND	operational autonomy
extremely tight culture (almost cult-like)	AND	ability to change, move, and adapt
investment for the long-term	AND	demands for short-term performance
philosophical, visionary, futuristic	AND	superb daily execution, "nuts and bolts"
organization aligned with a core ideology	AND	organization adapted to its environment.

We're not talking about mere balance here. "Balance" implies going to the midpoint, fifty-fifty, half and half. A visionary company doesn't seek balance between short-term and long-term, for example. It seeks to do very well in the short-term *and* very well in the long-term. A visionary company doesn't simply balance between idealism and profitability; it seeks to be highly idealistic *and* highly profitable. A visionary company doesn't simply balance between preserving a tightly held core ideology and stimulating vigorous change and movement; it does *both* to an extreme. In short, a highly visionary company doesn't want to blend yin and yang into a gray, indistinguishable circle that is neither highly yin nor highly yang; it aims to be distinctly yin *and* distinctly yang—*both* at the same time, all the time.

Irrational? Perhaps. Rare? Yes. Difficult? Absolutely. But as F. Scott Fitzgerald pointed out, "The test of a first-rate intelligence is the ability to hold two opposed ideas in the mind at the same time, and still retain the ability to function."[1] This is exactly what the visionary companies are able to do.

chapter 3

MORE THAN PROFITS

Our basic principles have endured intact since our founders conceived them. We distinguish between core values and practices; the core values don't change, but the practices might. We've also remained clear that profit—as important as it is—is not *why* the Hewlett-Packard Company exists; it exists for more fundamental reasons.

JOHN YOUNG, FORMER CEO, HEWLETT-PACKARD, 1992[1]

We are in the business of preserving and improving human life. All of our actions must be measured by our success in achieving this goal.

MERCK & COMPANY, INTERNAL MANAGEMENT GUIDE, 1989[2]

Putting profits after people and products was magical at Ford.

DON PETERSEN, FORMER CEO, FORD, 1994[3]

MRK

When Merck & Company reached its hundredth birthday, it published a book entitled *Values and Visions: A Merck Century.* Notice something? The title doesn't even mention what Merck does. Merck could have titled the book *From Chemicals to Pharmaceuticals: A Merck Century* or *A Hundred Years of Financial Success at Merck.* But it didn't. It chose instead to emphasize that it has been throughout its history a company guided and inspired by a set of ideals. In 1935 (decades before "values statements" became popular), George Merck II articulated those ideals when he said, "[We] are workers in industry who are genuinely inspired by the ideals of advancement of medical science, and of service to humanity."[4] In 1991—fifty-six years and three full generations of leadership later— Merck's chief executive P. Roy Vagelos sang the same idealistic tune: "Above all, let's remember that our business success means victory against disease and help to humankind."[5]

Cure for River blindness

With these ideals as a backdrop, we're not surprised that Merck elected to develop and give away Mectizan, a drug to cure "river blindness," a disease that infected over a million people in the Third World with parasitic worms that swarmed through body tissue and eventually into the eyes, causing painful blindness. A million customers is a good-sized market, except that these were customers who could not afford the product. Knowing that the project would not produce a large return on investment—if it produced one at all—the company nonetheless went forward with the hope that some government agencies or other third parties would purchase and distribute the product once available. No such luck, so Merck elected to give the drug away free to all who needed it.[6] Merck also involved itself directly in distribution efforts—at its own expense—to ensure that the drug did indeed reach the millions of people at risk from the disease.

Asked why Merck made the Mectizan decision, Vagelos pointed out that failure to go forward with the product could have demoralized Merck scientists—scientists working for a company that explicitly viewed itself as "in the business of preserving and improving human life." He also commented:

Streptomycin to Japan.

When I first went to Japan fifteen years ago, I was told by Japanese business people that it was Merck that brought streptomycin to Japan after World War II, to eliminate tuberculosis which was eating up their society. We did that. We didn't make any money. But it's no accident that Merck is the largest American pharmaceutical company in Japan today. The long-term consequences of [such actions] are not always clear, but somehow I think they always pay off.[7]

PRAGMATIC IDEALISM (NO "TYRANNY OF THE OR")

Did Merck's ideals—ideals that had consistently defined the company's self-identity since the late 1920s—drive the Mectizan decision? Or did Merck make the decision for pragmatic reasons—good long-term business and good PR? Our answer: *Both*. Merck's ideals played a substantial role in the decision and the evidence suggests that Merck would have gone ahead with the project *regardless of whether it created long-term business benefits for the company*. But the evidence also suggests that Merck acted on the assumption that such acts of goodwill "somehow . . . always pay off." This is a classic example of the "Genius of the AND" prevailing over the "Tyranny of the OR." Merck has displayed throughout most of its history both high ideals *and* pragmatic self-interest. George Merck II explained this paradox in 1950:

> I want to . . . express the principles which we in our company have endeavored to live up to. . . . Here is how it sums up: We try to remember that medicine is for the patient. We try never to forget that medicine is for the people. It is not for the profits. The profits follow, and if we have remembered that, they have never failed to appear. The better we have remembered it, the larger they have been.[8]

Merck, in fact, epitomizes the ideological nature—the pragmatic idealism—of highly visionary companies. Our research showed that a fundamental element in the "ticking clock" of a visionary company is a *core ideology*—core values and sense of purpose beyond just making money—that guides and inspires people throughout the organization and remains relatively fixed for long periods of time. In this chapter, we describe, support, and illustrate this crucial element that exists paradoxically with the fact that visionary companies are also highly effective profit-making enterprises.

Now, you might be thinking: "Of course it's *easy* for a company like Merck to proclaim and pursue inspirational ideals—Merck makes drugs that do in fact save lives, cure disease, and relieve suffering." Good point, and we agree. But in contrast to its comparison company, Pfizer—a company in the same industry, a company that also makes drugs that save lives, cure diseases, and relieve suffering—we found Merck to have been more ideologically driven.

Whereas Merck titled its history *Values and Visions*, Pfizer titled its history, *Pfizer . . . An Informal History*. Whereas Merck has explicitly and prominently articulated a consistent set of high ideals for four generations, we found no evidence of similar discussions at Pfizer until the late 1980s. Nor did we find at Pfizer any incident analogous to the Mectizan or streptomycin decisions at Merck.

Whereas George Merck II explicitly took a paradoxical view of profits ("medicine is for the patient . . . the profits follow"), John McKeen, president at Pfizer during the same era as George Merck II, displayed a somewhat more lopsided perspective: "So far as is humanly possible," he said, "we aim to get profit out of everything we do."[9] According to an article in *Forbes*, McKeen believed that "idle money was a sinfully non-productive asset." While Merck hoarded cash for investment in new research and drug development efforts, McKeen launched a frenetic acquisition binge, purchasing fourteen companies in four years and diversifying into such areas as farm products, women's toiletries, shaving products, and paint pigments. Why? To make more money, regardless of the line of business. "I would rather make 5% on $1 billion in sales than 10% on $300 million [in ethical drugs]," said McKeen. We don't mean to quibble over strategies here (diversification via acquisition versus focus and innovation via R&D); but the evidence suggests that Pfizer during this era displayed more of a purely pragmatic profit orientation than Merck.

Of course, a company like Merck could *afford* to have high ideals. As of 1925, when George Merck II took over from his father, the company already had a track record of substantial business success and a sizable financial cushion. Might it be, therefore, that having high ideals is merely a luxury for companies such as Merck that are so successful that they can afford to proclaim an ideology? No. We found that high ideals—a core ideology—often existed in the visionary companies not just when they were successful, but also when they were struggling just to survive. Consider the following two examples: Sony at its founding and Ford during the 1983 turnaround crisis.

When Masaru Ibuka started Sony among the ruins of a defeated and devastated 1945 Japan, he rented an abandoned telephone operator's room in the hollow remnants of a bombed and burned-out old department store in downtown Tokyo and, with seven employees and $1,600 of personal savings, began work.[10] But what should be his first priorities? What should he do first among the depressing ruins? Generate cash flow? Figure out what business to be in? Launch products? Develop customers?

Ibuka did indeed concentrate on these tasks (recall from Chapter 2 the failed rice cooker, sweetened bean-paste soup, and crude heating pads). But he also did something else—something remarkable for an entrepreneur wrestling with the problems of day-to-day survival: He codified an ideology for his newly founded company. On May 7, 1946, less than ten months after moving to Tokyo—and long before turning a positive cash flow—he created a "prospectus" for the company that included the following items (this is a partial translation, as the actual document is quite long):[11]

> If it were possible to establish conditions where persons could become united with a firm spirit of teamwork and exercise to their heart's desire their technological capacity . . . then such an organization could bring untold pleasure and untold benefits. . . . Those of like minds have naturally come together to embark on these ideals.

PURPOSES OF INCORPORATION

- To establish a place of work where engineers can feel the joy of technological innovation, be aware of their mission to society, and work to their heart's content.
- To pursue dynamic activities in technology and production for the reconstruction of Japan and the elevation of the nation's culture.
- To apply advanced technology to the life of the general public.

MANAGEMENT GUIDELINES

- We shall eliminate any unfair profit-seeking, persistently emphasize substantial and essential work, and not merely pursue growth.
- We shall welcome technical difficulties and focus on highly sophisticated technical products that have great usefulness in society, regardless of the quantity involved.
- We shall place our main emphasis on ability, performance, and personal character so that each individual can show the best in ability and skill.

Stop and think about this for a minute. How many entrepreneurial companies do you know that included such idealistic sentiments in their founding documents? How many corporate founders have you come across that think about such grand values and sense of purpose when simply struggling to bring in enough cash to keep the doors open? How many companies have you encountered that articulate a clear ideology at the start of the company, yet cannot articulate a clear idea of what products to make? (As an aside, if you're at the early stages in the development of a company and have been putting off articulating a corporate ideology until you've attained business success, you might pause to consider the Sony example.

We found that Ibuka's ideology laid down so early in the company's history played an important role in guiding the company's evolution.)

In 1976, Nick Lyons observed in his book *The Sony Vision* that the ideals embodied in the prospectus have "been a guiding force for the company these past thirty years, modified only slightly as [Sony] grew with extraordinary speed."[12] Forty years after Ibuka penned the prospectus, Sony chief executive Akio Morita rephrased the company's ideology in a simple, elegant statement, entitled the "Sony Pioneer Spirit":

Sony Pioneer Spirit

> Sony is a pioneer and never intends to follow others. Through progress, Sony wants to serve the whole world. It shall be always a seeker of the unknown. . . . Sony has a principle of respecting and encouraging one's ability . . . and always tries to bring out the best in a person. This is the vital force of Sony.[13]

Kenwood

In contrast to Sony stands Kenwood, Sony's comparison in the study. We attempted to obtain directly from Kenwood any and all documents that would describe the company's philosophy, values, visions, and ideals. Kenwood responded that it had no such documents and sent merely a set of recent and fairly standard annual reports. We tried to obtain external writings on this subject, but found none. Perhaps Kenwood has had a consistent, pervasive ideology that, like Sony's, traces back to the moment of the company's conception, but we could find no evidence of it. Whereas we had no trouble locating numerous books, articles, and documents—both internal and external—about Sony's ideology, we could find almost nothing similar published about Kenwood.

Sony Furthermore, we found substantial evidence of direct translations of Sony's ideology into tangible characteristics and practices, such as a highly individualistic culture and decentralized structure (relative to other Japanese companies) and product development practices that explicitly eschew traditional market research. "Our plan is to lead the market with new products, rather than ask them what kind of products they want. . . . Instead of doing a lot of market research, we . . . refine a product . . . and try to create a market for it by educating and communicating with the public."[14] And from these ideologically driven tangible practices came a series of decisions to launch products for which there was no proven demand, including the first magnetic tape recorder in Japan (1950), the first all-transistor radio (1955), the first pocket-sized radio (1957), the first home-use videotape recorder (1964), and the Sony Walkman (1979).[15]

Certainly, Sony wanted successful products; it didn't want to pioneer itself into bankruptcy. Nonetheless, the ideals of the "Sony Pioneer Spirit" trace their roots to the very early days of the company, long before it became a profitable venture, and have remained largely intact as a guiding force for nearly half a century. Yes, Sony made crude heating pads and sweetened bean-paste soup to keep itself alive (pragmatism), but it always dreamed and pushed toward making pioneering contributions (idealism).

Now let's look at a company at the other end of the spectrum—an aging giant in a desperate turnaround crisis. In the early 1980s, Ford Motor Company found itself reeling, bleeding red ink from wounds inflicted during the repeated thrashings it took from Japanese competitors. Pause for a moment and put yourself in the shoes of the Ford senior management team—a management team atop a company suffering from a $3.3 *billion* net loss (43 percent of its net worth) in three years. What should they do? What should be their highest priorities?

Naturally, the Ford team threw itself into a frenzy of emergency measures to stop the bleeding and keep the company breathing. But it also did something else—something unusual for a team facing such a tremendous crisis: It paused to clarify its guiding principles. According to Robert Schook (who researched and wrote a book on the 1980s Ford turnaround), "The objective was to create a proclamation that clearly stated what the Ford Motor Company stood for. At times the discussions . . . sounded more like a college class in philosophy than a business meeting."[16] (We found no evidence that General Motors, facing the same industry onslaught and also losing money, paused like Ford did in 1983 to have fundamental philosophical discussions.) Out of this process came Ford's "Mission, Values, Guiding Principles (MVGP)." Former Ford CEO Don Petersen commented:

> There was a great deal of talk about the sequence of the three P's— people, products, and profits. It was decided that people should absolutely come first [products second and profits third].[17]

If you're familiar with Ford's history, you may be skeptical of this ordering. Don't get us wrong here. We don't see Ford as exemplary throughout its entire history in labor relations and product quality. The bloody, brutal brawls with labor in the 1930s and the exploding Ford Pinto of the 1970s certainly leave Ford with a spotty record. Nonetheless, we found evidence that the Ford team's deliberations about the "three P's" reached back in time to reawaken an ideology espoused by Henry Ford in the early days of the company. The 1980s turnaround team wasn't inventing completely new ideals, but was, in part, breathing life back into ones that had long lain dormant. In describing the relationship between the "three P's" in the early days of the company, Henry Ford commented in 1916:

I don't believe we should make such an awful profit on our cars. A reasonable profit is right, but not too much. I hold that it is better to sell a large number of cars at a reasonably small profit . . . I hold this because it enables a larger number of people to buy and enjoy the use of a car and because it gives a larger number of men employment at good wages. Those are the two aims I have in life.[18]

Idealistic prattle? Cynical pronouncements to pacify the public? Perhaps. But keep in mind that Ford transformed the American way of life for 15 million families with the affordable Model T (the "people's car"), in large part by reducing prices by 58 percent from 1908 to 1916. At the time, Ford had more orders than it could fill and could have *raised* prices. Mr. Ford kept lowering them anyway, even in the face of a shareholder suit against the practice.[19] And, during the same era, he boldly introduced the $5 day for workers which, at roughly twice the standard industry rate, shocked and outraged the industrial world (as described by Robert Lacey in *Ford*):

$5 work day

The *Wall Street Journal* accused Henry Ford of "economic blunders if not crimes" which would soon "return to plague him and the industry he represents as well as organized society." In a naive wish for social improvement, declared the newspaper, Ford had injected "spiritual principles into a field where they do not belong"—a heinous crime and captains of industry lined up to condemn "the most foolish thing ever attempted in the industrial world."[20]

As an interesting aside, Henry Ford apparently embarked upon "the most foolish thing ever attempted in the industrial world" partly under the influence of the highly idealistic philosopher Ralph Waldo Emerson and, in particular, his essay "Compensation."[21] However, not being oppressed by the "Tyranny of the OR," Ford also embarked on this path with full recognition that workers earning $5 a day combined with lower car prices would lead to greater sales of Model Ts. Pragmatism? Idealism? Yes.

Again, we don't want to paint Ford as being in the same ideological league as Merck and Sony; it has a much spottier historical record on this dimension. But compared to GM, Ford has been much more ideologically guided. In fact, GM presents a fascinating case of how a clock-building orientation alone is not enough. Alfred P. Sloan, chief architect of GM, clearly had a strong clock-building orientation. But Sloan's clock had no soul; Sloan's clock was a cold, impersonal, inhuman, pure business, and totally pragmatic clock. Peter F. Drucker, who carefully studied GM and

GM

Sloan's clock - no soul.

Alfred Sloan for his landmark book *Concept of the Corporation*, summed it up this way:

> The failure of GM as an institution—for failure it is—is to a large extent the result of . . . an attitude that one might call "techno-cratic" . . . best exemplified in Alfred P. Sloan's own book, *My Years with General Motors*. . . . It focuses exclusively on policies, business decisions, and structure. . . . It is perhaps the most impersonal book of memoirs ever written—and this was clearly intentional. Sloan's book . . . knows only one dimension: that of managing a business so that it can produce effectively, provide jobs, create markets and sales, and generate profits. Business in the community; business as a life rather than a livelihood; business as a neighbor; and business as a power center—these are all absent in Sloan's world.[22]

In his book *Management: Tasks, Responsibilities, Practices*, Drucker added, "General Motors has stayed with Sloan's legacy. And in Sloan's terms . . . it has succeeded admirably. But it has also failed abysmally."[23]

CORE IDEOLOGY: EXPLODING THE PROFIT MYTH

Merck, Sony, and Ford each offer a different slice of a general pattern: the existence of a core ideology as a primary element in the historical development of visionary companies. Like the fundamental ideals of a great nation, church, school, or any other enduring institution, core ideology in a vision-ary company is a set of basic precepts that plant a fixed stake in the ground: "This is who we are; this is what we stand for; this is what we're all about." Like the guiding principles embodied in the American Declaration of Inde-pendence ("We hold these truths to be self-evident . . .") and echoed eighty-seven years later in the Gettysburg Address ("a . . . nation, conceived in Liberty, and dedicated to the proposition that all men are created equal"), core ideology is so fundamental to the institution that it changes seldom, if ever.

In some cases, like Sony, the ideology derives from the founding roots. In some cases, like Merck, it comes from the second generation. In other cases, like Ford, the ideology went dormant and was rekindled in later years. But in nearly all cases, we found evidence of a core ideology that existed not merely as words but as a vital shaping force. We will soon more thoroughly discuss the nuances of core ideology and its two component parts, core values and purpose, but first we will turn to explore one of our most intriguing findings.

Contrary to business school doctrine, *we did not find "maximizing shareholder wealth" or "profit maximization" as the dominant driving force or primary objective through the history of most of the visionary companies.* They have tended to pursue a cluster of objectives, of which making money is only one—and not necessarily the primary one. Indeed, for many of the visionary companies, business has historically been more than an economic activity, more than just a way to make money. Through the history of most of the visionary companies we saw a core ideology that transcended purely economic considerations. And—this is the key point—they have had core ideology *to a greater degree than the comparison companies in our study.*

A detailed pair-by-pair analysis showed that the visionary companies have generally been more ideologically driven and less purely profit-driven than the comparison companies in seventeen out of eighteen pairs. (See Table A.4 in Appendix 3.) This is one of the clearest differences we found between the visionary and comparison companies.

Of course, we're not saying that the visionary companies have been uninterested in profitability or long-term shareholder wealth (notice that we say that they are *"more* than" economic entities, not *"other* than"). Yes, they pursue profits. And, yes, they pursue broader, more meaningful ideals. Profit maximization does not rule, but the visionary companies pursue their aims profitably. They do *both.*

PROFITABILITY is a necessary condition for existence and a means to more important ends, but it is not the end in itself for many of the visionary companies. Profit is like oxygen, food, water, and blood for the body; they are not the *point* of life, but without them, there is no life.

Here are a few key examples of how the visionary companies embraced the "Genius of the AND"—ideology *AND* profits—to a greater degree than their comparison counterparts across a range of industries in our study.

Hewlett-Packard Versus Texas Instruments

Put yourself in the shoes of David Packard on March 8, 1960. Your company sold stock to the public for the first time three years earlier. The electronics revolution has launched your company into an explosive growth trajectory.

You've been wrestling with all the challenges of rapid growth, but you're particularly concerned about HP's ability to develop highly competent, homegrown managerial talent (you believe in a promote-from-within policy as a key element of your ticking clock). You've therefore initiated an HP management development program—a program that you consider central to the long-term health of the organization—and you're about to give a kickoff talk to the group of HP people responsible for that program. You want to imprint on their minds a key message to use as a guiding theme as they develop programs to socialize and train generation after generation of HP managers. What should be the theme of your talk? What message do you want these trainers to remember?

After a short preliminary welcome, Packard began his talk:

> I want to discuss *why* [emphasis his] a company exists in the first place. In other words, why are we here? I think many people assume, wrongly, that a company exists simply to make money. While this is an important result of a company's existence, we have to go deeper and find the real reasons for our being. As we investigate this, we inevitably come to the conclusion that a group of people get together and exist as an institution that we call a company so they are able to accomplish something collectively that they could not accomplish separately—they make a contribution to society, a phrase which sounds trite but is fundamental. . . . You can look around [in the general business world] and still see people who are interested in money and nothing else, but the underlying drives come largely from a desire to do something else—to make a product—to give a service—generally to do something which is of value. So with that in mind, let us discuss why the Hewlett-Packard Company exists. . . . The real reason for our existence is that we provide something which is unique [that makes a contribution].[24]

Those who worked with David Packard describe his management style as practical, no-nonsense, with a "let's roll up our sleeves and get down to work" attitude. He studied to be an engineer in college, not a philosophy professor. Nonetheless, we see David Packard ruminating about what we can best describe as corporate existentialism, pondering about the philosophical, noneconomic "reasons for being" of his company. "Profit," according to Packard, "is not the proper end and aim of management—it is what makes all of the proper ends and aims possible."[25]

David Packard perfectly exemplified the "Genius of the AND" by explicitly embracing the tension between profit and purpose beyond profit.

On the one hand, he made it crystal clear that the Hewlett-Packard Company should be managed "first and foremost to make a contribution to society"[26] and that "our main task is to design, develop, and manufacture the finest electronic [equipment] for the advancement of science and the welfare of humanity."[27] Yet, on the other hand, he made it equally clear that, because profit enables HP to pursue these broader aims, "anyone who cannot accept [profit] as one of the most important [objectives] of this company has no place either now or in the future on the management team of this company."[28]

Furthermore, he *institutionalized* this view, passing it along to John Young (HP chief executive from 1976 to 1992), who commented to us in an interview:

> Maximizing shareholder wealth has always been way down the list. Yes, profit is a cornerstone of what we do—it is a measure of our contribution and a means of self-financed growth—but it has never been the *point* in and of itself. The point, in fact, is to *win*, and winning is judged in the eyes of the customer and by doing something you can be proud of. There is a symmetry of logic in this. If we provide real satisfaction to real customers—we will be profitable.[29]

In comparing Texas Instruments with Hewlett Packard, we reviewed over forty historical articles and case studies and could find not one single statement that TI exists for reasons beyond making money. Such a statement might exist, but we found no evidence of it. Instead, TI appeared to define itself almost exclusively in terms of size, growth, and profitability—but very little on what David Packard called "the *why* of business." In 1949, TI's president Pat Haggarty issued his "dictum" for TI: "We are a good little company. Now we must become a good *big* company."[30] This obsessive focus on size and growth—and very little on "the why"—has persisted throughout TI's history. We noticed, for example, that all of TI's driving corporate goals, unlike HP's, were oriented purely to financial growth:

Texas Instruments Primary Corporate Goals
- Hit sales of $200 million (set in 1949).[31]
- Hit sales of $1 billion (set in 1961).[32]
- Hit sales of $3 billion (set in 1966).[33]
- Hit sales of $10 billion (set in 1973).[34]
- Hit sales of $15 billion (set in 1980).[35]

To be fair, we found similar financial goals in a few of the visionary companies, in particular Wal-Mart. But TI, unlike most of the visionary companies—and certainly unlike HP—appeared to make financial sales goals *the* driving force and put much less emphasis on the "why" of it all. For TI, bigger was better, period—even if the products were low-quality or made no technical contribution. For HP, bigger was better *only within the context of making a contribution.*[36] TI, for instance, moved into making cheap pocket calculators and $10 throwaway digital watches in an explicit "more is better" strategy in the 1970s; confronted with the same market opportunities, HP explicitly chose not to go after the cheap low end precisely because it offered no opportunity for technical contribution.[37]

Johnson & Johnson Versus Bristol-Myers

Johnson & Johnson, like HP, explicitly speaks first to ideals beyond profit, and then emphasizes the importance of profit within the context of those ideals. When Robert W. Johnson founded Johnson & Johnson in 1886, he did so with the idealistic aim "to alleviate pain and disease."[38] By 1908, he had expanded this into a business ideology that placed service to customers and concern for employees ahead of returns to shareholders.[39] Fred Kilmer, one of J&J's early research managers, explained in the early 1900s how this philosophy framed the role of the research department:

> The department is not conducted in any narrow, commercial spirit . . . and not kept going for the purpose of paying dividends or solely for the benefit of Johnson & Johnson, but with a view to aiding the progress of the art of healing.[40]

In 1935, Robert W. Johnson, Jr., echoed these sentiments in a philosophy that he called "enlightened self-interest," wherein "service to *customers* [italics his] comes first . . . service to *employees* and *management* second, and . . . service to *stockholders* last."[41] Later (in 1943), he added service to community to the list (still ahead of service to shareholders) and codified the J&J ideology in "Our Credo," printed on old-style parchment and captioned in the same lettering used in the American Declaration of Independence. "When these things have been done," he wrote, "the stockholders should receive a fair return."[42] Although J&J has periodically reviewed and slightly revised the wording of the credo since 1943, the essential ideology—the hierarchy of responsibilities descending from customers down to shareholders and the explicit emphasis on *fair* return rather than maximum return—has remained consistent throughout the history of the credo.[43]

J&J credo

Our Credo

WE BELIEVE THAT OUR FIRST RESPONSIBILITY IS TO THE DOCTORS, NURSES, HOSPITALS,
MOTHERS, AND ALL OTHERS WHO USE OUR PRODUCTS.
OUR PRODUCTS MUST ALWAYS BE OF THE HIGHEST QUALITY.
WE MUST CONSTANTLY STRIVE TO REDUCE THE COST OF THESE PRODUCTS.
OUR ORDERS MUST BE PROMPTLY AND ACCURATELY FILLED.
OUR DEALERS MUST MAKE A FAIR PROFIT.

OUR SECOND RESPONSIBILITY IS TO THOSE WHO WORK WITH US—
THE MEN AND WOMEN IN OUR PLANTS AND OFFICES.
THEY MUST HAVE A SENSE OF SECURITY IN THEIR JOBS.
WAGES MUST BE FAIR AND ADEQUATE,
MANAGEMENT JUST, HOURS REASONABLE, AND WORKING CONDITIONS CLEAN AND ORDERLY.
EMPLOYEES SHOULD HAVE AN ORGANIZED SYSTEM FOR SUGGESTIONS AND COMPLAINTS.
SUPERVISORS AND DEPARTMENT HEADS MUST BE QUALIFIED AND FAIR MINDED.
THERE MUST BE OPPORTUNITY FOR ADVANCEMENT—FOR THOSE QUALIFIED
AND EACH PERSON MUST BE CONSIDERED AN INDIVIDUAL
STANDING ON HIS OWN DIGNITY AND MERIT.

OUR THIRD RESPONSIBILITY IS TO OUR MANAGEMENT.
OUR EXECUTIVES MUST BE PERSONS OF TALENT, EDUCATION, EXPERIENCE, AND ABILITY.
THEY MUST BE PERSONS OF COMMON SENSE AND FULL UNDERSTANDING.

OUR FOURTH RESPONSIBILITY IS TO THE COMMUNITIES IN WHICH WE LIVE.
WE MUST BE A GOOD CITIZEN—SUPPORT GOOD WORKS AND CHARITY,
AND BEAR OUR FAIR SHARE OF TAXES.
WE MUST MAINTAIN IN GOOD ORDER THE PROPERTY WE ARE PRIVILEGED TO USE.
WE MUST PARTICIPATE IN PROMOTION OF CIVIC IMPROVEMENT,
HEALTH, EDUCATION AND GOOD GOVERNMENT,
AND ACQUAINT THE COMMUNITY WITH OUR ACTIVITIES.

OUR FIFTH AND LAST RESPONSIBILITY IS TO OUR STOCKHOLDERS.
BUSINESS MUST MAKE A SOUND PROFIT.
RESERVES MUST BE CREATED, RESEARCH MUST BE CARRIED ON,
ADVENTUROUS PROGRAMS DEVELOPED, AND MISTAKES PAID FOR.
ADVERSE TIMES MUST BE PROVIDED FOR, ADEQUATE TAXES PAID, NEW MACHINES PURCHASED,
NEW PLANTS BUILT, NEW PRODUCTS LAUNCHED, AND NEW SALES PLANS DEVELOPED.
WE MUST EXPERIMENT WITH NEW IDEAS.
WHEN THESE THINGS HAVE BEEN DONE THE STOCKHOLDER SHOULD RECEIVE A FAIR RETURN.
WE ARE DETERMINED WITH THE HELP OF GOD'S GRACE,
TO FULFILL THESE OBLIGATIONS TO THE BEST OF OUR ABILITY.

This is the text of the original 1943 Credo as penned by R.W. Johnson, Jr.

In the early 1980s, chief executive Jim Burke (who estimated that he spent fully 40 percent of his time as CEO communicating the credo throughout the company)[44] described the interplay between the credo and profits:

> All of our management is geared to profit on a day-to-day basis. That's part of the business of being in business. But too often, in this and other businesses, people are inclined to think, "We'd better do this because if we don't, it's going to show up on the figures over the short-term." This document [the Credo] allows them to say, "Wait a minute. I don't *have* to do that." The management has told me that they're . . . interested in me operating under this set of principles, so I won't.[45]

At Bristol-Myers, we found a much less ideologically guided company than at Johnson & Johnson. Whereas J&J formalized and published its credo in the early 1940s and had a clear sense of its ideology dating back to the early 1900s, we found no evidence whatsoever that Bristol-Myers had anything analogous to the credo until 1987, when it published the "Bristol-Myers Pledge" (which looks suspiciously like a paraphrased version of the J&J Credo). Nor did we find any evidence that the pledge, once stated, became anywhere near as pervasive a guiding document in Bristol-Myers. Whereas J&J employees spoke explicitly about the link between the credo and key decisions, we found no similar comments by Bristol-Myers employees.[46]

The Harvard Business School dedicated an entire case study to how J&J translated the credo into action—in organization structure, internal planning processes, compensation systems, strategic business decisions, and as a tangible guide in times of crisis. For example, J&J used the credo as the basis for its response to the 1982 Tylenol crisis, when the deaths of seven people in the Chicago area revealed that someone—not an employee—had tampered with Tylenol bottles, lacing them with cyanide. J&J immediately removed all Tylenol capsules from the entire U.S. market—even though the deaths occurred only in the Chicago area—at an estimated cost of $100 million and mounted a twenty-five-hundred-person communication effort to alert the public and deal with the problem. The Washington *Post* wrote of the crisis that "Johnson & Johnson has succeeded in portraying itself to the public as a company willing to do what's right, regardless of cost."[47]

Within days of the Tylenol crisis, Bristol-Myers faced an almost identical problem: Excedrin tablets had been tampered with in the Denver area. Instead of recalling all tablets from the entire U.S. market—as J&J had done—Bristol-Myers recalled tablets only from Colorado and did not launch a campaign to alert the public. Bristol-Myers' chairman Richard Gelb, who described himself as "a cautious manager who likes to count things down to the last bean," was quick to emphasize in Dun's *Business Month* that the Excedrin incident would "have a negligible effect on Bristol-Myers' earnings."[48] J&J had a codified ideology in place that guided its response to the crisis (for better or worse), whereas the evidence suggests that Bristol-Myers lacked a similar guidepost.

Boeing Versus McDonnell Douglas

To a far greater degree than McDonnell Douglas, Boeing has made key strategic decisions in its history as much out of an idealized view of its self-identity as out of strategic pragmatism. In particular, Boeing has a long history of taking huge gambles to build bigger and more advanced aircraft. These gambles have paid off, making Boeing a highly profitable company (more profitable than McDonnell Douglas)—pragmatic decisions indeed. But the evidence suggests that Boeing has not been fundamentally *about* profit, long-run or otherwise.[49] Boeing has been about pioneering aviation—about building big, fast, advanced, better-performing aircraft; about pushing the envelope of aviation technology; about adventure, challenge, achievement, and contribution; about having the Right Stuff. Boeing can't pursue these purposes without profits; but profit is not the "why" of it all—any more than Chuck Yeager test piloted jets just for the money. Bill Allen (chief executive from 1945 to 1968) commented on the purposes of work at Boeing:

> Boeing is always reaching out to tomorrow. This can only be accomplished by people who live, breathe, eat and sleep what they are doing. . . . [I am] associated with a large group of knowledgeable, dedicated [people] who eat, breathe, and sleep the world of aeronautics. . . . Man's objective should be opportunity for greater accomplishment and greater service. The greatest pleasure life has to offer is the satisfaction that flows from . . . participating in a difficult and constructive undertaking.[50]

Take, for example, Boeing's decision to make the 747. Sure, Boeing had economic motives; but it also had nonfinancial motives. Boeing built the 747 as much because of its self-identity as because of its desire for profits—because it believed it should be on the leading edge of air transportation, period. Why do the 747? "Because we're *Boeing!*" When Boeing director Crawford Greenwalt asked a member of senior management about the projected return on investment of the proposed 747, the manager told him that they'd run some studies, but couldn't recall the results. In *Legend and Legacy*, Robert Serling writes: "Greenwalt just put his head down on the table and muttered, 'My God, these guys don't even know what the return-on-investment will be on this thing.' "[51]

Motorola Versus Zenith

Motorola founder Paul Galvin viewed profitability as a necessary means to pursue the company's objectives, but not the ultimate aim. Yes, he continually pushed his engineers to drive costs down while improving quality so as to provide a profitable basis for the company. And yes, he believed that a businessperson needed to make a profit in order to get satisfaction from his or her efforts. But he never let profit become the primary, overriding objective of the company—nor did he think it should become so for any company.[52] During the 1930s Depression, Motorola—then a young, struggling company—confronted the common industry practice of misrepresenting company financial health and product benefits to distributors. Pressured to do the same, Paul Galvin responded that he didn't care about industry practices. "Tell them the truth," he said, "first because it is the right thing to do and second they'll find out anyway."[53] Galvin's response displays once again the dual nature—the pragmatic-idealism—of many of the visionary companies in our study. They are not purely idealistic; nor are they purely pragmatic. They are both.

> **VISIONARY** companies like Motorola don't see it as a choice between living to their values *or* being pragmatic; they see it as a challenge to find pragmatic solutions *and* behave consistent with their core values.

Furthermore, Paul Galvin institutionalized this paradoxical perspective at Motorola as a guiding force for future generations. In 1991, Robert W. Galvin (Paul's son and successor), wrote a series of essays to employees about "who and why we are." In thirty-one essays, he discussed the importance of creativity, renewal, total customer satisfaction, quality, ethics, innovation, and similar topics; *not once* did he write about maximizing profits, nor did he imply this was the underlying purpose—the "why" of it all.[54] Consistent with the above, Motorola's official statement of purpose (contained in an internal publication called "For Which We Stand: A Statement of Purpose, Principles, and Ethics") tied profit and broader purpose together, with the pursuit of adequate profit (versus maximum profit) in the supporting role:

> The purpose of Motorola is to honorably serve the community by providing products and services of superior quality at a fair price to our customers; to do this so as to earn an *adequate* profit which is required for the enterprise to grow, and by so doing provide the opportunity for our employees and shareholders to achieve their *reasonable* personal objectives. [emphasis ours]"[55]

At Zenith, in contrast, founder Commander Eugene F. McDonald did not pass along an enduring ideology to the company. Zenith's purpose during McDonald's era appears to have been primarily about being a toy and platform for its founder. After McDonald's death, the company languished with little guidance or inspiration of any kind, and defaulted to a classic profits-only perspective. In reviewing articles on Motorola and Zenith, we noticed that the articles on Motorola constantly emphasized "intangible" aspects of the company—its informality, egalitarianism, technological drive, and optimistic ever-forward feeling—whereas the articles on Zenith after McDonald's death put more emphasis on financial condition, market share, and other purely financial items. We found no document similar to Motorola's "For Which We Stand" at Zenith. In fact, we found no evidence of any significant ideology beyond the quest for increased market share and profit maximization in Zenith after McDonald's death in 1958.

Marriott Versus Howard Johnson

Marriott Corporation, like Motorola and HP, explicitly embraced the paradox of pragmatic idealism. When asked if he'd founded Marriott Corporation to make a million dollars or to build an empire, J. Willard Marriott, Sr., responded:

> No, not at all. I just had three general ideas in mind, all equally important. One was to render a friendly service to our guests. The second was to provide quality food at a fair price. The third was to work as hard as I could, day and night, to make a profit. . . . I wanted to reap the rewards of growth: jobs for more employees, money to take care of my family and to contribute to good causes.[56] . . . The service business is very rewarding. It makes a big contribution to

society. A good meal away from home, a good bed, friendly treatment. . . . It's important to make people away from home feel that they're among friends and are really wanted.[57]

And, as in the examples previously cited, Marriott institutionalized this perspective so that it would remain alive long after his death. He initiated elaborate employee screening and indoctrination processes to reinforce the ideology of employees as number one and customers as guests and created management development programs to ensure the continual availability of Marriott-indoctrinated management. He carefully groomed his successor and son, J. Willard Marriott, Jr., not only for the nuts and bolts of running the corporation, but also to carry on its values. A 1991 article commented: "With a certain solemnity, Marriott executives follow the 'Guideposts to Management' that J. Willard put in a letter to his son when he became executive-vice president in 1964."[58] We found a copy of that lengthy letter and noticed remarkable similarity between those guideposts and those espoused by his son two decades later (see below).

Consistent with the guiding principles laid down in the company years ago by his father, Marriott, Jr., commented that the motivating factor in the company "is not the money," but rather the sense of pride and accomplishment that comes from doing its work really well.[61] He pointed out that by taking superb care of employees and providing outstanding customer value

1964 J. Willard Marriott, Sr.[59]	1984 J. Willard Marriott, Jr.[60]
People are #1—their development, loyalty, interest, team spirit. [Their development] is your prime responsibility. . . . See the good in people and try to develop those qualities.	We are in the people business . . . teach them and help them and care about them. Give them a fair shake. Give them skills; help them succeed; make winners out of them.
Delegate and hold accountable for results. If . . . an employee is obviously incapable of the job, find a job he can do or terminate now. Don't wait.	Get good people and expect them to perform. Terminate them quickly and fairly if you make the wrong choice.
Manage your time . . . make every minute on the job count. . . . Keep a sense of humor. Make the business fun for you and others.	Work hard, but have fun. It's fun to do things and get things done. The key is to keep that going.

(treat them as guests), "attractive" (not "maximum") shareholder returns will follow as a natural result.[62]

Although the evidence suggests that Howard Johnson, Sr., also had an ideology (with emphasis on consistency and quality), we found no evidence that he passed this ideology along to his son (and successor) or to otherwise instill his ideals into the company as an enduring set of principles. There is no record of ideological coaching from first generation to second; nor is there any record of the deliberate development of ideological screening and indoctrination processes like Marriott's. By the mid-1970s, Howard Johnson, Jr., was actively running the company with a one-sided, purely financial focus (sales growth and return on investment) with little or no emphasis on customers or employees. According to three separate articles (two in *Business Week* and one in *Forbes*), Howard Johnson had squeezed captive turnpike customers with high prices for bland food, shoddy accommodations, and slow, sullen service.[63] Johnson, Jr., eventually sold the company to a British investor for a hefty eighteen times earnings.[64]

Philip Morris Versus R.J. Reynolds

At Philip Morris (relative to R.J. Reynolds), we found evidence of the company framing its work within the context of an ideology rather than just maximizing shareholder wealth. Ross Millhiser, vice chairman of Philip Morris in 1979, said:

I love cigarettes. It's one of the things that makes life really worth living. . . . Cigarettes supply some desire, some [aspect] of the fundamental human equation. The human equation is always trying to balance itself, and cigarettes play some part in that.[65]

Ideology or self-delusion? Merely good PR? It's impossible to tell. But we saw in Philip Morris an esprit de corps and sense of common purpose that we simply did not see over the last thirty years at R.J. Reynolds. Philip Morris executives have appeared far more passionate about their cigarettes than the executives at R.J. Reynolds. Philip Morris executives express much more defiance in their prosmoking ideology, whereas the RJR folks after about 1960 did not seem to care much about the products except as a way to make money. According to R.J. Reynolds' chairman in 1971, if the company could make more money for shareholders by getting out of cigarettes, then fine; unlike Millhiser, he had no ideological allegiance to tobacco.[66]

The Philip Morris executives, in contrast, framed the fight over cigarettes in almost self-righteous moral overtones: We have a *right* to smoke; it's a matter of freedom of choice. Don't take away our cigarettes. Don't tread on me! In our review of articles on Philip Morris, we noticed numerous photos of executives taking a rebellious pose—cigarettes in hand—glaring into the camera with a manner that conveys "Don't even *think* of asking me to put down this cigarette!" A *Fortune* magazine article noted:

> An almost defiant smoking culture permeates the executive floors, whose denizens yank from the pockets flip-top boxes . . . light up . . . and then toss their packs on the desk or table for all to see.[67]

It's as if they actually see themselves as the lone, fiercely independent cowboy depicted in their all-pervasive Marlboro billboards. An ex-Philip Morris employee described working at Philip Morris as "the cult of smoking" and told us that the company forced upon her and her co-workers boxes of cigarettes to take home with their paychecks. A Philip Morris board member told us (while fingering a box of filter-tips), "I really love being on the board of Philip Morris. It's a really great company; I mean a *great* company. It's like being part of something really special—it's a company that stands for something and being part of it is something you can really be proud of."[68] A *Forbes* article said of Philip Morris chairman Joseph Cullman in 1971:

> A good many people resent [Cullman] for his aggressive defense of cigarette smoking. Instead of apologizing for cigarettes, [he] points to the "beneficial effects of smoking" in the area of mental health.[69]

Please don't misinterpret us; we don't see Philip Morris as working altruistically for the good of humankind. The ideology at Philip Morris relates primarily to personal freedom of choice, individual initiative and hard work, merit-based opportunity, winning, and continuous self-improvement—earning the pride that comes from simply doing business extraordinarily well and ever better for its own sake. Michael Miles, who became Philip Morris chief executive in 1991 and whom *Fortune* magazine described as "a business junkie . . . pragmatic, ruthless, focused . . . cold-blooded,"[70] who "thinks about business every minute of his life,"[71] commented: "I see nothing morally wrong with the [tobacco] business. . . . I see nothing wrong with selling people products they don't need."[72] These are not particularly "soft" or "humanistic" values. And cigarettes, after all, don't cure river blindness.

But—and this may surprise you (it surprised us)—we found that Philip Morris shares with Merck an esprit de corps that is linked to a strong core ideology. To be sure, Philip Morris' ideology differs dramatically from Merck's, but both companies stand above their comparisons in the study in the extent to which they are ideologically guided. Along this key dimension,

Philip Morris has had more in common with Merck over the past forty years[73] than it has had in common with R.J. Reynolds, and Merck has had more in common with Philip Morris than it has had in common with Pfizer.

IS THERE A "RIGHT" IDEOLOGY?

The fact that both Merck and Philip Morris—companies at opposite ends of the spectrum in terms of what their products do to people—show up as visionary companies guided by strong, yet radically different ideologies, raises some interesting questions. Is there a "right" core ideology for being a visionary company? Does the content of the ideology matter? Are there any common elements or prevalent patterns across the core ideologies in the visionary companies?

We compiled in Table 3.1 the core ideologies of the visionary companies in our study and found that, although certain themes show up in a number of the visionary companies (such as contribution, integrity, respect for the individual employee, service to the customer, being on the creative or leading edge, or responsibility to the community), *no single item shows up consistently across all the visionary companies.*

- Some companies, such as Johnson & Johnson and Wal-Mart, made their *customers* central to their ideology; others, such as Sony and Ford, did not.
- Some companies, such as HP and Marriott, made concern for their *employees* central to their ideologies; others, such as Nordstrom and Disney, did not.
- Some companies, such as Ford and Disney, made their *products or services* central to their core ideology; others, such as IBM and Citicorp, did not.
- Some companies, such as Sony and Boeing, made audacious *risk taking* central to their ideology; others, such as HP and Nordstrom, did not.
- Some companies, such as Motorola and 3M, made *innovation* central to their ideology; others, such as P&G and American Express, did not.

> **IN** short, we did *not* find any specific ideological content essential to being a visionary company. Our research indicates that the *authenticity* of the ideology and the extent to which a company attains consistent alignment with the ideology counts more than the *content* of the ideology.

presence or absence is the key

In other words, it doesn't matter whether or not you like or agree with the Philip Morris ideology—not unless you work for Philip Morris. Nor does it matter whether outsiders agree with Merck's ideology, or Marriott's, or Motorola's, or Disney's, or HP's. We concluded that the critical issue is not whether a company has the "right" core ideology or a "likable" core ideology but rather whether it *has* a core ideology—likable or not—that gives guidance and inspiration to people *inside that company.*

Table 3.1

Core Ideologies in the Visionary Companies

3M[74]	• Innovation; "Thou shalt not kill a new product idea"
	• Absolute integrity
	• Respect for individual initiative and personal growth
	• Tolerance for honest mistakes
	• Product quality and reliability
	• "Our real business is solving problems"
American Express[75]	• Heroic customer service
	• Worldwide reliability of services
	• Encouragement of individual initiative
Boeing[76]	• Being on the leading edge of aeronautics; being pioneers
	• Tackling huge challenges and risks
	• Product safety and quality
	• Integrity and ethical business
	• To "eat, breathe, and sleep the world of aeronautics"
Citicorp[77]	• Expansionism—of size, of services offered, of geographic presence
	• Being out front—such as biggest, best, most innovative, most profitable
	• Autonomy and entrepreneurship (via decentralization)
	• Meritocracy
	• Aggressiveness and self-confidence
Ford[78]	• People as the source of our strength
	• Products as the "end result of our efforts" (we are *about* cars)
	• Profits as a necessary means and measure for our success
	• Basic honesty and integrity (NOTE: This is the order from 1980s Ford MVGP document. At different points in Ford's history, the order has varied.)

General Electric[79]	• Improving the quality of life through technology and innovation
	• Interdependent balance between responsibility to customers, employees, society, and shareholders (no clear hierarchy)
	• Individual responsibility and opportunity
	• Honesty and integrity

Hewlett-Packard[80]	• Technical contribution to fields in which we participate ("We exist as a corporation to make a contribution")
	• Respect and opportunity for HP people, including the opportunity to share in the success of the enterprise
	• Contribution and responsibility to the communities in which we operate
	• Affordable quality for HP customers
	• Profit and growth as a means to make all of the other values and objectives possible

IBM[81]	• Give full consideration to the individual employee
	• Spend a lot of time making customers happy
	• Go the last mile to do things right; seek superiority in all we undertake

Johnson & Johnson[82]	• The company exists "to alleviate pain and disease"
	• "We have a hierarchy of responsibilities: customers first, employees second, society at large third, and shareholders fourth" (see the credo reproduced elsewhere in this book)
	• Individual opportunity and reward based on merit
	• Decentralization = Creativity = Productivity

Marriott[83]	• Friendly service & excellent value (customers are guests); "make people away from home feel that they're among friends and really wanted"
	• People are number 1—treat them well, expect a lot, and the rest will follow
	• Work hard, yet keep it fun
	• Continual self-improvement
	• Overcoming adversity to build character

Merck[84]	• "We are in the business of preserving and improving human life. All of our actions must be measured by our success in achieving this goal."
	• Honesty and integrity
	• Corporate social responsibility
	• Science-based innovation, not imitation
	• Unequivocal excellence in *all* aspects of the company
	• Profit, but profit from work that benefits humanity

Table 3.1 (*continued*)
Core Ideologies in the Visionary Companies

Motorola[85]
- The company exists "to honorably serve the community by providing products and services of superior quality at a fair price"
- Continuous self-renewal
- Tapping the "latent creative power within us"
- Continual improvement in all that the company does—in ideas, in quality, in customer satisfaction
- Treat each employee with dignity, as an individual
- Honesty, integrity, and ethics in all aspects of business

Nordstrom[86]
- Service to the customer above all else
- Hard work and productivity
- Continuous improvement, never being satisfied
- Excellence in reputation, being part of something special

Philip Morris [87]
- The right to personal freedom of choice (to smoke, to buy whatever one wants) is worth defending
- Winning—being the best and beating others
- Encouraging individual initiative
- Opportunity to achieve based on merit, not gender, race, or class
- Hard work and continuous self-improvement

Procter & Gamble[88]
- Product excellence
- Continuous self-improvement
- Honesty and fairness
- Respect and concern for the individual

Sony[89]
- To experience the sheer joy that comes from the advancement, application, and innovation of technology that benefits the general public
- To elevate the Japanese culture and national status
- Being a pioneer—not following others, but doing the impossible
- Respecting and encouraging each individual's ability and creativity

Wal-Mart[90]
- "We exist to provide value to our customers"—to make their lives better via lower prices and greater selection; all else is secondary
- Swim upstream, buck conventional wisdom
- Be in partnership with employees
- Work with passion, commitment, and enthusiasm
- Run lean
- Pursue ever-higher goals

Walt Disney[91]
- No cynicism allowed
- Fanatical attention to consistency and detail
- Continuous progress via creativity, dreams, and imagination
- Fanatical control and preservation of Disney's "magic" image
- "To bring happiness to millions" and to celebrate, nurture, and promulgate "wholesome American values."

---

* This table presents the most historically consistent ideology for each of the visionary companies in our study. We did *not* merely paraphrase the company's most recent values, mission, vision, or purpose statement (if it had one) and we never relied on only one source; we looked for *historical consistency* through multiple generations of chief executives.

Words or Deeds?

How can we be sure that the core ideologies of highly visionary companies represent more than just a bunch of nice-sounding platitudes—words with no bite, words meant merely to pacify, manipulate, or mislead? We have two answers. First, social psychology research strongly indicates that when people publicly espouse a particular point of view, they become much more likely to behave consistent with that point of view *even if they did not previously hold that point of view.*[92] In other words, the very act of stating a core ideology (which the visionary companies have done to a far greater degree than the comparison companies) influences behavior toward consistency with that ideology.

Second—and more important—the visionary companies don't merely declare an ideology; they also take steps to make the ideology pervasive throughout the organization and transcend any individual leader. As we'll describe in subsequent chapters:

- The visionary companies more thoroughly indoctrinate employees into a core ideology than the comparison companies, creating cultures so strong that they are almost cult-like around the ideology.
- The visionary companies more carefully nurture and select senior management based on fit with a core ideology than the comparison companies.
- The visionary companies attain more consistent alignment with a core ideology—in such aspects as goals, strategy, tactics, and organization design—than the comparison companies.

Certainly, the visionary companies have not always found it easy to maintain and live to their ideologies. Jack Welch of GE described the difficulty of living with the tension between pragmatism and idealism, or what he calls "numbers and values":

Numbers and values. We don't have the final answer here—at least I don't. People who make the numbers and share our values go onward and upward. People who miss the numbers and share our values get a second chance. People with no values and no numbers—easy call. The problem is with those who make the numbers but don't share the values. . . . We try to persuade them; we wrestle with them; we agonize over these people.[93]

In fact, we did not find that the visionary companies have always been perfect exemplars of their ideologies. GE, for example, had a number of ethical and legal transgressions in the 1950s and 1960s, including collusion in a scandalous bid-rigging scheme with several utility companies in 1955. In 1991, P&G resorted to an insidious effort to seize Cincinnati phone records in an attempt to track down (and presumably punish) internal sources who spoke to a *Wall Street Journal* reporter[94]—a clear breach of its own highly touted value of "respect for the individual." Even Johnson & Johnson, with its famous credo, has struggled at times to keep its ideology alive and operating as a shaping force. In 1979, thirty-six years after Robert W. Johnson wrote the credo, J&J put itself through an extensive soul-search process with respect to the credo. According to then-chief executive Jim Burke:

People like my predecessors believed in the Credo with a passion, but the operating managers [in 1979] were not universally committed to it. . . . So I called a meeting of some 20 key executives and challenged them. I said, "Here's the Credo. If we're not going to live by it, let's tear it off the wall. . . . We either ought to commit to it or get rid of it." . . . By the end of the session, the managers had gained a great deal of understanding about and enthusiasm for the beliefs in the Credo. Subsequently, [we] met with small groups of J&J managers all over the world to challenge the Credo.[95]

The visionary companies have not always been perfect. But, as the J&J Credo rededication effort and the GE agony over numbers and values illustrate, the visionary companies, in general, have placed great emphasis on having a core ideology and have put much effort into preserving the core ideology as a vital shaping force. And—again the key point—they have done so more than the comparison companies in our study.

GUIDELINES FOR CEOS, MANAGERS, AND ENTREPRENEURS

A key step in building a visionary company is to articulate a core ideology. Drawing upon what we saw in the visionary companies, we've created a practical two-part definition of core ideology. Companies we've worked with have found this definition to be a useful guide for setting their own ideologies.

$$
\text{Core Ideology} = \text{Core Values} + \text{Purpose}
$$

Core Values = The organization's essential and enduring tenets—a small set of general guiding principles; not to be confused with specific cultural or operating practices; not to be compromised for financial gain or short-term expediency.

Purpose = The organization's fundamental reasons for existence beyond just making money—a perpetual guiding star on the horizon; not to be confused with specific goals or business strategies.

Core Values

Core values are the organization's essential and enduring tenets, not to be compromised for financial gain or short-term expediency. Thomas J. Watson, Jr., former IBM chief executive, commented on the role of core values (what he calls beliefs) in his 1963 booklet *A Business and Its Beliefs:*

> I believe the real difference between success and failure in a corporation can very often be traced to the question of how well the organization brings out the great energies and talents of its people. What does it do to help these people find common cause with each other? . . . And how can it sustain this common cause and sense of direction through the many changes which take place from one generation to another? . . . [I think the answer lies] in the power of what we call *beliefs* and the appeal these beliefs have for its

people. . . . I firmly believe that any organization, in order to survive and achieve success, must have a sound set of beliefs on which it premises all its policies and actions. Next, I believe <u>that the most important single factor in corporate success is faithful adherence to those beliefs</u>. . . . *Beliefs must always come before policies, practices, and goals. The latter must always be altered if they are seen to violate fundamental beliefs.* [emphasis ours][96]

In most cases, a core value can be boiled down to a piercing simplicity that provides substantial guidance. Notice how Sam Walton captured the essence of Wal-Mart's number one value: "[We put] the customer ahead of everything else. . . . If you're not serving the customer, or supporting the folks who do, then we don't need you."[97] Notice how James Gamble simply and elegantly stated P&G's core value of product quality and honest business: "When you cannot make pure goods of full weight, go to something else that is honest, even if it is breaking stone."[98] Notice how John Young, former HP chief executive, captured the simplicity of the HP Way: "The HP Way basically means respect and concern for the individual; it says 'Do unto others as you would have them do unto you.' That's really what it's all about."[99] <u>The core value can be stated a number of different ways, yet it remains simple, clear, straightforward</u>, and powerful.

Visionary companies tend to have only a few core values, usually between three and six. In fact, we found none of the visionary companies to have more than six core values, and most have less. And, indeed, we should expect this, for only a few values can be truly *core*—values so fundamental and deeply held that they will change or be compromised seldom, if ever.

This has important implications for articulating core values in your own organization. If you list more than five or six values, you might not be capturing those that are truly core. If you have a statement of corporate values, or are in the process of creating one, you might ask yourself: "Which of these values would we strive to live to for a hundred years *regardless* of changes in the external environment—*even* if the environment ceased to reward us for having these values, or perhaps even penalized us? Conversely, which values would we be willing to change or discard if the environment no longer favored them?" These questions can help you identify which values are authentically core.

A very important point. We strongly encourage you *not* to fall into the trap of using the core values from the visionary companies (listed in Table 3.1) as a source for core values in your own organization. Core ideology does not come from mimicking the values of other companies—even highly visionary companies; it does not come from following the dictates of outsiders; it does not come from reading management books; and it does not come from a sterile intellectual exercise of "calculating" what values would be most pragmatic, most popular, or most profitable. When articulating and codifying core ideology, the key step is to capture what is authentically believed, not what other companies set as their values or what the outside world thinks the ideology should be.

It's important to understand that core ideology exists as an *internal* element, largely independent of the external environment. To use an analogy, the founders of the United States didn't instill the core ideology of freedom and equality because the environment dictated it, nor did they expect the country to ever abandon those basic ideals in response to environmental conditions. They envisioned freedom and equality as timeless ideals independent of the environment ("We hold these truths to be *self*-evident . . .")—ideals to always work toward, providing guidance and inspiration to all future generations. The same holds true in visionary companies.

— Constant, No Justif. Req'd.

> **IN** a visionary company, the core values need no rational or external justification. Nor do they sway with the trends and fads of the day. Nor even do they shift in response to changing market conditions.

Robert W. Johnson, Jr. didn't write the credo because of a conceptual theory that linked credos with profits or because he read it in a book somewhere. He wrote the credo because the company embodied deeply held beliefs that he wanted to preserve. George Merck II deeply *believed* that medicine is for the patient, and he wanted every Merck person to share that belief. Thomas J. Watson, Jr. described IBM's core values as "bone deep" in his father: "As far as he was concerned, those values were the rules of life—to be preserved at all costs, to be commended to others, and to be followed conscientiously in one's business life."[100]

David Packard and Bill Hewlett didn't "plan" the HP Way or HP's "WHY of business"; they simply held deep convictions about the way a business *should* be built and took tangible steps to articulate and disseminate these convictions so they could be preserved and acted upon. And they held these beliefs *independent* of the current management fashions of the day. In sifting through the Hewlett-Packard Company archives, we came across the following statement made by David Packard:

[In 1949], I attended a meeting of business leaders. I suggested at the meeting that management people had a responsibility beyond that of making a profit for their stockholders. I said that we . . . had a responsibility to our employees to recognize their dignity as human beings, and to assure that they should share in the success which their work made possible. I pointed out, also, that we had a responsibility to our customers, and to the community at large, as well. I was surprised and shocked that not a single person at that meeting agreed with me. While they were reasonably polite in their disagreement, it was quite evident they firmly believed I was not one of *them*, and obviously not qualified to manage an important enterprise.[101]

Hewlett, Packard, Merck, Johnson, and Watson didn't sit down and ask "What business values would maximize our wealth?" or "What philosophy would look nice printed on glossy paper?" or "What beliefs would please the financial community?" No! They articulated what was inside them—what was in their gut, what was bone deep. It was as natural to them as breathing. It's not what they believed as much as *how deeply they believed it* (and how consistently their organizations lived it). Again, the key word is *authenticity*. No artificial flavors. No added sweeteners. Just 100 percent genuine authenticity. Authenticity

Purpose

Purpose is the set of fundamental reasons for a company's existence beyond just making money. Visionary companies get at purpose by asking questions similar to those posed by David Packard earlier in this chapter. ("I want to discuss *why* a company exists in the first place. In other words, why are we here? I think many people assume, wrongly, that a company exists simply to make money. While this is an important result of a company's existence, we have to go deeper and find the real reasons for our being.")

Purpose need not be wholly unique. It's entirely possible that two companies could have a very similar purpose, just as it's entirely possible that two companies can both share a rock-solid belief in a value like integrity. The primary role of purpose is to guide and inspire, not necessarily to differentiate. For example, many companies could share HP's purpose of making a contribution to society via electronic equipment for the advancement of science and the welfare of humanity. The question is, would they hold it as deeply and live it as consistently as HP? As with core values, the key is authenticity, not uniqueness.

When properly conceived, purpose is broad, fundamental, and enduring; a good purpose should serve to guide and inspire the organization for years, perhaps a century or more. Roy Vagelos—looking *one hundred years* into the future—described the enduring role of purpose at Merck & Company:

> Imagine that all of us were suddenly transported to the year 2091. Much [of our strategy and methods] would have been changed by developments we cannot anticipate. But no matter what changes might have occurred in the Company, I know we would find one thing had remained the same—and the thing that matters most: the . . spirit of Merck people. . . . A century from now, I believe we would feel the same esprit de corps. . . . I believe this, above all, because Merck's dedication to fighting disease, relieving suffering, and helping people is a righteous cause—one that inspires people to dream of doing great things. It is a timeless cause, and it will lead Merck people to great achievements during the next hundred years.[102]

Merck Spirit

Indeed, a visionary company continually pursues but never fully achieves or completes its purpose—like chasing the earth's horizon or pursuing a guiding star. Walt Disney captured the enduring, never-completed nature of purpose when he commented:

> Disneyland will never be completed, as long as there is imagination left in the world.[103]

Boeing can never be done pushing the envelope in aerospace technology; the world will always need a corporate Chuck Yeager. HP can never reach a point where it says, "There are no more contributions we can make." GE can never complete the task of improving the quality of life through technology and innovation.

Marriott can evolve—from A&W Root Beer stands, to food chains, to airline catering, to hotels, and to who-knows-what in the twenty-first century—yet never outgrow the fundamental task of "making people away from home feel that they're among friends and really wanted."

Motorola can evolve—from battery eliminators for home radios, to car radios, to home television, to semiconductors, to integrated circuits, to cellular communications, to satellite systems, and to who-knows-what in the twenty-first century—yet never outgrow its fundamental quest to "honorably serve the community by providing products and services of superior quality at a fair price."

Disney can evolve—from rinky-dink cartoons, to full-length animated

(o's   evolve

movies, to the Mickey Mouse club, to Disneyland, to box-office hits, to EuroDisney, and to who-knows-what in the twenty-first century—yet never outgrow the core task of "bringing happiness to millions."

Sony can evolve—from rice cookers and crude heating pads, to tape recorders, to transistor radios, to Trinitron color TVs, to VCRs, to the Walkman, to robotics systems, and to who-knows-what in the twenty-first century—yet never finish pursuing its core purpose of experiencing the sheer joy of applied technological innovation that brings about "untold pleasure and untold benefits . . . and the elevation of the [Japanese] culture."

In short, a visionary company can, and usually does, evolve into exciting new business areas, yet remain guided by its core purpose.

As an implication of this, if you're thinking about purpose for your own organization, we encourage you to not simply write a specific description of your product lines or customer segments ("We exist to make *X* products for *Y* customers"). For example, "We exist to make cartoons for kids" would have been a terrible purpose statement for Disney, neither compelling nor flexible enough to last one hundred years. But "to use our imagination to bring happiness to millions" can easily last one hundred years as a compelling purpose. The important step is to get at the deeper, more fundamental reasons for the organization's existence. An effective way to get at purpose is to pose the question "Why not just shut this organization down, cash out, and sell off the assets?" and to push for an answer that would be equally valid both now and one hundred years into the future.

We want to be clear: We did not find an explicit and formal statement of purpose in all of our visionary companies. We sometimes found purpose to be more implicitly or informally stated. Nonetheless, because purpose differs sufficiently from core values (which we saw explicitly in *all* eighteen cases) in its role and flavor—and because thirteen companies in our study did make purposelike statements (either formal/explicit or informal/implicit) at some point in their history—it's useful to identify purpose as a specific and distinct component of core ideology.[104] We've found that most companies benefit from articulating both core values *and* purpose in their core ideology, and we encourage you to do the same.

A Special Note to Non-CEOs

Although we've written this chapter from the perspective of the overall corporation, we've found the same ideas can apply to managers at *all* levels of an organization. There's absolutely no reason why you can't articulate a core ideology for your own work group, department, or division. If your company has a strong overall corporate ideology, then your group-level ideology will naturally be constrained by that ideology—particularly the core values. But you can still have your own flavor of ideology, and certainly you can articulate a purpose for your own suborganization. What is its reason for being? What would be lost if it ceased to exist?

And if your company *doesn't* have an overall corporate ideology, you can still set one at your level—and you'll probably have more freedom to do so. Just because the overall company lacks a clear ideology doesn't mean your group shouldn't have one! Furthermore, you can play a key role in pushing your company to articulate its ideology by setting one at your own level and letting it serve as a role model. We've seen subgroups in companies exert a great deal of pressure on the overall corporation by being role models from within.

A Special Note to Entrepreneurs and Small Business Managers

Not all of the visionary companies began life with a well-articulated core ideology. A few did. Robert W. Johnson, for example, had a sense of J&J's purpose from the moment he conceived the company ("to alleviate pain and disease").[105] So did Masaru Ibuka of Sony when he wrote the company's 1946 prospectus. But others, like HP and Motorola, didn't pin down their ideology until after the company had solidly passed the initial start-up phase, often a decade or so after founding (but usually before they became big companies). In the early stages, most visionary companies just tried to get off the ground and make a go of it and their ideology became clear only as the company evolved. So if you haven't yet articulated a core ideology because you've been in the throes of launching a company, that's okay. But the earlier, the better. In fact, if you've made time to read this book, then we encourage you to set aside the time to articulate your ideology *now*.

Core
values + Purpose

chapter 4

PRESERVE THE CORE/ STIMULATE PROGRESS

Paul Galvin urged us to keep moving forward, to be in motion for motion's sake. . . . He urged continuous renewal. . . . Change unto itself is essential. But, taken alone: it is limited. Yes, renewal is change. It calls for "do differently." It is willing to replace and redo. But it also cherishes the proven basics.[1]

ROBERT W. GALVIN, FORMER CEO, MOTOROLA, 1991

It is the consistency of principle . . . that gives us direction. . . . [Certain principles] have been characteristics of P&G ever since our founding in 1837. While Procter & Gamble is oriented to progress and growth, it is vital that employees understand that the company is not only concerned with results, but how the results are obtained.[2]

ED HARNESS, FORMER PRESIDENT,
PROCTER & GAMBLE, 1971

In the previous chapter, we presented core ideology as an essential component of a visionary company. But core ideology alone, as important as it is, does not—indeed *cannot*—make a visionary company. A company can have the world's most deeply cherished and meaningful core ideology, but if it just sits still or refuses to change, the world will pass it by. As Sam Walton pointed out: "You can't just keep doing what works one time, because everything around you is always changing. To succeed, you have to stay out in front of that change."[3] Similarly, Thomas J. Watson, Jr., embedded a huge caveat in his booklet *A Business and Its Beliefs:*

> If an organization is to meet the challenges of a changing world, *it must be prepared to change everything about itself except [its basic] beliefs as it moves through corporate life. . . . The only sacred cow in an organization should be its basic philosophy of doing business.* [emphasis ours][4]

We believe IBM began to lose its stature as a visionary company in the late 1980s and early 1990s in part because it lost sight of Watson's incisive caveat. Nowhere in IBM's "three basic beliefs"* do we see anything about white shirts, blue suits, specific policies, specific procedures, organizational hierarchies, mainframe computers—or computers at all, for that matter. Blue suits and white shirts are not core values. Mainframe computers are not core values. Specific policies, procedures, and practices are not core values. IBM should have much more vigorously changed *everything* about itself *except* its core values. Instead, it stuck too long to strategic and operating practices and cultural manifestations of the core values.

We've found that companies get into trouble by confusing core ideology with specific, noncore practices. By confusing core ideology with noncore practices, companies can cling too long to noncore items—things that should be changed in order for the company to adapt and move forward. This brings us to a crucial point: A visionary company carefully preserves and protects its core ideology, yet all the specific *manifestations* of its core ideology must be open for change and evolution. For example:

- HP's "Respect and concern for individual employees" is a permanent, unchanging part of its core ideology; serving fruit and doughnuts to all employees at ten A.M. each day is a noncore practice that can change.

---

* IBM's three basic beliefs are: Give full consideration to the individual employee, spend a lot of time making customers happy, and go the last mile to do things right.

- Wal-Mart's "Exceed customer expectations" is a permanent, unchanging part of its core ideology; customer greeters at the front door is a noncore practice that can change.
- Boeing's "Being on the leading edge of aviation; being pioneers" is a permanent, unchanging part of its core ideology; commitment to building jumbo jets is part of a noncore strategy that can change.
- 3M's "Respect for individual initiative" is a permanent, unchanging part of its core ideology; the 15 percent rule (where technical employees can spend 15 percent of their time on projects of their choosing) is a noncore practice that can change.
- Nordstrom's "Service to the customer above all else" is a permanent, unchanging part of its core ideology; regional geographic focus, piano players in the lobby, and overstocked inventory management are noncore practices that can change.
- Merck's "We are in the business of preserving and improving human life" is a permanent, unchanging part of its core ideology; its commitment to research targeted at specific diseases is part of a noncore strategy that can change.

It is absolutely essential to not confuse core ideology with culture, strategy, tactics, operations, policies, or other noncore practices. Over time, cultural norms must change; strategy must change; product lines must change; goals must change; competencies must change; administrative policies must change; organization structure must change; reward systems must change. Ultimately, the *only* thing a company should *not* change over time is its core ideology—that is, if it wants to be a visionary company.

This brings us to the central concept of this book: the underlying dynamic of "Preserve the core and stimulate progress" that's the essence of a visionary company. This is a brief chapter to introduce this fundamental concept and to present an organizing framework that provides a backdrop for the dozens of detailed stories and specific examples that fill the remaining six chapters.

DRIVE FOR PROGRESS

Core ideology in a visionary company works hand in hand with a relentless drive for progress that impels change and forward movement in all that is not part of the core ideology. The drive for progress arises from a deep human urge—to explore, to create, to discover, to achieve, to change, to improve. The drive for progress is not a sterile, intellectual recognition that "progress is healthy in a changing world" or that "healthy organizations should change and improve" or that "we should have goals"; rather, it's a deep, inner, compulsive—almost primal—*drive*.

It is the type of drive that led Sam Walton to spend time during the last precious few days of his life discussing sales figures for the week with a local store manager who dropped by his hospital room—a drive shared by J. Willard Marriott, who lived by the motto "Keep on being constructive, and doing constructive things, until it's time to die . . . make every day count, to the very end."[5]

It is the drive that motivated Citicorp to set the goal to become the most pervasive financial institution in the world when it was still small enough that such an audacious goal would seem ludicrous, if not foolhardy. It is the type of drive that led Walt Disney to bet its reputation on Disneyland with no market data to indicate demand for such a wild dream. It is the type of drive that impelled Ford to stake its future on the audacious goal "to democratize the automobile" and thereby leave an indelible imprint on the world.

It is the type of drive that spurred Motorola to live by the motto "Be in motion for motion's sake!" and propelled the company from battery eliminators and car radios to televisions, microprocessors, cellular communications, satellites circling the earth, and pursuit of the daunting "six sigma" quality standard (only 3.4 defects per *million*). Robert Galvin used the term "renewal" to describe Motorola's inner drive for progress:

> Renewal is the driving thrust of this company. Literally the day after my father founded the company to produce B Battery Eliminators in 1928, he had to commence the search for a replacement product because the Eliminator was predictably obsolete in 1930. He never stopped renewing. Nor have we. . . . Only those incultured with an elusive idea of renewal, which obliges a proliferation of new, creative ideas . . . and an unstinting dedication to committing to the risk and promise of those unchartable ideas, will thrive.[6]

It is the drive for progress that pushed 3M to continually experiment and solve problems that other companies had not yet even recognized *as* problems, resulting in such pervasive innovations as waterproof sandpaper, Scotch tape, and Post-it notes. It compelled Procter & Gamble to adopt profit-sharing and stock ownership programs in the 1880s, long before such steps became fashionable, and urged Sony to prove it possible to commercialize transistor-based products in the early 1950s, when no other companies had done so. It is the drive that led Boeing to undertake some of the boldest gambles in business history, including the decision to build the B-747 in spite of highly uncertain market demand—a drive articulated by William E. Boeing during the early days of the company:

It behooves no-one to dismiss any novel idea with the statement that it "can't be done." Our job is to keep everlastingly at research and experiment, to adapt our laboratories to production as soon as practicable, to let no new improvement in flying and flying equipment pass us by.[7]

Indeed, the drive for progress is never satisfied with the status quo, *even when the status quo is working well*. Like a persistent and incurable itch, the drive for progress in a highly visionary company can never be satisfied under *any* conditions, even if the company succeeds enormously: "We can always do better; we can always go further; we can always find new possibilities." As Henry Ford said, "You have got to keep doing and going."[8]

An Internal Drive

Like core ideology, the drive for progress is an *internal* force. The drive for progress doesn't wait for the external world to say "It's time to change" or "It's time to improve" or "It's time to invent something new." No, like the drive inside a great artist or prolific inventor, it is simply *there*, pushing outward and onward. You don't create Disneyland, build the 747, pursue six-sigma quality, invent 3M Post-it notes, institute employee stock ownership in the 1880s, or meet with a store manager on your deathbed because the outside environment demands it. These things arise out of an *inner* urge for progress. In a visionary company, the drive to go further, to do better, to create new possibilities *needs no external justification*.

Through the drive for progress, a highly visionary company displays a powerful mix of self-confidence combined with self-criticism. Self-confidence allows a visionary company to set audacious goals and make bold and daring moves, sometimes flying in the face of industry conventional wisdom or strategic prudence; it simply never occurs to a highly visionary company that it can't beat the odds, achieve great things, and become something truly extraordinary. Self-criticism, on the other hand, pushes for *self*-induced change and improvement *before* the outside world imposes the need for change and improvement; a visionary company thereby becomes its own harshest critic. As such, the drive for progress pushes from within for continual change and forward movement in everything that is not part of the core ideology.

Notice the ruthless self-imposed discipline captured in Bruce Nordstrom's response to the adulation the company had attained for its customer service standards: "We don't want to talk about our service. We're not as good as our reputation. It is a very fragile thing. You just have to do it every time, every day."[9] Notice the inner drive described by a

Hewlett-Packard marketing manager who never let his people rest on their laurels:

> We're proud of our successes, and we celebrate them. But the real excitement comes in figuring out how we can do even better in the future. It's a never-ending process of seeing how far we can go. There's no ultimate finish line where we can say "we've arrived." I never want us to be satisfied with our success, for that's when we'll begin to decline.[10]

PRESERVE THE CORE AND STIMULATE PROGRESS

Notice the dynamic interplay between core ideology and the drive for progress:

Core Ideology	Drive for Progress
Provides continuity and *stability*.	Urges continual *change* (new directions, new methods, new strategies, and so on).
Plants a relatively *fixed* stake in the ground.	Impels constant *movement* (toward goals, improvement, an envisioned form, and so on).
Limits possibilities and directions for the company (to those consistent with the content of the ideology).	*Expands* the number and variety of possibilities that the company can consider.
Has clear content ("*This* is our core ideology and we will not breach it").	Can be content-free ("*Any* progress is good, as long as it is consistent with our core").
Installing a core ideology is, by its very nature, a *conservative* act.	Expressing the drive for progress can lead to dramatic, radical, and *revolutionary* change.

The interplay between core and progress is one of the most important findings from our work. In the spirit of the "Genius of the AND," a visionary company does not seek mere balance between core and progress; it seeks to be *both* highly ideological and highly progressive at the same time, all the time. Indeed, core ideology and the drive for progress exist together in a visionary company like yin and yang of Chinese dualistic philosophy; each element enables, complements, and reinforces the other:

- The core ideology enables progress by providing a base of continuity around which a visionary company can evolve, experiment, and change. By being clear about what is core (and therefore relatively fixed), a company can more easily seek variation and movement in all that is not core.
- The drive for progress enables the core ideology, for without continual change and forward movement, the company—the carrier of the core—will fall behind in an ever-changing world and cease to be strong, or perhaps even to exist.

Although the core ideology and drive for progress usually trace their roots to specific individuals, a highly visionary company *institutionalizes* them—weaving them into the very fabric of the organization. These elements do not exist solely as a prevailing ethos or "culture." A highly visionary company does not simply have some vague set of intentions or passionate zeal around core and progress. To be sure, a highly visionary company does have these, but it also has concrete, tangible mechanisms to *preserve the core* ideology and to *stimulate progress.*

Walt Disney didn't leave its core ideology up to chance; it created Disney University and required every single employee to attend "Disney Traditions" seminars. Hewlett-Packard didn't just talk about the HP Way; it instituted a religious promote-from-within policy and translated its philosophy into the categories used for employee reviews and promotions, making it nearly impossible for anyone to become a senior executive without fitting tightly into the HP Way. Marriott didn't just talk about its core values; it instituted rigorous employee screening mechanisms, indoctrination processes, and elaborate customer feedback loops. Nordstrom didn't just philosophize about fanatical customer service; it created a cult of service reinforced by tangible rewards and penalties—"Nordies" who serve the customer well become well-paid heroes, and those who treat customers poorly get spit right out of the company.

Motorola didn't just preach quality; it committed to a daunting six-sigma quality goal and pursued the Baldrige Quality Award. General Electric didn't just pontificate about the importance of continuous technological innovation in the early 1900s; it created one of the world's first industrial R&D laboratories. Boeing didn't just dream about being on the leading edge of aviation; it made bold, irreversible commitments to audacious projects like the Boeing 747, in which failure could have literally killed the company. Procter & Gamble didn't just think self-imposed progress was a good idea; it installed a structure that pitted P&G product lines in fierce competition with each other, thus using institutionalized internal competition as a powerful mechanism to stimulate progress. 3M didn't just pay lip service to encouragement of individual initiative and innovation; it decentralized, gave researchers 15 percent of their time to pursue any project of their liking, created an internal venture capital fund, and instituted a rule that 25 percent of each division's annual sales should come from products introduced in the previous five years.

3M

Tangible. Concrete. Specific. Solid. Look inside a visionary company and you'll see a ticking, bonging, humming, buzzing, whirring, clicking, clattering clock. You'll see tangible manifestations of its core ideology and drive for progress everywhere.

> **INTENTIONS** are all fine and good, but it is the translation of those intentions into concrete items—mechanisms with teeth—that can make the difference between becoming a visionary company or forever remaining a wannabe.

We've found that organizations often have great intentions and inspiring visions for themselves, but they don't take the crucial step of translating their intentions into concrete items. Even worse, they often tolerate organization characteristics, strategies, and tactics that are misaligned with their admirable intentions, which creates confusion and cynicism. The gears and mechanisms of the ticking clock do not grind against each other but rather work in concert—in alignment with each other—to preserve the core and stimulate progress. The builders of visionary companies seek alignment in strategies, in tactics, in organization systems, in structure, in incentive systems, in building layout, in job design—in *everything*.

KEY CONCEPTS FOR CEOS, MANAGERS, AND ENTREPRENEURS

In working with practicing managers, we've found it useful to capture all of the key ideas from our findings into an overall framework that managers can use as a conceptual guide for diagnosing and designing their own organization.

Our framework, shown in Figure 4.A, has two layers. The top layer of the framework contains elements discussed in earlier chapters: a clock-building orientation (Chapter 2), the yin/yang symbol (No "Tyranny of the OR"), core ideology (Chapter 3), and the drive for progress (described earlier in this chapter). You can think of the top layer as a set of guiding intangibles that are necessary requirements to become a visionary company.

Figure 4.A

Conceptual Framework

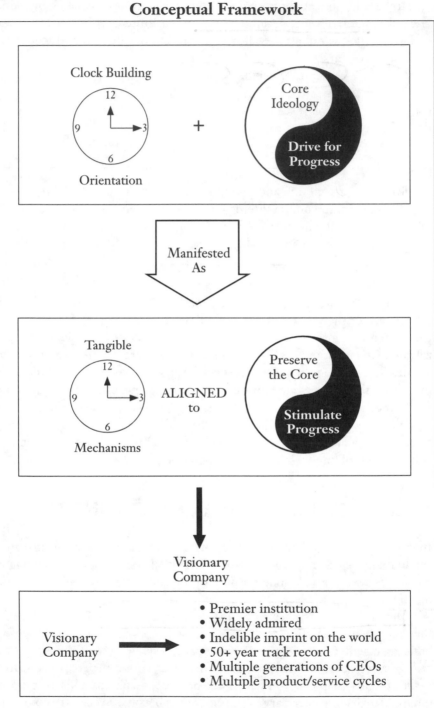

However, as important as they are, these intangible elements alone are not sufficient for becoming a visionary company. To become a visionary company requires translating these intangibles down into the second layer of the framework, and this is where most companies just fail to make the grade.

> **IF** you are involved in building and managing an organization, the single most important point to take away from this book is the critical importance of creating tangible mechanisms aligned to *preserve the core and stimulate progress.* This is the essence of clock building.

Tang' *Mech*

Indeed, if we had to distill our six-year research project into one key concept that conveys the most information about what it takes to build a visionary company, we would draw the following icon, which will appear atop all of the remaining chapters:

In the chapters that follow, we will describe the specific methods of preserving the core and stimulating progress that distinguished the visionary companies from the comparison companies, capped by a concluding chapter on alignment. They fall into five categories:

- *Big Hairy Audacious Goals (BHAGs)*: Commitment to challenging, audacious—and often risky—goals and projects toward which a visionary company channels its efforts (stimulates progress).
- *Cult-like Cultures:* Great places to work *only* for those who buy in to the core ideology; those who don't fit with the ideology are ejected like a virus (preserves the core).

- *Try a Lot of Stuff and Keep What Works:* High levels of action and experimentation—often unplanned and undirected—that produce new and unexpected paths of progress and enables visionary companies to mimic the biological evolution of species (stimulates progress).
- *Home-grown Management:* Promotion from within, bringing to senior levels only those who've spent significant time steeped in the core ideology of the company (preserves the core).
- *Good Enough Never Is:* A continual process of relentless self-improvement with the aim of doing better and better, forever into the future (stimulates progress).

We will provide examples, anecdotes, and systematic evidence to support and illustrate each of these methods. As you read each of these chapters, we encourage you to use our overall framework as a guide for diagnosing your own organization:

- Has it made the shift in perspective from time telling to *clock building*?
- Does it reject the "Tyranny of the OR" and embrace the "*Genius of the AND*"?
- Does it have a *core ideology*—core values and purpose beyond just making money?
- Does it have a *drive for progress*—an almost primal urge for change and forward movement in all that is not part of the core ideology?
- Does it *preserve the core and stimulate progress* through tangible practices, such as Big Hairy Audacious Goals, home-grown management, and the others described throughout the remainder of this book?
- Is the organization in *alignment*, so that people receive a consistent set of signals to reinforce behavior that supports the core ideology and achieves desired progress?

When you finish reading the next six chapters, you should have a sizable mental list of specific, tangible things that might make sense for you to implement in your own organization to make it more visionary. It doesn't matter whether you're a CEO, manager, individual contributor, or entrepreneur. You can put these ideas to work.

chapter **5**

BIG HAIRY AUDACIOUS GOALS

Preserve the Core

Stimulate Progress

Far better to dare mighty things, to win glorious triumphs, even though checkered by failure, than to take rank with those poor spirits who neither enjoy much nor suffer much, because they live in the gray twilight that knows not victory, nor defeat.

THEODORE ROOSEVELT, 1899[1]

We worked furiously [to realize our goals]. Because we didn't have fear, we could do something drastic.

MASARU IBUKA, FOUNDER, SONY CORPORATION, 1991[2]

Of all the things I've done, the most vital is coordinating the talents of those who work for us and pointing them toward a certain goal.

WALTER ELIAS DISNEY, FOUNDER, WALT DISNEY COMPANY, 1954[3]

Put yourself in the shoes of Boeing's management team in 1952. Your engineers have the idea to build a large jet aircraft for the commercial market. Your company has virtually no presence in the commercial market and your earlier commercial attempts have been failures.

You've been building aircraft primarily for the military (B-17 Flying Fortress, B-29 Superfortress, B-52 jet bomber) and four-fifths of your business comes from one customer—the Air Force.[4] Furthermore, your sales force reports that commercial airlines in both the United States and Europe have expressed little interest in the idea of a commercial jet from Boeing. The airlines have an anti-Boeing bias—a "they build great bombers, period" attitude. No other aircraft company has proved that there is a commercial market for jet aircraft. Rival Douglas Aircraft believes that propeller-driven planes will continue to dominate the commercial market. Your company still has memories of the painful layoffs from fifty-one thousand employees down to seventy-five hundred after the end of World War II.[5] And, for the clincher, you estimate that it will cost about three times your average annual after-tax profit for the past five years—roughly a quarter of your entire corporate net worth—to develop a prototype for the jet.[6] (Fortunately, you believe that you could also offer this jet aircraft to the military as a fueling plane for the military, but you still need to gamble the $15 million of your own money to develop the prototype.)[7]

What should you do?

If you're Boeing's management, you defy the odds and commit to the audacious goal of establishing yourself as a major player in the commercial aircraft industry. You build the jet. You call it the 707. And you bring the commercial world into the jet age.

In contrast, Douglas Aircraft (later to become McDonnell-Douglas, Boeing's comparison counterpart in our study) made the explicit decision to stick with piston propellers and take a cautious wait-and-see approach to commercial jet aircraft.[8] Douglas waited and saw Boeing fly right past and seize dominant control of the commercial market. Even as late as 1957—the year, according to *Business Week*, that the airlines "fell all over each other in their rush to replace piston planes"[9]—Douglas *still* did not have a jet ready for market. Finally, in 1958, Douglas introduced the DC-8, but never caught up to Boeing.

Perhaps you're thinking, "But might Boeing have just been lucky? Boeing looks smart in retrospect, but it could just as easily have been wrong." Good point. And we would be inclined to agree, except for one thing: Boeing has a long and consistent history of committing itself to big, audacious challenges. Looking as far back as the early 1930s, we see this bold commitment behavior at Boeing when it set the goal of becoming a major force in the military aircraft market and gambled its future on the P-26 military plane and then "bet the pot" on the B-17 Flying Fortress.[10]

Nor did this pattern end in the 1950s with the 707. During the development of the 727 in the early 1960s, Boeing turned the demands of a potential customer (Eastern Airlines) into a clear, precise—and nearly impossible—

challenge for its engineers: Build a jet that could land on runway 4-22 at La Guardia Airport (only 4,860 feet long—much too short for any existing passenger jet) *and* be able to fly nonstop from New York to Miami *and* be wide enough for six-abreast seating *and* have a capacity of 131 passengers *and* meet Boeing's high standards of indestructibility. Boeing's engineers made a significant breakthrough—the 727—largely because they were *given no other choice.*[11]

In contrast, Douglas Aircraft was slow to respond and didn't introduce the DC-9 until two years after the 727, putting it even further behind Boeing in the commercial jet market. And by then, Boeing had an even better short-range jet, the 737, in development. Theoretically, Douglas could have risen to the Eastern Airlines challenge just as quickly as Boeing, but it didn't. (As an aside, Boeing's original market-size estimate for the 727 was three hundred airplanes. It eventually sold over eighteen hundred, and the 727 became the short-range workhorse for the airline industry.)

In 1965, Boeing made one of the boldest moves in business history: the decision to go forward with the 747 jumbo jet, a decision that nearly killed the company. At the decisive board of directors meeting, Boeing Chairman William Allen responded to the comment by a board member that "if the [747] program isn't panning out, we can always back out."

"Back out?" stiffened Allen. "If the Boeing Company says we will build this airplane, we will build it even if it takes the resources of the entire company!"

Indeed, as it had with the P-26, B-17, 707, and 727, Boeing became irreversibly committed to the 747—financially, psychologically, publicly. During the 747 development, a Boeing visitor commented, "You know, Mr. Allen, [Boeing has] a lot riding on that plane. What would you do if the first airplane crashed on takeoff?" After a long pause, Allen replied, "I'd rather talk about something pleasant—like a nuclear war."[12]

Again, as with the DC-8 and DC-9, rival McDonnell Douglas was slow to commit to a jumbo jet project and fell into yet another round of catch-up with Boeing. The DC-10, McDonnell Douglas's response, never attained the same market position as the 747.

BHAGS: A POWERFUL MECHANISM TO STIMULATE PROGRESS

Boeing Corporation is an excellent example of how highly visionary companies often use bold missions—or what we prefer to call BHAGs (pronounced *bee-hags*, short for "Big Hairy Audacious Goals")—as a particularly powerful mechanism to stimulate progress. A BHAG is not the only powerful mechanism for stimulating progress, nor do all the visionary companies use it extensively (some, like 3M and HP, prefer to rely primarily on other mechanisms to stimulate progress, as we'll discuss in later chapters). Nonetheless, we found more evidence of this powerful mechanism in the visionary companies and less evidence of it in the comparison companies in fourteen out of eighteen cases. In three cases we found the visionary company and comparison company to be indistinguishable from each other with respect to BHAGs. In one case, we found more evidence for the use of BHAGs in the comparison company. (See Table A.5 in Appendix 3.)

All companies have goals. But there is a difference between merely having a goal and becoming committed to a huge, daunting challenge—like a big mountain to climb. Think of the moon mission in the 1960s. President Kennedy and his advisers could have gone off into a conference room and drafted something like "Let's beef up our space program," or some other such vacuous statement. The most optimistic scientific assessment of the moon mission's chances for success in 1961 was fifty-fifty and most experts were, in fact, more pessimistic.[13] Yet, nonetheless, Congress agreed (to the tune of an immediate $549 million and billions more in the following five years) with Kennedy's proclamation on May 25, 1961, "that this Nation should commit itself to achieving the goal, before this decade is out, of landing a man on the moon and returning him safely to earth."[14] Given the odds, such a bold commitment was, at the time, outrageous. But that's part of what made it such a powerful mechanism for getting the United States, still groggy from the 1950s and the Eisenhower era, moving vigorously forward.

A Clear—and Compelling—Goal

Like the moon mission, a true BHAG is clear and compelling and serves as a unifying focal point of effort—often creating immense team spirit. It has a clear finish line, so the organization can know when it has achieved the goal; people like to shoot for finish lines.

> **A BHAG** engages people—it reaches out and grabs them in the gut. It is tangible, energizing, highly focused. People "get it" right away; it takes little or no explanation.

The moon mission didn't need a committee to spend endless hours wordsmithing the goal into a verbose, meaningless, impossible-to-remember "mission statement." No, the goal itself—the mountain to climb—was so easy to grasp, so compelling in its own right, that it could be said one hundred different ways, yet easily understood by everyone. When an expedition sets out to climb Mount Everest, it doesn't need a three-page, convoluted "mission statement" to explain what Mount Everest is. Think about your own organization. Do you have verbose statements floating around, yet no stimulating bold goals with the compelling clarity of the moon mission, climbing Mount Everest, or the corporate BHAGs in this chapter? Most corporate statements we've seen do little to provoke forward movement (although some do help to preserve the core). To stimulate progress, however, we encourage you to think beyond the traditional corporate statement and consider the powerful mechanism of a BHAG.

Reflecting on the challenges facing a company like General Electric, CEO Jack Welch stated that the first step—before all other steps—is for the company to "define its destiny in broad but clear terms. You need an overarching message, something big, but simple and understandable."[15] Like what? GE came up with the following: "To become #1 or #2 in every market we serve and revolutionize this company to have the speed and agility of a small enterprise."[16] Employees throughout GE fully understood—and remembered—the BHAG. Now compare the compelling clarity of GE's BHAG with the difficult-to-understand, hard-to-remember "vision statement" articulated by Westinghouse in 1989:

General Electric[17]	Westinghouse[18]
Become #1 or #2 in every market we serve and revolutionize this company to have the speed and agility of a small enterprise.	Total Quality
	Market Leadership
	Technology Driven
	Global
	Focused Growth
	Diversified

The point here is not that GE had the "right" goal and Westinghouse had the "wrong" goal. The point is that GE's goal was clear, compelling, and more likely to stimulate progress, like the moon mission. Whether a company has the right BHAG or whether the BHAG gets people going in the right direction are not irrelevant questions, but they miss the essential point. Indeed, the *essential* point of a BHAG is better captured in such questions as: "Does it stimulate forward progress? Does it create momentum? Does it get people going? Does it get people's juices flowing? Do they find it stimulating, exciting, adventurous? Are they willing to throw their creative talents and human energies into it?" (NOTE: This doesn't mean that a visionary company pursues *any* random BHAG that occurs to it. An equally important question is, "Does it fit with our core ideology?" More on this at the end of the chapter.)

Take, for example, the case of Philip Morris versus R.J. Reynolds. In 1961, R.J. Reynolds had the largest market share (almost 35 percent), greatest size, and highest profitability in the tobacco industry. Philip Morris, on the other hand, was a sixth-place also-ran with less than 10 percent market share.[19] But Philip Morris had two things going for it that R.J. Reynolds didn't. First, and certainly not to be discounted, Philip Morris had recently repositioned a little-known women's cigarette called Marlboro as a general market cigarette with a cowboy mascot that would prove to be a huge success. And second, Philip Morris had *something to shoot for.*

Coming from behind, Philip Morris set the audacious goal for itself of becoming the General Motors of the tobacco industry.[20] (Back in the 1960s, becoming "the General Motors of the industry" meant becoming the dominant worldwide player.) Philip Morris then committed itself to this goal and rose from sixth to fifth, from fifth to fourth, and so on until it blasted longtime leader R.J. Reynolds out of first place. During this same time period, R.J. Reynolds displayed a stodgy, good-old-boy, clubby atmosphere and no clear, driving ambition for itself other than to attain a good return for shareholders.

Of course, Philip Morris had it easier than R.J. Reynolds: It's much more motivating to come from behind and topple industry giants—like David versus Goliath—than to simply hang on to number one. It's *exciting* to battle Goliath! It's even more exciting to beat him. But the fact remains that of the five also-ran tobacco companies in the 1960s, only one—Philip Morris—set and attained the ambitious goal of knocking Goliath on his rear and becoming the GM of the industry. To seriously entertain such ambitions as the distant sixth-place player in an industry dominated by entrenched players does not suggest timidity. Indeed, following the rational models of strategic planning, it would suggest arrogant stupidity, not farsighted wisdom. We've sometimes used the Philip Morris situation (disguised so as to not give away the punch line) with MBA students well schooled in strategic planning. Almost none of them think the company should go for the big cigar; as one student put it, "They don't have the right strategic assets and competencies; they should stick to their niche." Certainly, Philip Morris could have been wrong, long forgotten, and we wouldn't be writing about it in this book. But, equally certain, had Philip Morris timidly held to its industry niche and not challenged Goliath, we wouldn't be writing about them in this book, either.

AS in the Philip Morris case, BHAGs are bold, falling in the gray area where reason and prudence might say "This is unreasonable," but the drive for progress says, "We believe we can do it nonetheless." Again, these aren't just "goals"; these are *Big Hairy Audacious Goals.*

Another example, in 1907, Henry Ford, a forty-three-year-old businessman, stimulated his company forward with an astounding BHAG: "To democratize the automobile." Ford proclaimed:

> [To] build a motor car for the great multitude. . . . It will be so low in price that no man making a good salary will be unable to own one—and enjoy with his family the blessing of hours of pleasure in God's great open spaces. . . . everybody will be able to afford one, and everyone will have one. The horse will have disappeared from our highways, the automobile will be taken for granted.[21]

At the time of this BHAG, Ford was merely one of over thirty companies all clamoring for a slice of the emerging automobile market. No company had yet established itself as a clear leader in the chaos of the young industry, and Ford had only about 15 percent of the market. This outrageous ambition inspired the entire Ford design team to work at a ferocious pace till ten or eleven every night.[22] At one point, Charles Sorenson, a member of that team, remembered, "Mr. Ford and I [once] worked about forty-two hours without letup."[23]

During this period of time, General Motors (Ford's comparison in the study) watched its market share erode from 20 to 10 percent while Ford rose to the number one position in the industry.

Ironically, however, once Ford had achieved its big hairy goal of democratizing the automobile, it didn't set a new BHAG, became complacent, and watched GM set and achieve the equally audacious goal of overcoming Ford. We should emphasize here that *a BHAG only helps an organization as long as it has not yet been achieved.* Ford suffered from what we call the "we've arrived" syndrome—a complacent lethargy that can arise once a company has achieved one BHAG and does not replace it with another. (As an aside, if your organization has a BHAG, you might want to think about what's next before you complete the current one. Also, if you find your organization is in a state of malaise, you might ask yourself if you once had a BHAG—either implicit or explicit—that you've attained and not replaced with a new one.)

Let's look at another example of audacity in a young, small company. In the late 1950s, Tokyo Tsushin Kogyo (a relatively small company, largely unknown outside of its home country) took the costly step of discarding its original name in favor of a new one: Sony Corporation. The company's bank objected to the idea: "It's taken you ten years since the company's founding to make the name Tokyo Tsushin Kogyo widely known in the trade. After all this time, what do you mean by proposing such a nonsensical change?" Sony's Akio Morita responded simply that it would enable the company to expand worldwide, whereas the prior name could not be easily pronounced in foreign lands.[24]

You're probably thinking that such a move does not represent something particularly audacious; after all, most small to midsize companies eventually look to overseas markets. And it's not *that* big of a deal to change a corporate name from Tokyo Tsushin Kogyo to Sony. But look closely at the *reason* Akio Morita gave for this move, for therein lies an immense BHAG:

> Although our company was still small and we saw Japan as quite a large and potentially active market . . . it became obvious to me that if we did not set our sights on marketing abroad, we would not grow into the kind of company Ibuka and I had envisioned. We wanted to change the image [around the world] of Japanese products as poor in quality.[25]

In the 1950s, "Made in Japan" meant "cheap, junky, poor quality." In reading through materials on the company, we concluded that Sony not only wanted to be successful in its own right, but to become *the* company best known for changing the image of Japanese consumer products as being poor quality.[26] Having less than a thousand employees and no overseas presence to speak of, this was a nontrivial ambition.

This isn't the first example of a BHAG in Sony's history. In 1952, for example, it sent its limited engineering staff in pursuit of a seemingly impossible goal: to make a "pocketable" radio—a radio that could fit in a shirt pocket and could thereby become a pervasive product worldwide.[27] In the 1990s, we take such miniaturization for granted, but in the early 1950s, radios depended on vacuum tubes. To build such a miniature radio required long periods of painstaking trial and error and significant innovation. No company in the world had yet successfully applied transistor technology to a consumer radio.[28]

"Let's work on a transistor radio, whatever the difficulties we may face," proclaimed Masaru Ibuka. "I am sure we can produce transistors for radios."

When Ibuka told an outside adviser about the bold idea, the adviser responded: "Transistor radio? Are you sure? Even in America transistors are used only for defense purposes where money is no object. Even if you come out with a consumer product using transistors, who could afford to buy such a machine with such expensive devices?"

"That's what people think," responded Ibuka. "People are saying that transistors won't be commercially viable. . . . This will make the business all the more interesting."[29] In fact, Sony engineers *reveled* in the idea of doing something deemed by outsiders as foolhardy—perhaps even impossible—for such a small company. Sony made the pocketable radio and fulfilled its dream of creating a product that became pervasive world-wide. (As an outgrowth of this effort, one of Sony's scientists made break-throughs in the development of transistors that eventually led to a Nobel Prize.)[30]

Wal-Mart has had a similar pattern of audacious BHAGs, beginning as far back as Sam Walton's first five-and-dime store in 1945, for which his first goal was to "make my little Newport store the best, most profitable variety store in Arkansas within five years."[31] To achieve this goal required more than tripling the sales volume from $72,000 per year to $250,000 per year. The store attained this goal, becoming the biggest, most profitable store in Arkansas *and* in the surrounding five states.[32]

Walton continued to set similarly audacious goals for his organization, decade after decade. In 1977, he set the Big Hairy Audacious Goal of becoming a $1 billion company in four years (a more than doubling of the company's size).[33] Wal-Mart didn't stop there, however, continuing to set bold new targets for itself. In 1990, for example, Sam Walton set a new target: to double the number of stores and increase the sales volume per square foot by 60 percent by the year 2000.[34] After publishing this example in an article, we received the following letter from a proud Wal-Mart director:

January 10, 1992

You are correct that Sam Walton articulated a target to double the number of stores and increase the dollar volume per square foot by 60% by the fiscal year 2000.

The more important point—and what was missed—is that he did set a specific target of $125 billion! At the time, the largest retailer in the world had reached $30 billion. For the year ending January 1991, Wal-Mart reached $32.6 billion and became the largest retailer in the United States and the world. The only corporation anywhere which has attained a volume approaching $125 billion is General Motors.

I have been a director of Wal-Mart Stores since 1980 and have complete
confidence that the target set by Sam Walton will be attained. If
someone thought his original target set in 1977 was audacious, he or she
must be frightened by the present target.

> Sincerely,
> Robert Kahn
> Certified Management Consultant &
> Wal-Mart Director

Now, *that's* a BHAG!

Commitment and Risk

It's not just the presence of a goal that stimulates progress, it is also the level
of commitment to the goal. Indeed, *a goal cannot be classified as a BHAG
without a high level of commitment to the goal.* Doing the 747, for example,
would be a nice goal, maybe even an audacious goal. But the commitment to
"build this airplane even if it takes the resources of the entire company!"
turns it into a full-fledged BHAG. And, in fact, Boeing suffered terribly in
the early 1970s as sales of the "Big Bird" grew more slowly than expected.
During the three-year period from 1969 to 1971, Boeing laid off a total of
eighty-six thousand people, roughly 60 percent of its workforce.[35] During
those difficult days, someone placed a billboard near Interstate 5 in Seattle
which read:

> # Will the last person leaving Seattle please turn out the lights?

We all know now that the 747 became the flagship jumbo jet of the
airline industry, but the decision looks much different from the perspective
of the late 1960s. Yet—and this is the key point—Boeing was willing to
make the bold move in the face of the risks. As in Boeing's case, the risks do
not always come without pain. Staying in the comfort zone does little to
stimulate progress.

We see a similar pattern at Walt Disney Company, which has stimulated progress throughout its history by making bold—and often risky—commitments to audacious projects. In 1934, Walt Disney aimed to do something never before done in the movie industry: create a successful full-length animated feature film. In creating *Snow White*, Disney invested most of the company's resources and defied those in the industry that called it "Disney's Folly." After all, who would want to see a full-length feature cartoon? Two decades later, after a string of full-length animated films, including *Pinocchio*, *Fantasia*, and *Bambi*, Disney made yet another risky commitment to one of "Walt's screwy ideas": to build a radically new kind of amusement park, later to become known to all of us as Disneyland. In the 1960s, Disney repeated the process again, with a commitment to fulfill Walt's dying dream: EPCOT center in Florida.[36] Walt's brother, Roy, carried the commitment through, according to Michael Eisner:

> He virtually gave his life to fulfill his brother's dream of building Walt Disney World. He gave up his much deserved retirement, infused the park throughout with Disney quality, and saw the project through to completion, personally cutting the ribbon on opening day. He died within two months of that momentous event.[37]

Columbia Pictures, in contrast, did very little that was bold, visionary, or risky. It produced B-grade movies during the 1930s and 1940s. During the 1950s and 1960s, it made some good films, but was apparently unwilling to make committing moves into the future. While Disney was pushing forward into EPCOT, Columbia was being run by people who saw themselves "first, last, and always . . . as investors, not managers."[38] And whereas Columbia was eventually acquired in the early 1980s, Disney came roaring back after it defeated a set of hostile raiders and pursued new bold adventures, such as Japan Disney and EuroDisney.

IBM, like Disney, pulled ahead of rival Burroughs at critical junctures in its history via the mechanism of tangible—and, at times, risky—commitments to audacious goals. In particular, we point to IBM's BHAG to reshape the computer industry in the early 1960s. To attain this BHAG, IBM put itself at risk by making an all-or-nothing investment in a new computer called the IBM 360. At the time, the 360 was the largest privately financed commercial project ever undertaken; it required more resources than the United States spent on the Manhattan Project to develop the first atomic bomb. *Fortune* magazine called the 360 "IBM's $5,000,000,000 gamble . . . perhaps the riskiest business judgment of recent times." During the 360 introduction, IBM built up nearly *$600 million* of work-in-process inventory and almost needed emergency loans to meet payroll.

IBM 360

Furthermore, the 360 would make obsolete most of IBM's existing product lines. Upon public announcement of the 360, demand for IBM's existing products dried up and the company found itself committed to a long leap across a deep canyon with no going back. If the 360 failed, then, well, it wouldn't be a pretty sight. Wrote *Fortune*, "It was roughly as though General Motors had decided to scrap its existing makes and models and offer in their place one new line of cars covering the entire spectrum of demand, with a radically redesigned engine and an exotic fuel."[39] Tom Watson, Jr., wrote:

> There wasn't going to be much room for error. It was the biggest, riskiest decision I ever made, and I agonized about it for weeks, but deep down I believed there was nothing IBM couldn't do.[40]

Ironically, Burroughs (IBM's comparison in the study) had a technological lead over IBM in computers. However, when the time came to make a bold commitment to computers, Burroughs took the conservative approach, choosing instead to concentrate on older lines of accounting machines. Like Douglas Aircraft relative to Boeing, Burroughs then watched as IBM seized control of the market. In describing this phase in Burroughs' history, Ray MacDonald (Burroughs' president at the time), explained, "From 1964 to 1966 our major effort was to bring profitability up. The restraints on our computer program were temporary and were caused only by the fact that we needed to immediately improve earnings."[41]

Again, as discussed in the chapter on core ideology, we see that highly visionary behavior occurs when the company does not view business as ultimately about maximizing profitability. IBM had to be number one and go for the 360 not just to make money, but *because it was IBM*. But, of course, IBM wasn't always *IBM*.

Back in 1924, the Computing Tabulating Recording Company (CTR) was not much more than any of a hundred other fairly average midsize companies trying to make a go of it. In fact, it had been nearly bankrupt three years prior and only survived the 1921 recession through heavy borrowing.[42] It primarily sold time clocks and weighing scales, and only had fifty-two salesmen who met quota.[43] But Thomas J. Watson, Sr., had no interest in seeing CTR remain an average company. He wanted the company to raise its sights, to become more—much more—than the dreary little Computing Tabulating Recording Company. He wanted it to embark on the path of becoming a truly great company of global stature, so he changed the company's name. Today we think nothing of the name "International Business Machines"; but back in 1924, it seemed almost ludicrous. In the words of Thomas J. Watson, Jr.:

Father came home from work, gave mother a hug, and proudly announced that the Computing Tabulating Recording Company, henceforth would be known by the grand name International Business Machines. I stood in the doorway of the living room thinking, "*That* little outfit?" Dad must have had in mind the IBM of the future. The one he actually ran was still full of cigar-chomping guys selling coffee grinders and butcher scales.[44]

A name change per se isn't particularly audacious. But proclaiming itself to be *the* International Business Machines Corporation in 1924—and to *mean* it—represents sheer audacity. (For the record, Burroughs remained the "Burroughs Adding Machine Company" until 1953. We doubt that this name had the same impact on Burroughs employees' sense of their future as the name International Business Machines had over at IBM.)

Even highly conservative Procter & Gamble has periodically used bold BHAGs. In 1919, for example, P&G set the goal to reach a point where it could provide steady employment for its workers by revolutionizing the distribution system, bypassing wholesalers, and going straight to retailers. (Wholesalers ordered large quantities and then, like a snake digesting a large meal, would lie dormant for months, thus forcing P&G into hire-and-fire swings of high and slack demand.) According to Oscar Schisgall in *Eyes on Tomorrow: The Evolution of Procter & Gamble*, the internal debate on the goal went as follows:[45]

"We would need to increase the number of accounts from 20,000 to over 400,000," complained the accountants. "Do you realize what that will do to our accounting costs?"

"We'd have to open hundreds of warehouses around the country," the distribution team pointed out. "We'd have to hire trucking companies all over the United States to deliver to the retail stores."

"Will the wholesalers become so furious when their P&G business is taken away that they'll start to boycott and refuse to sell anything to stores that deal directly with P&G?" asked some managers. "That could ruin us."

"How can P&G possibly build a sales staff large enough to visit every little grocery store in America?" asked the sales people. "The sales division would have to be bigger than the U.S. Army!"

Richard Deupree, P&G president at the time, believed in P&G's ability to overcome the odds, and he saw the goal of steady employment as worth the risks. (His confidence was partly based on a successful experimental

effort to go directly to retailers in New England.) P&G went forward with
the idea and figured out how to make it work. By 1923, P&G had achieved
its goal. A newspaper article announced:

> On August 1, 1923, a statement of more than usual interest to the
> world of labor and industry was announced by Procter & Gamble
> Company. This was a guarantee of steady employment to the em-
> ployees of the company in plants and offices located in thirty cities
> in the United States. This epoch-making announcement meant that
> for the first time in American industry, the thousands of employees
> of one of the country's largest corporations were assured of steady
> employment the year round, regardless of seasonal depressions in
> business.[46]

In describing such commitments, Deupree explained:

> We like to try the impractical and impossible and prove it to be both
> practical and possible—if it's the right thing to do in the first
> place. . . . You do something you think is right. If it clicks, you give it
> a ride. If you hit, mortgage the farm and go for broke.[47]

Colgate, in contrast, showed much less self-initiative than P&G
throughout its history in launching new, audacious, or innovative projects.
As with the path straight to retailers, Colgate found itself time and again one
step behind P&G, in a reactive follow-the-leader mode. (We will more
thoroughly discuss the P&G/Colgate contrast in later chapters.)

The "Hubris Factor"

One of our research assistants observed that highly visionary companies
seem to have self-confidence bordering on hubris (the dictionary defines
hubris as "overbearing pride, confidence, or arrogance"). We came to call
this the "hubris factor." In mythological terms, you might think of it as
taunting the gods.

To set Big Hairy Audacious Goals requires a certain level of unreason-
able confidence. It's not reasonable to commit to the Boeing 707 or 747.
The IBM 360 was not prudent, nor was it humble for a midsize butcher-
scale seller to proclaim itself to be the International Business Machines
Corporation. It's not cautious to create Disneyland. It's not modest to
declare, "We will democratize the automobile." It was almost foolhardy for
Philip Morris—as the runt child of the tobacco industry—to take on R.J.
Reynolds. It's almost absurd to proclaim as a small company the goal of

becoming *the* company that changes the worldwide image of Japanese products as being of poor quality.

Therein lies one of the maddening paradoxes behind the visionary companies.

> **THE** BHAGs looked more audacious to *outsiders* than to insiders. The visionary companies didn't see their audacity as taunting the gods. It simply never occurred to them that they couldn't do what they set out to do.

Let's make an analogy to mountain climbing. Imagine watching a rock climber scale a cliff without a rope; if she falls, she dies. To the uninformed spectator, the climber looks bold and risk-seeking, if not foolhardy. But suppose that climber is on a climb that *to her* appears eminently doable, well within her range of ability. From the climber's perspective, she has no doubts that, with proper training and concentration, she can make the climb. To her, the climb is not too risky. It *does* stimulate her to know that if she falls, she dies; but she has confidence in her ability. The highly visionary companies in setting bold BHAGs are much like that climber.

THE GOAL, NOT THE LEADER (CLOCK BUILDING, NOT TIME TELLING)

We wish to emphasize that the key mechanism at work here is not charismatic leadership. Returning to the moon mission example, we cannot deny that John F. Kennedy had a charismatic leadership style, nor can we deny that he deserves much of the credit for seriously proposing the imaginative and bold goal of going to the moon and back before the end of the decade. Nonetheless, Kennedy's leadership style was not the primary mechanism at work for stimulating progress. Kennedy died in 1963; he was no longer present to urge, prod, inspire—to "lead" to the moon. After Kennedy's death, did the moon mission become any less inspiring? Did it grind to a halt? Did going to the moon cease to provide a sense of national momentum? Of course not! The beauty of the moon mission, once launched, was its ability to stimulate progress regardless of whoever happened to be president. Was it any less exciting to land on the moon with Richard Nixon in office than John F. Kennedy? No. The *goal itself* became the motivating mechanism.

Let's return for a moment to our letter from Robert Kahn, the Wal-

Mart director. He wrote the letter on January 10, 1992—the same time that Sam Walton was in the final months of his battle with bone cancer, which ended his life on April 5, 1992. Nonetheless, even with Walton's rapidly deteriorating health, Kahn expressed "complete confidence" that Wal-Mart would meet the goal. Whether Wal-Mart will become a $125 billion company by the year 2000 remains to be seen as we write these words, but the goal still exists—pulling the company forward like a magnet—even without the charismatic leadership of Sam Walton. By setting such an audacious BHAG, Walton left behind a powerful mechanism for stimulating progress. The goal transcended the leader.

The goal also transcended the leader at Boeing. Certainly, William Allen played a key role in getting the company committed to the 747, but the goal itself became the stimulus for vigorous movement, not William Allen. In fact, T. A. Wilson, William Allen's successor, became Boeing's president and chief executive officer in 1968, with the 747 still in development and the company yet to face the nearly fatal task of surviving the initial slow sales of the big bird. Boeing did not grind to a halt or become lethargic after Allen's retirement, not with the very survival of the company at stake, and certainly not with the most amazing commercial airplane in history yet to be born. Keep in mind that Boeing used this mechanism for stimulating progress long before William Allen (the P-26, the B-17, and others) and long after the tenure of William Allen (the completion of the 747, and then the 757 and 767). The repeated commitment to BHAGs has been a key mechanism—part of the "ticking clock"—at Boeing through (so far) six generations of leadership.

In contrast, McDonnell Douglas' lack of forward progress relative to Boeing can be traced in large part to the personal leadership style of James McDonnell. *Business Week* ran an article on McDonnell Douglas in 1978 entitled "Where Management Style Sets Strategy," wherein it detailed how "Mr. Mac's" style of "measuring every risk carefully, being highly conservative . . . produce[s] a strategy without debating it around the table."[48] At Boeing, audacious commitments to bold, daring projects became a *characteristic of the institution*—regardless of the leader in charge. At McDonnell Douglas, the risk-averse, stick-in-the-mud approach to commercial aircraft was a characteristic of the individual leader in charge. Again, we see clock building at Boeing and time telling at McDonnell Douglas (and not even good time telling, at that).

Sony also made the use of BHAGs an institutionalized habit—*a way of life*. Nick Lyons, who delved into the inner workings of Sony's management processes for his book *The Sony Vision*, wrote: "Target. A word I heard repeated over and over—in English—[inside Sony]."[49] Dr. Makato Kikuchi, Sony's director of research in the mid-1970s, described to Lyons the importance of this embedded process (paraphrased):

Though it is widely rumored that Sony spends a vastly greater proportion of gross sales on research than other firms, this is simply not so. . . . The difference between our efforts and those of other Japanese companies lies not in the level of technology, or the quality of the engineers, or even in the amount of money budgeted for development (about 5% of sales). The main difference lies in . . . the establishment of mission-oriented research and proper *targets*. Many other companies give their researchers *full* freedom. We don't; we find an aim, a very real and clear *target* and then establish the necessary task forces to get the job done. Ibuka taught us that, once the commitment to go ahead is made, *never* give up. This pervades all the research and development work at Sony.[50]

BHAGs and the "Postheroic Leader Stall"

Corporations regularly face the dilemma of how to maintain momentum after the departure of highly energetic leaders (often founders). We saw this "postheroic leader stall" at a number of comparison companies in our study: Burroughs (after Boyer), Chase Manhattan (after Rockefeller), Columbia (after Cohn), Howard Johnson (after Johnson, Sr.), Melville (after Melville), TI (after Haggarty), Westinghouse (after George Westinghouse), and Zenith (after MacDonald). We didn't see this pattern as much in the visionary companies—only two clear cases stand out: Walt Disney (after Walt Disney) and Ford Motor (after Henry Ford, Sr.). The visionary companies offer a partial solution: Create BHAGs that take a life of their own and thereby act as a stimulus through multiple generations of leadership. (If you are a soon-to-retire chief executive, we encourage you to take a hard look at this lesson. Does your company have a BHAG to which it is committed and that will provide momentum long after you're gone? And, even more important, *does it have the ability to continually set bold new goals for itself long into the future?*)

In examining Citicorp, for example, we noticed that the company continually used bold, audacious goals to move itself forward through multiple generations of leadership. In the 1890s, City Bank (as Citicorp was then named) was an unspectacular regional bank with only a president, a cashier, and a handful of employees. Yet president James Stillman set the almost ludicrous (but certainly stimulating) aim "to become a great national bank."[51] A financial journalist wrote in 1891:

[He] dreams of a great national bank, and thinks he can make one of the City Bank. It is what he is trying to do, it is what occupies his mind, and animates his actions. He is running his bank not toward dividends, but towards an ideal . . . to make it great in domestic and in international finance: that is the dream of James Stillman."[52]

Although we can certainly trace the conception of this BHAG to Stillman himself, it took a life of its own and propelled the company forward long into future generations. Frank Vanderlip, Stillman's successor as president, wrote in 1915 (a quarter of a century after Stillman's "dream" and six years after Stillman moved to Paris in retirement):

> I am perfectly confident that it is open to us to become the most powerful, the most serviceable, the most far-reaching world financial institution that has ever been.[53]

A bold goal indeed, especially for a bank that a year earlier had only "eight vice presidents, ten junior officers, and fewer than five hundred other employees . . . at a single location on Wall Street."[54] Then, in the next generation, Charles Mitchell echoed the same go-forward tune in a 1922 speech to employees: "We are on our way to bigger things. The National City Bank's future is brighter than it has ever been. . . . We are getting ready now to go full speed ahead."[55] Going "full speed ahead"—in pursuit of the great ambitions first dreamed in the late 1880s—City Bank grew from $352 million total assets in 1914 to $2.6 billion of assets in 1929, an average annual growth rate of over 35 percent.

City Bank, like most banks, struggled through the 1930s, but after World War II it flew forward—through five further generations of leadership—with heightened energy toward Stillman and Vanderlip's ambition of becoming "the most far reaching financial institution there has ever been." George Moore (president from 1959 to 1967) sounded a lot like his predecessors of half a century earlier when he said:

> Around 1960 . . . [we decided that] we would seek to perform every useful financial service, anywhere in the world.[56]

Note the consistency across the generations. Yes, each generation had a chief executive. And yes, the original Citicorp dream traces back to an original architect. But the goal itself transcended that architect, and the predisposition to go for the audacious became an embedded pattern in the institution.

Chase Manhattan (Citicorp's comparison in the study) had similar ambitions and, in fact, the two banks vied with each other as fierce rivals. Throughout the twentieth century, Citicorp and Chase were evenly matched, racing side by side. During the 1960s, the two banks battled with

each other for end-of-year first-place honors in terms ...
1954 to 1969 they ran almost dead even.[57] Not until 1.
Citicorp pull ahead of Chase for good, eventually reaching tw
Chase. We acknowledge that Citicorp stumbled in the late 198
1990s. But so did Chase, and they had a lot of company, as a 1.
commercial banks had hard times in the 1980s.

Yet, even with their similarities, there was a significant differenc...between Citicorp and Chase in the tone and strategies supporting their ambitious goals—a difference that perhaps explains in part their different trajectories after 1968. David Rockefeller became president of Chase in 1960, and the goal to beat Citibank was viewed more as *Rockefeller's* goal than Chase's goal.

The Citicorp chief executives, unlike those at Chase, used primarily organizational (clock-building) strategies in their stewardship of the bank toward its goals. Stillman concentrated on management succession and organization structure. Vanderlip commented that "the one limitation that I can see, lies in the quality of management" and he put most of his effort into organization design and initiated a management development program.[58] George Moore focused first and foremost on making "Citicorp an institution" built largely around procedures for finding, training, and promoting personnel. "Without the capable people these procedures developed," he wrote, "none of our goals would have been attainable."[59] Chase, in contrast, concentrated primarily on market and product strategies (time telling) rather than clock-building strategies.

Like Boeing and Citicorp, Motorola presents an excellent example of BHAGs as part of a multigenerational ticking clock. Founder Paul Galvin often used BHAGs to push his engineers to do the impossible. When Motorola moved into the television market in the late 1940s, for example, Galvin set a challenging BHAG for the television group: to profitably sell one hundred thousand TVs in the first year at a price of $179.95.

"Our new plant hasn't nearly the capacity for that kind of production," exclaimed one of his managers. "We'll never sell that quantity; that would make our industry position third or fourth, and the best we've ever been in home radio is seventh or eighth," complained another. "We're not even sure we can break $200 [in cost]," said a production engineer.

"We'll sell them," Galvin responded. "I don't want to see any more cost sheets until you provide me with a profit at that price and that volume. We'll work ourselves into it."[60]

Motorola did indeed rise to fourth in the television industry within the year. But even more important, Galvin instilled an *institutional* drive for progress that resulted in a repeating pattern of BHAGs within the company.

.n grooming his son for the CEO job, he continually emphasized the importance of "keeping the company moving" and that vigorous movement in *any* direction is better than sitting still; always have something to shoot for, he advised.[61]

Decades after his death in 1959, Galvin's company still uses BHAGs, including the goal of becoming a major force in advanced electronics, the goal of attaining six-sigma quality performance and the goal of winning the Malcolm Baldrige Quality Award. Galvin's son and successor used the word "renewal" to capture the idea of continual transformations, often (although not exclusively) attained through commitments to audacious projects. Bob Galvin then passed along to the next generation of leadership the imperative that "at times we must engage in an act of faith that key things are doable that are not provable."[62]

The same little company that began life doing B-battery eliminator repairs for Sears radios and making jerry-built car radios has continually propelled itself forward via bold goals and reinvented itself over and over again, far beyond the life of its founder. That same little company has moved far from radios and TVs. That same company eventually created the powerful M68000 microprocessors that Apple Computer selected as the brains of the Macintosh Computer on which we're writing this book. And, as we write these very words, that same company moves forward with the biggest BHAG of its life to date: the task of launching Iridium, a $3.4 billion commercial gamble taken in joint venture with other companies to create a worldwide satellite system that would allow phone calls between any two points on earth.[63]

Zenith, like Motorola, did have a few BHAGs in its early history: the goal to make FM radio a pervasive reality, early commitment to be a major player in televisions, and an expensive bet on pay TV. But—and this is the crucial point—Zenith, unlike Motorola, did not display an *organizational* propensity for setting bold, audacious goals after the death of its founder in 1958. By the early 1970s, "innate cautiousness" pervaded Zenith, as described by its controller in 1974:

> It's hard to explain why a decision is made *not* to do something. There are a number of reasons behind it—including innate cautiousness. For one thing, we've always had our hands full with [our current markets] and we've always tended to stick with what appeared to be the biggest payoff and what we knew how to do best. . . . We didn't feel we could compete . . . in those [new] markets unless we were willing to sacrifice some of our margin, and we were unwilling to do that. We are basically a U.S. company and likely to stay that way.[64]

Zenith chief executive John Nevin echoed the same view in talking about the company's slow move into new technologies, like solid-state electronics: "I think you also have to say that Zenith has been more cautious than some of its competitors in bringing innovations to market. . . . We are now involved in an extraordinary effort to bring [solid-state] to market, but we are in doubt as to whether it will come to fruition."

Zenith's Commander McDonald, unlike Motorola's Paul Galvin, did not leave behind a company with the ability to continually reinvent itself with bold goals. Commander McDonald was a great leader—a great time teller—but he died a long time ago. Paul Galvin's company, on the other hand, lives and thrives thirty-five years after his death. Galvin built a clock.

GUIDELINES FOR CEOS, MANAGERS, AND ENTREPRENEURS

Although we've written this chapter primarily from a corporate perspective, BHAGs can be applied to stimulate progress at any level of an organization. Individual product line managers at P&G frequently set BHAGs for their brands. Nordstrom systematically sets BHAGs all up and down the company—from regions, to stores, to departments, to individual salespeople. 3M product champions thrive on overcoming all odds, skeptics, and naysayers to prove that their quirky inventions can make it in the market. An organization can have any number of BHAGs. It does not need to limit itself to only one BHAG at a time; Sony and Boeing, for instance, usually pursued multiple BHAGs simultaneously, often at different levels of the corporation.

BHAGs are particularly well suited to entrepreneurs and small companies. Recall Sam Walton and his goal to make his first dime store the most successful in Arkansas within five years. Recall Sony's goal to make a "pocketable radio" in its early years. Or Tom Watson, Sr.'s goal to transform his tiny one-building company into International Business Machines Corporation. Indeed, most entrepreneurs have a built-in BHAG: To just get off the ground and reach a point where survival is no longer in question is huge and audacious for most start-ups.

We've covered most of the key points about BHAGs as we've moved through the text of this chapter. Here are a few key take-away points you might want to keep in mind as you consider BHAGs for your own organization:

- A BHAG should be so clear and compelling that it requires little or no explanation. Remember, a BHAG is a *goal*—like climbing a mountain or going to moon—not a "statement." If it doesn't get people's juices going, then it's just not a BHAG.

- A BHAG should fall well outside the comfort zone. People in the organization should have reason to believe they can pull it off, yet it should require heroic effort and perhaps even a little luck—as with the IBM 360 and Boeing 707.
- A BHAG should be so bold and exciting *in its own right* that it would continue to stimulate progress even if the organization's leaders disappeared before it had been completed—as happened at Citibank and Wal-Mart.
- A BHAG has the inherent danger that, once achieved, an organization can stall and drift in the "we've arrived" syndrome, as happened at Ford in the 1920s. A company should be prepared to prevent this by having follow-on BHAGs. It should also complement BHAGs with the other methods of stimulating progress.
- Finally, and most important of all, a BHAG should be consistent with a company's core ideology.

Preserve the Core and Stimulate Progress

BHAGs alone do not make a visionary company. Indeed, progress alone— no matter what the mechanism used to stimulate progress—does not make a visionary company. *A company should be careful to preserve its core while pursuing BHAGs.*

For example, the 747 was an incredibly risky venture but along the way, Boeing maintained its core value of product safety and applied the most conservative safety standards, testing, and analysis ever to a commercial aircraft. No matter what the financial pressures, Walt Disney preserved its core value of fanatical attention to detail while working on *Snow White*, Disneyland, and Disney World. Merck, in keeping with its core value of imagination, sought preeminence primarily by creating new breakthrough innovations, not by creating me-too products. Jack Welch at GE made it clear that attaining number one or number two in a market at the expense of integrity would be unacceptable. Citicorp continually reinforced its belief in meritocracy and internal entrepreneurship throughout its expansive quest to become the "most far-reaching world financial institution that has ever been." Motorola never abandoned its basic belief in the dignity of and respect for the individual throughout all of its big, hairy, self-selected challenges.

Furthermore, the visionary companies didn't launch blindly toward *any* random BHAG, but only toward those that reinforced their core ideologies and reflected their self-concept. Notice the link between core and BHAG in the following list:

Core to Preserve	☯	BHAG(s) to Stimulate Progress
Being on the leading edge of aviation; being pioneers; risk-taking	(Boeing) ⟷	Bet the pot on the B-17, 707, 747.
Seek superiority in all we undertake; Spend a lot of time making customers happy.	(IBM) ⟷	Commit to a $5 billion gamble on the 360; meet the emerging needs of our customers.
We are *about* cars—especially cars for the average person.	(Ford) ⟷	"Democratize the automobile."
Tapping the "latent creative power within us"; self-renewal; continual improvement; honorably serve the community via great products.	(Motorola) ⟷	Invent a way to sell 100,000 TVs at $179.95; Attain six-sigma quality; win the Baldridge Award; launch Iridium.
Winning—being the best and beating others; Personal freedom of choice is worth defending.	(Philip Morris) ⟷	Slay Goliath and become the front-runner in the tobacco industry, despite the social forces against smoking.
Elevation of the Japanese culture and national status; being a pioneer, doing the impossible.	(Sony) ⟷	Change the worldwide image of Japanese products as poor quality; create a pocketable transistor radio.
"Bring happiness to millions"; fanatical attention to detail; creativity, dreams, imagination.	(Disney) ⟷	Build Disneyland—and build it to *our* image, not industry standards.
Preserving and improving human life; medicine is for the patient, not for the profits; imagination and innovation.	(Merck) ⟷	Become the preeminent drug maker worldwide, via massive R&D and new products that cure disease.

Revolutionizing the railroad business would certainly have been a BHAG for Ford in 1909; but Ford wasn't *about* railroads, it was about cars. Creating the cheapest radios in history, regardless of quality or innovation, would certainly have been a BHAG for Sony in 1950, but it wouldn't have fit with Sony's self-image as pioneers of innovation and key players in the task of elevating Japan's status in the world. Reinventing itself entirely away from the tobacco industry after the Surgeon General's reports would certainly have been a BHAG for Philip Morris in the 1960s, but how would it have fit with the company's self-conception as the defiant, fiercely independent, free-thinking, free-choosing, individualistic Marlboro cowboy? It wouldn't.

Yes, any BHAG exciting to people inside your company would stimulate change and movement. But the BHAGs should also be a powerful statement about the company's ideology. In fact, BHAGs can help to reinforce one of the key sets of mechanisms for preserving the core ideology: a cult-like culture, the subject of our next chapter. To defy the odds, to take on big hairy challenges—especially if rooted in an ideology—does much to make people feel that they belong to something special, elite, different, better.

We return once again to a key aspect of a visionary company: the powerful interplay between core ideology and the drive for progress which exist together like the yin and yang of Chinese dualistic philosophy. Each element complements and reinforces the other. Indeed, the core ideology enables progress by providing a base of continuity from which a visionary company can launch the corporate equivalent of the moon mission; likewise, progress enables the core ideology, for without change and movement forward, the company will eventually cease to be viable. Again, it's not *either* core *or* progress. It's not even a nice balance between core and progress but rather two powerful elements, inextricably linked and both working at full force to the ultimate benefit of the institution. A GE employee eloquently described the dynamic interplay between core and progress while discussing the company's BHAG to "become #1 or #2 in every market we serve and revolutionize this company to have the speed and agility of a small enterprise":

> "GE . . . We bring good things to life." Most wouldn't admit it, but everyone at GE gets chills when they hear that jingle. The simple, corny phrase captures how they feel about the company. . . . It means jobs and growth for the economy, quality and service for the customer, benefits and training for the employee, and challenge and satisfaction for the individual. It means integrity, honesty, and loyalty at all levels. *And without this reservoir of values and commitment, Welch could not have pulled off his revolution.* [emphasis hers][65]

chapter **6**

CULT-LIKE CULTURES

Preserve the Core

Stimulate Progress

Now, I want you to raise your right hand—and remember what we say at Wal-Mart, that a promise we make is a promise we keep—and I want you to repeat after me: From this day forward, I solemnly promise and declare that every time a customer comes within ten feet of me, I will smile, look him in the eye, and greet him. So help me Sam.

SAM WALTON, TO OVER ONE HUNDRED THOUSAND WAL-MART ASSOCIATES VIA TV SATELLITE LINK-UP, MID-1980s[1]

IBM is really good at motivating its people; I see that through Anne. [She] might be brainwashed by some people's standards, but it's a good brainwashing. They really do instill a loyalty and drive to work.

SPOUSE OF IBM EMPLOYEE, 1985[2]

So why do you want to work at Nordstrom?" the interviewer asks.

"Because my friend, Laura, tells me it's the best place she's ever worked," Robert responds. "She gushes about the excitement of working with the very best—being part of the elite of the elite. She's almost a mission-ary for you folks. Very proud to call herself a Nordstrom employee. And she's been rewarded well. Laura started in the stockroom eight years ago and now she gets to manage an entire store; she's only twenty-nine.[3] She told me that people here make a lot more than salespeople at other stores, and that the best salespeople working on the floor can make over $80,000 a year."*[4]

"Yes, it's true that you can make more money here than working at other department stores. Our salespeople generally make almost double the na-tional average for retail sales clerks—and a few make a lot more than that.[5] But you know, of course, not everyone has what it takes to really make it here as a member of the Nordstrom corporate family," explains the interviewer. "We're selective, and a lot don't make it. You prove yourself at every level, or you leave."[6]

"Yes. I've heard that 50 percent of new hires are gone after one year."[7]

"Something like that. Those who don't like the pressure and the hard work, and who don't buy into our system and values, they're gone. But if you have the drive, initiative, and—above all else—the ability to produce and serve the customer, then you'll do well.[8] The key question is whether Nord-strom is right for you. If not, you'll probably hate it here, fail miserably, and leave."[9]

"What positions would I be eligible for?"

"The same as every other new hire—you start at the bottom, working the stockroom and the sales floor."

"But I have a bachelor's degree, Phi Beta Kappa, from University of Washington. Other companies will let me begin as a management trainee."

"Not here. *Everybody* starts at the bottom. Mr. Bruce, Mr. Jim, and Mr. John—the three Nordstrom brothers that make up the chairman's office—they all started on the floor. Mr. Bruce likes to remind us that he and his brothers were all raised sitting on a shoe sales stool in front of the customer; it's a literal and figurative posture that we all keep in mind.[10] You get a lot of operational freedom here; no one will be directing your every move, and you're only limited by your ability to perform (within the bounds of the Nordstrom way, of course). But if you're not willing to do whatever it takes to make a customer happy—to personally deliver a suit to his hotel room, get down on your knees to fit a shoe, force yourself to smile when a customer is a real jerk—then you just don't belong here, period. Nobody *tells* you to be a customer service hero; it's just sort of expected."[11]

---

* "Robert"—a typical Nordstrom new hire—is a composite character, but the experience described is authentic. We created a description of Robert's experience based on interviews with employees and ex-employees, transcript notes from an interview with co-chairman Jim Nordstrom, company documents, book excerpts, and articles.

Robert took the job at Nordstrom, excited at the prospect of joining something special, thrilled to be at *the* place to work. He was proud to receive personalized professional business cards, rather than a name tag.[12] The handout depicting Nordstrom's "Company Structure" as an upside down pyramid made him feel even more important.[13]

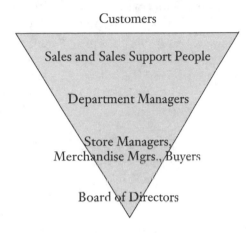

He also received a copy of Nordstrom's employee handbook, which consisted of a single five-by-eight-inch card and read, in its entirety:[14]

WELCOME TO NORDSTROM

We're glad to have you with our Company.
Our number one goal is to provide
outstanding customer service.
Set both your personal and professional goals high.
We have great confidence in your ability to achieve them.

Nordstrom Rules:
Rule #1: **Use your good
judgment in all situations.**
There will be no additional rules.

Please feel free to ask your department manager,
store manager or division general manager
any question at any time.

During his first few months, Robert became immersed in the world of a dedicated "Nordie," as many employees called themselves.[15] He found that he spent most of his time at the store, at Nordie functions, or socializing with other Nordies; they became his support group.[16] He heard dozens of stories about heroic customer service: the Nordie who ironed a new-bought shirt for a customer who needed it for a meeting that afternoon; the Nordie who cheerfully gift wrapped products a customer bought at Macy's; the Nordie who warmed customers' cars in winter while the customers finished shopping; the Nordie who personally knit a shawl for an elderly customer who needed one of a special length that wouldn't get caught in the spokes of her wheelchair; the Nordie who made a last-minute delivery of party clothes to a frantic hostess; and even the Nordie who refunded money for a set of tire chains—although Nordstrom doesn't sell tire chains.[17] He learned about the notes called "heroics" that Nordstrom salespeople wrote about each other, and that were used—along with customer letters and employee thank-you notes to customers—to determine which stores should receive monthly prizes for the best service.[18]

His manager explained about the all-important customer letters: "Customer letters are real important around here. You never, ever want to get a bad one; that's a real sin. But good ones can lead you to become a 'Customer Service All Star.' You think Phi Beta Kappa was a big deal, but to become a Customer Service All Star, now *that's* a really big deal. You get a personal handshake from one of the Nordstrom brothers, your picture goes on the wall, and you get prizes and discounts. It makes you the top of the top.[19] And if you become a productivity winner, you become a Pacesetter, complete with new business cards so designated and 33 percent merchandise discounts.[20] Only our very top people become Pacesetters."

"How do I become a Pacesetter?" Robert asked.

"Simple. You set very high sales goals, and then you exceed them,"[21] she explained. Then she asked, "By the way, what are your sales goals for today?"[22]

Sales goals. Productivity. Achievement. Robert noticed "reminders" posted on the walls in the employee back rooms: "Make a daily to do list!" or "List goals, set priorities!"[23] or "Don't let us down!" or "Be a top dog pacesetter; Go for the milk bones!"[24]

He learned quickly about the all important SPH (sales per hour) calculation. "If you exceed your target SPH, you'll get a ten percent commission on net sales," his manager explained. "If not, you'll just get your base hourly wage rate. And if you have a high SPH, you'll get to work more attractive hours and have better odds of being promoted. You can track your SPH on computer printouts we keep in the back office. We list all the SPHs in rank order, so you can keep track and make sure you're not falling behind. Your SPH will also appear on your pay stub."[25]

At the end of his first pay period, employees gathered around a bulletin board in the back room on which was posted a ranking of SPH by employee number; a few had dropped below a red line marked on the paper.[26] Robert quickly understood that he should do all that he could to avoid falling behind. He woke up one night in a cold sweat from a vivid nightmare of walking into the back room and seeing his name at the bottom of the list. He worked furiously during the day to not be left behind by his peers.[27]

Soon after the first pay period, Robert noticed that one of the salespeople in his area had left work early. "Where's John?" he asked.

"Sent home for the day . . . penalized for getting irritated with a customer," said Bill, a fellow salesperson who had won a recent Smile Contest and thereby got his picture on the wall.[28] "It's kind of like being sent to your room without dinner. He'll be back tomorrow, but they'll be watching him closely for a few weeks."[29]

At age twenty-six, Bill was already a five-year Nordstrom veteran, a Pacesetter, and an All Star. Bill clearly had that rare "what it takes" quality to thrive at Nordstrom. "When people shop at Nordstrom, they deserve the best attitude," he explained. "I always have my smile, for anybody, everybody."[30] Bill dressed almost exclusively in Nordstrom clothes and, in addition to the Smile Contest, he'd also won a "Who Looks the Most Nordstrom Contest"[31] the prior year. He basked in the glory of public praise one day as the store manager read aloud a letter about Bill from a satisfied customer—to the applause and cheers of fellow employees.

Bill loved his job at Nordstrom, always quick to point out, "Where else could I get paid so well and have so much autonomy? Nordstrom is one of the first places I've ever felt like I really belong to something special. Sure, I work really hard, but I like to work hard. No one tells me what to do, and I feel I can go as far as my dedication will take me. I feel like an entrepreneur."[32]

Bill had earlier moved—along with over a hundred other Nordstrom people—from Nordstrom stores on the West Coast to one of its new store openings on the East Coast.[33] "We wouldn't want non-Nordies to open a new store, even if it's all the way across the country," he explained. He described the excitement of opening day: "Employees were clapping. Customers came in and they were clapping, too. There was so much energy and adrenaline flowing—it was an emotional 'look what I'm part of' atmosphere that made you feel really special."[34]

Bill was a great Nordie role model for Robert. He told Robert about how he attended a Nordstrom motivational seminar, where he learned to write upbeat "affirmations," which he repeated over and over to himself: "I feel proud to be a Pacesetter." Bill had the goal of becoming a store manager, so he chanted to himself the affirmation "I enjoy being a store manager at Nordstrom ... I enjoy being a store manager at Nordstrom ... I enjoy being a store manager at Nordstrom."[35]

Bill explained that being a Nordstrom manager would be tough and demanding. He described how store managers must publicly declare their sales goals at quarterly meetings. "Mr. John, he sometimes wears a sweater with a giant *N* on the front and stirs up the crowd. Then someone unveils the sales target for each store set by a secret committee. I've heard that those managers who set goals below those set by the secret committee get booed; those who set goals higher than the committee get cheered."[36]

Bill was also a great source of information and guidance about the Nordstrom Way. "Be very careful about talking to outsiders," Bill cautioned. "The company's very sensitive about its privacy and likes to keep tight control on what information goes to the outside world. That comes from the very top. How we do things around here is not anybody else's business."[37]

"By the way," Bill asked as they were closing up shop late one evening, "did you know that we had a 'secret shopper' in here today?"

"A what?"

"A secret shopper. That's a Nordstrom employee who pretends to be a customer—secretly—and checks on your demeanor and service. She came by you today. I think you did fine, but watch the frown. You have a tendency to frown when you're working hard. Just remember to smile; don't frown. A frown can be a black mark in your file."[38]

"Rule number two," Robert thought to himself. "Don't frown, be happy."

Over the following six months, Robert found himself increasingly uncomfortable at Nordstrom. When he found himself at a seven A.M. department meeting with Nordies chanting "We're number one!" and "We want to do it for Nordstrom!"[39] he thought back to the opening paragraph of the write-up on Nordstrom in *The Best 100 Companies to Work for in America*, which said, "If you don't like to work in a gung-ho atmosphere where people are always revved up, then this is not the place for you."[40] He found himself doing okay—never falling to the bottom of the SPH listings—but, tellingly, not great. He'd never received a handshake from Mr. Jim or Mr. John or Mr. Bruce. He had not become a Pacesetter or an All Star, and feared that he would once again frown for a secret shopper or that he might get a negative customer letter. And worst of all, he was being left behind by those who were just much more Nordstrom than he. They had the right Nordstrom stuff; he didn't. He just didn't fit.

Robert quit eleven months into his career at Nordstrom. A year later, however, he was thriving as a department manager at another store. "Nordstrom was a great experience, but it wasn't for me," he explained. "I know some of my friends are incredibly happy there; they really love it. And there's no doubt about it—Nordstrom's a really great company. But I fit better here."

"EJECTED LIKE A VIRUS!"

When we began our research project, we speculated that our evidence would show the visionary companies to be great places to work (or at least better places to work than the comparison companies). However, we didn't find this to be the case—at least not for everyone. Recall how well Bill and Laura fit and flourished at Nordstrom; for them, it was a truly great place to work. But notice how Robert just couldn't fully buy in; for him, Nordstrom was not a great place to work. Nordstrom is only a great place to work for those truly dedicated—and well suited to— the Nordstrom way.

The same is true for many of the other visionary companies that we studied. If you're not willing to enthusiastically adopt the HP Way, then you simply don't belong at HP. If you're not comfortable buying into Wal-Mart's fanatical dedication to its customers, then you don't belong at Wal-Mart. If you're not willing to be "Procterized," then you don't belong at Procter & Gamble. If you don't want to join in the crusade for quality (even if you happen to work in the cafeteria), then you don't belong at Motorola and you certainly can't become a true "Motorolan."[41] If you question the right of individuals to make their own decisions about what to buy (such as cigarettes), then you don't belong at Philip Morris. If you're not comfortable with the Mormon-influenced, clean-living, dedication-to-service atmosphere at Marriott, then you'd better stay away. If you can't embrace the idea of "wholesomeness" and "magic" and "Pixie dust," and make yourself into a "clean-cut zealot,"[42] then you'd probably hate working at Disneyland.

We learned that you don't need to create a "soft" or "comfortable" environment to build a visionary company. We found that the visionary companies tend to be more demanding of their people than other companies, both in terms of performance and congruence with the ideology.

"VISIONARY," we learned, does not mean soft and undisciplined. Quite the contrary. Because the visionary companies have such clarity about who they are, what they're all about, and what they're trying to achieve, they tend to not have much room for people unwilling or unsuited to their demanding standards.

During a research team meeting, one of our research assistants made the observation, "Joining these companies reminds me of joining an extremely tight-knit group or society. And if you don't fit, you'd better not join. If you're willing to really buy in and dedicate yourself to what the company stands for, then you'll be very satisfied and productive—probably couldn't be happier. If not, however, you'll probably flounder, feel miserable and out-of-place, and eventually leave—ejected like a virus. It's binary: You're either in or you're out, and there seems to be no middle ground. It's almost cult-like."

The observation rang true enough that we decided to examine the literature on cults and see if the visionary companies have indeed had more characteristics in common with cults than the comparison companies. We found no universally accepted definition of *cult* in the literature; the most common definition is that a cult is a body of persons characterized by great or excessive devotion to some person, idea, or thing (which certainly describes many of the visionary companies). Nor did we find any universally accepted checklist of what separates cults from noncults. We did, however, find some common themes, and in particular we found four common characteristics of cults that the visionary companies display to a greater degree than the comparison companies.[43]

- Fervently held ideology (discussed earlier in our chapter on core ideology)
- Indoctrination
- Tightness of fit
- Elitism

Look at Nordstrom versus Melville. Notice the heavy-duty indoctrination processes at Nordstrom, beginning with the interview and continuing with Nordie customer service heroic stories, reminders on the walls, chanting affirmations, and cheering. Notice how Nordstrom gets its employees to write heroic stories about other employees and engages peers and immediate supervisors in the indoctrination process. (A common practice of cults is to actively engage recruits in the socializing of others into the cult.) Notice how the company seeks to hire young people, mold them into the Nordstrom way from early in their careers, and promote only those who closely reflect the core ideology. Notice how Nordstrom imposes a severe tightness of fit—employees that fit the Nordstrom way receive lots of positive reinforcement (pay, awards, recognition)—and those who don't fit get negative reinforcement (being "left behind," penalties, black marks). Notice how Nordstrom draws clear boundaries between who is "inside" and who is "outside" the organization, and how it portrays being "inside" as being part of something special and elite—again, a common practice of cults. Indeed, the very term "Nordie" has a cultish feel to it. We found no evidence that Melville cultivated and maintained through its history anywhere near such clear and consistent use of practices like these.

Nordstrom presents an excellent example of what we came to call "cultism"—a series of practices that create an almost cult-like environment around the core ideology in highly visionary companies. These practices tend to vigorously screen out those who do not fit with the ideology (either before hiring or early in their careers). They also instill an intense sense of loyalty and influence the behavior of those remaining inside the company to be congruent with the core ideology, consistent over time, and carried out zealously.

Please don't misunderstand our point here. We're *not* saying that visionary companies are cults. We're saying that they are more cult-*like*, without actually being cults. The terms "cultism" and "cult-like" can conjure up a variety of negative images and connotations; they are much stronger words than "culture." But to merely say that visionary companies have a culture tells us nothing new or interesting. All companies have a culture! We observed something much stronger than just "culture" at work. "Cultism" and "cult-like" are *descriptive*—not pejorative or prescriptive—terms to capture a set of practices that we saw more consistently in the visionary companies than the comparison companies. We're saying that these characteristics play a key role in preserving the core ideology.

An analysis of the visionary versus comparison companies revealed the following (see Table A.6 in the Appendix 3):

- In eleven out of eighteen pairs, the evidence shows *stronger indoctrination* into a core ideology through the history of the visionary company than the comparison company.*
- In thirteen out of eighteen pairs, the evidence shows *greater tightness of fit* through the history of the visionary company than in the comparison company—people tend to either fit well with the company and its ideology or tend to not fit at all ("buy in or get out").
- In thirteen out of eighteen pairs, the evidence shows *greater elitism* (a sense of belonging to something special and superior) through the history of the visionary company.
- Summing up across all three dimensions (indoctrination, tightness of fit, and elitism), the visionary companies have shown *greater cultism through history than the comparison companies in fourteen out of eighteen pairs* (four pairs are indistinguishable).

---

* We found that the visionary companies put more emphasis on employee training in general. Not just ideological orientation, but also skills and professional development training. We will return to this point in a later chapter.

The following three examples—IBM, Disney, and Procter & Gamble—show these characteristics at work in the development of visionary companies.

IBM'S RISE TO GREATNESS

Thomas J. Watson, Jr., former IBM chief executive, described the environment at IBM during its rise to national prominence in the first half of the twentieth century as a "cult-like atmosphere."[44] This atmosphere traces back to 1914, when Watson's father (Thomas J. Watson, Sr.) became chief executive of the small, struggling company, and consciously set about to create an organization of dedicated zealots.* Watson plastered the wall with slogans: "Time lost is time gone forever"; "There is no such thing as standing still"; "We must never feel satisfied"; "We sell service"; "A company is known by the men it keeps." He instituted strict rules of personal conduct—he required salespeople to be well groomed and wear dark business suits, encouraged marriage (married people, in his view, worked harder and were more loyal because they had to provide for a family), discouraged smoking, and forbade alcohol. He instituted training programs to systematically indoctrinate new hires into the corporate philosophy, sought to hire young and impressionable people, and adhered to a strict promote-from-within practice. Later, he created IBM-managed country clubs to encourage IBMers to socialize primarily with other IBMers, not the outside world.[45]

Similar to Nordstrom, IBM sought to create a heroic mythology about employees who best exemplified the corporate ideology and placed their names and pictures—along with stories of their heroic deeds—in company publications. A few exemplars even had corporate songs composed in their honor![46] And, also like Nordstrom, IBM emphasized the importance of individual effort and initiative within the context of the collective effort.

By the 1930s, IBM had fully institutionalized its indoctrination process and created a full-fledged "schoolhouse" that it used to socialize and train future officers of the company. In *Father, Son & Co.*, Watson, Jr., wrote:

> Everything about the school was meant to inspire loyalty, enthusiasm, and high ideals, which IBM held out as the way to achieve success. The front door had [IBM's ubiquitous] motto "THINK"

---

*NOTE: for an excellent account of IBM's early history, see Robert Sobel, *IBM: Colossus in Transition* (New York: Truman Talley Books, 1981).

written over it in two foot high letters. Just inside was a granite staircase that was supposed to put students in an aspiring frame of mind as they stepped up to the day's classes.[47]

Veteran employees in "regulation IBM clothes" taught the classes and emphasized IBM values. Each morning, surrounded by posters with corporate mottos and slogans, students would rise and sing IBM songs out of the songbook *Songs of the IBM*, which included "The Star-Spangled Banner" and, on the facing page, IBM's own anthem, "Ever Onward."[48] IBMers sang such lyrics as:[49]

> *March on with I.B.M.*
>
> *Work hand in hand,*
>
> *Stout hearted men go forth,*
>
> *In every land.*

Although IBM eventually evolved beyond singing corporate songs, it retained its intensely values-oriented training and socialization processes. Newly hired IBMers always learned the "three basic beliefs" (described in an earlier chapter) and experienced training classes that emphasized company philosophy as well as skills. IBMers learned language unique to the culture ("IBM-speak") and were expected at all times to display IBM professionalism. In 1979, IBM completed a twenty-six-acre "Management Development Center" that, in IBM's own words, "might pass for a monastic retreat—until you find yourself in its busy classrooms."[50]

IBM's profile in the 1985 edition of *The 100 Best Companies to Work For* described IBM as a company that "has institutionalized its beliefs the way a church does. . . . The result is a company filled with ardent believers. (If you're not ardent, you may not be comfortable.) . . . Some have compared joining IBM with joining a religious order or going into the military. . . . If you understand the Marines, you understand IBM. . . . You must be willing to give up some of your individual identity to survive."[51] A 1982 *Wall Street Journal* article noted that the IBM culture "is so pervasive that, as one nine-year [former] employee put it, 'leaving the company was like emigrating.' "[52]

Indeed, throughout its history (at least to the time of this book), IBM imposed a severe tightness of fit with its ideology. Former IBM marketing vice president Buck Rodgers explained in his book *The IBM Way:*

> IBM begins imbuing its employees with its . . . philosophy even before they're hired, at the very first interview. To some, the word "imbuing" connotes brainwashing, but I don't think there's

anything negative . . . in what is done. Basically, anyone who wants to work for IBM is told: "Look this is how we do business. . . . We have some very specific ideas about what that means—and if you work for us we'll teach you how to treat customers. If our attitude about customers and service is incompatible with yours, we'll part ways—and the quicker the better." [53]

Elitism also ran throughout the entire history of the company. Beginning in 1914, long before the company had any national stature, Watson, Sr., sought to instill the perspective that the company was a superior and special place to work. "You cannot be a success in any business," he exhorted, "without believing that it is the greatest business in the world."[54] (And recall from the BHAG chapter how he tangibly buttressed this elitist attitude by changing the name of the company from the dreary-sounding Computer Tabulating Recording Company to The International Business Machines Corporation.) In 1989, three-quarters of a century after Watson, Sr., initiated the company's self-concept as something elite and special, Watson, Jr., came full circle to the same theme in an essay for a seventy-fifth anniversary publication entitled *IBM: A Special Company:*

If we believe that we're working for just another company, then we're going to be like another company. We have got to have a concept that IBM is special. Once you get that concept, it's very easy to give the amount of drive to work toward making it continue to be true.[55]

You might be wondering whether IBM's cult-like atmosphere and tight adherence to its three basic beliefs contributed to IBM's difficulties in the early 1990s. Was cultism a primary cause of IBM's difficulty to adapt to the dramatic changes in the computer industry? Upon close inspection, the evidence does not support this view. IBM was strongly cult-like in the 1920s, yet was able to adapt to the dramatic shift to automated accounting procedures. IBM was incredibly cult-like in the 1930s, yet was able to adapt to the demands of the Depression without a single layoff. IBM maintained its cult-like culture in the 1950s and 1960s, yet was able to adapt to the rise of computers, perhaps the most dramatic shift in IBM's history. IBM still had a cultish feel in the early 1980s, yet—unlike any other old-line computer company—adapted to the personal computer revolution and established itself as a major player. If anything, IBM's cult-like culture—its fanatical preservation of its core values—*declined* as the company headed toward trouble.

> **IBM** attained its greatest success—and displayed its greatest ability to adapt to a changing world—during the same era that it displayed its strongest cult-like culture.

Furthermore, Burroughs (IBM's comparison) displayed little of the cultism we saw in the history of IBM. It had no Burroughs indoctrination center to "imbue" employees with corporate values. We found no indication that Burroughs sought to impose severe tightness of fit around a central ideology, nor did we see any evidence that Burroughs saw itself as elite and special in the scheme of American enterprise. IBM gave itself a clear self-identity, however cult-like. Burroughs did not. And IBM consistently pulled ahead of Burroughs at critical junctures in the evolution of the industry, even though Burroughs had a better early start in life.

THE MAGIC OF WALT DISNEY

Like IBM and Nordstrom, the Walt Disney Company has made extensive use of indoctrination, tightness of fit, and elitism as key parts of preserving its core ideology.

Disney requires every single employee—no matter what level or position—to attend new employee orientation (also known as "Disney Traditions") taught by the faculty of Disney University, the company's own internal socialization and training organization.[56] Disney designed the course so that "new members of the Disney team can be introduced to our traditions, philosophies, organization, and the way we do business."[57]

Disney pays particular attention to thoroughly screen and socialize hourly workers into its theme parks. Potential recruits—even those being hired to sweep the floor—must pass at least two screenings by different interviewers.[58] (In the 1960s, Disney required all applicants to take an extensive personality test.)[59] Men with facial hair and women with dangling earrings or heavy makeup need not apply; Disney enforces a strict grooming code.[60] (In 1991, members of the Disneyland staff went on strike to protest the grooming code; Disney fired the strike leader and kept the rule intact.)[61] Even as far back as the 1960s, Disneyland imposed strict tightness-of-fit guidelines in hiring, as Richard Schickel described park employees in his 1967 book *The Disney Version:*

[They] present a rather standardized appearance. The girls are generally blonde, blue-eyed and self-effacing, all looking as if they stepped out of an ad for California sportswear and are heading for suburban motherhood. The boys . . . are outdoorsy, All-American types, the kind of vacuously pleasant lad your mother was always telling you to imitate.[62]

All new hires at Disneyland experience a multiday training program where they quickly learn a new language:

Employees are "cast members."

Customers are "guests."

A crowd is an "audience."

A work shift is a "performance."

A job is a "part."

A job description is a "script."

A uniform is a "costume."

The personnel department is "casting."

Being on duty is "onstage."

Being off duty is "backstage."

The special language reinforces the frame of mind Disney imposes via carefully scripted orientation seminars delivered by well-practiced "trainers" who drill new cast members with questions about Disney characters, history, and mythology, and who constantly reinforce the underlying ideology:

TRAINER: What business are we in? Everybody knows McDonald's makes hamburgers. What does Disney make?

NEW HIRE: It makes people happy.

TRAINER: Yes, exactly! *It makes people happy.* It doesn't matter who they are, what language they speak, what they do, where they come from, what color they are, or anything else. We're here to make 'em happy. . . . Nobody's been hired for a job. Everybody's been cast for a role in our show.[63]

The orientation seminars take place in specially designed training rooms, plastered with pictures of founder Walt Disney and his most famous characters (such as Mickey Mouse, Snow White and the Seven Dwarfs). They aim, in the words of a Tom Peters Group video, "to create the illusion that Walt himself is present in the room, welcoming the new hires to his personal domain. The object is to make these new employees feel like partners with the Park's founder."[64] Employees read from the University Textbooks, which have included such exhortations as: "At Disneyland we get tired, but never bored, and even if it's a rough day, we appear happy. You've got to have an honest smile. It's got to come from within. . . . If nothing else helps, remember that you get paid for smiling."[65]

After in-class orientation, each new cast member doubles up with an experienced peer who further socializes him or her into the nuances of the specific job. Throughout, Disney enforces strict codes of behavior and conduct, demanding that the cast member quickly sand off any personality quirks that do not fit their specific script.[66] *Training* magazine observed: "At Disney there is no such thing as an unplanned moment for new hires. The first days following the Disney orientation program are filled with costume (uniform) fittings, script rehearsals (training) and meeting fellow cast members. And it is all as carefully orchestrated and thought-out as any performance staged for theme park guests."[67]

Disney's fanatical preservation of its self-image and ideology has shown itself most clearly in the theme parks, but it also extends far beyond the theme parks. *All* employees in the company must attend a Disney Traditions orientation seminar. A Stanford MBA who spent a summer at Disney doing financial analysis, strategic planning, and other similar work, described:

> I recognized the magic of Walt's vision on my first day at the Walt Disney Company. . . . At Disney University, through videos and "pixie dust," Walt shared his dreams and the magic of Disney's "world." Disney archives treasure Walt's history for cast members to enjoy. After orientation, I stopped at the corner of Mickey Avenue and Dopey Drive—I felt the magic, the sentimentality, the history. I believed in Walt's dream and shared this belief with others in the organization.[68]

No employee anywhere in the company could cynically or flagrantly denounce the ideal of "wholesomeness" and survive.[69] Company publications constantly emphasize that Disney is "special," "different," "unique," "magical." Even the company's annual reports to shareholders have been peppered with such terms and phrases as "dreams," "fun," "excitement," "joy," "imagination," and "magic is the essence of Disney."[70]

Disney shrouds much of its inner workings in secrecy, which further contributes to a sense of mystery and elitism—only those deep on the "inside" get to peek behind the curtain to see the mechanics of the "magic." No one except specific cast members (who are sworn to secrecy), for example, can observe the training of characters at Disneyland. Writers who cover Disney have encountered fiercely protective gatekeepers to the secrets of the Magic Kingdom. "Disney is a strangely closed corporation," wrote one author. "It [has] a level of controlling paranoia I had never encountered in my years of writing about American business."[71]

Disney's intensive screening and indoctrination of employees, its obsession with secrecy and control, and its careful cultivation of a mythology and image as something special—and important—to the lives of children around the world, all help to create a cultish following that extends even to its customers. A loyal Disney customer once noticed a slightly discolored Disney character doll at a retail store and seethed, "If Uncle Walt saw that, he'd be ashamed."[72]

Indeed, when examining Disney, it can be hard to keep in mind that it is a corporation, not a social or religious movement. Joe Fowler wrote in his book *Prince of the Magic Kingdom:*

> This is not a corporate history. It is a history of a deeply human struggle over ideas, values, and hopes for which men and women were willing to give themselves over, values at times so evanescent that some people could dismiss them as silly, values so deep that others became students of them, dedicated their careers to making them come alive, became enraged and embittered when they seemed to be violated, and turned poetic and inspired in their defense. This is what is impressive about the name "Disney": no one is neutral. . . . Walt Disney was a genius or a charlatan, a hypocrite or an exemplar, a snake-oil salesman or a beloved father figure to generations of children.[73]

The company's cult-like culture does, in fact, trace to founder Walt Disney, who saw the relationship between himself and employees as like that between father and children.[74] He expected complete dedication from Disney employees, and he demanded unblemished loyalty to the company *and* its values. A dedicated and—above all—*loyal* Disneyite could make honest mistakes and be given a second (and often, third, fourth, and fifth) chance.[75] But to breach the sacred ideology or to display disloyalty . . . well, these were *sins*, punishable by immediate and unceremonious termination. According to Marc Eliot's biography *Walt Disney*, "When someone did, on occasion, slip in Walt's presence and use a four-letter word in mixed company, the result was always immediate dismissal, no matter what type of professional inconvenience the firing caused."[76] When Disney animators went on strike in 1941, Walt felt betrayed by his workers and saw the union not so much as an economic force but as an intrusion into his carefully controlled "family" of loyal Disneyites.[77]

Walt had a rage for order and control that he translated into tangible practices to maintain the essence of Disney. The personal grooming code, the recruiting and training processes, the fanatical attention to the tiniest details of physical layout, the concern with secrecy, the exacting rules about preserving the integrity and sanctity of each Disney character—these all trace their roots to Walt's quest to keep the Disney Company completely within the bounds of its core ideology. Walt described the roots of the Disneyland processes:

> The first year I leased out the parking concession, brought in the usual security guards—things like that. But I soon realized my mistake. I couldn't have outside help and still get over my idea of hospitality. So now we recruit and train every one of our employees. I tell the security officers, for instance, that they are never to consider themselves cops. They are there to help people. . . . Once you get the policy going, it grows.[78]

And grow it did. Even though the company languished after Walt's death, it never lost its core ideology, due in large part to the tangible processes laid in place before he died. And when Michael Eisner and the New Disney Team took over in 1984, the core—carefully preserved—formed the bedrock of Disney's resurgence in the following decade.

Columbia Pictures, in contrast, had neither a core ideology nor any core preservation mechanisms in place after Cohn's death in 1958. Walt didn't build a perfectly ticking clock, but he *did* have a core ideology, and he *did* clock-build mechanisms (however cultish) to preserve the core ideology. Cohn did not. Disney eventually rebounded after Walt's death as an independent institution built on his legacy; Columbia Pictures ceased to exist as an independent company.

COMPLETE IMMERSION AT PROCTER & GAMBLE

Throughout most of its history, Procter & Gamble has preserved its core ideology through extensive use of indoctrination, tightness of fit, and elitism. P&G has long-standing practices of carefully screening potential new hires, hiring young people for entry-level jobs, rigorously molding them into P&G ways of thought and behavior, spitting out the misfits, and making middle and top slots available only to loyal P&Gers who grew up inside the company. *The 100 Best Companies to Work for in America* states:

> Competition to get into P&G is tough. . . . Recruits, when they sign on, may feel they have joined an institution, rather than a company. . . . No one ever comes into P&G at a middle or top-management level who has garnered his or her experience at another company. It just doesn't happen. This is an up-through-the-ranks company with a vengeance.[79] . . . There is a P&G way of doing things, and if you don't master it or at least feel comfortable with it, you're not going to be happy here, not to speak of being successful.[80]

Indoctrination processes are both formal and informal. P&G inducts new employees into the company with training and orientation sessions and expects them to read its official biography *Eyes on Tomorrow* (also known to insiders as "The Book"), which describes the company as "an integral part of the nation's history" with "a spiritual inheritance" and "unchanging character . . . that [has] remained solidly based on the principle, the ethics, the morals so often pronounced by the founders [and] has become a lasting heritage."[81] Internal company publications, talks by executives, and formal orientation materials stress P&G's history, values, and traditions.[82] Employees cannot miss seeing the "Ivorydale Memorial" overlooking the Ivorydale plant—a life-size marble sculpture of William Cooper Procter, grandson of cofounder William Procter, striding forward from the inscribed words: "He lived a life of noble simplicity, believing in God and the inherent worthiness of his fellow men."[83]

New hires—especially those in brand management (the central function of the company)—immediately find nearly all of their time occupied by working or socializing with other members of "the family," from whom they further learn about the values and practices of P&G. The company's relatively isolated location in a P&G-dominated city (Cincinnati) further reinforces the sense of complete immersion into the company. "You go to a strange town, work together all day, write memos all night, and see each other on weekends," described one P&G alum.[84] P&Gers are expected to socialize primarily with other P&Gers, belong to the same clubs, attend similar churches, and live in the same neighborhoods.[85]

P&G has a long historical track record of paternalistic and progressive employee pay and benefit programs, which bind its people closely to the company.[86]

- In 1887, P&G introduced a profit-sharing plan for workers, making it the oldest profit-sharing plan in continuous operation in American industry.
- In 1892, P&G introduced an employee stock ownership plan, one of the first in industrial history.
- In 1915, P&G introduced a comprehensive sickness-disability-retirement-life-insurance plan—again, one of the first companies to do so.

The company has used these programs not only as a means of rewarding employees, but also as mechanisms to influence behavior, gain commitment, and ensure tightness of fit. A P&G publication described how it used the early profit-sharing plan:

[William Cooper Procter] concluded that workers who showed indifference to the need for greater work effort should be deprived of their share of profits—that their shares should be turned over to those who cared. So he set up four classifications—based on the degree of a worker's cooperation as decided by management. That helped considerably [to ensure the proper attitude]![87]

By encouraging employees to purchase shares in the employee stock ownership program, the company garnered a high level of psychological commitment. After all, what better way to gain "buy in" to the organization than to have employees literally buy in with some of their own hard-earned income? In 1903, to further reinforce this buy-in process, P&G restricted its profit-sharing program only to those willing to make a significant stock purchase commitment:

Profit sharing would [henceforth] be tied directly to employee ownership of P&G common stock. To be eligible for profit sharing, an employee had to buy stock *equivalent at current value to his annual wage* [emphasis ours], but could spread payment over several years with a minimum payment of four percent of his annual wage. At the same time, the Company contributed 12 percent of the employee's annual wage toward purchase of that stock.[88]

By 1915, fully 61 percent of employees had bought in to the stock program—and thereby bought full psychological membership in P&G. Throughout its history, P&G has used a myriad of tangible mechanisms to enforce desired behavior, ranging from strong dress codes and office layouts that allow little privacy to P&G's famous "one-page memo"* that mandates consistency in communication style.

P&G's tightness of fit applies across the company, at all locations, in all countries, and in all world cultures. An ex-employee who joined P&G directly out of business school to work in Europe and Asia commented: "Procter's culture extends to all corners of the globe. When going overseas, it was made very clear to me that I must first and foremost adapt to the P&G culture, and secondarily adapt to the national culture. Belonging to P&G is like belonging to a nation unto itself."[89] At a company meeting in 1986, chief executive John Smale echoed a similar theme:

> Procter & Gamble people all over the world share a common bond. In spite of cultural and individual differences, we speak the same language. When I meet with Procter & Gamble people—whether they are in Sales in Boston, Product Development at the Ivorydale Technical Center, or the Management Committee in Rome—I feel I am talking to the same kind of people. People I know. People I trust. Procter & Gamble people.[90]

Like Nordstrom, IBM, and Disney, Procter & Gamble has displayed an intense penchant for secrecy and control of information. Managers routinely admonish, scold, or penalize employees for working on airplanes, using luggage ID cards that reveal them as P&G employees, and for talking about business in public places. The 1991 management stock option plan stipulates that if the recipient of the options discloses unauthorized information about P&G to the outside world, the options will be revoked.[91]

The company's secretive nature reinforces an elitism cultivated throughout much of its history. P&G people feel proud to be part of an organization that describes itself as "special," "great," "excellent," "moral," "self-disciplined," full of "the best people," "an institution," and "unique among the world's business organizations."[92] In describing a particularly difficult project, a P&G manager commented: "If there was one characteristic I saw demonstrated by everyone [throughout the project] it was the pride in being the best."[93]

The contrast between P&G and Colgate is not as stark as between Nordstrom and Melville, IBM and Burroughs, or Disney and Columbia. For one thing, up until the early 1900s, Colgate placed great emphasis on a

---

*All memos are supposed to be kept to one page, plus exhibits. Most P&Gers conform to this rule, although some P&Gers have in fact seen memos longer than one page.

paternalistic culture built around the Colgate family values.[94] Nonetheless, there is a difference, particularly over the past sixty years. We found no evidence that Colgate imposes the same rigorous screening or tightness-of-fit criteria upon new hires. Nor did we find any evidence of the same level of indoctrination into the "character" of P&G and the guiding principles laid down by its founders. Whereas P&G has always defined itself in terms of its *own* core ideology and deep heritage—constantly emphasizing its specialness and uniqueness—Colgate has increasingly defined itself *in relation to P&G*. Procter has continually reinforced a sense of being the elite of the elite; Colgate has come to see itself as "second to Procter" and on a quest to become "another P&G."[95]

THE MESSAGE FOR CEOS, MANAGERS, AND ENTREPRENEURS

You might find yourself somewhat uncomfortable with the findings in this chapter. We share some of that discomfort, and we wish to be clear that we're certainly *not* advocating (or even describing) the extreme Jim Jones, David Koresh, or Reverend Sun Myung Moon type of situation. It is important to understand that, unlike many religious sects or social movements which often revolve around a charismatic cult leader (a "cult of personality"), visionary companies tend to be cult-like *around their ideologies*. Notice, for example, how Nordstrom created a zealous and fanatical reverence for its core values, shaping a powerful mythology about the customer service heroics of its employees, rather than demanding slavish reverence for an individual leader. Disney's zealous protection of its values transcended Walt and remained largely intact decades after his death. P&G remained tightly dedicated to its principles for over 150 years, through nine generations of top management. Cultism around an individual personality is time telling; creating an environment that reinforces dedication to an enduring core ideology is clock building.

THE point of this chapter is *not* that you should set out to create a cult of personality. That's the last thing you should do.

Rather, the point is to *build an organization* that fervently preserves its core ideology in specific, concrete ways. The visionary companies translate their ideologies into *tangible* mechanisms aligned to send a consistent set of reinforcing signals. They indoctrinate people, impose tightness of fit, and create a sense of belonging to something special through such practical, concrete items as:

- Orientation and ongoing training programs that have ideological as well as practical content, teaching such things as values, norms, history, and tradition
- Internal "universities" and training centers
- On-the-job socialization by peers and immediate supervisors.
- Rigorous up-through-the-ranks policies—hiring young, promoting from within, and shaping the employee's mind-set from a young age
- Exposure to a pervasive mythology of "heroic deeds" and corporate exemplars (for example, customer heroics letters, marble statues)
- Unique language and terminology (such as "cast members," "Motorolans") that reinforce a frame of reference and the sense of belonging to a special, elite group
- Corporate songs, cheers, affirmations, or pledges that reinforce psychological commitment
- Tight screening processes, either during hiring or within the first few years
- Incentive and advancement criteria explicitly linked to fit with the corporate ideology
- Awards, contests, and public recognition that reward those who display great effort consistent with the ideology. Tangible and visible penalties for those who break ideological boundaries
- Tolerance for honest mistakes that do not breach the company's ideology ("non-sins"); severe penalties or termination for breaching the ideology ("sins")
- "Buy-in" mechanisms (financial, time investment)
- Celebrations that reinforce successes, belonging, and specialness
- Plant and office layout that reinforces norms and ideals
- Constant verbal and written emphasis on corporate values, heritage, and the sense of being part of something special

Preserve the Core AND Stimulate Progress

At this point, you might thinking: But isn't a tight, cult-like culture dangerous? Does it lead to group-think and stagnation? Does it drive away talented people? Does it stifle creativity and diversity? Does it inhibit change? Our answer: Yes, a cult-like culture *can* be dangerous and limiting if not complemented with the other side of the yin-yang. *Cult-like cultures, which preserve the core, must be counterweighted with a huge dose of stimulating progress.* In a visionary company, they go hand in hand, each side reinforcing the other.

A cult-like culture can actually *enhance* a company's ability to pursue Big Hairy Audacious Goals, precisely because it creates that sense of being part of an elite organization that can accomplish just about anything. IBM's cultish sense of itself contributed greatly to its ability to gamble on the IBM 360. Disney's cult-like belief in its special role in the world enhanced its ability to launch such radical BHAGs as Disneyland and EPCOT center. Without Boeing's dedication to being an organization of people who "live, breathe, eat and sleep what they are doing," it could not have successfully launched the 707 and 747 projects. Without Sony's almost fanatical belief that it was a unique organization with a special role to play in the world, it could not have taken its bold steps with transistors in the 1950s. Merck's cult- like dedication to its ideology gave its people a sense that they were part of something more than just another corporation—and it is largely out of this sense that they were inspired to put forth the effort required to establish Merck as the preeminent pharmaceutical company in the world.

Furthermore, it's important to understand that you can have a cult-like culture of innovation, or a cult-like culture of competition, or a cult-like culture of change. You can even have a cult-like culture of zaniness. We think that's exactly what executives at Wal-Mart do through such actions as leading thousands of screaming associates in the Wal-Mart cheer: "Give Me a W! Give Me an A! Give Me an L! Give Me a Squiggly! (Employees twist and squiggle their hips.) Give me an M! Give Me an A! Give Me an R! Give Me a T! What's that spell? Wal-Mart! What's that spell? Wal-Mart! Who's number one? THE CUSTOMER!"[96]

Cult-like tightness and diversity can also work hand in hand. Some of the most cult-like visionary companies have received accolades as being the best major corporations for women and minorities. Merck, for example, has a long track record of progressive equal opportunity programs. At Merck, diversity is a form of progress that nicely complements its deeply cherished core. You can be any color, size, shape, or gender at Merck—just as long as you believe in what the company stands for.

IDEOLOGICAL CONTROL/OPERATIONAL AUTONOMY

In a classic example of the "Genius of the AND" prevailing over the "Tyranny of the OR," visionary companies impose tight ideological control *and* simultaneously provide wide operating autonomy that encourages individual initiative. In fact, as we will discuss in the next chapter, we found that the visionary companies were significantly more decentralized and granted greater operational autonomy than the comparison companies as a general pattern, even though they have been much more cult-like.[97] *Ideological* control preserves the core while *operational* autonomy stimulates progress.

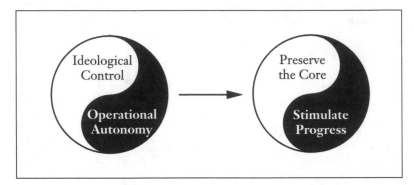

Recall the Nordstrom one-page employee handbook described at the beginning of this chapter. Notice how, on the one hand, the company constricts behavior to that consistent with the Nordstrom ideology. Yet, on the other hand, it grants immense operating discretion. When asked during a visit to a Stanford Business School class how a Nordstrom clerk would handle a customer attempting to return a dress that had obviously been worn, Jim Nordstrom replied:

> I don't know. That's an honest answer. But I do have a high level of confidence that it would be handled in such a way that the customer would feel well treated and served. Whether that would involve taking the dress back would depend on the specific situation, and we want to give each clerk a lot of latitude in figuring out what to do. We view our people as sales professionals. They don't need rules. They need basic guideposts, but not rules. You can do anything you need to at Nordstrom to get the job done, just so long as you live up to our basic values and standards.[98]

Nordstrom reminds us of the United States Marine Corps—tight, controlled, and disciplined, with little room for those who will not or cannot conform to the ideology. *Yet, paradoxically, those without individual initiative and entrepreneurial instincts will just as likely fail at Nordstrom as those who do not share the ideological tenets.* The same holds at other ideologically tight visionary companies like 3M, J&J, Merck, HP, and Wal-Mart.

This finding has massive practical implications. It means that companies seeking an "empowered" or decentralized work environment should first and foremost impose a tight ideology, screen and indoctrinate people into that ideology, eject the viruses, and give those who remain the tremendous sense of responsibility that comes with membership in an elite organization. It means getting the right actors on the stage, putting them in the right frame of mind, and then giving them the freedom to ad lib as they see fit. It means, in short, understanding that cult-like tightness around an ideology actually *enables* a company to turn people loose to experiment, change, adapt, and—above all—to *act*.

chapter 7

TRY A LOT OF STUFF AND KEEP WHAT WORKS

To my imagination it is far more satisfactory to look at [well-adapted species] not as specially endowed or created instincts, but as small consequences of one general law leading to the advancement of all organic beings—namely, multiply, vary, let the strongest live and the weakest die.

CHARLES DARWIN, *ORIGIN OF SPECIES*, 1859[1]

Our company has, indeed, *stumbled* onto some of its new products. But never forget that you can only stumble if you're moving.

RICHARD P. CARLTON, FORMER CEO, 3M CORPORATION, 1950[2]

Failure is our most important product.

R. W. JOHNSON, JR., FORMER CEO, JOHNSON & JOHNSON, 1954[3]

In examining the history of the visionary companies, we were struck by how often they made some of their best moves not by detailed strategic planning, but rather by experimentation, trial and error, opportunism, and—quite literally—accident. What looks in hindsight like a brilliant strategy was often the residual result of opportunistic experimentation and "purposeful accidents." Consider the following examples at Johnson & Johnson, Marriott, and American Express.

Johnson & Johnson's Accidental Move into Consumer Products

In 1890, Johnson & Johnson—then primarily a supplier of antiseptic gauze and medical plasters—received a letter from a physician who complained about patient skin irritation from certain medicated plasters. Fred Kilmer, the company's director of research, quickly responded by sending a packet of soothing Italian talc to apply on the skin. He then convinced the company to include a small can of talc as part of the standard package with certain products. To the company's surprise, customers soon began asking to buy more of the talc directly. J&J responded by creating a separate product called "Johnson's Toilet and Baby Powder," which became a famous household staple around much of the world. According to J&J's own official history, "the Johnsons got into the baby powder business quite by accident."[4] Even more significant, the company thereby took a tiny incremental step that eventually mushroomed into a significant strategic shift into consumer products—an "accident" which eventually grew to become 44 percent of J&J's revenues—and as important to its growth as medical supplies and pharmaceutical products.[5]

Later, J&J stumbled upon another famous product by accident. In 1920, company employee Earle Dickson created a ready-to-use bandage—made of surgical tape with small pieces of gauze and a special covering so it would not stick to the skin—for his wife who had a knack for cutting herself with kitchen knives. When he mentioned his invention to the marketing people, they decided to experiment with the product on the market. Eventually, after a slow start and a never-ending process of tinkering, Band-Aid products became the biggest selling category in the company's history and further solidified J&J's "accidental" strategic move into consumer products.[6]

Marriott's Opportunistic Step into Airport Services

In 1937—ten years after opening his first root beer stand—J. Willard Marriott had built a chain of nine profitable restaurants staffed by two hundred zealous employees trained in the company's meticulous methods of customer service. Marriott clearly had a system that worked. With plans to double the number of restaurants over the next three years, the future prospects of the emerging company never looked brighter. J. Willard and his management team would certainly attain great success—and, just as certain, have their hands full—if they simply focused on executing the restaurant expansion plan.

But what to do about the odd emerging situation at Marriott shop number eight? Located near Hoover Airport in Washington, D.C., number eight had attracted an entirely different clientele than other Marriott shops: Passengers on their way to catch a flight began purchasing meals and snacks which they stuffed in pockets, paper bags, and carry-on luggage. "Well how about that," said Marriott during an inspection visit to number eight. "Coming in here and buying things to eat on the plane?"[7]

"Every day," his store manager explained, "we get a few more of them."

Marriott pondered the situation overnight, according to Robert O'Brian in the book *Marriott*. The very next day, he paid a visit to Eastern Air Transport and created a new business arrangement whereby shop number eight would deliver prepackaged box lunches directly onto the tarmac in a bright orange truck with Marriott's logo and lettering on the side. Within a few months, the service expanded to American Airlines and catered twenty-two flights per day. Marriott soon put a full-time manager in charge of the emerging business, with the mission to fully develop it at Hoover and expand it to other airports. Airport services evolved from the seed of that unexpected opportunity to become a major business for Marriott Corporation, eventually reaching more than a hundred separate airports.[8]

Marriott could have bogged down in long meetings and strategic analyses to decide what to do. The unusual clientele at number eight presented Marriott with an odd variation to its traditional customer base. The company could have ignored it, but chose instead to experiment—to actually test and see if this "odd variation" might prove to be a *favorable* variation. Marriott made an incremental shift in corporate strategy by quick, vigorous action taken to seize upon a stroke of unexpected good luck. The step looks brilliant in retrospect, but in reality was simply the result of an opportunistic experiment that happened to work out.

American Express's Unintended Evolution into Financial and Travel Services

American Express began life in 1850 as a regional freight express business (essentially the nineteenth-century equivalent of the United Parcel Service). In 1882, the company took a small, incremental step that turned out to be the genesis of a dramatic strategic shift. Due to the increasingly popular postal money order, American Express faced declining demand for its cash-shipping services (similar to an armored car service). In response, AmEx created its own money order. The "Express Money Order" became an unexpected success—11,959 of them sold during the first six weeks. AmEx aggressively seized the opportunity and began selling the product not only at its own offices, but also at railroad stations and general stores, and thereby began—unwittingly—to transform itself into a financial services company.[9]

A decade later, in 1892, American Express president J. C. Fargo took a European vacation, where he found it difficult to translate his letters of credit into cash—a problem (and therefore an opportunity) which impelled a further shift in the company's trajectory. In his book *American Express 1850–1950*, Alden Hatch wrote:

> On his return, [Fargo] stalked through the corridors of 65 Broadway with more than his usual preoccupation. . . . He walked right past his own office to that of [employee Marcellus] Berry. "Berry," he said, omitting a salutation and going straight to the point, "I had a lot of trouble cashing my letters of credit. The moment I got off the beaten track they were no more use than so much wet wrapping paper. If the president of American Express has that sort of trouble, just think what ordinary travelers face. Something has got to be done about it."[10]

Berry did indeed do something about it. He created an elegant solution which required simply a signature upon purchase and a countersignature upon redemption, which eventually became known around the world as the ubiquitous "American Express Travelers Cheque." The mechanics of the traveler's check gave American Express an unexpected bonus: Due to lost checks and delays, the company sold more orders than it redeemed each month, which created a cash cushion. According to Jon Friedman and John Meehan in *House of Cards:*

> Unintentionally, AmEx had invented the 'float.' . . . A mere $750 at the beginning, the float would eventually top $4 billion by 1990, generating $200 million in revenue. The company had virtually [and accidentally] created a new international currency.[11]

In what started as just another incremental, opportunistic step, the traveler's check further evolved American Express toward financial services. AmEx didn't plan to become a financial services company. Nonetheless, it became one.

The traveler's check also contributed to the company's completely unintentional evolution into a travel services company. In fact, president J. C. Fargo issued a clear, unambiguous dictum that American Express was *not* going into the travel/tourism business: "We want it distinctly kept in mind at all times and in all places and by all the company's forces, that *this company is not and does not intend going into the touring* [*travel services*] *business* [emphasis ours]."[12]

In spite of Fargo's dictum, that's exactly what AmEx did. The company had developed a pattern of solving customer problems and quickly exploiting opportunities—an impulse guided by its core ideology of heroic customer service—that could not be easily suppressed, even by the CEO. Soon after the company opened its first European traveler's check office in Paris in 1895, an entrepreneurial employee named William Dalliba began expanding the company's activities in response to the needs of American travelers that always crammed the Paris office clamoring for check cashing, mail services, travel schedules, tickets, advice, and so on. Dalliba had to be careful and low-profile, of course, so as not to raise the ire of J. C. Fargo. So he moved incrementally, experimenting with ticket windows to sell berths on steamships. Using his successful experiment as a foot in the door, Dalliba convinced the company to open a "Travel Department" and began selling train tickets, packaged tours, and a range of travel services.[13] By 1912, AmEx had "firmly established itself as a great travel organization, *though even yet it did not admit the fact* (emphasis ours)."[14] By the early 1920s, Dalliba's experiments had turned travel-related services into the second most important strategic pillar of the company, behind financial services.

Thus, through a series of incremental steps—most of them opportunistic and certainly not part of any grand plan—American Express had evolved into something entirely different from its original founding concept as a freight express business.

CORPORATIONS AS EVOLVING SPECIES

What should we make of these examples from J&J, Marriott, and American Express? We might be tempted to just ignore them as weird aberrations, but they weren't the only such examples we found. Bill Hewlett told us that HP "never planned more than two or three years out" during the pivotal 1960s.[15] Nor did the company have any grand plan in mind when making its watershed strategic move into the computer business. Quite the opposite. In 1965, HP designed its first small computer simply to add power to its line of instruments products.[16] Explained former chief executive John Young:

It was basically an under the bench thing. We didn't even call it a computer. We called it an "instrument controller." Although we knew computers would be important in the future, we wanted to maintain our reputation as an instrument company and did not want to be known as a computer company.[17]

Similarly, Motorola initially entered the field of advanced electronics (transistors, semiconductors, integrated circuits) simply as a natural outgrowth of its small Phoenix laboratory set up in 1949 to develop a few electronic components for use in the company's televisions and radios.[18] Only later, in 1955, did Motorola make a conscious strategic choice to move into the electronics business—and that simply because the company could not afford to build an advanced plant unless it sold some of the output to outside customers.

We could go on with examples from Citicorp, Philip Morris, GE, Sony, and others. Don't get us wrong. We're not saying that these companies never had plans. But we were surprised to find so many examples of key moves by the visionary companies that came about by some process other than planning. Nor do these examples merely represent random luck. No, we found something else at work.

These provocative examples led us to a second type of progress (the first was BHAGs) stimulated by the visionary companies to a greater degree than the comparison companies: *evolutionary progress*. The word "evolutionary" describes this type of progress because it closely resembles how organic species evolve and adapt to their natural environments. Evolutionary progress differs from BHAG progress in two key ways. First, whereas BHAG progress involves clear and unambiguous goals ("We're going to climb *that* mountain"), evolutionary progress involves ambiguity ("By trying lots of different approaches, we're bound to stumble onto something that works; we just don't know ahead of time what it will be"). Second, whereas BHAG progress involves bold discontinuous leaps, evolutionary progress usually begins with small *incremental* steps or mutations, often in the form of quickly seizing unexpected opportunities that eventually grow into major—and often unanticipated—strategic shifts.

Why lead into the topic of evolutionary progress with examples of unplanned strategies? Because evolutionary progress is *unplanned* progress. Indeed, if we looked at species in the natural world through the lens of strategic planning, we might easily conclude that they were the result of well-executed plans: They're so well adapted, they *must* have been created exactly that way as part of a brilliant overall strategic plan. How else could we explain them? But, from the perspective of modern biology, such a conclusion would be dead wrong. After the Darwinian revolution, biologists came to understand that species were not directly created in a specific preplanned form; they *evolved*. Not only that, they evolved by a process with remarkable similarity to how some of our visionary companies became well adapted to their environments.

Darwin's Theory of Evolution Applied to Visionary Companies

The central concept of evolutionary theory—and Charles Darwin's great insight—is that species evolve by a process of undirected *variation* ("random genetic mutation") and natural *selection*. Through genetic variation, a species attains "good chances" that some of its members will be well suited to the demands of the environment. As the environment shifts, the genetic variations that best fit the environment tend to get "selected" (that is, the well-suited variations tend to survive and the poorly suited tend to perish—that's what Darwin meant by "survival of the fittest"). The selected (surviving) variations then have greater representation in the gene pool and the species will evolve in that direction. In Darwin's own words: "Multiply, vary, let the strongest live, and the weakest die."*

Now consider a company—say, American Express—as analogous to a species. By the early twentieth century, American Express found its traditional freight business under siege. Government regulators eroded the company's monopolistic rate structure and in 1913 the U.S. Post Office began a competing parcel-post system. Profits fell 50 percent.[19] Then in 1918 the U.S. government nationalized all freight express businesses, creating a cataclysmic industry change.[20] Most freight companies disappeared as the government snatched away their core business. But for American Express, its experiments in financial and travel services (described earlier) proved to be favorable—albeit unplanned—*variations* that were better suited to the changed environment than its traditional freight business. These variations were then *selected* as the path to evolve beyond its traditional—and now obsolete—line of business and on which to base its future prosperity.[21]

WE like to describe the evolutionary process as "branching and pruning." The idea is simple: If you add enough branches to a tree (variation) and intelligently prune the deadwood (selection), then you'll likely evolve into a collection of healthy branches well positioned to prosper in an ever-changing environment.

---

* For a more detailed discussion of evolutionary theory, we highly recommend reading books by Stephen J. Gould, especially *Hen's Teeth and Horse's Toes* and *The Panda's Thumb*, and books by Richard Dawkins, especially *The Blind Watchmaker*.

To this day, Johnson & Johnson consciously encourages branching and pruning. It tries lots of new things, keeps those that work, and quickly discards those that don't. It stimulates variation by fostering a highly decentralized environment that encourages individual initiative and allows people to experiment with new ideas. At the same time, J&J imposes rigorous selection criteria. Only those experiments that prove to be profitable and that fit with J&J's core ideology get to remain in the company's portfolio of businesses.

With his oft-repeated statement "Failure is our most important product," R. W. Johnson Jr., understood that companies must accept failed experiments as part of evolutionary progress. And, in fact, J&J has had a number of prominent failures to "prune away" in its history, including a foray into kola stimulants (made from sherry and kola nut extract) and colored casts for children that "met an early demise when the pure food dyes turned bed linens into a symphony of colors and hospital laundries into bedlam."[22] It has also had more recent failed ventures in heart valves, kidney dialysis equipment, and ibuprofen pain relievers.[23] Failures at J&J have been an essential price to pay in creating a healthy branching tree within the context of its core ideology. In spite of these setbacks, the company has never posted a loss in its 107-year history. J&J's financial success makes the company look to outsiders like it was all mapped out by a strategic genius. In reality, J&J's history is filled with favorable accidents, trial and error, and periodic failures. Summed up chief executive Ralph Larsen in 1992: "Growth is a gambler's game."[24]

Similarly, Wal-Mart's phenomenal success in the 1970s and 1980s can better be understood by an evolutionary perspective than a creationist perspective. In fact, the folks at Wal-Mart have always been somewhat amused by the primary explanation of Wal-Mart's success frequently taught in microeconomics textbooks and MBA strategic planning courses. As Jim Walton summed up:

> We all snickered at some writers who viewed Dad [Sam Walton] as a grand strategist who intuitively developed complex plans and implemented them with precision. Dad thrived on change, and no decision was ever sacred.[25]

Indeed, the tools taught in most corporate strategy courses utterly fail to capture how the company's strategic competitive advantage came to be—how Wal-Mart attained its "brilliant" system in the first place. The Wal-Mart system came into being not primarily by a strategic plan formulated by economic genius, but largely by an evolutionary process of variation and selection: "Multiply, vary, let the strongest [experiments] win, and the weakest die."[26] That's exactly what Wal-Mart made a habit of doing from the time Sam Walton opened his first store in 1945. Wal-Mart *looks* like it had brilliant foresight, just as it *looks* like a species was preplanned and created. As a Wal-Mart executive described: "We live by the motto, 'Do it. Fix it. Try it.' If you try something and it works, you keep it. If it doesn't work, you fix it or try something else."[27]

Wal-Mart's famous people greeters, for example, did not come from any grand plan or strategy. A store manager in Crowley, Louisiana, was having trouble with shoplifting, so he tried an experiment: He put a friendly older gentleman by the front door to "greet" people on their way in and out. The "people greeter" made honest people feel welcome: "Hi! How are ya? Glad you're here. If there's anything I can tell you about our store, just let me know." At the same time, the greeter sent a message to potential shoplifters that someone would see them if they tried to walk out with stolen merchandise. No one at Wal-Mart—including Sam Walton—had conceived of anything like the greeter concept before the Crowley manager put it in place. Nonetheless, this odd experiment proved effective and eventually became standard practice across the company and a competitive advantage for Wal-Mart.

Using Wal-Mart as an example, we can rephrase Darwin's quote at the beginning of the chapter so it might read like this:

> It might be far more satisfactory to look at well-adapted visionary companies not primarily as the result of brilliant foresight and strategic planning, but largely as consequences of a basic process— namely, try a lot of experiments, seize opportunities, keep those that work well (consistent with the core ideology), and fix or discard those that don't.

Of course, we should be careful about making a wholesale analogy from biology to business. We do not think all visionary company adaptation and progress comes from an undirected evolutionary process. Certainly it would be inaccurate to view corporations as *exactly* like biological species.

For one thing, companies do in fact have the ability to set goals and plan. Species do not. And certainly our visionary companies do set goals and make plans—even Wal-Mart, which has simultaneously pursued both BHAGs *and* evolutionary progress throughout its history. It uses BHAGs to define a mountain to climb, and uses evolution to invent a way to the top. Jack Welch at General Electric embraced this paradoxical mixture of goals and evolution in a management idea labeled "planful opportunism," as described by Tichy and Sherman in *Control Your Own Destiny or Someone Else Will:*

Instead of directing a business according to a detailed . . . strategic plan, Welch believed in setting only a few clear, overarching goals. Then, on an ad hoc basis, his people were free to seize any opportunities they saw to further those goals. . . . [Planful opportunism] crystallized in his mind . . . after he read Johannes von Moltke, a nineteenth century Prussian general influenced by the renowned military theorist Karl von Clausewitz [who] argued that detailed plans usually fail, because circumstances inevitably change.[28]

For another thing, the process of variation and selection in human organizations differs from a purely Darwinian process in the natural world. Darwinian selection with species is *natural* selection—an entirely *unconscious* process whereby the variations that best fit with the environment survive and the weakest variations perish. In other words, species in the natural world do not consciously choose what variations to select; the environment selects. Human organizations, on the other hand, can make *conscious* selections. Furthermore, evolution in the natural world has no goal or ideology other than sheer survival of the species. Visionary companies, on the other hand, stimulate evolutionary progress toward desired ends within the context of a core ideology—a process we call *purposeful evolution.*

Of course, all companies evolve to some degree. Evolution "happens" whether we purposefully stimulate it or not. The real world is full of chance events that affect the trajectory of life. It happens to individual people. It happens to organizations. It happens to entire economic systems. But—and this is the crucial point—visionary companies more aggressively *harness* the power of evolution. This brings us to the key point of the chapter:

> **IF** well understood and consciously harnessed, evolutionary processes can be a powerful way to stimulate progress. And that's exactly what the visionary companies have done to a greater degree than the comparison companies.

Of course, purposeful evolution is not the only type of progress stimulated by visionary companies, nor do all of them use it extensively. Some, such as Boeing, IBM, and Disney, have relied more heavily on BHAG stimulated progress. (After all, it would be difficult to build an incremental

Boeing 747!) Others, such as Merck, Nordstrom, and Philip Morris, have relied more on continuous self-improvement, as shown in a later chapter. Nonetheless, wherever they fall along the continuum, the visionary companies have harnessed the power of evolution to a greater degree than the comparison companies in fifteen out of eighteen comparative cases. (See Table A.7 in Appendix 3.)

3M: "THE MUTATION MACHINE FROM MINNESOTA"*
AND HOW IT BLEW AWAY NORTON

During our interview with Bill Hewlett of HP, we asked him if there is any company that he greatly admired and saw as a role model. He responded without hesitation: "3M! No doubt about it. You never know what they're going to come up with next. The beauty of it is that *they* probably don't know what they're going to come up with next, either. But even though you can never predict what exactly the company will do, you know that it will continue to be successful." We agree with Hewlett. Indeed, if we had to bet our lives on the continued success and adaptability of any single company in our study over the next fifty to one hundred years, we would place that bet on 3M.

The great irony, of course, is that 3M began life as a failure—a big mistake. Dealt a nearly lethal blow when its initial concept to mine corundum failed (see Appendix 2), the tiny company tried for months to come up with something—*anything*—that might prove viable. According to Virginia Tuck in her book, *Brand of the Tartan—The 3M Story:*

> The board of directors met every week during the cold November of 1904, seeking a solution. The founders were determined not to give up [on the company]. Fortunately their employees felt the same way. Everyone offered some personal sacrifice [including some working for free] to keep the company going.[29]

Finally, the board agreed to the suggestion by one of its investors that 3M should shift away from mining and become a manufacturer of sandpaper and grinding wheels. (What else could it do with all that unusable, low-grade grit coming out of its failed mine?) So, out of desperation more than careful planning, 3M gave up mining and made a strategic shift to abrasives.

---

*3M's official name is Minnesota Mining and Manufacturing Company.

Enter William McKnight

From 1907 to 1914, the company struggled with quality problems, low margins, excess inventory, and cash flow crises. But under the quiet and deliberate urgings of a bookish young accountant-turned-sales-manager named William McKnight, the company began tinkering and experimenting with product improvements that kept the company viable—just barely.

In 1914, the company promoted McKnight, still in his twenties, to general manager. An instinctive clock builder, McKnight quickly set aside a five-by-eleven-foot corner storage room, invested $500 for a sink and glue bath for experiments and testing, and thereby created 3M's first "laboratory."[30] After months of experimentation with an artificial mineral, 3M introduced a new and highly successful cloth abrasive, called "Three-M-Ite"[31]—a product that propelled 3M to its first-ever dividend and was still listed in 3M's product directory seventy-five years after its invention.[32]

Although shy and unobtrusive on the outside, McKnight carried within an insatiable curiosity and unrelenting drive for progress, frequently working seven days a week to further the cause of the fledgling 3M Corporation and always looking for new opportunities that the company might pursue.[33] For example, in January 1920, McKnight opened an unusual letter that read:

> Please send samples of every mineral grit size you use in manufacturing sandpaper [to] Francis G. Okie, Manufacturer of printing inks, bronze powders, and gold ink liquids, Philadelphia.[34]

3M didn't sell raw materials, so there was no business to transact. But McKnight—curiosity piqued and on the prowl for interesting new ideas that might move the company forward—asked a simple question: "*Why does Mr. Okie want these samples?*"[35]

3M thereby stumbled into one of the most important products in its history, for Mr. Okie had invented a revolutionary waterproof sandpaper that would prove immensely useful to automobile manufacturers and repaint shops around the world. (As an aside, Okie had requested samples from numerous mineral and sandpaper companies, but none—except 3M—had bothered to ask why he wanted the samples.) 3M quickly acquired rights to the technology and began selling "Wetodry" brand sandpaper.

But that's not all 3M acquired. Indeed, Wetodry wasn't even the most valuable part of the transaction. McKnight—the consummate clock builder who always focused on building the organization—didn't just sign an agreement with Okie and thank him. He hired him! Okie closed his shop in Philadelphia, moved to St. Paul, and became a key player in developing new inventions at 3M until his retirement nineteen years later.[36]

"BRANCHING AND PRUNING" AT 3M

3M's near-fatal early days had made a big impression on McKnight. He therefore wanted 3M to have enough internal variation to protect itself:

> Our eggs were all in one basket at the beginning [the failed mine]. . . . By diversifying products . . . it was unlikely a trade war would hit them all at once [and] at least part of our business would always be profitable.[37]

But, as his hiring of Okie illustrates, McKnight did not want the evolution and expansion of the company to depend only on himself. He wanted to create an *organization* that would continually self-mutate from within, impelled forward by employees exercising their individual initiative. McKnight's approach was captured in phrases that would be chanted often by 3Mers throughout its history:[38]

> "Listen to anyone with an original idea, no matter how absurd it might sound at first."
>
> "Encourage; don't nitpick. Let people run with an idea."
>
> "Hire good people, and leave them alone."
>
> "If you put fences around people, you get sheep. Give people the room they need."
>
> "Encourage experimental doodling."
>
> "Give it a try—and quick!"

McKnight intuitively understood that encouraging individual initiative would produce the raw material of evolutionary progress—undirected variation. He also understood that not all such variation would prove favorable:

> Mistakes will be made [by giving people the freedom and encouragement to act autonomously], but . . . the mistakes he or she makes are not as serious in the long run as the mistakes management will make if it is dictatorial and undertakes to tell those under its author-

ity exactly how they must do their job. Management that is destruc-
tively critical when mistakes are made kills initiative and it's essential that we have many people with initiative if we are to continue to
grow.[39]

In fact, 3M's first attempt at self-mutation beyond sandpaper—a foray
into automobile wax and polish introduced in 1924—proved to be a costly
mistake, and the company eventually discontinued the line.[40]

But its second mutation proved wildly successful. Working in the give-
it-a-try atmosphere created by McKnight, a young 3M employee named
Dick Drew visited a customer site—an auto paint shop—and overheard a
violent explosion of particularly vivid profanity. Two-tone auto paint jobs
had become popular, but the improvised glues and adhesive tapes separating
the two colors failed to mask properly, leaving behind ugly blotches and
uneven lines.

"Can't anyone give us *something* that will work?" yowled the paint man,
storming across the paint shop.

"We can!" responded the 3M visitor. "I'll bet we can adapt something at
our lab to make foolproof masking tape."[41]

Drew discovered, however, that 3M had no such readily adaptable
product in the lab. So, like any true 3Mer, he invented one: 3M masking
tape. In response to an opportunity disguised as a problem—a process to be
repeated thousands of times—3M had finally made its first incremental shift
away from sandpaper. Five years later, in response to companies that had
contacted 3M looking for a waterproof packaging tape, Drew built on the
masking tape technology and invented a product destined to become a
household item worldwide: Scotch cellophane tape.

Scotch tape wasn't planned. No one at 3M had any idea in 1920 that 3M
would enter the tape business, and certainly no one expected that it would
become the most important product line in the company by the mid-1930s.
Scotch was a natural outgrowth of the organizational climate McKnight
created, not the result of a brilliant strategic plan.

Even more important than Scotch tape itself, however, was the fact that
3M institutionalized the evolutionary process that led to Scotch tape. Richard P. Carlton, director of research and later president of 3M, codified the
strategy of "variation and selection" in 3M's technical guidance manual as
early as 1925:

> [We] must possess a two-fisted generating *and* testing [process] for
> ideas.... Every idea evolved should have a chance to prove its
> worth, and this is true for two reasons: 1) if it is good, we want it; 2) if
> it is not good, we will have purchased our insurance and peace of
> mind when we have proved it impractical.[42]

Figure 7.A
A Branching Evolutionary Tree at 3M

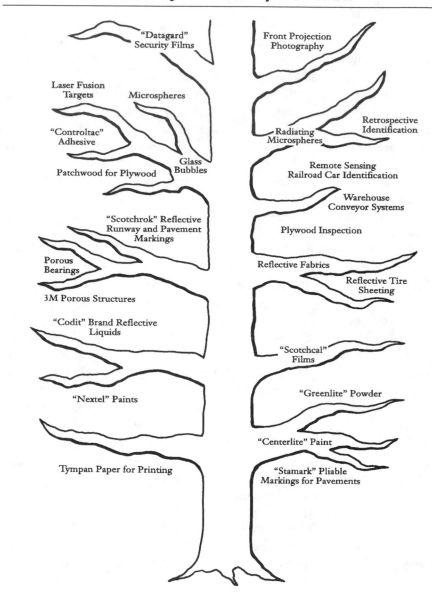

Product Evolution from Scotchlite Reflective Sheeting Technology
as of the mid-1970s, as depicted by 3M corporation in its official history.[46]

Carlton also added two other key criteria for evaluating and selecting ideas—criteria based on 3M's core ideology. First, for an idea to be selected, it had to be basically *new;* 3M only wanted to select innovative ideas. Second, it had to meet a demonstrable human need—to solve a real problem. Innovation that didn't "turn into products and processes that someone somewhere will find *useful*" would be of no interest to 3M.[43]

Interestingly, however, 3M did not select innovations based strictly on market size. With mottoes like "Make a little, sell a little" and "Take small steps,"[44] 3M understood that big things often evolve from little things; but since you can't tell ahead of time which little things will turn into big things, you have to try *lots* of little things, keep the ones that work and discard the ones that don't. Operating "on a simple principle that no market, no end product is so small as to be scorned,"[45] 3M adopted a policy of allowing people to sprout tiny "twigs" in response to problems and ideas. Most twigs wouldn't grow into anything. But anytime a twig showed promise, 3M would allow it to grow into a full branch—or perhaps even a full-fledged tree. This branching approach became so conscious at 3M that it sometimes explicitly depicted its product families in "branching tree" form (Figure 7.A presents an example.)

The beauty of the 3M story is that the company transcended McKnight, Okie, Drew, Carlton, and all the other original individuals from the early days of 3M. They created a *company*—a mutation machine—that would continue to evolve independent of whoever happened to be chief executive. Although 3M's leaders could never predict *where* the company would go in the future, they had little doubt that it would go far. It became a ticking, whirring, clicking, clattering clock with a myriad of tangible mechanisms well aligned to stimulate continual evolutionary progress. For example:

Mechanisms to Stimulate Progress at 3M

"15 percent rule"—a long-standing tradition that encourages technical people to spend up to 15 percent of their time on projects of their own choosing and initiative.[47]

To stimulate unplanned experimentation and variation that might turn into successful, albeit unexpected, innovations.

"25 percent rule"—each division is expected to generate 25 percent of annual sales from new products and services introduced in the previous five years. (Upped to 30 percent and shortened to the previous four years, beginning in 1993.)[48]

To stimulate continuous new product development (in 1988, for example, 32 percent of 3M's $10.6 billion came from new products introduced in the prior five years).[49]

"Golden Step" award, granted to those responsible for successful new business ventures originated within 3M.[50]

To stimulate internal entrepreneurship and risk taking.

"Genesis Grants"—internal venture capital fund that distributes parcels of up to $50,000 for researchers to develop prototypes and market tests.[51]

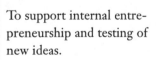

To support internal entrepreneurship and testing of new ideas.

Technology sharing awards, granted to those who develop a new technology and successfully share it with other divisions.[52]

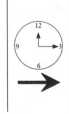

To stimulate internal dissemination of technology and ideas.

Mechanisms to Stimulate Progress at 3M (*continued*)

"Carlton Society"—a technical honor society whose members are chosen in recognition for their outstanding and original technical contributions within 3M.[53]		To stimulate the development of new technologies and innovation.
"Own business" opportunities—3Mers who successfully champion a new product then get the opportunity to run it as his or her own project, department, or division (depending on sales levels of product).[54]		To stimulate internal entrepreneurship.
"Dual ladder" career track that allows technical and professional people to move up without sacrificing their research or professional interests.[55]		To stimulate innovation by allowing top professional and technical people to "advance" without having to switch to a managerial track.
New product forums, where all divisions share their latest products.[56]		To stimulate new ideas across divisions.
Technical forums, where 3M people present technical papers and exchange new ideas and findings with each other.[57]		To stimulate cross-fertilization of ideas, technology, and innovation.

Mechanisms to Stimulate Progress at 3M (*continued*)

"Problem-solving missions"—small hit teams sent out to customer sites in response to specific, idiosyncratic customer problems.[58]	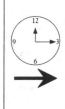	To stimulate innovation via customer problems that are the seeds of new opportunities, perpetually replicating the process by which 3M stumbled onto masking tape in the 1920s.
"High Impact Programs"—each division selects one to three priority products to get to market within a short, specified time frame.[59]		To speed product development and market introduction cycles, which thereby increases evolutionary "variation and selection" cycles.
Small, autonomous divisions and units—42 product divisions in 1990, each with average annual sales of about $200 million; plants—median size 115 people—are spread across forty states, mostly in small towns.[60]		To stimulate individual initiative by promoting a "small company within a big company" feel.
Early use of profit sharing (introduced to key employees in 1916, expanded to almost all employees in 1937).[61]		To stimulate a sense of individual investment in the overall financial success of the company, and thereby stimulate individual effort and initiative.

Propelled by these mechanisms, 3M had branched into over sixty thousand products and over forty separate product divisions by 1990. These spanned such wide-ranging categories as roofing granules, reflective highway signs, video recording tape, overhead projection systems, computer storage diskettes, bioelectronic ears, and 3M Post-it notes.

Indeed, the ubiquitous Post-it notes present just one more example of

3M living according to the philosophy that you often get to where you're going by stumbling, but you can only stumble if you're moving. Post-it coinventor Art Fry described:

> One day in 1974, while I was singing in church choir, I had one of those creative moments. To make it easier to find the songs we were going to sing at each Sunday's service, I used to mark the places with little slips of paper [but they would flutter out at just the wrong time, leaving me frantic]. I thought, "Gee, if I had a little adhesive on these bookmarks, that would be just the ticket," so I decided to check into . . . Spence Silver's adhesive.[62]

Using the 15 percent rule and following the principle of "experimental doodling," Spence Silver had invented the aberrant adhesive by just experimenting in the lab—mixing certain chemicals together "just to see what would happen." He explained:

> The key to the Post-it™ adhesive was doing the experiment. If I had factored it out beforehand, and thought about it, I wouldn't have done the experiment. If I had really seriously cracked the books and gone through the literature, I would have stopped. The literature was full of examples that said you can't do this.[63]

Reflecting on this somewhat chaotic process, 3M executive Geoffrey Nicholson pointed out that "a lot of the things [that led to the Post-it] were accidental." But had Art Fry not been in an environment where people were doodling around with weird adhesives on their 15 percent time, he would not have come up with the product. Furthermore, had Fry and Silver been in an environment that discouraged persistence—had 3M forbidden them from continuing to work on their crazy idea when initial market surveys indicated that the product would fail—3M Post-it notes wouldn't exist as a commercial product.[64] And that is precisely the point—indeed, *the* key point from 3M:

ALTHOUGH the invention of the Post-it note might have been somewhat accidental, the creation of the 3M environment that allowed it was anything but an accident.

The Stark Contrast at Norton

Founded on a good concept, Norton—unlike 3M—made money from the start and, by its fifteenth birthday, had multiplied its investor capital fifteen-fold (see Appendix 2). While 3M was fighting simply to survive during the period 1902 to 1914, Norton became the industry leader in bonded abrasives and produced superb financial returns year after year.[65] In 1914, Norton was fully ten times the size and significantly more profitable than the struggling 3M company.

Yet, despite its vastly superior early life, Norton failed to keep pace with 3M's "perpetual motion machine."[66] 3M gradually overtook and eventually far surpassed Norton in both size and profitability:

Size Comparison	3M	Norton	Ratio: 3M/Norton
1914 Revenues ($000):	264	2,734	.10
1929 Revenues ($000):	5,500	20,300	.27
1943 Revenues ($000):	47,200	131,300	.36
1956 Revenues ($000):	330,807	165,200	2.00
1966 Revenues ($000):	1,152,630	310,472	3.71
1976 Revenues ($000):	3,514,259	749,655	4.69
1986 Revenues ($000):	8,602,000	1,107,100	7.77
1990 Revenues ($000):	13,021,000	Norton Acquired	Norton Acquired
Profitability Comparison			
Return on Assets, 1962–86:	34.36%	17.72%	1.94
Return on Equity, 1962–86:	23.22%	11.25%	2.06
Return on Sales, 1962–86:	20.27%	9.42%	2.15

How did this happen? How did Norton lose its seemingly insurmountable lead over the failed mine from Minnesota?

Norton first laid the groundwork for its decline relative to 3M during the period 1914 to 1945. While 3M installed management practices that encouraged individual initiative and experimentation, Norton created no explicit practices or mechanisms whatsoever to stimulate experimentation and unplanned evolution. While 3M had a relentless drive for progress and impulse for activity ("Give it a try, and quick!"), Norton became a highly centralized and bureaucratic firm characterized by "routinization and stagnation."[67] While 3M seized opportunities that led to waterproof sandpaper and Scotch tape, Norton had an explicit policy *not* to encourage pursuit of new opportunities outside of its traditional product lines.[68] In 1928, 85 percent of Norton sales and 90 percent of profits came from Charles Norton's grinding wheel line, first introduced *a quarter of a century* earlier.[69] As a Norton research scientist described:

> Although we would play with the idea of doing research on new, radically different products, almost all work . . . involved . . . making better grinding wheels. . . . *You could work on anything you wanted as long as it was round and had a hole in it.* [emphasis ours][70]

During the late 1940s and 1950s, 3M pulled ahead, never to look back. While 3M decentralized and installed mechanisms to stimulate continued evolutionary progress, Norton remained centralized and concentrated primarily on cost cutting and efficiency.[71] While 3M branched into seven separate product divisions by 1948, with less than 30 percent of revenues coming from abrasives, Norton still derived nearly 100 percent of its revenues from its traditional abrasives line.[72] While 3M's Scotch product family generated high cash flow used to fund the development of exciting new technologies like Scotchlite reflective sheeting and Thermo-fax copying technology, Norton's abrasives products faced a mature market with slowing growth, overcapacity, price cutting, and declining margins.

In the late 1950s, Norton made a few feeble attempts to branch away from the maturing abrasives industry, but most of these were thwarted by lack of resources and institutional encouragement. Interestingly, Norton tried at one point to follow 3M's lead into adhesives, introducing a cellophane tape in 1957 (twenty-seven years after 3M!). But 3M's Scotch brand proved too entrenched and, according to a Norton sales manager, "We never got so bloody in our entire lives [as competing against Scotch]."[73]

By 1962, 3M had attained over three times the revenues and nearly twice the profit margins of Norton. Furthermore, whereas 3M had a wide array of attractive business units—stable cash generators like adhesives, high growth businesses like Scotchguard fabric protector and magnetic recording tapes, and emerging markets like microfilm and fax—Norton still derived over 75 percent of its sales from its old-line abrasives business.[74] Even more important, 3M's mutation machine was clicking into full gear, ensuring that it would continue to stumble into thousands of new opportunities long into the future. Norton, in contrast, had ground to a virtual standstill (2 percent sales growth, 0 percent profit growth) with no significant drive for progress or tangible mechanisms to stimulate progress. Wrote Charles W. Cheape in his well-researched historical account of Norton:

By the 1960s, management was largely a caretaker operation to maintain existing modest profit levels and the possibility of [selling the company].[75]

Finally, in response to declining stock multiples relative to 3M and Carborundum, Norton decided to make a concerted effort to diversify and progress—like 3M.[76] Unlike 3M, however, Norton elected to attain this array primarily by corporate strategic planning and diversification by acquisition—instead of by evolution. In fact, Norton became one of the first major clients and a dedicated disciple of the Boston Consulting Group (BCG) and its "portfolio management" techniques.* Instead of installing mechanisms to stimulate internal progress, Norton sought simply to *buy* progress. As *Forbes* magazine described, "Norton runs its operations the way most investors run their portfolios."[77]

Indeed, one of the great ironies in comparing 3M and Norton comes in the fact that 3M has consistently had a "portfolio" of business units that would be the envy of any strategic planning consulting firm. 3M's portfolio *looks* beautifully planned (just as species look perfectly created), but it actually came about largely by an undirected evolutionary process of variation and selection. 3M presents yet another classic example of how a creationist strategic planning perspective can so easily confuse the "why" and "how."

IF we mapped 3M's portfolio of business units on a strategic planning matrix, we could easily see *why* the company is so successful ("Look at all those cash cows and strategic stars!"), but the matrix would utterly fail to capture *how* this portfolio came to be in the first place.

Throughout the 1970s and 1980s, 3M continued to evolve into new—and often unexpected—arenas by encouraging individual initiative. Norton, in contrast, relied primarily on studies and planning models handed down from its consultants.[78] While 3M continued to stimulate progress by allowing people like Spence Silver to create new markets in part by "acci-

---

* This involved categorizing of businesses units into a matrix of "cash cows," "stars," "question marks," and "dogs," based on market share and market growth. Using this categorization, a company would make investments, acquisitions, and divestitures.

dents, not calculations,"[79] Norton's president proclaimed that "planning must become a way of life."[80] While 3M encouraged "scientific playfulness," Norton's management described its strategic method as "It's all derived from military planning."[81] While 3M diversified primarily by selecting the best incremental opportunities that emerged from its fruitful and self-stimulated research efforts, Norton primarily emphasized wholesale acquisitions, "because [internal] technology and research resources offered limited opportunity."[82]

Finally, in 1990, 3M sailed on to top $13 billion in sales and hundreds of innovative new product introductions. Norton, in contrast, found itself the target of an unfriendly takeover bid and ceased to exist as an independent entity.

LESSONS FOR CEOS, MANAGERS, AND ENTREPRENEURS

Using 3M as a blueprint for evolutionary progress at its best, here are five basic lessons for stimulating evolutionary progress in a visionary company.

1. *"Give it a try—and quick!"* For 3M, unlike Norton, the modus operandi became: When in doubt, vary, change, solve the problem, seize the opportunity, experiment, try something new (consistent, of course, with the core ideology)—even if you can't predict precisely how things will turn out. Do something. If one thing fails, try another. Fix. Try. Do. Adjust. Move. Act. No matter what, *don't sit still*. Vigorous action—especially in response to unexpected opportunities or specific customer problems—creates variation. Had McKnight not asked why Okie sent his cryptic letter requesting grit samples, or had Dick Drew not impulsively promised a solution for two-tone paint jobs, or had Spence Silver not done the experiment that textbooks said could not work, or had Art Fry not tried to solve his church choirbook problem—and so on for a thousand such "ifs"—then 3M wouldn't be a visionary company.

2. *"Accept that mistakes will be made."* Since you can't tell ahead of time which variations will prove to be favorable, you have to accept mistakes and failures as an integral part of the evolutionary process. Had 3M nailed Okie and Drew to the wall (or fired them) for the failed car wax business, then 3M probably wouldn't have invented Scotch tape. Remember Darwin's key phrase: "Multiply, vary, let the strongest live, and the weakest die." In order to have healthy evolution, you have to try enough experiments (multiply) of different types (vary), keep the ones that work (let the strongest live), and discard the ones that don't

(let the weakest die). In other words, you cannot have a vibrant self-mutating system—you cannot have a 3M—without lots of failed experiments. As former 3M CEO Lewis Lehr put it: "The secret, if there is one, is to dump the flops as soon as they are recognized. . . . But even the flops are valuable in certain ways. . . . You can learn from success, but you have to work at it; it's a lot easier to learn from a failure."[83] Keep in mind J&J's paradoxical perspective, described earlier in the chapter, that failures and mistakes have been an essential price to pay in creating a healthy branching tree that has not once posted a loss in 107 years. At the same time, keep in mind a lesson from the chapter on cult-like cultures: A visionary company tolerates mistakes, but not "sins," that is, breaches of the core ideology.

3. *"Take small steps."* Of course, it's easier to tolerate failed experiments when they are just that—*experiments*, not massive corporate failures. Keep in mind that small incremental steps can form the basis of significant strategic shifts. McKnight's simple answer to Okie led to waterproof sandpaper, opening a large market in the auto industry, leading to Dick Drew's masking tape and then to Scotch cellophane tape, which spawned recording tape, and so on. If you want to create a major strategic shift in a company, you might try becoming an "incremental revolutionary" and harnessing the power of small, visible successes to influence overall corporate strategy. Indeed, if you really want to do something revolutionary, it might be best to ask simply for permission to "do an experiment." Recall American Express's incremental steps in financial services that eventually became the primary strategic pillar of the company, and how William Dalliba used small experiments to incrementally revolutionize the company into travel services. Keep in mind the image of "twigs and branches." Or consider the image of "seeds and fruit" used by Masaru Ibuka at Sony to convey the concept of small, idiosyncratic problems as the starting point of great big opportunities.[84*]

4. *"Give people the room they need."* 3M provided greater operational autonomy and maintained a more decentralized structure than Norton—a key step that enabled unplanned variation. When you give people a lot of room to act, you can't predict precisely what they'll do—and this is *good*. 3M had no idea what Silver, Fry, and Nicholsen would do with their 15 percent "discretionary time." In fact, the visionary companies decentralized more and provided greater opera-

---

* Richard Dawkins does a beautiful job of describing incrementalism as a potent evolutionary force in Chapter 3 of *The Blind Watchmaker* (New York: Norton, 1986).

tional autonomy than the comparison companies in twelve out of eighteen cases. (Five were indistinguishable.) To this lesson, we'd add a corollary: Allow people to be persistent. Although the Post-it clan had trouble convincing other 3Mers that their weird sticky little notes had merit, no one ever told them to *stop* working on it.

5. *Mechanisms—build that ticking clock!* The beauty of the 3M story is that McKnight, Carlton, and others translated the previous four points into tangible mechanisms working in alignment to stimulate evolutionary progress—a step Norton never took. Look back at the list of mechanisms at 3M. Notice how concrete they are. Notice how they send a consistent set of reinforcing signals. Notice how they have teeth. If you're a division manager, you damned well better meet the 30 percent new product goal. If you want to become a technical hero at 3M, you'd better share your technology around the company. If you want to receive a Golden Foot Award and become an entrepreneurial hero, you've got to create a successful new venture with actual products, satisfied customers, and profitable sales. Good intentions alone simply won't cut it. 3M doesn't just throw a bunch of smart people in a pot and hope that something will happen. 3M lights a hot fire under the pot and stirs vigorously!

We find that managers often underestimate the importance of this fifth lesson and fail to translate their intentions into tangible mechanisms. They erroneously think that if they just set the right "leadership tone," people will experiment and try new things. No! It takes more than that. It requires putting in place items that will continually stimulate and reinforce evolutionary behavior. Tick, bong, click, whirr!

What Not to Do

We also found a number of cases where the comparison companies actively suppressed evolutionary progress at critical stages in their history—lessons of what *not* to do.

Chase Manhattan. Ruled by an obsessively controlling David Rockefeller during the 1960s and 1970s, Chase Manhattan (known as "David's Bank") became a fear-filled environment where managers spent most of their time in meetings—not on making decisions and taking action. Chase managers lived with the mentality, "Whew! One more day gone and I'm not in trouble." Even in the late 1980s, many senior managers at the bank wouldn't try new ideas because "David might not like it."[85] In contrast, Citibank during the same era was a "loosely structured corporation fueled by a chaotic kind of creativity . . . a corporate survival of the fittest" among highly talented people well rewarded for championing innovative ideas.[86]

Burroughs. During the critical early stages of the computer industry, Burroughs president Ray W. Macdonald stifled individual initiative. He drove away nearly all talented people who had a penchant for experimentation and publicly humiliated managers for failures and mistakes. A man "who [had] to prove he's the boss every day," Macdonald centralized all power and decisions in himself—making the product managers "almost a direct extension of his office." Instead of viewing customer problems as opportunities for evolution (like 3M did), Macdonald prided himself on keeping customers "sullen but not rebellious." Even though Burroughs had a technical lead over IBM in computers in the early 1960s, Macdonald inhibited his managers from seizing one of the biggest business opportunities of the century.[87]

Texas Instruments. During the 1950s and 1960s, Texas Instruments attained well-deserved acclaim as a highly innovative company under the guidance of chief executive Patrick Haggerty, who created an environment where ideas and innovations bubbled up from the lowest levels of the company.[88] However, Haggerty's successors, Mark Shepard and Fred Bucy, reversed this approach and instituted a top-down, autocratic approach that obliterated TI's entrepreneurial culture through fear and intimidation. If they saw something in a presentation they didn't like, they'd interrupt by saying, "That's bullshit! If that's all you have to say, we don't want to hear it." They'd yell, pound tables, and throw objects across the room. As an ex-TI manager described: "[Shepard and Bucy] don't have faith in their people. . . . Lower managers lost a great deal of authority. Much of their control [was] shifted into headquarters. Proposed products were defined and redefined there ad infinitum. Eventually, you were just given a product that was a square peg and told to fit it into the round hole of the market."[89] During the late 1970s and 1980s, TI lost its position as one of the most respected companies in America and suffered significant losses, while HP continued to be widely admired and highly profitable.

STICK TO THE KNITTING? STICK TO THE CORE!

In their 1982 book *In Search of Excellence*, Peters and Waterman counseled "Stick to the Knitting," meaning, in their words, "the odds for excellent performance seem strongly to favor those companies that stay reasonably close to the businesses they know."[90] On the surface, such a precept does not square with the evolutionary perspective we've presented in this chapter. Indeed, if 3M had defined its knitting as mining or sandpaper, then 3M wouldn't be what it is today—nor would we have those fabulous Post-it tape flags that have helped us keep organized while writing this book. From our standpoint, thank goodness 3M didn't stick to its knitting! Furthermore,

Norton stuck much closer to its knitting than 3M—and just look at the results. Zenith, too, stuck much closer to its knitting (television and radio) than Motorola—right into decline. J&J had no consumer goods experience when it began selling baby powder. Marriott had no background in hotels when it branched into that business. HP had no expertise in the computer business in the 1960s when it launched its first computer product. Disney had no knowledge of the theme park business when it created Disneyland. IBM had no background in electronics when it moved into computers. Boeing had virtually no experience in the commercial aircraft business when it did the 707. Had American Express stuck to its knitting (freight express), it probably wouldn't exist today.

We're not saying that evolutionary progress equals wanton diversification, or even that a focused business strategy is necessarily bad. Wal-Mart, for example, has thus far remained resolutely focused on one industry—discount retailing—while simultaneously stimulating evolution within that narrow focus. Nor are we saying that the concept of "Stick to the knitting" makes no sense. The real question is: *What* is the "knitting" in a visionary company? Our answer: Its core ideology.

Preserve the Core/Stimulate Progress

To the five lessons just given we must therefore add a sixth: Never forget to preserve the core while stimulating evolutionary progress. Keep in mind that evolution involves both variation *and* selection. In a visionary company, like 3M, selection involves two key questions. The first is simply pragmatic: Does it work? But just as important is the second question: Does it fit with our core ideology?

Since the time of William McKnight, 3M has sought to create innovative solutions to real human problems—that's what the company is all about. Variations at 3M must be new, useful, and reliable (key elements of 3M's core ideology) in order to stand a good chance of being selected. Certainly no one at 3M would stop Spence Silver from spending his 15 percent experimental doodling time on his bizarre glue that didn't glue. But, equally important, 3M didn't select the mutant adhesive until Silver married it to Art Fry's church choir problem, demonstrated to other 3Mers that the weird little Post-it notes were useful, and proved that they could be produced with 3M quality and reliability. You can't win a "Genesis Grant" to develop a me-too product at 3M. You don't become a member of the Carlton Society without an *original* technical contribution. You'll never survive as a division manager if your products prove consistently unreliable in customer hands. 3M stimulates progress with awesome vigor for a $13 billion company, but just as tenaciously preserves its core ideology.

Similarly, if a Wal-Mart experiment doesn't add value to customers, it will not be selected. If a J&J branch grows contrary to the credo, it will be pruned away. If a zealous marketing manager at Hewlett-Packard tries to launch a mutant new business that makes no technical contribution, he or she will find little support. If a Marriott opportunity would cause the company to veer wildly from its purpose of "making people away from home feel that they're among friends and really wanted," it will look instead for other opportunities. If a Sony "seed" leads only to technically mundane or low-quality "fruit," the company will sow other seeds.

Core ideology serves as a bonding glue and guiding force that holds a visionary company together while it mutates and evolves. For all its mutations, far-flung enterprises, and small divisions, we found a remarkable cohesion at 3M. Indeed, 3Mers bond to their company with the same almost cult-like dedication we saw at P&G, Disney, and Nordstrom. The same holds true for HP, Motorola, and Wal-Mart—three companies that rival 3M as self-mutation machines, yet cling tenaciously to their core ideologies.

Like the genetic code in the natural world, which remains fixed while species vary and evolve, core ideology in a visionary company remains unchanged throughout all its mutations. Indeed, it is the very presence of these fixed, guiding ideals that gives a visionary company something extra that evolving species in the natural world can never have: a purpose and a spirit. In the words of William McKnight reflecting on his sixty-five-year relationship with 3M and its ideals:

> It is proper to emphasize how much we depend on each other [and our shared values]. Our challenge, while stressing this important lesson of humanity, lies in maintaining, at the same time, a proper respect for the individual. . . . To continue our progress and service to America and the world, we need a healthy appreciation for those who exercise . . . the option for excellence, permitting the creation of something for all of us, enriching lives with new ideas and products. The best and hardest work is done in the spirit of adventure and challenge.[91]

chapter **8**

HOME-GROWN MANAGEMENT

From now on, [choosing my successor] is the most important decision I'll make. It occupies a considerable amount of thought almost every day.
JACK WELCH, CEO, GENERAL ELECTRIC, SPEAKING ABOUT SUCCESSION PLANNING IN 1991—*NINE YEARS* BEFORE HIS ANTICIPATED RETIREMENT,[1]

One responsibility [we] considered paramount is seeing to the continuity of capable senior leadership. We have always striven to have proven backup candidates available, employed transition training programs to best prepare the prime candidates, and been very open about [succession planning]. . . . We believe that continuity is immensely valuable.
ROBERT W. GALVIN, FORMER TEAM MEMBER OF THE CHIEF EXECUTIVE OFFICE, MOTOROLA CORPORATION, 1991[2]

In 1981, Jack Welch became chief executive of the General Electric Company. A decade later, he had become legendary in his own time, "widely acknowledged," according to *Fortune* magazine, "as the leading master of corporate change in our time."[3] To read the myriad of articles on Welch's revolution, we might be tempted to picture him as a savior riding in on a white horse to rescue a severely troubled company that had not changed significantly since the invention of electricity. If we did not know Welch's background or GE's history, we might be lured into thinking that he must have been brought in from the outside as "new blood" to shake up a lumbering, complacent behemoth.

Nothing could be further from the truth.

For one thing, Welch was pure GE home-grown stock, having joined the company directly out of graduate school one month before his twenty-fifth birthday. It was his first full-time job, and he worked at GE for twenty consecutive years before becoming chief executive.[4] Like every single one of his predecessors, Welch came from deep *inside* the company.

Nor did Welch inherit a grossly mismanaged company. Quite the opposite. Welch's immediate predecessor, Reginald Jones, retired as "the most admired business leader in America."[5] A survey of his peers in *U.S. News and World Report* found Jones to be "the most influential person in business today"—not once, but twice, in 1979 and 1980. Similar surveys in the *Wall Street Journal* and *Fortune* magazine also listed Jones at the top, and a Gallup poll named Jones CEO of the Year in 1980.[6] In financial terms, such as profit growth, return on equity, return on sales, and return on assets, GE performed as well under Jones's eight-year tenure as during Welch's first eight years.[7]

Furthermore, Welch is not the first change agent or management innovator in GE's panoply of chief executives. Under Gerard Swope (1922–1939), GE moved dramatically into home appliances. Swope also introduced the idea of "enlightened management"—new at the time to GE—with balanced responsibilities to employees, shareholders, and customers.[8] Under Ralph Cordiner (1950–1963) and his slogan "Go for it," GE exploded into a vast array of new arenas—a twentyfold increase in the number of market segments served.[9] Cordiner radically restructured and decentralized the company, instituted management by objective (one of the first companies in America to do so), created Crotonville (GE's now-famous management training and indoctrination center), and wrote the influential book *New Frontiers for Professional Managers*.[10] Fred Borch's tenure (1964–1972) was "a time of creative ferment" and a willingness to make bold, risky investments in such areas as jet aircraft engines and computers.[11] Reginald Jones (1973–1980) became a leader in changing the relationship between business and government.

Indeed, Welch comes from a long heritage of managerial excellence atop GE. Using pretax return on equity (ROE) as a basic benchmark of financial performance, GE under Welch's predecessors performed as well on average since 1915 as GE during Welch's first decade in office—26.29 percent for Welch and 28.29 percent for his predecessors.[12] In fact, when we ranked GE chief executive eras by return, the Welch era came in *fifth* place out of seven. (Every single GE chief executive, including Welch, outperformed rival Westinghouse in ROE during their tenure.) Of course, a straight ROE calculation doesn't take into account the ups and downs of industry cycles, wars, depressions, and the like. So we also rank-ordered GE chief executive eras in terms of average annual cumulative stock returns *relative* to the market and Westinghouse.[13] On this basis, we found Welch in second and fifth* place, respectively, relative to his predecessors. An excellent performance, but not the best in GE history. (See Table A.9 in Appendix 3.)

This is no way detracts from Welch's immense achievements. He ranks as one of the most effective chief executive officers in American business history. But—and this is the crucial point—*so do his predecessors*. Welch changed GE. So did his predecessors. Welch outperformed his counterparts at Westinghouse. So did his predecessors. Welch became widely admired by his peers—a "management guru" of his age. So did his predecessors. Welch laid the groundwork for the future prosperity of GE. So did his predecessors. We respect Welch for his remarkable track record. But we respect GE even more for *its* remarkable track record of continuity in top management excellence over the course of a hundred years.

> **TO** have a Welch-caliber CEO is impressive. To have a century of Welch-caliber CEOs all grown from inside—well, that is one key reason why GE is a visionary company.

In fact, the entire selection process that resulted in Welch becoming CEO was traditional GE at its best. Welch is as much a reflection of GE's heritage as he is a change agent for GE's future. As longtime GE consultant Noel Tichy and *Fortune* magazine editor Stratford Sherman described in *Control Your Own Destiny or Someone Else Will*:†

---

* Given GE's recent superb performance in the early 1990s and Westinghouse's decline, we expect that the Welch era ranking will improve significantly on this dimension.
† Two books cover the Welch selection process in detail. One is Tichy and Sherman's. The other is *The New GE*, by Robert Slater. In this section, we have drawn background data from both of these fine books.

The management-succession process that placed venerable General Electric in Welch's hands exemplifies the best and most vital aspects of the old GE culture. [Prior CEO Reginald] Jones spent years selecting him from a group of candidates so highly qualified that almost all of them ended up heading major corporations. . . . Jones insisted on a long, laborious, exactingly thorough process that would carefully consider every eligible candidate, then rely on reason alone to select the best qualified. The result ranks among the finest examples of succession planning in corporate history.[14]

Jones took the first step in that process by creating a document entitled "A Road Map for CEO Succession" in 1974—*seven years* before Welch became CEO. After working closely with GE's Executive Manpower Staff, he spent two years paring an initial list of ninety-six possibilities—*all* of them GE insiders—down to twelve, and then six prime candidates, including Welch. To test and observe the candidates, Jones appointed each of the six to be "sector executives," reporting directly to the Corporate Executive Office. Over the next three years, he gradually narrowed the field, putting the candidates through a variety of rigorous challenges, interviews, essay contests, and evaluations.[15] A key part of the process included the "airplane interviews," wherein Jones asked each candidate: "You and I are flying in a company plane. It crashes. You and I are both killed. Who should be chairman of General Electric?" (Jones learned this technique from his predecessor, Fred Borch.)[16] Welch eventually won the grueling endurance contest over a strong field; runner-up candidates went on to become president or CEO of such companies as GTE, Rubbermaid, Apollo Computer, and RCA.[17] As an interesting aside, more GE alumni have become chief executives at American corporations than alumni of any other company.[18]

Westinghouse, in contrast to GE, has been rocked by periods of turmoil and discontinuity at the top. Westinghouse has had nearly twice as many CEOs as GE, some with tenure of less than two years. The average Westinghouse CEO remained in office eight years, compared to fourteen years at GE. Furthermore, Westinghouse has periodically resorted to hiring CEOs from the outside, rather than building on internal talent, as GE has *always* done. George Westinghouse was kicked out of the company in 1908 and replaced by two outsiders (both bankers) during a reorganization.[19] In 1946, another outsider (again a banker) became CEO.[20] Then in 1993, Westinghouse went outside yet again for a CEO—bringing in an ex-PepsiCo executive to run the company after it posted billion-dollar losses in 1991 and 1992.[21]

We would like to comment more explicitly about the internal succession process at Westinghouse, but we found scant material on this topic in outside publications or from the company itself. But that, too, is an interesting point. GE has paid such prominent, conscious attention to leadership continuity that both the company and outside observers have commented greatly on it. Westinghouse has paid significantly less attention to management development and succession planning.

PROMOTE FROM WITHIN TO PRESERVE THE CORE

Throughout this book, we've downplayed the role of leadership in a visionary company. Yet it would be outright wrong to state that top management doesn't matter at all. It would be naive to suggest that any random person could become CEO of a visionary company, and it would still continue to tick along in top form. Top management *will* have an impact on an organization—in most cases, a significant impact. The question is, will it have the *right kind* of impact? Will management preserve the core while making its impact?

Visionary companies develop, promote, and carefully select managerial talent grown from inside the company to a greater degree than the comparison companies. They do this as a key step in preserving their core. Over the period 1806 to 1992, we found evidence that only two visionary companies (11.1 percent) ever hired a chief executive directly from outside the company, compared to thirteen (72.2 percent) of the comparison companies. Of 113 chief executives for which we have data in the visionary companies, only 3.5 percent came directly from outside the company, versus 22.1 percent of 140 CEOs at the comparison companies. In other words, *the visionary companies were six times more likely to promote insiders to chief executive than the comparison companies.* (See Table 8.1 in the text and Table A.8 in Appendix 3.)

> **PUT** another way, across *seventeen hundred years* of combined history in the visionary companies, we found only *four* individual cases of an outsider coming directly into the role of chief executive.

In short, it is not the quality of leadership that most separates the visionary companies from the comparison companies. It is the *continuity* of quality leadership that matters—continuity that preserves the core. Both the visionary companies and the comparison companies have had excellent top management at certain points in their histories. But the visionary com-

Table 8.1

Companies that Put Outsiders into Chief Executive Roles[22]
1806−1992

Visionary Companies	Comparison Companies
Philip Morris	Ames
Walt Disney	Burroughs
	Chase Manhattan
	Colgate
	Columbia
	General Motors
	Howard Johnson
	Kenwood
	Norton
	R.J. Reynolds
	Wells Fargo
	Westinghouse
	Zenith

NOTE: IBM hired an outsider as CEO (Louis Gerstner) in 1993, the year after we cut off the data for our analysis. We did not count William Allen at Boeing as an outsider because he had been actively involved in major management decisions (such as reorganizations, R&D investments, financing structures, and business strategy) for twenty years as the company's lawyer and fourteen years as a highly active director prior to becoming chief executive—a post he then held for twenty-three years. We are indebted to Morten Hansen for his background analysis for this table.

panies have had better management development and succession planning—key parts of a ticking clock. They thereby ensured greater continuity in leadership talent grown from within than the comparison companies in fifteen out of eighteen cases. (See Table A.8 in Appendix 3.)

You can think of it as a continuous self-reinforcing process—a "leadership continuity loop":

Leadership Continuity Loop

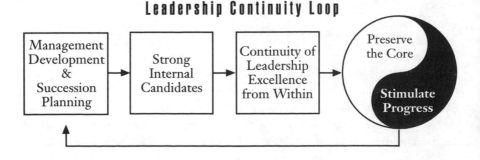

Absence of any of these elements can lead to management discontinuities that force a company to search outside for a chief executive—and therefore pull the company away from its core ideology. Such discontinuities can also impede progress, as a company stalls due to turmoil at the top. In fact, we saw a pattern common in the comparison companies that stands in contrast to the "management continuity loop" in the visionary companies. We came to call this pattern the "leadership gap and savior syndrome":

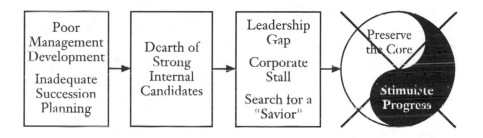

Consider the following examples of Colgate versus P&G and Zenith versus Motorola.

Discontinuity at Colgate Versus Talent Stacked Like Cordwood at P&G

Up until the early 1900s, Colgate was an extraordinary company. Founded in 1806, the company had attained over a century of steady growth and was roughly the same size as P&G. It also had the strongest early statement of core ideology of any comparison company in our study, complete with core values and an enduring purpose articulated by Sidney Colgate.[23] By the 1940s, however, Colgate had fallen to less than half the size and less than one-fourth the profitability of P&G, and remained at that ratio on average for the next four decades. It also drifted from its strong core ideology and became a company with a much weaker self-identity than Procter.

What happened? The answer lies partly in poor succession planning and resulting management discontinuities at Colgate relative to P&G. Colgate had been run entirely by insiders (all members of the Colgate family) for its first four generations of top management. However, the company failed in its management development and succession planning during the early 1900s. By the late 1920s, Colgate faced such a shortage of well-developed successors that it resorted to a merger with Palmolive-Peet which "put an alien management in office."[24] As a 1936 *Fortune* article described:

The brothers Colgate were getting old. Gilbert, the President, was seventy, Sidney was sixty-six. And Russell, who was only fifty-five, took no great part in the management. . . . Sidney's son, Bayard Colgate, was . . . barely six years out of Yale. That, for a Colgate, was *too* young. So the brothers listened attentively when Charles Pearce offered to merge Palmolive-Peet with Colgate. . . . [After the merger], they resigned themselves to virtual retirement.

Pearce, who became chief executive of the combined company, proved to be a disaster. Driven by "a mania for expansion,"[25] Pearce concentrated on an unsuccessful attempt to merge Colgate into a giant conglomerate with Standard Brands, Hershey, and Kraft. Distracted by his quest for sheer size, Pearce ignored the fundamentals of Colgate's business and its basic values. He even moved headquarters from Jersey City, New Jersey (where it had resided close to the soap making operations for eighty-one years), to Chicago.[26] During Pearce's reign from 1928 to 1933, Colgate's average return on sales declined by more than half (9.0 to 4.0 percent). During the same period P&G's return on sales actually *increased* slightly (11.6 to 12.0 percent), despite the Depression.[27]

Pearce severely breached Colgate's core ideology, especially its core value of fair dealing with retailers, customers, and employees.[28] He drove such hard bargains with retailers that they revolted:

> Druggists were especially irate: they had long been accustomed to the conservative dealings of the Colgates. The tactics of the Pearce . . . management pleased them not at all. And since Colgate . . . was depending on substantial profits from its toilet articles, . . . the defection of the druggists . . . was a ruinous blow.[29]

Finally, according to *Fortune*, the Colgate family "roused up from its lethargy to look astonished on what Charles Pearce had done."[30] Bayard Colgate (age thirty-six) replaced Pearce as chief executive, moved the headquarters back to New Jersey, and tried to reawaken the Colgate values and reestablish forward progress. However, Pearce's reign of havoc made the CEO job particularly difficult for the young Colgate, who had not been prepared or groomed for such a role. He held the post for only five years, before passing the job to international sales manager Edward Little. Colgate fell behind P&G, never to catch up. During the decade immediately after the Pearce era, P&G grew twice as fast and attained four times the profits as Colgate.[31]

With the Pearce debacle, Colgate began a pattern of poorly handled top management succession. Edward Little (chief executive from 1938 to 1960) ran Colgate as a one-man show.[32] "Colgate was dominated by [Little]—and 'dominate' is not too strong a term," wrote *Forbes*.[33] We found no evidence that Little could imagine Colgate without himself at the helm, or that the company had any succession plan in place. Finally, at age seventy-nine, Little retired, and Colgate had to call home one of its international vice presidents to ride in as a "White Knight" to turn around the company whose domestic operations were in serious trouble.[34]

In 1979, Colgate experienced yet another tumultuous transition at the top when chief executive David Foster was removed—against his will—by the Colgate board. Like his predecessors before him, Foster "carried on a tradition of one-man rule at Colgate, and it suited his temperament."[35] In fact, Foster actually *impeded* succession planning, according to an article in *Fortune:*

> To the end, David Foster did his best to give his heir apparent the least possible power—or even visibility. . . . Foster [sought] an effective way to silence the board on the matter of succession. Colgate had an unwritten policy at the time calling for top executives to leave at sixty. Foster was then fifty-five and was saying he would adhere to the policy, but it is a telling comment that when [his potential heir] received an offer to become president of [another company], he took it.[36]

Rocked again by turmoil at the top, Colgate slid further behind P&G in both sales and profitability during the decade after Foster's ouster, dropping to one-fourth the size of P&G in both sales and profits. Certainly factors other than chaotic management contributed to Colgate's relative decline, including P&G's superior R&D efforts and greater economies of scale. But—and this is the crucial point—Colgate first lost its chance to run even with P&G during the Pearce turmoil, and then continued with fits and stalls at critical transition points.

P&G, in contrast, suffered no lurches in management like those at Colgate, even though the two companies faced exactly the same challenge of moving beyond family governance at precisely the same point in history. During the 1920s, while the Colgate brothers neglected to develop worthy successors, Cooper Procter had been carefully preparing Richard Deupree—an insider who had joined P&G in 1909—to assume the role of chief executive.[37] Under Cooper Procter's watchful eye and coaching, Deupree assumed ever greater responsibility, eventually becoming chief operating officer in 1928 (the exact same year that Colgate "put an alien management in office"). In 1930, Deupree began a successful eighteen-year stint as chief executive—the first nonfamily CEO in P&G's history. Then, like Procter before him, Deupree ensured continuity from generation to generation, as John Smale (CEO 1981–1989) described:

Deupree held a pivotal role in carrying out and handing down the character of the Company. He knew—and learned from—the only two people to precede him as Chief Executive Officer since Procter & Gamble was incorporated in 1890. And he also knew—and helped teach—the next four people to hold the job after him. I am one of these four people—only the seventh Chief Executive of this Company in the nearly 100 years since it's been incorporated.[38]

P&G understood the importance of constantly developing managerial talent so as to never face gaps in succession at *any* level, and therefore to preserve its core throughout the company. *Dun's Review* once commented that "P&G's program for developing managers is so thoroughgoing and consistent that the company has talent stacked like cordwood—in every job and in every level."[39] All the way to senior management ranks, P&G aims at all times to "have two or three people equally capable of assuming responsibility of the next step up."[40] Deupree's successor, Neil McElroy, explained: "Our [development] of people who . . . will be the management of the future goes on year after year, in good times and bad. If you don't do it, X years from now we will have a gap. And we can't stand a gap."[41]

Leadership Gaps at Zenith Versus Motorola's Deep Bench

"Commander" Eugene F. McDonald, Jr., the brilliant and domineering mastermind founder of Zenith Corporation, had developed no capable successors by the time he died in 1958. McDonald's closest associate, Hugh Robertson, took over as chief executive, but he was already past the age of seventy. *Fortune* magazine commented in 1960, "Zenith is traveling largely on momentum imparted by . . . forceful personalities that belong to its past rather than its future."[42] Robertson held on for two years and passed the company to the highly conservative corporate counsel Joseph Wright, who allowed the company to drift away from its core value of fanatical dedication to high quality.[43] Insider Sam Kaplan became chief executive in 1968, but died suddenly in 1970. Facing yet another management vacuum at the top, Zenith felt the need to find an outside savior to rescue the company. After an intensive search, Zenith hired John Nevin from Ford.[44]

After an unspectacular tenure and continued drift from the company's original values, Nevin resigned in 1979, forcing ex-chairman Wright to come out of retirement at age sixty-eight "to try to put the company back on its feet."[45] Wright elevated Revone Kluckman to chief executive, but he—like Kaplan before him—died suddenly two years into his tenure, forcing yet another crisis transition.

In contrast, Motorola had none of the same turmoil—a model example of management continuity that preserves the core. Founder Paul Galvin began grooming his son Bob Galvin years before the formal transfer of power. The younger Galvin began work at Motorola in 1940 while still in high school, sixteen years before becoming president and nineteen years before becoming chief executive.[46] Paul Galvin made sure that his son grew up from deep inside the business, having him begin as a stock clerk with a minimum of special privileges. When young Bob reported to the personnel office at seven A.M. to apply for a summer job, a manager offered to take him directly—out of turn—to see the head of personnel. Galvin declined. He wanted to go through the process from the bottom, just like every other Motorolan had to.[47]

Bob Galvin moved up through the business, finally sharing presidential duties for the three years preceding his father's death. "In time, my father . . . announced we would act as one. Either of us could act on any issue. The other would support."[48] Paul Galvin's biographer wrote that the transfer of experience from one generation to the next was a daily process that lasted years.[49] Then, almost immediately after his father's death in 1959, Bob Galvin began thinking about management development and succession planning for the next generation—*a quarter of a century* before he would pass the reins.

To reinforce the concept of leadership continuity from within, Bob Galvin discarded the traditional concept of a chief executive officer in favor of the concept of a Chief Executive *Office* occupied by "team members." "Members" plural is not a misprint. Galvin envisioned an office held by *multiple* team members (usually three) at any one time, rather than a single leader. Galvin did this in part to ensure that the company would have capable insiders well positioned to assume leadership responsibility at any point in time. "There was always a private but clear understanding of succession hierarchy," wrote Galvin. "We were prepared for unschedulable change throughout that quarter of a century [that I was a member of the Chief Executive Office.]"[50]

Motorola implemented this "Office Of" concept not only at the chief executive level, but also at lower levels (with two or three team members per office)—a key mechanism for management development and leadership continuity throughout the company. Aware that such an approach was controversial among management thinkers—not to mention awkward to manage—Galvin argued that the benefits far outweighed the costs, as he wrote in 1991:

> If an Office Of at the top was to succeed, it needed candidates who had experienced and adapted to such a . . . role earlier in their career. It followed that the experience base had to be provided by similar assignments at business unit levels. . . . The Office Of has its

disadvantages. Some incumbents just plain don't prefer it. . . . Mixed signals can emanate from the office. . . . As a consequence, periodically some Office Ofs have not clicked. Some players departed or were benched. But it has worked well more often. . . . The proof is in the using. On balance it is a figure of merit. It has consistently provided the best informed succession answers. It absolutely helped to provide the proven source of Chief Executive Office candidates.[51]

In sixty-five years of history, Motorola has suffered no leadership discontinuities like those at Zenith. Motorola has continually reinvented itself (from battery repair for Sears radios to integrated circuits to satellite communications systems), yet displayed unbroken continuity in top management excellence steeped in its core values, *even when it has unexpectedly lost top management talent.* For example, in 1993, George Fisher—a key member of the Chief Executive Office—left Motorola to become chief executive at Kodak. At most companies, the unexpected departure of such a capable chief executive would cause disarray, turmoil, and a management gap—as happened at Zenith when CEOs died unexpectedly. But not at Motorola. The other two members of the chief executive office (Gary Tooker, age fifty-four, and Christopher Galvin, age forty-three) simply clicked into place to shoulder the extra responsibilities. Simultaneously, Motorola began an internal process to select a new third team member from its deep bench of well-trained managerial talent. In an article appropriately titled "Motorola Will Be Just Fine, Thanks," the *New York Times* summed up: "Mr. Fisher had the luxury of making his move secure in the knowledge that Motorola could hardly be better positioned to absorb such a surprise."[52]

Management Turmoil and Corporate Decline

Westinghouse, Colgate, and Zenith and are not the only examples of top management turmoil and discontinuity in our study. We found numerous such examples in the comparison companies.

It happened at Melville Corporation in the 1950s, when Ward Melville found he hadn't adequately prepared any successors. Desperate to pass the company to somebody—anybody—because he was "anxious to retire," Melville gave the job to a production manager who was ill prepared and didn't even want the job. The company declined precipitously. "I was shocked to see how fast the numbers can deteriorate when the men are wrong," Melville commented later.[53] Melville then launched a year-long search for an outside CEO to come in and turn around the company. Fortunately, Melville had the wisdom to abandon the outside search and turn instead to developing a promising young insider who, over time, proved to be a very capable CEO.[54]

It happened at Douglas Aircraft in the late 1950s, as founder Donald Douglas turned his company over to an inadequately prepared Donald Douglas, Jr. "The younger Douglas could not possibly fill his old man's shoes," wrote one biographical account. "The son retaliated against those he considered his enemies [i.e., most of his father's management], and . . . replaced experienced administrators with those who joined his team."[55] As Douglas, Jr., placed key friends in high positions, talented managers left the company when it needed them most to face the ever-growing onslaught from Boeing. During the early 1960s, the loss of managerial talent caught up with Douglas as it tried desperately—and unsuccessfully—to catch up to Boeing. Facing an epic crisis in 1966, Douglas, Jr., sought salvation in the form of a merger with McDonnell Aircraft.

It happened at R.J. Reynolds in the 1970s, as company director J. Paul Sticht— ex president of Federated Department Stores—"helped torpedo the planned succession of an heir apparent, then maneuvered himself into the presidency," according to *Business Week*.[56] Sticht assumed chief executive responsibility and restocked the management team almost entirely with outsiders.[57] Later, in one of the most famous senior management disasters in corporate history, Ross Johnson (a truly alien element to the company's heritage) became CEO after RJR acquired Nabisco Brands in 1985. Well-documented in *Barbarians at the Gate: The Fall of RJR Nabisco* by Bryan Burroughs and John Helyar, the Johnson era ended with a junk-bond-financed takeover by financiers Kohlberg Kravis Roberts & Co., who brought in yet another outside CEO.

It happened at Ames, as the founding family watched its creation destroyed by outsiders who were brought in due to lack of capable successors. It happened at Burroughs with its importation of outsider W. Michael Blumenthal from Bendix, when the company faced "an obvious gap in our management structure," brought on because "new managers were not groomed during the years of [Ray W.] Macdonald's dictatorial rule."[58] It also happened at Chase Manhattan, Howard Johnson, and Columbia Pictures.

It also happened at two recent high-profile cases in our visionary companies: Disney and IBM.

At Disney, Walt developed no capable successor, and the company floundered during the 1970s as managers ran around asking themselves, "What would Walt do?" To save the company, the board hired outsiders Michael Eisner and Frank Wells in 1984. We'd like to point out, however, that Disney consciously did its best to preserve ideological continuity even while selecting an outsider. Ray Watson, who guided the CEO search, wanted Eisner for the job not only because he had a stellar track record in the industry, but also because Eisner understood and appreciated—indeed, had unabashed enthusiasm for—the Disney values.[59] As one Disneyite summed up: "Eisner turned out to be more Walt than Walt."[60]

The Disney case illustrates an important point. If you're involved with an organization that feels it must go outside for a top manager, then look for candidates who are highly compatible with the core ideology. They can be different in managerial style, but they should share the core values at a gut level.

What should one make of IBM's 1993 decision to replace its internally grown CEO with Louis V. Gerstner—an outsider from R.J. Reynolds with no industry experience? How does this massive anomaly fit with what we've seen in our other visionary companies? It doesn't fit. IBM's decision simply doesn't make any sense to us—at least not in the context of the seventeen hundred cumulative years of history we examined in the visionary companies.

Perhaps IBM's board was operating under the assumption that dramatic change requires an outsider. To that assumption we respond simply: Jack Welch. The "leading master of corporate change in our time" spent his entire career inside the company that made him CEO. IBM has had one of the most thorough management development programs of any corporation on the planet. It has a long track record of hiring extraordinarily talented people. We simply cannot believe that IBM didn't have at least one Welch-caliber change agent inside the company. Indeed, we would be surprised if there weren't at least a dozen insiders equally capable as anyone IBM could attract from the outside.

AS companies like GE, Motorola, P&G, Boeing, Nordstrom, 3M, and HP have shown time and again, a visionary company absolutely does not need to hire top management from the outside in order to get change and fresh ideas.

IBM's board and search committee wanted dramatic change and progress. With Mr. Gerstner, they'll probably get it. But the real question for IBM—indeed, the pivotal issue over the next decade—is: *Can Gerstner preserve the core ideals of IBM* while simultaneously bringing about this momentous change? Can Gerstner be to IBM what Eisner has been to Disney? If so, then IBM might regain its revered place among the world's most visionary companies.

THE MESSAGE FOR CEOS, MANAGERS, AND ENTREPRENEURS

Simply put, our research leads us to conclude that it is extraordinarily difficult to become and remain a highly visionary company by hiring top management from outside the organization. Equally important, there is absolutely no inconsistency between promoting from within and stimulating significant change.

If you're the chief executive or board member at a large company, you can directly apply the lessons of this chapter. Your company should have management development processes and long-range succession planning in place to ensure a smooth transition from one generation to the next. We urge you to keep in mind how the Walt Disney Company—an American icon—got itself in a terrible fix because Walt neglected to build this vital part of a ticking clock. We urge you to not repeat the mistakes made at Colgate, Zenith, Melville, Ames, R.J. Reynolds, and Burroughs. Do not fall into the trap of thinking that the only way to bring about change and progress at the top is to bring in outsiders, who might dilute or destroy the core. The key is to develop and promote insiders who are highly capable of stimulating healthy change and progress, while preserving the core.

If you're a manager, the essence of this chapter also applies to you. If you're building a visionary department, division, or group within a larger company, you can also be thinking about management development and succession planning, albeit on a smaller scale. If you were hit by a bus, who could step into your role? What are you doing to help those people develop? What planning have you done to ensure a smooth and orderly transition when you move up to higher responsibilities? (You can also be asking those at higher levels what steps *they* have taken to ensure a smooth succession.) Finally, if you find a visionary company that you fit really well with, it might be worth your while to develop your skills within that company rather than job hop.

How does this chapter apply to smaller companies and entrepreneurs? Clearly, a small company cannot have a chief executive succession process that begins with ninety-six candidates, as happened at GE. Nonetheless, small to midsize companies can be developing managers and planning for succession. Motorola was still a small company when Paul Galvin began carefully grooming his son to become chief executive. The same holds true for family transitions during the early days of Merck, P&G, J&J, Nordstrom, and Marriott. Sam Walton began thinking about future management of the company before the company had even fifty stores.[61] Bill Hewlett and Dave Packard began formal management development programs and thoughtful succession planning in the 1950s, when the company had five hundred employees.[62]

Interestingly, nearly all of the key early architects in the visionary companies remained in office for long periods of time (32.4 years on average), so few of the companies faced actual succession while still young and small. Nonetheless, many of them were planning for succession long before the actual moment of succession. If you're a small-business person, this indicates taking a very long-term view. The entrepreneurial model of building a company around a great idea, growing quickly, cashing out, and passing the company off to outside professional managers will probably not produce the next Hewlett-Packard, Motorola, General Electric, or Merck.

From the perspective of building a visionary company, the issue is not only how well the company will do during the current generation. The crucial question is, how well will the company perform in the *next* generation, and the next generation after that, and the next generation after that? All individual leaders eventually die. But a visionary company can tick along for centuries, pursuing its purpose and expressing its core values long beyond the tenure of any individual leader.

chapter **9**

GOOD ENOUGH
NEVER IS

Don't bother just to be better than your
contemporaries or predecessors. Try to be better
than yourself.

WILLIAM FAULKNER[1]

People would always say to my father, "Gee whiz,
you've done real well. Now you can rest." And he
would reply, "Oh, no. Got to keep going and do it
better."

J. WILLARD MARRIOTT, JR., CHAIRMAN, MARRIOTT, 1987[2]

The critical question asked by a visionary company is
not "How well are we doing?" or "How can we do well?" or "How well do
we have to perform in order to meet the competition?" For these companies, the critical question is *"How can we do better tomorrow than we did
today?"* They institutionalize this question as way of life—a habit of mind
and action. Superb execution and performance naturally come to the visionary companies not so much as an end goal, but as the residual result of a
never-ending cycle of self-stimulated improvement and investment for the
future. There is no ultimate finish line in a highly visionary company. There

is no "having made it." There is no point where they feel they can coast the rest of the way, living off the fruits of their labor.

Visionary companies, we learned, attain their extraordinary position not so much because of superior insight or special "secrets" of success, *but largely because of the simple fact that they are so terribly demanding of themselves.* Becoming and remaining a visionary company requires oodles of plain old-fashioned discipline, hard work, and a visceral revulsion to any tendency toward smug self-satisfaction. As J. Willard Marriott, Sr., summed up while reflecting on the essence of success:

> Discipline is the greatest thing in the world. Where there is no discipline, there is no character. And without character, there is no progress. . . . Adversity gives us opportunities to grow. And we usually get what we work for. If we have problems and overcome them, we grow tall in character, and the qualities that bring success.[3]

During the 1980s, "continuous improvement" became a management catchphrase. But at the visionary companies, the concept has been common-place for decades—over a century in some cases. William Procter and James Gamble, for example, used the concept of continuous improvement as far back as the 1850s![4] William McKnight brought the concept to life at 3M in the 1910s. J. Willard Marriott embraced the concept soon after opening his first root beer stand in 1927. David Packard incessantly used the term "continuous improvement" beginning in the 1940s.

Our research findings clearly support the concept of continuous improvement, but not as a program or management fad. In a visionary company, it is an institutionalized habit—a disciplined way of life—ingrained into the fabric of the organization and reinforced by tangible mechanisms that create discontent with the status quo. Furthermore, visionary companies apply the concept of self-improvement in a much broader sense than just process improvement. It means long-term investments for the future; it means investment in the development of employees; it means adoption of new ideas and technologies. In short, it means doing *everything* possible to make the company stronger tomorrow than it is today.

MECHANISMS OF DISCONTENT

You're probably getting the impression that the visionary companies are not exactly comfortable places. And that's precisely the impression you should be getting.

COMFORT is not the objective in a visionary company. Indeed, visionary companies install powerful mechanisms to create *dis*comfort—to obliterate complacency—and thereby stimulate change and improvement *before* the external world demands it.

Like great artists or inventors, visionary companies thrive on discontent. They understand that contentment leads to complacency, which inevitably leads to decline. The problem, of course, is how to avoid complacency—how to remain self-disciplined once a company has attained success or become number one in its field. How can a company keep alive that "fire that burns from within" that impels people to keep pushing, to never be satisfied, and to always search for improvement?

Richard Deupree at Procter & Gamble pondered these exact questions, worried that P&G's rise to prominence in the early twentieth century might cause the company to become fat, happy, and complacent. What to do? He could have gone around giving passionate speeches about the importance of remaining disciplined. He could have written memos and pamphlets about the dangers of complacency. He could have met personally with managers throughout the company to impress upon them the inherent value of change and self-improvement. But Deupree knew that the company needed something more than just good intentions to improve for the future. He wanted something with teeth in it, something that would continually impel progress from within.

He therefore responded favorably to a radical proposal made in 1931 by marketing manager Neil McElroy, namely to create a brand management structure that would allow P&G brands to compete directly with other P&G brands, almost as if they were from different companies. P&G already had the best people, the best products, the best marketing muscle. So why not pit the best of P&G against the best of P&G? If the marketplace doesn't provide enough competition, why not create a system of internal competition that makes it virtually impossible for any brand to rest on its laurels? Implemented in the early 1930s, the competing brand management structure became a powerful mechanism at P&G for stimulating change and improvement from within. The structure proved so effective that it was eventually copied in one form or another by virtually every American consumer products company, including Colgate—but not until nearly three decades later.[5]

The point here is not that a successful company should necessarily create internal competition in order to keep itself vibrant. The point is that it should have some sort of discomfort mechanisms in place to combat the disease of complacency—a disease that inevitably begins to infect all success-ful organizations. Internal competition is one such mechanism, but not the only one. We found a variety of mechanisms across the visionary companies.

Merck in the 1950s embraced a strategy of consciously *yielding* market share as products became low-margin commodities, thus *forcing* itself to produce new innovations in order to grow and prosper.[6] Motorola used an innovate-or-die mechanism similar to Merck's, with its practice of cutting off mature product lines that accounted for significant sales volume, thus forcing itself to fill the gap with new products. Motorola did this with televisions and car radios.[7] (Chairman Robert Galvin kept the last car radio made at its U.S. plant on his desk as a reminder of Motorola's "refounding as a front-runner in higher technologies.")[8] Motorola filled the gaps via a mechanism called "Technology Road Maps"—a comprehensive tool for benchmarking technology progress versus competitors and anticipated mar-ket needs up to ten years into the future.[9]

General Electric institutionalized internal discomfort with a process called "work out." Groups of employees meet to discuss opportunities for improvement and make concrete proposals. Upper managers are not al-lowed to participate in the discussion, but must make on-the-spot decisions about the proposals, in front of the whole group—he or she cannot run, hide, evade, or procrastinate.[10]

Boeing created discomfort for itself with a planning process that we came to call "eyes of the enemy." It assigns managers the task of developing strategy as if they worked for a competing company with the aim of oblit-erating Boeing. What weaknesses would they exploit? What strengths would they leverage? What markets could be easily invaded? Then, based on these responses, how should Boeing respond?[11]

Early in Wal-Mart's history, Sam Walton began using a mechanism called "Beat Yesterday" ledger books (see example p. 189). These ledger books tracked sales figures on a daily basis in comparison to the exact same day of the week one year earlier. Wal-Mart used these ledgers as a stimulus to push the standards up and up, forever.[12]

Nordstrom created an environment where people can never stop trying to improve. Sales per hour (SPH) rankings measure success relative to one's peers. Thus, there are no absolute standards that, once achieved, allow an employee to relax. Nordstrom also carefully tracks customer feedback and links employee compensation and advancement to the trends.[13] Bruce Nordstrom explained:

> If you really listen to your customers, they're never happy—they'll let you know what you're doing wrong—and it just forces you to get better. Fat headedness is what bothers me most. I think we get so

much press about our service and all this stuff and we start believing it and then we think we're better than the customer. And then we're dead right there.[14]

Hewlett-Packard also has a history of ranking employees relative to their peers. Managers must argue for the rankings of their people in group ranking sessions with other managers who are just as intent on arguing that *their* people should get the top rankings. The process continues until all the managers agree on a pooled ranking from top to bottom. It's a tough, draining, and uncomfortable process that makes it virtually impossible for any employee to attain a high rating and then coast the rest of the way.[15]

HP also installed a powerful mechanism called "pay as you go" (a policy against taking out any long-term debt). Sophisticated financial models have shown this policy to be totally irrational—that a company like HP should take out debt in order to maximize its value. But such models fail to account for the powerful internal effect of a no-debt policy: *It enforces discipline.* By refusing to take on long-term debt in order to fund growth, HP forced itself to learn how to fund its 20-plus percent average annual growth (not to mention its ongoing 10 percent of sales investment in R&D) entirely from within. Such a mechanism may not be considered rational, but it produced a whole company of incredibly disciplined general managers skilled at operating with a level of leanness and efficiency usually

Wal-Mart "Beat Yesterday" ledger book

November				
1964	**1965**	**1966**	**1967**	**1968**
1st Monday				
1st Tuesday				
1st Weds.				
1st Thursday				
1st Friday				
1st Saturday				
1st Sunday				
1st WEEK				

only found in small, cash-constrained companies. As an HP vice president described:

> This philosophy [pay-as-you-go] provides great discipline all the way down. If you want to innovate, you must bootstrap. It is one of the most powerful, least understood influences that pervades the company.[16]

And the comparison companies? We found no evidence that they installed mechanisms of discomfort to the same degree as the visionary companies. The sense of ruthless self-discipline simply does not show up as consistently in their history. Indeed, we found that some of the comparison companies consciously took the comfortable road, at times milking the company in the short-term at the expense of the long-term—a behavior pattern almost unheard of in the visionary companies.

BUILD FOR THE FUTURE (AND DO WELL TODAY)

Put yourself in the shoes of Bill Hewlett and David Packard in 1946. You have a small company, less than ten years old. You've just watched your revenue decline by 50 percent as defense contracts dried up at the end of World War II. You face an imminent cash flow crisis that threatens the very survival of the company, and you have no prospects in commercial markets that would immediately solve the problem. David Packard described the situation:

> We were all celebrating the end of the war but, at the same time, we realized there was going to be a very serious problem. Our sales dropped from about a million and a half to something like half of that in 1946, and we were very worried as I remember about whether we could hold on or not.[17]

What would you do in the same situation? What do you think they did?

First, they cut payroll by approximately 20 percent. Faced with evaporating government contracts, they simply *had* to reduce headcount in order to save the company. Second, they vowed that they would never again allow themselves to become overly dependent on the hire-and-fire government contract business.[18]

Hewlett and Packard didn't stop there, however. They took a remarkably bold and farsighted step for a small company reeling from a 40 percent decline in business: They decided to take advantage of the fact that *all* defense-funded institutions were facing hard times, and they therefore set out to hire talented scientists and engineers who had been engaged at government-funded research laboratories during the war. They also decided to keep their best and most expensive in-house talent, not wanting to make cuts that would have been damaging in the long term. Packard explained:

> Even though our business was going down, we decided we were going to hire . . . these bright young engineers. We hired Ralph Lee and Bruce Wholey and Art Fong and Horace Overacker and several other people right at the time when our company was going down because we were convinced that this was a time to get some good technical people.[19]

The remarkable thing about this decision was that Hewlett and Packard were not at all sure whether the postwar business climate would provide enough support for their talented staff. It was a gamble. And, in fact, the company struggled through a painful postwar adjustment and didn't start to grow rapidly again until 1950. But HP's farsighted investment in 1946 paid off handsomely over the next two decades as its engineering team introduced a slew of innovative and profitable new products.[20]

As the company grew, Bill Hewlett and David Packard constantly emphasized the importance of never compromising the long-term principles and health of HP for the sake of quick, expedient profits. For example, David Packard pointed out in 1976 that anytime he discovered an employee had violated HP's ethical principles in order to increase short-term divisional profits, the individual involved was fired—no exceptions, no matter what the circumstance, no matter what the impact on the immediate bottom line.[21] HP's long-term reputation, in Packard's view, had to be protected under all circumstances. Yet Hewlett and Packard never mistook their farsighted perspective as a reason to let up the pressure and coast complacently through the current year. To illustrate, here are two quotes from Packard speaking to HP managers in the 1970s:

David Packard Fifty-Year Perspective	David Packard One-Year Perspective
"If we continue our dedication to the principles that have carried us through the first 50 years, we will be assured of our continuing success over the next 50 years. I'm sure I speak for Bill as well as myself, in saying we are very, very proud of what you're doing and we expect you to do even better in the future."[22]	"It is just as easy to make a profit today as it will be tomorrow. Actions taken which result in reducing short-term profit in the hope of increasing long-term profit are very seldom successful. Such actions are almost always the result of wishful thinking and almost always fail to achieve an overall optimum performance."[23]

In fairness, Patrick Haggarty—Texas Instrument's counterpart to David Packard—also guided his company with a long-term perspective. In fact, he also hired top scientists from research labs in 1946—though TI was not facing a dire financial crisis like that at HP.[24]

However, as TI evolved beyond Haggarty, it veered away from the difficult challenge put forth at HP, namely to manage with a fifty-year horizon *and* perform extremely well in the current year. In the 1970s, TI, unlike HP, began introducing cheap consumer products and making drastic, unexpected price cuts—often at the expense of its dealers—in a bid to grab market share. One dealer commented in 1979, "TI is so bent on getting the price down that when it comes to the consumer, they squeeze the quality out."[25] The strategy backfired, leaving TI with financial losses and a damaged reputation. Whereas HP never lost sight of either the short or long term, TI's quest for sheer size and growth in the short term eroded its foundation and heritage as a creator of excellent and innovative products and severely damaged its long-term prospects.[26]

Hewlett-Packard versus Texas Instruments illustrates one of the key differences we saw between the visionary and comparison companies. Visionary companies habitually invest, build, and manage for the long term to a greater degree than the comparison companies in our study. "Long term" at a visionary company does not mean five or ten years; it means multiple decades—*fifty* years is more like it. Yet, at the same time, they do not let themselves off the hook in the short term.

MANAGERS at visionary companies simply do not accept the proposition that they must choose between short-term performance *or* long-term success. They build first and foremost for the long term while *simultaneously* holding themselves to highly demanding short-term standards.

Again, comfort is not the objective in a visionary company.

Greater Long-Term Investment in the Visionary Companies

Taking a systematic look across the entire set of companies in our study, we found substantial evidence that the visionary companies invested for the future to a greater degree than the comparison companies. By analyzing annual financial statements dating back to the year 1915, we found that the visionary companies consistently invested more heavily in new property, plant, and equipment as a percentage of annual sales than the comparison companies (thirteen out of fifteen cases).* They also plowed a greater percentage of each year's earnings back into the company, paying out less in cash dividends to shareholders (twelve out of fifteen cases, plus one indistinguishable case).* (See Table A.10 in Appendix 3.)

Few of our companies reported R&D expenditures as a separate line item for long periods of their history, and some, such as Wal-Mart and Marriott, simply don't have R&D in the conventional sense. However, for those pairs on which we have information, the visionary companies invested more heavily in R&D as a percentage of sales in every single case (eight out of eight).[27] In the pharmaceutical industry, where basic research is arguably the most important factor in long-term corporate health, our visionary companies outinvested our comparison companies in R&D as a percentage of sales by over 30 percent. Merck, for example, has consistently invested more heavily in basic research as a percentage of sales than Pfizer since the 1940s and more heavily than *every* other company in the industry since the late 1960s—a key reason for Merck's preeminent position in the 1980s.[28]

The visionary companies also invested much more aggressively in human capital via extensive recruiting, employee training, and professional development programs. Merck, 3M, P&G, Motorola, GE, Disney, Marriott, and IBM all made significant investments in their "universities" and "education centers" for intensive training and development programs. (The comparison companies invested in training, but not as early or to the same degree.) Motorola, for example, targets forty hours per week of training per employee per year and requires that every division spend 1.5 percent of payroll on training.[29] All managers at Merck attend a three-day training course on recruiting and interviewing techniques; Merck CEO Roy Vagelos routinely begins meetings with the question: "Whom did you recruit lately?"[30] In general, we noticed that the visionary companies tended to have much more elaborate and extensive recruiting and interviewing processes than the comparison companies, requiring a significant professional and managerial time investment. At HP, for instance, potential new employees usually interview with at least eight people in the division where they will eventually work.

Finally, the visionary companies invest earlier and more aggressively than the comparison companies in such aspects as technical knowhow, new technologies, new management methods, and innovative industry practices. Instead of waiting for the world to impose the need for change, they're likely

---

* Number of cases varies based on information consistently available. Financial and entertainment companies, for example, report different accounting line items than industrial companies. We excluded Sony/Kenwood.

to be earlier adopters than the comparison companies. Throughout its history, GE embraced new management methods—management by objectives, decentralization, employee empowerment—earlier than Westinghouse. In fact, GE has historically been a leader in adopting new management methods. In 1956, GE published and distributed to all its managers a two-volume work entitled *Some Classic Contributions to Professional Managing*. The volumes contained a collection of thirty-six papers representing the most significant management thinking to date and were designed to spread powerful management ideas throughout the ranks of GE.

Merck was one of the first American companies in history to fully embrace a "zero defects" TQM process—back in 1965.[31] Merck was also the first to adopt state-of-the-art financial analysis techniques based on Monte Carlo computer simulations that allow it to make strategic decisions with extraordinarily long time horizons.[32] Philip Morris adopted state-of-the art production technologies more quickly than R.J. Reynolds during the pivotal 1960–1985 era.[33] Motorola committed to new technologies that would likely be important down the road, while Zenith held back until forced by the market to adopt them. Walt Disney habitually invested in new film technologies, quickly seizing upon them while its rivals fearfully contemplated their possible drawbacks.[34] Citibank consistently invested in important new methods earlier than Chase Manhattan—three decades earlier in some cases:

Adopted Earlier at Citibank Than at Chase Manhattan

Divisional profitability statements

Merit pay

Management training programs

College recruiting programs

Organization by industry (versus geography)

National charter

Automated teller machines

Credit cards

Retail branches

Foreign branches

Not only were the comparison companies slower and more timid, but in a number of cases management shirked investment for the future or, worse, milked the company at a crucial stage in its history. For example, during the 1970s and 1980s, while Philip Morris relentlessly invested in its goal of becoming number one (see the BHAGs chapter), R.J. Reynolds executives used the company primarily as a platform for their own self-aggrandizement and enrichment.[35] They bought a fleet of corporate jets (referred to as the "RJR Air Force"), built expensive airport hangars (dubbed the "Taj Mahal of corporate hangars"), constructed elaborate and unneeded corporate offices (called the "Glass Menagerie"), decorated with expensive antique furniture and exquisite artwork ("the only company I've ever worked for without a budget," according to one vendor), and sponsored celebrity athletes and sporting events with dubious marketing value. When asked about the wisdom of these expenses, CEO F. Ross Johnson responded simply: "A few million dollars are lost in the sands of time."[36]

McDonnell Douglas consistently demonstrated a penny-wise, pound-foolish fanatical attention to the short-term bottom line that has inhibited bold leaps into the future (including hesitation on building a jumbo jet). By the 1970s, this conservatism had become a repetitive historical pattern at McDonnell Douglas. A 1978 *Business Week* article characterized McDonnell Douglas as "infused with a penchant for penny-pinching" and described how its conservative, short-term, bottom-line orientation led to the company's decision to abandon development of new generation jetliners: "Known for frugality and prudence, McDonnell-Douglas is concentrating on derivative designs . . . rather than launch costly new development programs."[37] The contrast between "reaching out to tomorrow" at Boeing versus the "penny-pinch conservatism" at McDonnell Douglas has expressed itself in key decisions for over half a century.

For decades, Colgate neglected investments in new product development, marketing programs, and plant modernization. Here are representative quotes from *Forbes* and *Fortune*, commenting on Colgate across time:

1966: "Turning out new products that succeed requires a finely-tuned marketing machine. Colgate simply did not have one after 22 years of Little's rule [1938–1960]. Lesch launched a crash program to create almost overnight what it had taken P&G 30 years to nurture and perfect."[38]

1969: "The company had not produced any major new products in years. None were even in the works, and between 1956 and 1960, Colgate's domestic volume had actually declined."[39]

1979: "Foster, desperate to keep earnings rising, was cutting back on advertising and holding down on research and development spending—the lifeblood of any marketing company. In short, he was borrowing from the future with the hope that tomorrow would bring a stronger economy to bail him out."[40]

1982: "Colgate is now virtually the only consumer products company in the country with no new major product program."[41]

1987: "Profits from the core business propped up Foster's acquisitions. That squeezed financially and stifled important things such as new product development and plant modernization."[42]

1991: "Developing breakthrough products costs big money. But Mark, an accomplished cost cutter, may not be willing to pay the price that other companies are paying. Colgate sets aside less than 2% of its revenues for research and development. Compare that with P&G's almost 3%."[43]

MARRIOTT VERSUS HOWARD JOHNSON: THE DECLINE OF A GREAT AMERICAN FRANCHISE

In 1960, Howard Johnson, Sr., abruptly retired from the company he built, leaving it in the hands of his son, Howard, Jr. "I've never seen anything like it," said a longtime associate. "Most men don't want to let go of what they've built. He just walked away, and that was that."[44] He left behind one of the best-known American businesses, with seven hundred restaurants and hotels dotting highways around the country, all of them adorned with eye-catching bright orange roofs and beloved by middle America. J. Willard Marriott, Jr., commented at the time that he hoped the company he had inherited from his father could one day be as successful as Howard Johnson.[45] By 1985, Marriott had not only become as successful as Howard Johnson, but had far surpassed it—by a factor of seven times.

What happened? The answer lies largely in Marriott's relentless self-discipline as a continuous improvement machine versus Howard Johnson's complacency. As Howard Johnson, Jr. described in a 1975 interview: "We are a reacting company. We don't try to anticipate the future. In this business, you can't look too far ahead, maybe two years."[46] Unlike Marriott, Howard Johnson refused to invest in restaurants and hotels tailored to specific market segments and eventually found itself "segmented to death." While Marriott continued to invest and build for the future even during recessions, Howard Johnson became overly focused on cost control, efficiency, and short-term financial objectives.[47] While Marriott pushed itself to continually improve the quality and value of its service, Howard Johnson became "overpriced and understaffed purveyors of pallid food, hamstrung by outdated ideas."[48] A former Howard Johnson executive commented: "Ho Jo always seemed to have ideas to upgrade the restaurants and hotels, but they never wanted to spend the money."[49] An executive from Imperial Group, the company that bought Howard Johnson in 1979, explained why it sold the company six years later for less than half the acquisition price:

> Profits were artificially high. Its reinvestment had been neglected. Pennies had been pinched on staffing, menus and renewal. It was milking the business by not reinvesting.[50]

At one point, Johnson, Jr., moved to elegant quarters in New York's Rockefeller Center (leaving the rest of his management team in Boston) and spent the bulk of his time socializing in elite society.[51] Summed up a competitor:

> Every time I saw Howard Johnson he was always telling me how he was going to cut costs. I don't think he spent enough time at his restaurants. If he'd eaten at his own restaurants more instead of lunching at 21 [a fashionable New York restaurant], he might have learned something.[52]

In contrast, Marriott, Jr., lived a relatively modest lifestyle guided by what he calls "the Mormon work ethic" (seventy hours per week) that drove him to personally visit up to two hundred Marriott facilities per year—and to expect similar travel schedules from other top managers.[53]

Even more important, Marriott, Jr., *translated his personal drive for progress into the very fabric of the institution.* Here is a short list of mechanisms for stimulating improvement we saw at Marriott during this era, but *not* at Howard Johnson:

- "Guest Service Index" (GSI) reports based on customer comment cards and detailed surveys of customers selected at random. Managers can track their GSI by computerized reports and make corrective adjustments. GSI reports affect bonus compensation and promotion opportunities.[54]
- Annual performance reviews for every employee—hourly and managerial.[55]

- Incentive bonuses reaching all the way down to coffee shop managers; bonuses based on service, quality, and cleanliness in addition to cost effectiveness.[56]
- Profit-sharing program available to employees at all levels of the company; participation in the program where individual employees invest up to 10 percent of their wages in a profit-sharing trust, thus creating a tangible link between the individual employee's welfare and the progress of the company.[57]
- Investment in extensive interviewing and screening to hire quality employees; new Marriott hotels routinely interview over a thousand employees for one hundred openings.[58]
- Management and employee development programs; by the early 1970s, Marriott was spending up to 5 percent of pretax profits on management development.[59]
- Investment in a full-scale corporate "Learning Center" (built in 1970) equipped with state-of-the-art audio/visual/computerized teaching technologies. A 1971 *Forbes* article described: "Hundreds of Marriott managers stream in and out for refresher courses, right along with new employees involved in 'total immersion' training on how to prepare and serve."[60]
- "Phantom Shoppers"—inspectors that pose as customers. If the service has been good, the phantom pulls out an ID card and hands the server the card with a $10 bill clipped to the back. If the service needs improvement, there's no $10 bill and the card says "Oops!" People who get an "Oops!" are sent to retraining. Each employee gets up to three chances to improve.[61]

THE MESSAGE FOR CEOS, MANAGERS, AND ENTREPRENEURS

The decline of Howard Johnson relative to Marriott presents an excellent example of nearly all the lessons of this chapter. But we could have selected any number of examples. We could describe how Ames always lagged behind Wal-Mart in adopting new retailing innovations, and how it delayed investment in new technologies such as bar code scanning because the payback period was longer than two years.[62] We could describe how Norton milked certain divisions to such an extent that windows had not been washed for months because everyone expected each day to be the last.[63] We could describe in detail how Zenith neglected to invest in solid-state electronics (the last company to switch to printed circuit boards in the 1950s), dragged its feet into color TVs, cut R&D to keep earnings up, and milked Zenith's reputation for quality—all while Motorola and the Japanese kept improving themselves. And on and on.

Indeed, the discipline of self-improvement stands out as one of the most clear differences between the visionary and comparison companies. Taking into account mechanisms of discomfort and long-term investments for the future, we found that the visionary companies have driven themselves harder for self-improvement in sixteen out of eighteen cases (see Table A.10 in Appendix 3).

If you're involved in building and managing a company, we urge you to consider the following questions:

- What "mechanisms of discontent" can you create that would obliterate complacency and bring about change and improvement from within, yet are consistent with your core ideology? How can you give these mechanisms sharp teeth?
- What are you doing to invest for the future *while* doing well today? Does your company adopt innovative new methods and technologies before the rest of the industry?
- How do you respond to downturns? Does your company continue to build for the long-term even during difficult times?
- Do people in your company understand that *comfort is not the objective*—that life in a visionary company is not supposed to be easy? Does your company reject doing well as an end goal, replacing it with the never-ending discipline of working to do better tomorrow than it did today?

We see good news and bad news in this chapter. The good news is that one of the key elements of being a visionary company is strikingly simple: Good old-fashioned hard work, dedication to improvement, and continually building for the future will take you a long way. It's pretty straightforward stuff, easily within the grasp of every manager. The bad news is that creating a visionary company requires huge quantities of good old-fashioned hard work, dedication to improvement, and continually building for the future. There are no shortcuts. There are no magic potions. There are no work-arounds. To build a visionary company, you've got to be ready for the long, hard pull. Success is never final. It's a lesson Howard Johnson never learned.

THE PARABLE OF THE BLACK BELT

Picture a martial artist kneeling before the master sensei in a ceremony to receive a hard-earned black belt. After years of relentless training, the student has finally reached a pinnacle of achievement in the discipline.

"Before granting the belt, you must pass one more test," says the sensei.

"I am ready," responds the student, expecting perhaps one final round of sparring.

"You must answer the essential question: What is the true meaning of the black belt?"

"The end of my journey," says the student. "A well-deserved reward for all my hard work."

The sensei waits for more. Clearly, he is not satisfied. Finally, the sensei speaks. "You are not yet ready for the black belt. Return in one year."

A year later, the student kneels again in front of the sensei.

"What is the true meaning of the black belt?" asks the sensei.

"A symbol of distinction and the highest achievement in our art," says the student.

The sensei says nothing for many minutes, waiting. Clearly, he is not satisfied. Finally, he speaks. "You are still not ready for the black belt. Return in one year."

A year later, the student kneels once again in front of the sensei. And again the sensei asks: "What is the true meaning of the black belt?"

"The black belt represents the beginning—the start of a never-ending journey of discipline, work, and the pursuit of an ever-higher standard," says the student.

"Yes. You are now ready to receive the black belt and *begin* your work."

chapter 10

THE END OF THE BEGINNING

This is not the end. It is not even the beginning of
the end. But it is, perhaps, the end of the
beginning.

WINSTON S. CHURCHILL[1]

I t's become fashionable in recent decades for com-
panies to spend countless hours and sums of money drafting elegant vision
statements, values statements, mission statements, purpose statements, aspiration statements, objectives statements, and so on. Such pronouncements
are all fine and good—indeed, they can be quite useful—but they're not the
essence of a visionary company. *Just because a company has a "vision statement"
(or something like it) in no way guarantees that it will become a visionary company!*
If you walk away from this book thinking that the most essential step in
building a visionary company is to write such a statement, then you will have
missed the whole point. A statement might be a good first step, but it is *only* a
first step.

The essence of a visionary company comes in the translation of its core
ideology and its own unique drive for progress into the very fabric of the
organization—into goals, strategies, tactics, policies, processes, cultural
practices, management behaviors, building layouts, pay systems, accounting
systems, job design—into *everything* that the company does. A visionary

company creates a total environment that envelops employees, bombarding them with a set of signals so consistent and mutually reinforcing that it's virtually impossible to misunderstand the company's ideology and ambitions.

We've made this point in a number of ways in preceding chapters. But it is an important enough point—indeed, it just might be the most important point to take away from this book—that we choose to bring our findings to a close with this short capstone chapter illustrating the central concept of *alignment* that has run throughout these pages. By "alignment" we mean simply that all the elements of a company work together in concert within the context of the company's core ideology and the type of progress it aims to achieve—its vision, if you like. (We see vision as simply a combination of an enduring core ideology plus envisioned progress for the future.) Consider the following three examples of alignment at its best.

THE POWER OF ALIGNMENT: FORD, MERCK, AND HEWLETT-PACKARD

Ford

We wrote in an earlier chapter about how executives at the Ford Motor Company wrote a statement of "Mission, Values, and Guiding Principles" (MVGP) as a key part of its remarkable 1980s turnaround. The MVGP listed people and products ahead of profits and emphasized the central importance of quality improvement, employee involvement, and customer satisfaction. But the MVGP statement did *not* bring about the turnaround, at least not by itself. Had Ford not dramatically translated the MVGP into reality—had it not aligned its operations, strategies, and tactics to be consistent with the MVGP—then Ford would have failed in the turnaround and we wouldn't be writing about it in this book.

For the first time in its history, Ford fully implemented statistical quality control and instructed production managers to shut down a line in the event of a bad part or faulty material.[2] But Ford didn't stop with its own plants. It also carried the drive for quality to its suppliers with its "Q1" program that screened suppliers based on quality ratings *and* whether the supplier had also implemented statistical quality control. Ford provided education seminars and hands-on assistance for its suppliers to help them meet Q1 standards, which Ford continually increased over time.[3]

Ford created employee involvement programs, thus making line employees key team members of the quality improvement effort. Not only that, it created participative management programs to instruct managers and supervisors in how to support the employee involvement programs. It further reinforced these programs by placing greater emphasis on participative management skills as a factor in promotions.[4] To keep employees better informed and therefore feeling more involved with the company, Ford invested in a satellite television system to communicate Ford news and information to employees before they would have a chance to see it on TV or read it in the newspaper.[5] To forge a direct link between employees and the success of the company, Ford negotiated a profit-sharing clause with labor—the first ever in its contract with the United Auto Workers.[6] Ford's relationship with labor improved to such an extent in the early 1980s that the union made Philip Caldwell an honorary member upon his retirement—the first CEO of an American car company to ever be inducted into the UAW.[7]

To get the company back to its "car" roots, Ford created a separate group with the BHAG of creating a completely new car, truly world-class in its segment and designed with the customer more in mind than at any time since the Model T. Ford backed what became known as the Taurus/Sable program with a $3.25 billion budget, the largest in Ford's history by a factor of four times. With Taurus/Sable, Ford began soliciting input from production workers about the design years before it was ready for production.[8] To reinforce the importance of customer input and satisfaction, Ford's highest-ranking executives attended focus group sessions to hear directly what customers had to say. The company instituted an extensive "Quality-Commitment-Performance" follow-up program to solicit customer input on the quality of dealer service and created the prestigious President's Award to recognize dealerships with the highest customer ratings.[9]

In hundreds of ways—big and small—Ford translated the MVGP into daily practice, into reality. And that is the real force behind Ford's remarkable turnaround. Can you imagine the cynicism that would have erupted had Ford published the MVGP but then not translated the rhetoric into reality? Labor would have been cynical. Customers would have been cynical. Shareholders would have been cynical. And the whole turnaround probably would have failed.

Merck

In the late 1920s, George W. Merck formulated the backbone of Merck's vision. Building upon core values of integrity, contribution to society, responsibility to customers and employees, and the unequivocal pursuit of quality and excellence, he envisioned Merck as a world-class company that benefits humanity through innovative contributions to medicine—a company that makes superb profits not as the primary goal, but as a residual result of succeeding at that task. At the 1933 opening of the Merck Research Laboratory, he said:

We believe that research work carried on with patience and persistence will bring to industry and commerce new life; and we have faith that in this new laboratory, with the tools we have supplied, science will be advanced, knowledge increased, and human life win ever a greater freedom from suffering and disease. . . . *We pledge our every aid that this enterprise shall merit the faith we have in it. Let your light so shine—that those who seek the Truth, that those who toil that this world may be a better place to live in, that those who hold aloft that torch of Science and Knowledge through these social and economic dark ages, shall take new courage and feel their hands supported.* [emphasis his][10]

We're certainly impressed with George Merck's visionary pronouncement—especially given that he spoke these words over sixty years ago, long before "vision statements" became popular. But his words and sentiments alone, as inspiring and impressive as they are, do not—indeed, *could not*—make Merck a visionary company. The truly outstanding thing about Merck is how consistently it has aligned itself with the core ideology and the type of progress envisioned by George Merck.

For example, the company didn't just create a standard industrial R&D lab. Instead, it set the BHAG of creating a research capability so outstanding that it could "talk on equal terms with the universities and research institutes."[11] In fact, Merck explicitly designed the research laboratories to have an academic atmosphere and appearance—to look so much like a college that it quickly became known as the "Merck Campus."[12] Furthermore, instead of keeping its pure research behind locked doors, Merck encouraged its research scientists to publish in scientific journals—a key move that attracted many a top scientist.[13] It also encouraged its researchers to collaborate with scientists at academic and noncompeting industrial research laboratories outside of Merck—an unusual step that improved the quality of their published work. The company recruited prominent academic scientists to serve on the board of directors[14] and created a dual career track that allowed scientists to pass up promotions into management without financial penalty.[15] Merck even went so far as to list the scientific publications of its researchers in recruiting materials, much as an academic institution lists the publications of its faculty. As one scientist summed up:

Merck is like MIT or Harvard or any other academic institution with an outstanding reputation for research. You have to want to do your science intensely.[16]

To further encourage scientific exploration and experimentation, Merck gave research scientists "the greatest possible latitude and scope in pursuing their investigations, the utmost freedom to follow promising leads—no matter how unrelated to ... practical returns."[17] Unlike most American corporations, Merck *prohibited* marketing input into the pure research process until products had clearly entered the development stage.[18] As CEO P. Roy Vagelos put it:

> We keep basic research *exclusively* in the hands of research. We keep marketing out of the way until products are being tested on humans. We don't want concerns about "market potential" to get in the way of basic scientific exploration and experimentation that can lead to big break-throughs.[19]

These and similar practices have remained essentially intact at Merck for six decades, even though many of them fly in the face of conventional business doctrine. Along the way, Merck has added other practices that, although unconventional, make perfect sense at Merck. For instance, Merck explicitly *rejected* budgets as a planning or control tool in R&D. It creates new product project teams and explicitly does *not* give them a budget. Instead, team leaders ("champions") must persuade people from a variety of disciplines to join the team and to commit *their* resources to the project. This process creates a survival-of-the-fittest selection process where the best projects attract resources and the weakest perish.[20] Unlike its more diversified competitors, Merck adopted the unconventional strategy of being one of the *least* diversified pharmaceutical companies, placing all bets on its ability to innovate new, breakthrough drugs.[21] Merck lives with the self-imposed requirement that new products must be significantly better than the competition, else they cannot be introduced to the market—a highly risky strategy that can produce long droughts if nothing good comes down the pipe.[22]

In fact, throughout its history, Merck has set BHAGs that—bold as they might be—were aligned perfectly with its ideology:

Early 1930s: BHAG to build a research capability so outstanding that it could "talk on equal terms with the universities and research institutes" (described earlier).[23]

Early 1950s: BHAG to transform itself into a fully integrated pharmaceutical company in order to participate fully in the dramatic changes in medicine—backed by a "bet the company" acquisition of pharmaceutical giant Sharp & Dohme that gave Merck a well-established distribution and marketing network.[24]

Late 1970s: BHAG "to establish Merck as the pre-eminent drug maker worldwide in the 1980s."[25]

Late 1980s: BHAG to become the first drug maker with advanced research in every disease category.[26]

Early 1990s: BHAG to "redefine the pharmaceutical paradigm" with a $6 billion acquisition of Medco to create more of a direct link with end customers.[27]

Merck also has a long track record of being well aligned with its ideology of corporate responsibility. A lot of companies talk about corporate social responsibility, equal opportunity, and other such lofty ideals. But how many of these companies were one of the first to donate to the United Negro College Fund, as Merck did in 1944?[28] How many were the first in their industry to establish an Office of Minority Affairs, as Merck did in the 1960s?[29] How many companies in the 1970s required that all senior executives include affirmative action goals in their annual objectives and tied them to bonuses, stock options, ratings, and merit increases?[30] How many were recognized by the National Organization for Women for "vigorous programs to recruit, develop, and promote women and minorities"? How many were selected by *Black Enterprise* and *Working Mother* as one of the best places for women and minorities to work in America?[31] How many large industrial companies have a woman as a chief financial officer?[32] How many companies would have brought streptomycin to Japan—at no profit—to eliminate a serious outbreak of tuberculosis after the end of World War II?[33] How many companies would have made the decision to develop Mectizan to cure river blindness and to give it away free?[34] How many have set an explicit environmental BHAG, such as "to reduce our release of toxins into the environment by 90% by 1995"?[35] Indeed, to a far greater degree than most companies, Merck has consistently translated its social conscience into practice.

Merck doesn't just envision progress and excellence in its employees. It *commits* to progress and excellence. Getting a job at Merck is like applying to graduate school—rigorous and thorough. Merck often requires candidates to deliver multiple written recommendations about their qualifications for working at Merck—just like applying to a top-flight educational institution.[36] Merck invests heavily in employee recruiting, development, and retention. It rates managers on their success at recruiting and retaining top talent. By the 1980s, Merck had one of the lowest turnover rates in industry (5 percent versus the U.S. average of 20 percent).[37]

Finally, Merck consistently reinforces its core ideology, decade after decade, day after day—in shareholder reports, in recruiting materials, in employee manuals, in self-published books, in historical videos, in executive speeches, in orientation seminars, in articles for outside magazines and journals, and in a myriad of internal magazines and newsletters. When we asked Merck to send us any documents that might describe its values and purpose, Merck provided us with no fewer than eighty-five distinct items, some dating back to the turn of the century. In 1991, the company put on an extensive and elaborate centennial celebration, with publication of books, articles, speeches, videos, historical analyses—all with tremendous emphasis on the company's heritage and values. It is simply impossible to work at Merck and not be immersed in the ideology; it pervades *everything*, and has done so for nearly a century. As Jeffrey L. Sturchio, Merck's director of science and technology policy, summed up:

> I used to work at another major American corporation before coming to Merck. The basic difference I see between the two companies is rhetoric versus reality. The other company touted values and visions and all the rest, but there was a big difference between rhetoric and reality. At Merck, there is no difference.[38]

Hewlett-Packard

Bill Hewlett and Dave Packard envisioned HP as a role-model corporation, known for progressive personnel practices, innovative and entrepreneurial culture, and an unbroken string of products that make a technical contribution. "Our main task," wrote Dave Packard, "is to design, develop, and manufacture the finest [electronic equipment] for the advancement of science and the welfare of humanity. We intend to devote ourselves to that task."[39] HP director Fred Terman used the lofty phrase "Model Social Institution" to describe the company's aspirations.[40] Later, Hewlett boiled down HP's guiding principles into what he called the "Four Musts": The company *must* attain profitable growth; the company *must* make its profit through technological contribution; the company *must* recognize and respect the personal worth of employees and allow them to share in the success of the company; and the company *must* operate as a responsible citizen of the general community.[41]

All fine and good, but Hewlett and Packard's vision would have been essentially useless if not translated into practice. Like Merck, HP stands out not as much for its lofty values and aspirations, but for the comprehensive and consistent way it aligned with them.

For example, HP has a long history of showing respect for employees in a multitude of tangible ways. In the 1940s, it introduced a "production bonus" (essentially a profit-sharing plan) that paid the same percentages to the janitor as to the CEO, and created a catastrophic medical insurance plan for all employees—actions virtually unheard of at that time, especially in a small company.[42] When the company went public in the 1950s, *all* employees at *all* levels with six months of tenure received an automatic stock grant and became eligible for a stock option program.[43] Soon thereafter, HP instituted an employee stock purchase program, with a 25 percent subsidy from the company.[44] To reduce the chance of layoffs, HP passed up large government contract opportunities—profitable as they might be—if they would lead to "hire-and-fire" tactics.[45] It required divisions to hire HP insiders first before looking to the outside, providing further secure employment across the entire company (not to mention keeping the culture tight).[46] When facing corporate-wide downturns, HP generally asked all employees to take every other Friday off and reduce their pay by 10 percent, rather than imposing a 10 percent layoff.[47] HP was one of the first American companies to introduce flextime opportunities for employees at all levels and to conduct extensive employee surveys to gauge and track employee concerns.[48] It was also one of the first American companies to introduce an open-door policy in which employees could bring grievances all the way to the top without retribution.[49] To promote communication and informality and to deemphasize hierarchy, HP created a wide-open floor plan; no manager at any level would be allowed to have a private office with a door— a very unusual practice in the 1950s. Not surprisingly, HP has remained nonunionized, as one HPer described:

> Several attempts at unionization were made but failed dismally. What union could make headway in a company whose employees felt an integral part of management, and who invited the pickets in out of the cold to share hot coffee and doughnuts at coffee breaks?[50]

Similarly, HP took many steps to reinforce the importance of technological contribution and to promote an entrepreneurial environment. Beginning in the 1950s, HP sought to hire only top 10 percent graduating seniors from respected engineering schools, rather than hiring more experienced but less talented engineers from industry.[51] (Thirty years later, HP was still viewed at top engineering schools as *the* elite job offer.)[52] Like 3M, HP pursued a strategy of producing new and better products each year as its primary source of growth, rather than seeking to ride the product life cycle and maximize unit volume of older products. In 1963, more than 50 percent of HP's sales came from products introduced in the previous five years; by 1990, this had improved to 50 percent of sales from products introduced in the previous *three* years.[53] And they couldn't be just *any* new products; me-too or copycat products were always weeded out, *no matter what the market potential.* "If you had the opportunity to listen in on one of our management sessions," explained Bill Hewlett, "you would find that many approaches are rejected because people feel there is not enough of a technical contribution to justify bringing a particular product to market."[54] This tough, self-imposed standard led HP to bypass high-volume markets—such as IBM-compatible personal computers—until it could figure out a way to enter with a technological contribution. What follows is an actual conversation between a seasoned lab manager and a young product manager at HP in 1984:[55]

PRODUCT MANAGER: "We've got to introduce an IBM-compatible personal computer *now*. That's where the market is going. That's where the volume is. That's what customers primarily want."

LAB MANAGER: "But where's the technological contribution? Until we figure out a way to make an IBM-compatible personal computer with a clear technical advantage, then we just can't do it—no matter how big the market."

PRODUCT MANAGER: "But what if that's not what customers want? What if they just want to run their software and don't really care about technical contribution? And what if the market window will close unless we act now?"

LAB MANAGER: "Then we shouldn't be in that business. That's not who we are. We simply shouldn't be in markets that don't value technical contribution. That's just not what the Hewlett-Packard Company is all about."

The lab manager won hands down, as they almost always do at HP. "As important as they are," said Bill Hewlett, "marketing people must play a secondary role in the question of product definition."[56] For years, HP shunned market input in favor of the "Next Bench Syndrome"—a strategy of engineers solving their own technical problems as the primary means of identifying opportunities for technical and market contribution.[57] In the 1950s and 1960s, HP titled its product lists "*Contribution to the Test Equipment Field*" [emphasis ours]—an interesting and revealing detail.[58] Corporate-wide hero recognition programs were generally geared toward the engineers who invented new gadgets, not those who sold them. Career advancements also reflected the technological emphasis; over 90 percent of division general managers at HP hold technical degrees.[59]

To promote an entrepreneurial culture, HP early on adopted a management method of "provide a well-defined objective, give the person as much freedom as possible in working toward that objective, and finally, provide motivation by seeing that the contribution of the individual is recognized throughout the organization."[60] Later, as the company rapidly expanded in the 1950s, it extended this management method into a decentralized structure of highly autonomous divisions set up as little businesses with self-control over their own R&D, production, and marketing strategies and wide discretion in operating decisions (within the bounds, of course, of the HP ideology). When entering a new business, HP would usually create a new division and turn it loose to figure out how best to enter the market. According to Hewlett:

> We simply said, "Here's the field we want to enter; now you define the particular item you can build." The presumption was that they would design it on the best technology available.[61]

To further reinforce entrepreneurship, HP dispersed its divisions into several states, rather than locating them all near headquarters. The company then allocated R&D funds to reward innovation—the most innovative divisions getting the most resources. (Even though HP has a central laboratory called "HP Labs," it allocated the vast majority of R&D funds to its divisions.)[62] Facilities that began as manufacturing plants could only attain full divisional status by creating (with boot-strapped funds) an innovative new product and taking it to market.[63] And, unlike most companies, HP encouraged its international divisions to develop R&D capabilities, rather than merely remaining sales and distribution centers.[64]

Equally important as what HP did do is what it did *not* do, regardless of prevailing management theories or fads. Recall, for instance, how HP shunned corporate debt (even though such a practice is "irrational") because Hewlett and Packard believed debt would erode entrepreneurial discipline. Unlike many high-technology companies, HP avoided outside investors like venture capitalists because "they can push companies to grow too fast, and if you grow too fast, you can lose your values."[65] In stark contrast to most corporations, HP forbade the personnel department from getting involved in personnel problems:

> Taking care of his or her people is the most important part of every management job. . . . In no case is the personnel department expected to handle the manager's personnel problems—he or she must accept and handle the personnel responsibility to be a good manager.[66]

A particularly revealing example of HP following its own vision and not falling prey to management fads and fashions of the day came in the 1970s, when the "learning-curve/market-share" theory of corporate strategy swept American business. Touted by prestigious management consulting firms and taught at top-flight business schools, it became a pervasive management tool adopted by thousands of executives across the corporate landscape. Operating under the theory that greater market share leads to lower costs and eventually greater profits, managers at a wide range of companies began cutting prices in order to gain market share. For roughly a decade, this theory dominated strategic thinking. *But not at HP,* which explicitly rejected the learning curve theory and held itself to a different standard: "If a product isn't good enough to make an excellent gross margin in the first year, then it's not a product with a significant technical advantage and the Hewlett-Packard Company shouldn't be making it, period."[67] Packard explained to his managers in 1974: "If I hear anybody talking about how big their share of the market is or what they're trying to do to increase their share of the market, I'm going to personally see that a black mark gets put in their personnel folder."[68]

Finally, HP—like Ford and Merck—has gone to great lengths to continually immerse employees in the tenets of what became known as the "HP Way." Hewlett and Packard took all their managers off-site in the 1950s to the "Sonoma Conferences," where they penned HP's ideology and ambitions into a document "somewhat similar to the U.S. Constitution—a document expressing basic ideals subject to current interpretation and to amendment."[69] Soon thereafter, HP began a strict promote-from within policy, implemented extensive interviewing processes that emphasize "adaptability and fit" to the HP Way, and created a program to indoctrinate first-line supervisors. "We recognized very early that it was important to have your first line managers indoctrinated or oriented toward the philosophy because ... they're the company to most people," explained Dave Packard.[70]

We found no less than a hundred separate documented incidents of HP managers talking explicitly about HP's values and purpose—in internal talks, in external speeches, in written materials, in individual conversations. They simply talked and acted on them constantly for decades. We also encountered dozens of "Bill and Dave stories" recounted over the years to convey the essence of the HP Way. For instance, when Bill Hewlett found a storeroom chain-locked on a weekend, he chopped and shredded the chain with a pair of bolt cutters and left it on the manager's desk with a terse note that locked storerooms do not fit with HP's notion of respect for its employees—or so the story goes.[71] True or not, the stories illustrate how HP's management worked continually to make the HP Way a genuine way of life. Barney Oliver, longtime general manager of HP Laboratories, summed up HP during its rise to prominence:

> When I first joined HP in 1952 it was immediately apparent that nearly all of its 400 employees were enthusiastic about, loyal to, and proud of *their* company to an unusual degree. . . . As one employee put it, "I have the impression that Bill and Dave are working for me, rather than the other way around." What surprises visitors today is that this same spirit has survived HP's growth. It is unusual to find such spirit in a company with over 17,000 employees, but it is not surprising. For in a deeper sense, what was going on in those early days was a process of education in management. . . . Most of the early employees became extensions of Bill and Dave's personalities and philosophies, and put these philosophies and techniques to good use when they took their places as line leaders, supervisors or division heads. . . . We all believe in [these philosophies] and practice them. They are part of our way of life.[72]

LESSONS OF ALIGNMENT FOR CEOS, MANAGERS, AND ENTREPRENEURS

We applaud if you go off-site to discuss your corporate ideology, like Hewlett and Packard did in the 1950s. We encourage you to set lofty ambitions for your company, like George Merck did in the 1930s. We hope you will want to put to paper the guiding vision of your company, like Ford did. But never forget that such steps do not in themselves make a visionary company. You never attain final alignment. You never reach final success. You have to work at it constantly. Here are some guideposts.

1. Paint the Whole Picture

You're probably feeling a bit overwhelmed by all the comprehensive detail about Ford, Merck, and HP. *And that in itself is precisely the point!*

VISIONARY companies do not rely on any one program, strategy, tactic, mechanism, cultural norm, symbolic gesture, or CEO speech to preserve the core and stimulate progress. It's the whole ball of wax that counts.

It's the remarkable comprehensiveness and consistency over time that counts. It's the nearly overwhelming set of signals and actions—signals to continually reinforce the core ideology and to stimulate progress—that lead to a visionary company. Taken in isolation, each fact about Ford, Merck, and HP would be trivial, and certainly wouldn't account for their visionary status. But in the context of hundreds of other facts, they add up to a consistent overall picture.

It would be a mistake to conclude that you could implement any single chapter of this book in isolation and have a visionary company. Core ideology alone cannot do it. The drive for progress alone cannot do it. A BHAG alone will not do it. Evolution through autonomy and entrepreneurship by itself will not do it. Home-grown management alone does not make a visionary company, nor a cult-like culture, nor even living the concept that good enough never is.

A visionary company is like a great work of art. Think of Michelangelo's scenes from Genesis on the ceiling of the Sistine Chapel or his statue of David. Think of a great and enduring novel, like *Huckleberry Finn* or *Crime and Punishment.* Think of Beethoven's Ninth Symphony or Shakespeare's *Henry V.* Think of a beautifully designed building, like the masterpieces of Frank Lloyd Wright or Ludwig Mies van der Rohe. You can't point to any one single item that makes the whole thing work; it's the *entire* work—all the pieces working together to create an overall effect—that leads to enduring greatness. And it's not just the big pieces, but also the itty-bitty details—the turn of phrase, the change in pace at just the right moment, the perfect off-center placement of a window, a subtle expression sculpted into the eyes. As the great architect Mies van der Rohe put it, "God is in the details."

2. Sweat the Small Stuff

People don't work day-to-day in the "big picture." They work in the nitty-gritty details of their company and its business. Not that the big picture is irrelevant, but it's the little things that make a big impression, that send powerful signals. Little things, like business cards for salespeople at Nordstrom to send the signal, "We want you to be a sales *professional.*" Little things, like Wal-Mart giving employees at the lowest level complete departmental financial reports to send the signal, "You are a partner in the company and we want you to run your department as your own little business." Little things, like Motorola's chairman sitting in for the quality improvement reports (which always topped the agenda) and then leaving for the financial reports to send the signal, "Quality improvement is our crusade, not just profits." Little things, like allowing key divisions at Johnson & Johnson to put their own logos on their products—and leave off the J&J

logo—to send the signal, "We want you to operate with the psychology of autonomous, entrepreneurial business units." Little things, like Philip Morris sending employees home with a box of cigarettes along with their paycheck to send the signal "We're *proud* of our product, no matter what the Surgeon General says."

Social cognition research shows that individuals pick up on *all* the signals in their work environment—big and small—as cues for how they should behave. People notice little things. People remember stories not so much about grand heroics, but about little events like shredding the chain of a locked storeroom. People want to believe in their company's vision, but will be ever watchful for the tiny inconsistencies that allow them to say "Aha! See, there you go. I knew management was just blowing smoke. They don't really believe their own rhetoric."

3. Cluster, Don't Shotgun

Visionary companies don't put in place any random set of mechanisms or processes. They put in place pieces that reinforce each other, clustered together to deliver a powerful combined punch. They search for synergy and linkages. Notice the clustering at Ford: statistical quality control methods *reinforced by* employee involvement programs *reinforced by* participative management training programs *reinforced by* promotion criteria based on participative management skills. Notice the clustering at Merck: recruiting of top scientists *reinforced by* allowing them to publish *reinforced by* allowing them to collaborate with outside scientists *reinforced by* the "Merck Campus" *reinforced by* the dual career track. Notice how it would be impossible to work at HP and not get the message that managers had better treat their people well or that divisions had better make profits by technical contribution. Working at HP is like being in a sound room equipped with not one but ten speakers working to amplify each other and send the same consistent messages from the floor, the ceiling, to the right, to the left, front, back, and sideways.

4. Swim in Your Own Current, Even if You Swim Against the Tide

Recall how Merck and HP took steps that flew in the face of conventional business practices in order to remain true to themselves. Alignment means being guided first and foremost by one's own internal compass, not the standards, practices, conventions, forces, trends, fads, fashions, and buzz-words of the outer world. Not that you should ignore reality—quite the contrary—but your company's own self-defined ideology and ambitions should guide all of its dealings with reality. If done right, you will likely astonish competitors, journalists, business professors, and others with idiosyncratic practices and strategies that, however unusual, make perfect sense *for your company*.

Johnson & Johnson, for example, made the decision to place its new headquarters right smack in the middle of blighted New Brunswick, New Jersey, in the 1970s not because it made the best business sense (it didn't), but because it made the most sense in the context of the J&J Credo. Boeing held itself to aircraft design safety standards that far exceeded its competitors' not because the market demanded it, but because Boeing's ideology demanded it. 3M rejected the conventional business wisdom that a small growing company should concentrate on one line of business; a focus strategy simply didn't fit with the type of innovative company 3Mers wanted to build. The learning-curve/market-share model may have become the latest rage among corporate executives in the 1970s, but it just didn't make sense for HP.

The point here is not that the visionary companies pursue "good" practices and other companies pursue "bad" practices. "Good or bad" puts the wrong frame on it. What might be "good" at HP might be "bad" at Merck or 3M or Marriott or P&G.

THE real question to ask is not "Is this practice good?" but "Is this practice *appropriate* for us—does it fit with our ideology and ambitions?"

---

5. Obliterate Misalignments

If you look around your company right now, you can probably put your finger on at least a dozen specific items misaligned with its core ideology or that impede progress—"inappropriate" practices that have somehow crept through the woodwork. Does your incentive system reward behaviors inconsistent with your core values? Does the organization's structure get in the way of progress? Do goals and strategies drive the company away from its basic purpose? Do corporate policies inhibit change and improvement? Does the office and building layout stifle progress?

Attaining alignment is not just a process of adding new things; it is also a never-ending process of identifying and doggedly *correcting misalignments* that push a company away from its core ideology or impede progress. If the building layout impedes progress, change the building layout or move. If the strategy is misaligned with the core, change the strategy. If the organization structure inhibits progress, change the organization structure. If the incentive system rewards behavior inconsistent with the core, change the incentive system. Keep in mind that the only sacred cow in a visionary company is its core ideology. Anything else can be changed or eliminated.

6. Keep the Universal Requirements While Inventing New Methods

A company *must* have a core ideology to become a visionary company. It must also have an unrelenting drive for progress. And finally, it must be well designed as an organization to preserve the core and stimulate progress, with all the key pieces working in alignment. These are universal requirements for visionary companies. They distinguished visionary companies a hundred years ago. They distinguish visionary companies today. And they will distinguish visionary companies in the twenty-first century. If we were to rewrite this book in the year 2095, we would find these same basic elements to distinguish the most enduring and successful corporations from the rest of the pack.

However, the specific *methods* visionary companies use to preserve the core and stimulate progress will undoubtedly change and improve. BHAGs, cult-like cultures, evolution through experimentation, home-grown management, and continuous self-improvement—these are all proven methods of preserving the core and stimulating progress. But they are not the *only* effective methods that can be invented. Companies will invent new methods to complement these time-tested ones. The visionary companies of tomorrow are already out there today experimenting with new and better methods. They're undoubtedly already doing things that their competitors might find odd or unusual, but that will someday become common practice.

And that's exactly what you should be doing in the corporations you work with—that is, if you want them to enter the elite league of visionary companies. It doesn't matter whether you're an entrepreneur, manager, CEO, board member, or consultant. You should be working to implement as many methods as you can think of to preserve a cherished core ideology that guides and inspires people at all levels. And you should be working to invent mechanisms that create dissatisfaction with the status quo and stimulate change, improvement, innovation, and renewal—mechanisms, in short, that infect people with the spirit of progress. If you can think of new methods to preserve the core that we haven't written about in this book, then by all means put them in place. If you can invent powerful new mechanisms to stimulate progress, then give them a try. Use the proven methods *and* create new methods. Do both.

THIS IS NOT THE END

We've done our best to discover and teach here the fundamental underpinnings of truly outstanding companies that have stood the test of time. We've given you an immense amount of detail and evidence in this book, and we expect that few readers will remember every little item in these pages. But as you walk away from reading this book, we hope you will take away four key concepts to guide your thinking for the rest of your managerial career, and to pass on to others. These concepts are:

1. Be a clock builder—an architect—not a time teller.
2. Embrace the "Genius of the AND."
3. Preserve the core/stimulate progress.
4. Seek consistent alignment.

We feel a bit like Dorothy in the *Wizard of Oz*, who after her long journey in search of the wizard, pulls back the curtain and discovers that the wizard isn't a wizard after all. He's just a normal human being. Like Dorothy, we discovered that those who build visionary companies are not necessarily more brilliant, more charismatic, more creative, more complex thinkers, more adept at coming up with great ideas—in short, more wizardlike—than the rest of us. What they've done is within the conceptual grasp of *every* manager, CEO, and entrepreneur in the world. The builders of visionary companies tend to be simple—some might even say simplistic—in their approaches to business. Yet simple does not mean *easy*.

We think this has profound implications for what you take away from this book. It means that no matter who you are, you can be a major contributor in building a visionary company. You don't have to wait for the great charismatic visionary to descend from the mount. You don't have to hope for the lightning bolt of creative inspiration to strike with the "great idea." You don't have to accept the debilitating perspective of "Well, let's face it. Our CEO just isn't a charismatic visionary leader. It's hopeless." You don't have to buy into the belief that building visionary companies is something mysterious that only other people do.

It also means that life will probably be more difficult for you from here on. It means helping those around you to understand the lessons of this book. It means accepting the frightening truth that *you* are probably as qualified as anyone else to help your organization become visionary. And it means recognizing that you can begin right now—today—to apply the lessons of this book. Finally, and perhaps most important of all, it means working with a deep and abiding respect for the corporation as an important social institution in its own right—an institution that requires the care and attention we give to our great universities or systems of government. For it is through the power of human organization—of individuals working together in common cause—that the bulk of the world's best work gets done.

So this is not the end. Nor even the beginning of the end. But it is, we hope, the end of the beginning—the beginning of the challenging and arduous, but eminently doable task of building a visionary company.

FREQUENTLY ASKED QUESTIONS

While conducting seminars, giving talks, and working as consultants to companies, we've encountered a number of questions about our findings and ideas. Here are the most common, and our brief answers.

Q: WE WANT OUR COMPANY TO BECOME A VISIONARY COMPANY. WHERE SHOULD WE BEGIN?

First, and above all else, pin down your core ideology. Start by articulating your organization's core values. And we mean *core* values. If you articulate more than five or six, there's a good chance you're not getting down to only the core essentials. Remember, these values must stand the test of time. After you've drafted a preliminary list of the core values (or if you went through this exercise sometime in the past), ask about each one: "If the circumstances changed and *penalized* us for holding this core value, would we still keep it?" If you can't honestly answer yes, then it's not core and should be dropped.

For example, a high-technology company we worked with wondered whether it should put "Quality" on its list of core values. We asked: "Suppose in ten years quality doesn't make a hoot of difference in your markets. Suppose the only thing that matters is sheer speed and horsepower, but not quality. Would you still want to put quality on the list as a core value?" The management team looked around at each other and finally said, "To be honest, no." Quality stayed *off* the list as a core value. Quality stayed in the current *strategy* of the company—and quality improvement programs remained in place as a mechanism for stimulating progress—but it did not make the list of core values. Remember, strategies can change as market conditions change, but core values remain intact in a visionary company. This same group of executives then wrestled with whether it should put "Leading-edge innovation" on its list of core values. We asked the same question: "Would you keep it on the list as a core value, no matter how the world around you changes?" This time, the management team gave a resounding "Yes! We always want to do leading-edge innovation. That's who we are. It's really important to us, and always will be. No matter what." Leading-edge innovation went *on* the list of core values, and will stay there forever.

Also, try to pin down the second component of core ideology: purpose—the organization's fundamental reason for being. Ask the question: "Suppose we could shut this company down with no adverse economic consequences to employees or owners. Why shouldn't we do so? What would the world lose if the company ceased to exist? What would we lose if it ceased to exist?" And answer this question so that it would be equally valid now and a hundred years from now. For example, a pharmaceutical company we worked with considered stating their purpose as "To make drugs for human therapy." We asked: "Would that purpose still hold a hundred years from now?" One manager pointed out that the company might well discover or invent new ways of improving human therapy besides traditional drugs. Another pointed out that the company would likely invent solutions for animal therapy sometime in the next few decades. A third executive pointed out, "Well, I'm not here just to make stuff for therapy. I'm here to make significant *improvements* in therapy—to leave a mark beyond just what everyone else has done. Otherwise, what's the point?" So the company captured its purpose as: "We exist to provide significant improvements in therapy." The company will always be in pursuit of this guiding star, or at least for the next hundred years.

A very important point: You do not "create" or "set" core ideology. You *discover* core ideology. You get at it by *looking inside*. It has to be authentic. You can't fake an ideology. Nor can you just intellectualize it. Core values and purpose must be passionately held on a gut level, else they are not core.

Who should be involved in articulating the core ideology varies depending on the size and age of the company, but in many situations we like to suggest a "Mars Group." It works like this: Suppose you wanted to re-create the company on another planet, but only had room on the spaceship for a fixed number of people—say between six and fifteen (a dozen is a nice number). You want these people to be a representative slice of the "genetic code" of the company—to be gut-level exemplars of what the company stands for. The group should almost certainly not be just the top twelve people in the organization, although it will include some of them. If choosing the group presents political or ego challenges, we've found a widespread employee nomination process works well for selecting representatives.

Once you're clear about the core ideology, you should feel free to change absolutely *anything* that is not core. From then on, anytime someone says something shouldn't change because "it's part of our culture" or "we've always done it that way" or any of the other excuses for resisting change, remind them of this simple rule: If it's not core, it's up for change. Or the strong version of this rule: If it's not core, change it!

Of course, articulating core ideology is just a starting point. You've also got to determine what type of progress you want to stimulate. Do you want to pursue BHAGs, like Boeing did? Do you want to become an evolutionary branching tree, like 3M? Do you want to be a self-improvement machine, like Marriott? We suggest considering all three, plus any other methods of stimulating progress you can concoct. We think it's a good idea to put in place BHAGs (or at least a BHAG), *and* mechanisms to stimulate people to "try a lot of stuff and keep what works," *and* mechanisms to stimulate continuous self-improvement. Motorola, for example, has artfully used all three forms of progress throughout its life.

Most important, you've got to then align the organization to preserve the core and stimulate progress. *Far and away the biggest mistake managers make is ignoring the crucial importance of alignment.* If you decide to build a visionary company by taking a team off-site to articulate a core ideology and envision progress for the future, then you should come back with at least a half dozen specific, concrete changes to make in the organization to increase alignment. What can you add to the organization to better preserve the core and stimulate progress? And, just as important, what should you obliterate in your organization that's currently driving you away from the core and/or blocking progress?

Most managers we've worked with do a good job at adding new mechanisms to preserve the core and stimulate progress, but they fall short in obliterating misalignments. If you state teamwork as a core value, but you compensate primarily on individual performance, then you've got to change the compensation structure. If you state innovation as a core value, yet have market share as the dominant strategic objective, then you've got to change your strategy. If you want to encourage people to try a lot of stuff and keep what works, then you have to remove penalties for honest mistakes.

Keep in mind that this is a never-ending process. As misalignments crop up, you've got to kill them as quickly as possible. Think of misalignments as like cancer cells. It's best to get in there and cut them out before they spread too far.

Q: I'M NOT CEO. WHAT CAN I DO WITH THESE FINDINGS?

Plenty.

First, you can apply most of our findings in your work area, albeit on a smaller scale. You can be a clock builder at any level, for this is a state of mind as much as a method of operating. Instead of instinctively jumping in to solve a problem in the heroic leader mode, ask first, "What *process* should we use to solve this problem?" You can build a cult-like culture around a strong ideology at any level. Of course, it will be constrained somewhat by the ideology of the overall organization, but it can be done. And if the overall company doesn't have a clear ideology, then all the more reason (and freedom) to put one in place at your level! *Just because the corporation as a whole might not have a strong core ideology doesn't mean your group should be deprived.* One manufacturing manager for a computer company told us: "I got tired of waiting for those on top to get their act together, so I just went ahead with my people. We now have a very distinct set of values here in my group, and we manage by them. It gives my people a greater sense of meaning in their work. We have a strong self-identity within the company, and we interview people with an eye to how they'll fit with our team. People feel they belong to something special. We even have our own jackets and caps."

You can also stimulate progress at any level. We've seen BHAGs work particularly well at midlevels. A real estate operations manager within a larger company asks every single employee and manager in her group to set a personal BHAG for each year. She also sets a BHAG for the entire group. And there's no reason why you can't create a group culture that encourages people to try a lot of stuff and keep what works. Why not put in place a 3M-style 15 percent rule in your group? Why not invent mechanisms of discontent to stimulate change and improvement before you're forced to change and improve? One manager running an internal components operation that had captive customers within a larger company went to the divisions his group supplied and said: "From now on, we're not going to hold you to the policy that you have to get all of your components from us. If you can get better components, faster turnaround, better service, or higher quality from outside vendors, then okay. Knowing that you can go elsewhere will *force* us to get better."

Another powerful step you can take is to educate those around you about the key findings from the companies we studied. Help them understand the importance of building the organization, rather than just building the next great product. Help them understand the concept of preserving the core and stimulating progress. Point out to people where the organization is misaligned and why alignment is so vital. Help them reject the Tyranny of the OR. For example, one middle manager we know frequently gets people unstuck during meetings by saying, "Hey, I think we're succumbing to the 'Tyranny of the OR' here. Let's find a way to embrace the 'Genius of the AND.' " And they usually do.

You can use the visionary companies as a source of immense credibility. For example, if senior executives resist articulating core values or purpose as too "soft" or "new age," point to Hewlett-Packard, Merck, 3M, Procter & Gamble, Sony, and others in this book—and point to how they've done this for decades. How can any hard-nosed executive argue with the long-term track record of these companies? Indeed, you can use these companies as credibility to virtually *demand* that senior management pay attention. What executive could not be interested in attaining the enduring stature of these companies?

Q: IS THERE HOPE FOR OLD, LARGE, NONVISIONARY CORPORATIONS?

Yes, but the task is probably more difficult than building a visionary company from the ground up. For one thing, there will be entrenched processes and practices that need to be changed or obliterated in order to align with an ideology. The older and larger the company, the more entrenched the misalignments.

Yet we've seen a number positive examples. Even in our own study, we saw a visionary company that strayed from its ideology, yet returned to it decades later and pulled off an amazing realignment: Ford. And Philip Morris did not display many characteristics of a visionary company until about the late 1940s—at about its one hundredth birthday. Additionally, we've seen remarkable progress at companies we've worked with. One large bank, for instance, began working with our preliminary findings a few years ago and—for the first time in its history—pinned down its core ideology and began a long process of aligning itself to preserve the core and stimulate progress. One of its executive vice presidents explained: "I've worked at this company my entire life, and I'd begun to lose hope. But once we became clear in our own minds about what we really stand for and began to change the organization to fit with that, well, the release of human energy has been amazing. People all the way down to the individual branch level feel that their work has more meaning than it used to. And now that we know what is core and should remained fixed, we've felt *liberated* to change anything else—to slay sacred cows that had really been getting in our way. It's like awakening a sleeping giant. We're not at the level of your visionary companies yet, but we've come a long way."

Being a visionary company is a continuum. It is not static. Any company at any time can move along that continuum and become *more* visionary— even if it has a long way to go. Again, it's a long-term process. The race goes to those who persist and never quit moving in that direction. Our findings do not represent a quick fix, or the next fashion statement in a long string of management fads, or the next buzzword of the day, or a new "program" to introduce. No! The only way to make any company visionary is through a *long-term* commitment to an eternal process of building the organization to preserve the core and stimulate progress.

Q: WHAT GUIDANCE WOULD YOU GIVE TO A VISIONARY COMPANY THAT SEEMS TO BE LOSING ITS VISIONARY STATUS—LIKE, SAY, IBM?

IBM's a great case, because it was arguably one of the most visionary companies in the world for nearly seventy years. IBM shows that not only can companies move *forward* on the continuum of visionary status, they can also move *backward*. Once a visionary company does not necessarily mean always a visionary company! Like democracies, visionary companies require eternal vigilance.

A company like IBM should learn the lessons of its own past. For decades, IBM cherished and fanatically protected its core values (called the "Three Basic Beliefs") while simultaneously being one of the most progressive companies on the planet. IBM committed to some of the most audacious BHAGs in history, including a bet-the-company decision to go with the IBM 360 and render obsolete nearly all of its prior product lines. Bold! Yet then IBM got conservative in the 1980s, protecting its mainframe line. It lost sight of its own past.

If we were sitting down with the senior executives at IBM, we'd challenge them to set a BHAG of boldness equal to that of the IBM 360. We'd challenge IBM to once again obsolete itself, to bet the company on the success or failure of that BHAG, just like it did on the 360. We'd challenge them to have faith that IBM people would come through and achieve the impossible again, just like they did on the 360. IBM has great people, and they would undoubtedly rise to the task.

We'd also challenge the IBM executives to revisit the three basic beliefs, just like J&J revisited its credo in the 1970s. We'd challenge them to have the top one hundred managers and a thousand IBMers chosen at random to attend a rededication to the beliefs and all sign a giant printed version of them. We'd challenge them to cast that giant signed document in bronze, reproduce it, and place replicates of it in every single IBM facility in the world. We'd challenge them to ask every employee in the company to personally rededicate himself or herself to the three basic beliefs—in writing.

Finally, we'd challenge them to set up a realignment process for preserving the core and stimulating progress. We'd challenge them to identify at least *fifty* specific misalignments with the three basic beliefs. We'd challenge them to identify at least *fifty more* specific misalignments that inhibit progress. And then we'd challenge them to not just change these misalignments, but eliminate them entirely.

We believe IBM has the roots to regain its stature as one of the most visionary companies in the world. If IBM reembraces the basic lessons of being a visionary company, then we believe it will regain its stature and hold it for the next seven decades. If, on the other hand, it does not reembrace these lessons then we believe it will continue to decline in the long term, even though it might bounce back in the short term.

Although the specifics would be different, we'd give the same guidance to any visionary company on the decline. We'd ask them to learn the lessons of their own past. We'd ask them to reclarify and recommit to their ideology—to get back to their basic roots. And we'd ask them to make dramatic, bold moves forward. Most important, we'd put them on a ruthless realignment program to preserve the core and stimulate progress.

Q: ARE THERE ANY PEOPLE WHO *CAN'T* BUILD A VISIONARY COMPANY?

Few. The only people who can't do it are those unwilling to persist for the long haul, those who like to rest on their laurels, those with no core ideology, and those who do not care about the health of the company after they're gone. If you want to start a company, build it quickly, make a lot of money, cash out, and retire, then building a visionary company is not for you. If you don't have a drive for progress—an internal urge to never stop improving and going forward for its own sake—then building a visionary company is not for you. If you don't have any interest in a values-driven company with a sense of purpose beyond just making as much money as possible, then building a visionary company is not for you. If you don't care about building the company so that it will be strong not only during your tenure but also decades after you're gone, then building a visionary company is not for you. But beyond these four, we see no other prerequisites.

Q: DO YOUR FINDINGS APPLY TO NONPROFIT ORGANIZATIONS?

Yes. They can apply in *any* type of organization, although the form might vary. We're employed by a nonprofit organization (Stanford University) and Jerry is an associate dean there. We've found our findings to apply quite well. We've also seen executives at for-profit corporations take our findings and apply them in nonprofit organizations. One CEO of a visionary company directly applies the ideas at his church. Another executive brings them to a hospital of which she is a director. We even think the architects of the United States used the concepts of visionary companies.

Q: HOW DOES YOUR BOOK FIT OTHER WORKS, SUCH AS *IN SEARCH OF EXCELLENCE*?

In Search of Excellence stands out as one of the outstanding books of the past two decades, and deservedly so. Everyone should read it. We found a lot of compatibility between Peters and Waterman's work and ours. But there are also some key differences. One difference is in method: Unlike their research project, we looked at companies throughout their entire life spans and in direct comparison to other companies. Another key difference is that we boiled all of our findings into a framework of underlying ideas. In particular, the concept of preserving the core and stimulating progress provides an umbrella over virtually everything we observed. We found some of their "eight attributes" to be well supported in our research, in particular: Hands-On/Value-Driven, Autonomy & Entrepreneurship, A Bias for Action, and Simultaneous Loose-Tight Properties. But we also found some of the eight attributes less well supported, in particular: Stick to the Knitting and Close to the Customer. If you define the "Knitting" as the core ideology, then yes, visionary companies stick to the knitting. But as long as they don't breach the core, anything is fair game—and that can take companies like Motorola and 3M far afield from where they started. And with Close to the Customer, we found a number of our companies to be much more technology-driven than customer-driven: Sony, HP, and Merck immediately come to mind. It's not that they don't care for their customers or serve them well; quite the contrary. But all three of these companies will ignore customer demands if those demands pull them away from their ideology, as HP did when it ignored customers clamoring for cheap IBM-compatible computers or cheap pocket calculators. Close to the customer yes, but never at the expense of the core.

We also found extensive compatibility with the work of Peter Drucker. In fact, we came away with immense respect for Drucker's prescience. Read his classic works: *Concept of the Corporation* (1946), *The Practice of Management* (1954), and *Managing for Results* (1964), and you'll get one heck of a jolt in seeing how far ahead of today's management thinking he was. In fact, as we did our research, we came upon a number of companies that were tremendously influenced by Drucker's writings: HP, GE, P&G, Merck, Motorola, and Ford to name a few.

Finally, we also found compatibility with other works, such as Edgar Schein's *Organizational Culture and Leadership* (1985) and John Kotter and James Heskett's *Corporate Culture and Performance* (1992). Schein writes about cultural "hybrids"—managers that grow up in the core of the company, yet are able to bring about cultural change (without losing the core values). Our chapter on home-grown management fits well with Schein's findings, especially our discussion of Jack Welch at GE. Kotter and Heskett explored the relationship between strong cultures and organizational performance, which dovetails with our findings about cult-like cultures in high-performing organizations.

Q: YOU STUDIED THE PAST. DO YOU WORRY THAT YOUR FINDINGS MIGHT BECOME OBSOLETE IN THE TWENTY-FIRST CENTURY?

No. If anything, we believe our findings will apply *more* in the twenty-first century than in the twentieth. In particular, the essential ideas to come from our work—clock building, the Genius of the AND, preserving the core/stimulating progress, and alignment—will continue to be key concepts long into the future. We cannot easily picture a scenario where they would become obsolete.

Take clock building, for example. The concept of focusing on building the characteristics of the organization versus coming up with a great idea or being a great charismatic leader will become even more important. With the accelerating rate of technological change, increasing global competition, and dramatically shorter product life cycles, the life span of any specific idea will continue to decline. No matter how great the idea, it will become obsolete more quickly than at any time in the past.

And as for the charismatic leader model, we think the world is heading in exactly the opposite direction. Just look at the twentieth century. Nearly the entire world has moved toward democracy. Democracy is a *process*. The very essence of democracy is to avoid overdependence on any single leader and put the primary focus on the process. Even Churchill—perhaps the single greatest leader of this century—was secondary to the nation and its processes, kicked out of office at the end of World War II. Hitler, Stalin, Mussolini, Tōjō—these were charismatic leaders who did not understand that they were fundamentally *less* important than the institutions they served. And even if you don't buy the analogy between the shift to democracy and the evolution of corporations, the great charismatic leader model has one fundamental flaw that will not ever go away—not now, not in the twenty-first century, not in a thousand years: *All leaders die.* And to transcend this unchanging reality, the focus must be first and foremost on building the characteristics of the organization.

Our key framework concept, preserving the core/stimulating progress, will also become increasingly important in the twenty-first century. Look at the trends of business organization: flatter, more decentralized, more geographically dispersed, greater individual autonomy, more knowledge workers, and so on. More than at any time in the past, companies will not be able to hold themselves together with the traditional methods of control: hierarchy, systems, budgets, and the like. Even going into the office will become less relevant as technology enables people to work from remote sites. The corporate bonding glue will increasingly become *ideological*. People still have a fundamental human need to belong to something they can feel proud of. They have a fundamental need for guiding values and sense of purpose that gives their life and work meaning. They have a fundamental need for connection with other people, sharing with them the common bond of beliefs and aspirations. More than any time in the past, employees will demand operating autonomy while also demanding that the organizations they're connected to *stand* for something.

And look at the trends of the outer world: fragmentation, segmentation, chaotic change, unpredictability, increased entrepreneurship, and so on. Only those companies particularly adept at stimulating progress will be able to thrive. Companies will need to continually renew themselves, perhaps through awesome BHAGs, in order to remain exciting places to work. Companies in search of greatness will need to relentlessly push themselves for *self*-stimulated change and improvement *before* the world demands change and improvement. Companies that mimic the evolution of well-adapted species—those that try a lot of stuff and keep what works—will have better odds of survival in an unpredictable, changing environment; others will likely become extinct. We think the visionary companies of the twenty-first century will need to become increasingly fanatical about preserving their core ideology *and* becoming increasingly aggressive in granting operational autonomy to individual employees. More than ever before, companies will need to embrace the yin and yang dynamic of preserving the core and stimulating progress.

That said, companies must apply the general findings from our work *with imagination*. We deliberately chose not to write a "ten-step program" style of book. It would have been a terrible disservice to our readers and our research. Indeed, the last thing a visionary company would ever do is follow a cookbook recipe for success, any more than Michelangelo would have bought a paint-by-numbers kit. Building a visionary company is a *design* problem, and great designers apply general principles, not mechanical lock-step dogma. Any specific how-to will almost certainly become obsolete. But the general concepts—adapted, of course, to changing conditions—can last as guiding principles well into the next century. We doubt that the basic elements underlying companies like Merck, Motorola, Procter & Gamble, and 3M will be any different a century from now. The form will undoubtedly change, but not the essential elements.

RESEARCH ISSUES

"PLAYING WITH FIRE" (WHAT ABOUT BANKRUPT VISIONARY COMPANIES?)

Our research would not capture companies that have visionary characteristics yet fail. Might it be that a higher percentage of companies that share the visionary characteristics go bankrupt than those companies that do not share the visionary characteristics? To use an analogy, suppose we studied the climbing techniques of two groups of mountain climbers: "visionary climbers" who successfully climb Mount Everest and "comparison climbers" who do not successfully climb Mount Everest. Further suppose that we found differences between the two groups (such as in philosophy, in training, or in risk taking). It's entirely possible that the "visionary climbers" die at a more frequent rate than the "comparison climbers," but since we're only studying climbers that lived, we wouldn't catch that fact in the study. So, although we could give good guidance as to what it takes to be a visionary climber, we might (unwittingly) also be giving guidance that increases the odds of death. Similarly, suppose having the characteristics of a visionary company results in a 75 percent bankruptcy rate (allowing that 25 percent do go on to become super-premier institutions) and having comparison company characteristics results in only a 50 percent failure rate (allowing that the surviving 50 percent do not become super-premier institutions). Under these circumstances, perhaps some managers would want to forgo being visionary and increase the chances of simple survival.

We have two responses to this concern. First, some climbers do indeed die while trying to climb Mount Everest, but only those who fully try to climb Mount Everest (whatever the risks) do in fact ever reach the summit. We cannot deny the possibility that some companies with visionary characteristics have died out there on the corporate landscape. But so what? We're not writing about mere survival in this book. We don't find mere survival to be a very interesting topic. We're interested in how companies might attain entrance to that special category of premier institutions, and we readily admit that it *might* require a risky path to get there.

But—and this is our second response—we believe (although we cannot prove) that the visionary characteristics might actually increase both the odds of greatness *and* the odds of survival. We return again to our historical perspective. We're not writing about one-shot companies here. We're writing about enduring companies that have faced massive change and prospered for decades. If being visionary is risky, then why has this risk not caught up with these companies and killed them at some point during their very long lives?

IS "VISIONARY" JUST ANOTHER WORD FOR "SUCCESSFUL"?

Using the CEO survey implicitly assumes financial success. We readily acknowledge this. After all, would CEOs describe unprofitable companies as highly visionary? Probably not. This raises a legitimate chicken-and-egg question: Do we simply ascribe the term "visionary" to any company that turns out to be successful? No. There are many financially successful companies that did not show up on our list of visionary companies. We did an extensive analysis of corporate performance of *Fortune* 500 companies for the decade prior to our survey. This analysis showed that the visionary companies were not the *only* highly successful companies during that time frame. In fact, if you just took the top eighteen companies in the *Fortune* 500 Industrial plus *Fortune* 500 Service listings in terms of return to investors during the period 1978–1988 (the decade preceding our survey), the list looks quite different than our visionary company list, as shown below.

Top 18 Fortune Industrial and Service Companies
Return to Investors, 1978–1988

1. Hasbro
2. The Limited
3. Wal-Mart*

*Visionary company

4. Affiliated
5. Tele-Communications
6. Giant Food
7. Toys "R" Us
8. Marion Laboratories
9. State Street Boston Corp
10. Berkshire Hathaway
11. DCNY
12. Macmillan
13. Cooper Tire & Rubber
14. Tyson Foods
15. Philips Industries
16. MCI Communications
17. Dillard Department Stores
18. Food Lion

The evidence suggests that our surveyed CEOs saw a visionary company as *more* than just a highly profitable company (else we would have simply had a one-for-one linkage between the top financial performers in 1978–1988 and the CEO responses). Of course, from the period 1926–1990, our visionary companies outperformed just about everyone. This suggests that if the CEOs were thinking only in terms of financial success, they were thinking in terms of very long-term success, which fits with our picture of a visionary company as an enduring great institution.

CAN WE TRUST THE CEO SURVEY TO GIVE US THE RIGHT COMPANIES?

Doing a survey—even a survey of highly thoughtful and knowledgeable people such as leading CEOs—is an imperfect method. Our survey attempted to minimize bias, but did not eliminate bias entirely. For one thing, companies that received significant positive press coverage around the time of the survey may have received undue representation in the survey results. For example, American Express received fabulous press—some of it labeling the company as "visionary"—in the few months immediately prior to the survey. This perhaps influenced some of the CEO responses and gave American Express unduly high representation in the survey data. As we compare American Express to the other companies on our list, it shares fewer characteristics of a visionary company.

We also acknowledge that relying on a survey assumes that visionary companies are, by definition, widely known and admired. This, in turn, introduces a bias toward large, publicly held companies. (Notice that all of the companies in our final sample set are publicly traded.) But might there be highly visionary companies (perhaps even more visionary than those in our study) that prefer to remain small or out of the public eye? For example, L.L. Bean and Granite Rock (1992 winner of the Malcolm Baldrige quality award—quite a feat for a rock quarry) appear to share many of the traits of our visionary companies, but they remain privately held and somewhat secluded institutions.

Though acknowledging these difficulties, we still believe that the CEO survey, while less than perfect, was the best available method for constructing a study set. Since we didn't know ahead of time the key characteristics of a visionary company (that's what we were trying to find out!), we couldn't construct a precise scientific screening device. Most important, the survey had the benefit of a wide population of discerning judges who didn't share our idiosyncratic prejudices.

In a related point, some have asked whether our survey merely re-created *Fortune* magazine's list of "Most Admired" companies (which also uses a CEO survey), rather than a list of "visionary companies." No. We thoroughly analyzed the *Fortune* "Most Admired" lists for the years 1983– 1990 and, although the visionary companies are well represented in the *Fortune* survey, we did not find a one-for-one correlation. In 1989 all of the visionary companies common to both lists fell in the top 30 percent of the *Fortune* list, but not in a one-for-one correlation with the top eighteen. (Only two of the comparison companies showed up in the top 30 percent of the *Fortune* list.) Of course, the visionary companies *are* admired (as we would expect), but visionary companies are not merely a regurgitation of the *Fortune* "Most Admired" list.

CORRELATIONS VERSUS CAUSES

We identified certain characteristics that tend to distinguish the visionary companies from the comparison companies in this particular sample set. We can therefore claim that there is a *correlation* between these differences and the visionary companies. However, we cannot claim a *causal* link. We cannot *prove* that the characteristics of visionary companies will necessarily lead to enduring success in all cases. Nor do we know definitively that the companies in our study have discovered an optimal approach to business— perhaps there are a number of privately held companies that no one has studied that were even more successful for longer periods of time, yet relied on a different set of dynamics. We cannot claim to have definitively found cause and effect. Tightly controlled experiments simply do not exist in the real world of corporations, and it is therefore impossible to ever claim cause and effect with 100 percent certainty. Our comparison analyses give us *greater* confidence that we have identified causes and not just random correlations than we would have had without comparisons, but they cannot give us certain confidence.

We'd like to emphasize, however, that *the basic elements we found to distinguish the visionary companies usually appeared in the companies long before they became hugely successful premier institutions.* Indeed, the fact that such characteristics generally *preceded* ultimate success (a fact that shows again the power of the historical approach) gives us confidence that we have found more than chance correlations.

TROUBLED TIMES AT THE VISIONARY COMPANIES

In the early 1990s, the majority of the visionary companies in our study were undeniably premier institutions in their industries. Nonetheless, a few of the visionary companies were having difficulty. Does this undermine the basic validity of our findings? We don't think so, for two reasons.

First, it's important to keep in mind that *all* the highly visionary companies in our study, even the ones doing well in the 1990s, received black eyes at points in their history. Highly visionary companies are not immune to setbacks and difficult times, yet they display resiliency and have built remarkable long-term track records.

Consider IBM, for example. Whatever IBM's problems in the 1990s, the company had an impressive seven-decade track record that included two world wars, the Depression, and the invention of computers. No company in the business machines industry matched IBM stride for stride over that seventy-year period. Even in IBM's darkest hours, the business press referred to it as "a national treasure." A company does not attain such status by accident, and we believe that there are many lessons to be learned from IBM's history—its successes *and* its difficulties. What lessons should IBM learn from its *own* past? What does it need to do to regain its prior status?

Second, keep in mind that throughout our study we continually compared one company to another. So, although no company is perfect (all have their warts), some companies do attain superior status over the long haul. For example, when Burroughs languished and lost its own unique identity, no one wrote about the demise of "a national treasure." For most people, Burroughs was just another company. Why did IBM rise to an elevated status while Burroughs never reached a similar status in the American psyche or world economy? Whatever their imperfections, the fact remains that the visionary companies have outshined the general market and a carefully selected control set of comparison companies over the long course of history. We can learn much from the contrast.

LARGE COMPANIES VERSUS SMALL COMPANIES

Is the study biased toward large companies? Yes and no. Yes, the list consists only of large corporations. But every single company on the list *was once a small company.* We looked at these companies not only when they were large, but also when they were small, and we sought to gain insights that would apply to small companies as well as large companies. Keep in mind that we also surveyed CEOs of small to midsize companies (from the *Inc.* 500 and *Inc.* 100); even the small-company CEOs wanted to learn lessons from companies that became large.

UNEVEN INFORMATION

The quality and quantity of historical information varied across companies. Some companies, such as Hewlett-Packard and Merck, opened their archives to us and provided multiple boxes of primary source materials. Most companies (even the comparison companies) cooperated freely, although the quality of information varied. In a few cases, however, the company refused to cooperate in the study and we therefore relied entirely on secondary sources. Furthermore, the secondary sources varied in quality and quantity across the companies. For example, we found no books written specifically about Nordstrom, but we found stacks of books on such companies as Ford, IBM, Disney, and GE. We did our best to locate all possible sources on each and every company, and we found substantial sources on all but one company (Kenwood). There is no such thing as perfect information. But, given the magnitude of information we did have, we're confident that our findings would not change significantly given perfect information. If anything, we suspect they would be further reinforced.

UNITED STATES BIAS

We surveyed only American CEOs and only examined one pair of non-U.S. companies (Sony versus Kenwood). We believe that the *basic dynamics* of being a visionary company will hold up across cultures and nationalities, but we also suspect that the *flavor* of those dynamics will vary—perhaps dramatically—across cultures. We freely acknowledge this fact and encourage future research into cross-cultural differences in visionary companies.

FOUNDING ROOTS OF VISIONARY COMPANIES AND COMPARISON COMPANIES

3M[1]

Year founded: 1902

Founder(s): Five Minnesota investors—two railroad operators, a physician, a meat-market operator, and an attorney

Location: Crystal Bay, MN

Founding Concept: To open and operate a mine to extract corundum as an abrasive to export to grinding-wheel manufacturers.

Initial Results: Mining business failed after selling only one ton of material; no further purchasers could be found. Company stumbled along via personal accounts of the investors and saved by a new investor (Louis Ordway), who helped the company shift to sandpaper production in 1905. 3M could not afford to pay its president (Edgar Ober) a salary during his first eleven years.

Norton[2]

Year founded: 1885

Founder(s): Seven investor-managers of diverse business backgrounds

Location: Worcester, MA

Founding Concept: Purchased small grinding-wheel company from Frank Norton to capitalize on the growing market for grinding wheels for the expanding machine tools industry.

Initial Results: Early growth and success; paid steady annual dividends in all but one of its first fifteen years of operations and multiplied its capital fifteen times over during the same time. By 1890, Norton had become the number one company in its industry.

American Express[3]

Year founded: 1850

Founder(s): Henry Wells (age unknown), William Fargo (age unknown), John Butterfield (age unknown)

Location: New York, NY

Founding Concept: To eliminate "wasteful competition" between three rival companies (Wells & Company; Livingston, Fargo & Company; and Butterfield, Wasson & Company) in the freight express business, the three companies agreed to join forces into one, somewhat monopolistic, company.

Initial Results: Immediately profitable and rapidly growing (not surprising with a near monopoly).

Wells Fargo[4]

Year founded: 1852

Founder(s): Henry Wells (age unknown), William Fargo (age unknown)

Location: San Francisco, CA

Founding Concept: To provide express (package delivery) and banking services in the expanding California market (expansion due to the gold rush).

Initial Results: One of the only companies to survive the California banking shakeout of 1855, and emerged in strong position with few competitors after the panic. Expanded rapidly from 1855 to 1866.

Boeing[5]

Year founded: 1915

Founder(s): William E. Boeing (age 35)

Location: Seattle, WA

Founding Concept: From the articles of incorporation: "To be a general manufacturing business . . . to manufacture goods, wares, and general merchandise of every kind, especially airplanes and vehicles of aviation . . . to operate a flying school and act as a common carrier of passengers and freight by aerial navigation." Bill Boeing entered the business as an ex-lumber merchant.

Initial Results: Bill Boeing's first airplane (the B&W) failed its Navy tests. Boeing then sold fifty of its second plane (the Model C) to the Navy, but could not extend the contract and the company spiraled downward through 1919–1920. Boeing lost $300,000 in 1920 and kept itself alive through loans from Bill Boeing and making furniture and speedboats.

Douglas Aircraft[8]

Year founded: 1920

Founder(s): Donald W. Douglas (age 28)

Location: Los Angeles, CA

Founding Concept: To design and build an aircraft for the first nonstop flight across the United States (the Cloudster). Company reorganized in 1921 into a new corporation to transfer technology from Cloudster to fulfill contract for experimental torpedo bombers for the Navy.

Initial Results: Successfully gained quantity contract from the Navy for eighteen torpedo bombers and soon thereafter obtained further contracts from the U.S. and Norwegian governments. The company attained early success and grew at an average annual rate of 284 percent per year during its first four years of operations.

Citicorp[7]

Year founded: 1812

Founder(s): Samuel Osgood (age unknown)

Location: New York, NY

Founding Concept: Essentially a private credit union for its merchant-owners, who used it to finance their own ventures.

Initial Results: No coherent strategy and continued to operate like a private bank for nearly seventy years. Didn't begin process of becoming a national bank until the 1890s under the guidance of James Stillman.

Chase Manhattan[8]

Year founded: 1799 for Bank of Manhattan and 1877 for Chase Bank.

Founder(s): Aaron Burr (age unknown) for Bank of Manhattan and John Thompson (age unknown) for Chase Bank

Location: New York, NY

Founding Concept: To be a bank.

Initial Results: Bank of Manhattan flourished from 1808 on. The Chase Bank didn't become prominent until 1911.

Other Comments: Chase and Manhattan merged in 1955.

Ford[9]

Year founded: 1903

Founder(s): Henry Ford (age 40) and Alex Malcomson (age unknown)

Location: Detroit, MI

Founding Concept: To make automobiles based on Henry Ford's mechanical expertise and, in particular, to capitalize on vertical piston technology. One of 502 firms founded in the United States between 1900 and 1908 to make automobiles.

Initial Results: First car, the Model A, proved successful; reached sales of over six hundred units per month by the end of the first year of operations. Introduced five models (A, B, C, F, and K) before introducing the Model T in 1908, which revolutionized the industry and made Ford the number one car maker.

Other Comments: Although Ford did not found the company specifically to build the Model T, it appears that he had considered the idea of the mass-production line manufacturing process as early as 1903.

General Motors[10]

Year founded: 1908

Founder(s): William Durant (age unknown)

Location: Detroit, MI

Founding Concept: To acquire and organize a range of smaller automakers into one company with the strategy of providing a variety of cars for a variety of tastes and incomes and capitalizing on shared financial and other resources.

Initial Results: Between 1908 and 1910, Durant acquired seventeen companies—including Oldsmobile, Cadillac, and Pontiac—to complement Buick Motors. Added Chevrolet in 1918. Bumpy road with strong growth but financial crises; Durant ousted in 1920.

Other Comments: From 1921 to 1927, GM under the guidance of Alfred Sloan, caught and passed Ford to became the number one automaker.

General Electric[11]

Year founded: 1892

Founder(s): Thomas Edison (age 45), Elihu Thomson (age 39), Charles Coffin (age 48)

Location: New York, NY

Founding Concept: Consolidation of Edison General Electric Company (founded in 1878 to develop and commercialize Edison's electricity and lighting research) and Thomson-Houston Electric Company (founded in 1883 as a conglomerate of electricity-related businesses).

Initial Results: Successful first year ($3 million earnings in seven months); financial difficulties and cash shortage in 1893 due to national depression, recovered and grew steadily through the next two decades aided, in part, by evolving to the AC system.

Westinghouse[12]

Year founded: 1886

Founder(s): George Westinghouse (age 39)

Location: Pittsburgh, PA

Founding Concept: To develop and commercialize alternating current (AC) electricity technology and the concept of central power systems—a technology that eventually proved superior to Edison's DC system—and thereby make the AC system the primary system throughout the world.

Initial Results: Superior technology concept led to substantial early success, turning the company into the number two company in the industry, and George Westinghouse was able to finance initial growth for two decades without losing control of the company.

Other Comments: Financial trouble during the national panic of 1907 led bankers to oust Westinghouse from his own company in 1910.

Hewlett-Packard[13]

Year founded: 1937

Founder(s): William Hewlett (age 26) and David Packard (age 26)

Location: Palo Alto, CA

Founding Concept: Initial approach was "strictly opportunistic" within the broadly defined "radio, electronic, and electrical engineering field." Initial products considered in early years included welding equipment, shock machines for weight reduction, automatic urinal flushers, bowling alley sensors, radio transmitters, public address systems, air-conditioning equipment, clock drives for telescopes, medical equipment, and oscilloscopes.

Initial Results: Kept itself alive in the first year via contract engineering jobs and lean operations (in a garage). In 1939, sold a few audio oscilloscopes. First-year sales: just above $5,100 with a profit of $1,300. Moved out of garage in 1940. Seventeen people employed in 1941. World War II boosted employment to 144 people; shrank twenty percent after the war. Sales in 1948: $2.1 million.

Texas Instruments[14]

Year founded: 1930

Founder(s): Dr. J. Clarence Karcher (age unknown) and Eugene McDermott (age 31)

Location: Newark, NJ

Founding Concept: Began life as Geophysical Service, Inc., "the first independent company to make reflection seismograph surveys of potential oil fields, and its Texas labs developed and produced instruments for such work." The company moved to Dallas, Texas, in 1934 to solidify its position in the oil exploration business. Changed its name to Texas Instruments in 1951.

Initial Results: Quickly became the market leader in geophysical exploration business. Grew and prospered in the early and mid-1930s. Stumbled in the early 1940s when it tried to move into the oil exploration business directly. Saved itself by applying seismic technology to signal search for the military. Recovered well during World War II.

IBM[15]

Year founded: 1911 (1890 for root companies)

Founder(s): Charles Flint (age unknown)

Location: New York, NY

Founding Concept: Merger of two small companies into a mini-conglomerate of measuring scales, time clocks, and tabulating machines for clerks and accountants (named the "Computing, Tabulating, Recording Company," or CTR.)

Initial Results: Floundered for three years and the board seriously discussed liquidation. In 1914, hired Thomas J. Watson, Sr., who gradually improved the health of the company and turned it into the market leader in tabulating machines by 1930.

Other Comments: Changed name to the International Business Machines Corporation in 1925.

Burroughs[16]

Year founded: 1892

Founder(s): William Burroughs (age unknown), Joseph Boyer (age unknown)

Location: St. Louis, MO

Founding Concept: William Burroughs invented the first-ever recording and adding machine and formed a company (named the American Amirthmometer Company) to market it.

Initial Results: Once on the market, the product proved a success and the company grew. Burroughs consolidated its position in the industry through new products and acquisitions. In 1914, the company had ninety products. In 1920, it was viewed as a "mainstay of the office-machine industry."

Other Comments: William Burroughs received the Franklin Institute's John Scott Medal for his invention; he died in 1898 from tuberculosis; company renamed "Burroughs Adding Machine Company" in his memory in 1905.

Johnson & Johnson[17]

Year founded: 1886

Founder(s): Robert W. Johnson (age 41), James Johnson, E. Mead Johnson (younger brothers of Robert W.; ages unknown)

Location: New Brunswick, NJ

Founding Concept: Manufacture of medical products, with particular emphasis on antiseptic surgical dressings and medical plasters; first catalog had thirty-two pages "crammed with an array of products."

Initial Results: The company began with fourteen employees in 1886; in 1888, the company employed 125 workers; in 1894, the company employed 400. Early success based on a wide range of innovative products, emergence of hospitals, and cultivation of a strong brand image.

Bristol-Myers[18]

Year founded: 1887

Founder(s): William McLaren Bristol (age early 20s), John Ripley Myers (early 20s)

Location: Clinton, NY

Founding Concept: Acquired for $5,000 "a failing drug manufacturing firm called the Clinton Manufacturing Company." Neither Bristol nor Myers had any background in pharmaceuticals.

Initial Results: Struggled early on; in 1889, the company employed only nine employees; did not earn a profit during its first twelve years of operations. The company did not begin to grow rapidly until 1903, when it introduced new hit products: Sal Hepatica (a laxative salt) and Ipana (the first-ever disinfectant toothpaste).

Marriott[19]

Year founded: 1927

Founder(s): J. Willard Marriott (age 26), Allie Marriott (age 22)

Location: Washington, DC

Founding Concept: To be in business for themselves. Began with a nine-seat A&W root beer stand. To attract additional business, they added hot food (mostly Mexican) and named the restaurant the Hot Shoppe.

Initial Results: Built on sixteen-hour days, the store proved profitable during the first year, with $16,000 gross receipts. By 1929, had expanded to three outlets running twenty-four hours per day. Expanded to Baltimore in 1931. Had eighteen Hot Shoppes by 1940.

Howard Johnson[20]

Year founded: 1925

Founder(s): Howard Johnson (age 27)

Location: Wollaston, MA

Founding Concept: Acquired a soda fountain and adopted his mother's ice-cream formula, which proved a hit with New Englanders.

Initial Results: Within six months, demand exceeded his production capacity. By 1928, ice-cream sales reached $240,000. In 1933, he expanded to the famous roadside orange-tiled restaurants. Built to 125 units by 1940.

Other Comments: Once Howard Johnson had the basic concept of his road restaurants down, he expanded and fully capitalized on that idea to the fullest.

Merck[21]

Year founded: 1891

Founder(s): George Merck (age 23).

Location: New York City, NY

Founding Concept: Sales branch for German chemical company, E. Merck. Traces roots back to Merck family apothecary in Darmstadt, Germany, 1668.

Initial Results: Solid sales success ($1 million by 1897) of imported chemicals from parent company; didn't manufacture its own chemicals until its second decade of life. Began manufacturing iodides and other staple pharmaceuticals at new facility in Rahway, New Jersey, in about 1903. Revenue in 1910 $3 million.

Pfizer[22]

Year founded: 1849

Founder(s): Charles Pfizer (age 25) and Charles Erhart (age 28)

Location: Brooklyn, NY

Founding Concept: Manufacture of high-quality chemicals not then produced in the United States, thus leveraging off a tariff advantage over imports; first product was Santonin, a compound to combat parasitic worms.

Initial Results: Santonin appears to have sold well, giving the company a basis for expansion; in 1855, the company began manufacturing iodine-based products, and by 1860 the company manufactured at least five product lines. In 1857 the company opened an office in downtown Manhattan and between 1857 and 1888 Pfizer purchased seventy-two lots of land for expansion.

Motorola[23]

Year founded: 1928

Founder(s): Paul V. Galvin (age 33)

Location: Chicago, IL

Founding Concept: Battery eliminators for radios, including a repair business for Sears, Roebuck radio battery eliminators that came back to Sears for service under warranty. Galvin "knew that the eliminator was not going to provide a market for very long," so he began looking early for other markets.

Initial Results: The company kept itself barely alive in the first year on the eliminator manufacture and repair business. Almost bankrupt at the end of 1929. Conceived of car radio concept in 1930. Lost money in 1930, then became profitable in 1931 and grew steadily from then on.

Zenith[24]

Year founded: 1923

Founder(s): Eugene F. MacDonald (age 37)

Location: Chicago, IL

Founding Concept: Sales and marketing of radios to capitalize on the emerging radio industry (commercial radio broadcasts began in 1920, and radios were in short supply); in 1923, took out an exclusive license to sell radios made by the Chicago Radio Lab; in 1924, introduced the world's first portable radio.

Initial Results: Early innovations fueled sales growth (1924: first portable radio; 1926: first home radio to operate from an AC outlet; 1927: first push-button tuning). Lax asset management, however, led to liquidity and credit problems in the mid-1920s.

Nordstrom[25]

Year founded: 1901

Founder(s): John Nordstrom (age 30), Carl Wallin (age unknown)

Location: Seattle, WA

Founding Concept: In the words of John Nordstrom: "I was still not certain what I wanted to do. . . . I started looking around for some small business to get into. Mr. Wallin was a shoemaker by trade and . . . had set up a shoe repair shop. . . . I often visited Mister Wallin in his shop and one day he suggested that we join a partnership and open a shoe store."

Initial Results: Became profitable early. Changed location three times in the first fifteen years, but remained a single-unit business until 1923, when the partners added a second store.

Other Comments: John Nordstrom sold out his share of the company to two of his sons (Everett and Elmer) in 1928.

Melville[26]

Year founded: 1892

Founder(s): Frank Melville (age unknown)

Location: New York, NY

Founding Concept: Frank Melville, a traveling shoe wholesaler, acquired three shoe stores "when the owner skipped town without paying Melville for a shipment of shoes."

Initial Results: Appears to have been profitable from early on. Began expanding into a chain concept in 1895. By 1923 it had 31 retail outlets; by 1935 it had 571 retail outlets. Largest retailer of shoes in the United States by the early 1930s.

Procter & Gamble[27]

Year founded: 1837

Founder(s): William Procter (age 36) and James Gamble (age 34)

Location: Cincinnati, OH

Founding Concept: Procter, a candle-maker, and Gamble, a soapmaker, relied on the same animal fat raw materials to make their products; as brothers-in-law, they decided to pool their efforts and formed a partnership to sell soap and candles.

Initial Results: The company grew slowly, requiring fifteen years before outgrowing their modest office, production facility, and store on "Main Street, 2nd door off Sixth Street." Although not spectacular in growth, the company appears to have been profitable; in 1847, the company earned $20,000. Two decades after founding, the company employed eighty factory workers.

Other Comments: At its founding, P&G was one of eighteen companies that sold soap and/or candles in Cincinnati.

Colgate[28]

Year founded: 1806

Founder(s): William Colgate (age 23)

Location: New York, NY

Founding Concept: According to Colgate's chairman in 1956, "At that period in American history [1806], at least 75 percent of the soap used was home made. . . . Soap made at home was crude, coarse, rough to the skin, and hardly pleasant in aroma. William Colgate undertook to make a soap that would be pleasant to the senses and yet available to the average person."

Initial Results: Little information available; no indication that the company was significantly more or less successful than P&G during its first two decades of life.

Other Comments: One of the first companies in the United States to manufacture soap for sale.

Philip Morris[29]

Year founded: 1847

Founder(s): Philip Morris (age unknown)

Location: London, England

Founding Concept: Tobacco shop on Bond Street in London.

Initial Results: Remained a simple retail shop until 1854, when Philip Morris began making cigarettes. Little indication of substantial early growth. Introduced its cigarettes in the United States in 1902. American investors purchased rights to the Philip Morris name in 1919.

Other Comments: Marlboro brand introduced as a women's cigarette in 1924.

R.J. Reynolds[30]

Year founded: 1875

Founder(s): Richard J. Reynolds (age 25)

Location: Winston, NC

Founding Concept: To develop and sell chewing tobacco based on a newly developed "flue-cured leaf that made the best chewing tobacco."

Initial Results: In the first year of operations, his company turned out 150,000 pounds of product. "From then on, about every other year, a new addition had to be made to the factory to keep up with a nation of chewers." By the mid-1880s, R.J. Reynolds had amassed a personal fortune in excess of $100,000.

Other Comments: Introduced Camel brand cigarettes in 1913; became No. 1 U.S. brand by 1917.

Sony[31]

Year founded: 1945

Founder(s): Masaru Ibuka (age 37)

Location: Tokyo, Japan

Founding Concept: No clear idea other than the vague concept to apply technology to the creation of consumer products.

Initial Results: Struggled with a failed rice cooker, failed tape recorder system; stayed alive via crude heating pads and then a hodgepodge of products on contract for Japan Broadcasting, such as voltmeters and control consoles for studios. Developed first hit consumer product (pocket radio) in 1955. Took a dozen years to reach five hundred employees.

Kenwood[32]

Year founded: 1946

Founder(s): Not listed in history

Location: Komagane City, Japan

Founding Concept: To be a specialist pioneer in audio technology.

Initial Results: Quickly established itself as a leader in audio technology. Its first products, specialized radio components, were successful and immediately established the company. Its high-frequency transformer is the first product made in Japan to pass the approval standards of the Japan Broadcasting Corporation (1949).

Wal-Mart[33]	Ames[34]
Year founded: 1945	*Year founded:* 1958
Founder(s): Sam Walton (age 27)	*Founder(s):* Milton Gilman (age 33) and Irving Gilman (age unknown)
Location: Newport, AR	*Location:* Southbridge, MA
Founding Concept: Acquired a franchise license for a single-unit Ben Franklin five-and-dime store in a small town; no evidence of plans to be anything than a single-unit outlet.	*Founding Concept:* Mortgaged family farm specifically to launch discount retailing chain in small towns.
Initial Results: First year sales: $80,000; third year sales $225,000. Lost his lease in 1950, and thereby lost his store. Moved to Bentonville, Arkansas, and opened a small five-and-dime store he called "Walton's." Expanded to two units in 1952.	*Initial Results:* First-year sales $1 million; within two years, Ames expanded to multi-unit chain in New York and Vermont.
Other Comments: Opened first large-scale rural discount store in 1962.	*Other Comments:* Opened first large-scale rural discount store in 1958.

Walt Disney[35]

Year founded: 1923

Founder(s): Walter E. Disney (age 21), Roy O. Disney (age 27)

Location: Los Angeles, CA

Founding Concept: Walt moved from Kansas City to Los Angeles to get into the movie business, but could not land a job, so he rented a camera, made an animation stand, set up a studio in his uncle's garage, and decided to go into the animation business for himself. According to Disney biographer Schickel, "He was at least halfway convinced that he was too late, by perhaps six years, to break into animation, but [it] was the only area in which he had any prior experience."

Initial Results: First film series (*Alice*) provided barely enough cash flow (due to frugal expenses) to keep going. Second product (*Oswald the Rabbit*, 1927) did better, but lost control of product in bad business arrangement. In 1928, he introduced Micky Mouse.

Columbia Pictures[36]

Year founded: 1920

Founder(s): Harry Cohn (age 29) and Jack Cohn (age unknown)

Location: Los Angeles, CA

Founding Concept: Harry and Jack Cohn founded the company in 1920 initially to make cartoons and short films to show the off-screen activities of movie stars and publicize the current pictures of the stars. Then moved into full-length feature films.

Initial Results: Only moderate success with the initial shorts concept. First feature-length films more successful: $130,000 income for cost of $20,000 on first full-length feature; between August 1922 and December 1923, the company produced ten profitable full-length feature movies.

Founding Roots Summary	Founded with a "Great Idea"?*		Which company had greater initial success during the entrepreneurial phase: Visionary or Comparison?
	Visionary	Comparison	
3M vs. Norton	No	Yes	Comparison Company
American Express vs. Wells Fargo	No	No	Visionary Company
Boeing vs. McDonnell Douglas	No	Yes	Comparison Company
Citicorp vs. Chase	No	No	Indistinguishable
Ford vs. GM	Yes	No	Visionary Company
GE vs. Westinghouse	Yes	Yes	Indistinguishable
HP vs. TI	No	Yes	Comparison Company
IBM vs. Burroughs	No	Yes	Comparison Company
Johnson & Johnson vs. Bristol-Myers	Yes	No	Visionary Company
Marriott vs. Howard Johnson	No	No	Indistinguishable
Merck vs. Pfizer	No	Yes	Indistinguishable
Motorola vs. Zenith	No	Yes	Comparison Company
Nordstrom vs. Melville	No	No	Comparison Company
Procter & Gamble vs. Colgate	No	Yes	Indistinguishable
Philip Morris vs. R.J. Reynolds	No	Yes	Comparison Company
Sony vs. Kenwood	No	Yes	Comparison Company
Wal-Mart vs. Ames	No	Yes	Comparison Company
Walt Disney vs. Columbia	No	No	Comparison Company
Overall	3 Yes 15 No	11 Yes 7 No	3 Visionary Company 5 Indistinguishable 10 Comparison Company

*Defined as a specific, innovative, and highly successful product or service.

APPENDIX 2 NOTES

1. *Our Story So Far* (St. Paul, MN: 3M Company, 1977), 51–56.
2. Charles W. Cheape, *Norton Company: a New England Enterprise* (Cambridge, MA: Harvard University Press, 1985), 12
3. Alden Hatch, *American Express 1850–1950* (Garden City, NY: Country Life Press, 1950); "About American Express," corporate publication; Peter G. Grossman, *American Express: The Unofficial History of the People Who Built the Great Empire* (New York: Crown, 1987).
4. *International Directory of Corporate Histories* (Chicago: St. James Press, 1988), 380.
5. E. E. Tauber, *Boeing in Peace and War* (Enumaclaw, WA: TABA, 1991), 19; Robert J. Serling, *Legend and Legacy* (New York: St. Martin's Press, 1992), 2–6.
6. René Francillon, *McDonnell Douglas Aircraft Since 1920* (Annapolis, MD: Naval Institute Press, 1988), 1–12.
7. Harold van B. Cleveland and Thomas F. Huertas, *Citibank 1812–1970* (Cambridge, MA: Harvard University Press, 1985); *International Directory of Corporate Histories* (Chicago: St. James Press, 1988), 253.
8. *International Directory of Corporate Histories* (Chicago: St. James Press, 1988), 247.
9. Alfred Chandler, *Giant Enterprise: Ford, General Motors, and the Automobile Industry* (Cambridge, MA: M.I.T. Press, 1964); Arthur Kuhn, *GM Passes Ford, 1918–38* (University Park, PA: Pennsylvania State University Press, 1986); Robert Lacey, *Ford: The Men and the Machine* (New York: Ballantine Books, 1986)
10. Alfred Sloan, *My Years with General Motors* (New York: Anchor Books, 1972), Alfred Chandler, *Giant Enterprise: Ford, General Motors, and the Automobile Industry* (Cambridge, MA: M.I.T. Press, 1964); Maryann Keller, *Rude Awakening* (New York: Morrow, 1986); Arthur Kuhn, *GM Passes Ford, 1918–38* (University Park, PA: Pennsylvania State University Press, 1986); Arthur Pund, *The Turning Wheel: The Story of General Motors Through 25 Years, 1908–1933* (Garden City, NY: Doubleday Doarn, 1934).
11. *The General Electric Story* (Schenectady, NY: Hall of History Foundation, 1981), volumes 1–2.
12. Henry G. Prout, *A Life of George Westinghouse* (New York: American Society of Mechanical Engineers, 1921), 1–150.
13. Materials courtesy Hewlett-Packard Company Archives.
14. "Research Packed with Ph.D.'s," *Business Week*, 22 December 1956, 58; *Hoover's Handbook, 1991*, (Emeryville, CA: The Reference Press, 1990), 528; John McDonald, "The Men Who Made T.I.," *Fortune*, November 1961, 118–119.
15. Thomas J. Watson, Jr., *Father, Son & Company* (New York: Bantam Books, 1990), 13–17; *International Directory of Corporate Histories* (Chicago: St. James Press, 1988), 147.
16. *International Directory of Corporate Histories* (Chicago: St. James Press, 1988), 165.

17. Lawrence G. Foster, *A Company that Cares* (New Brunswick, NJ: Johnson & Johnson, 1986), 9–27.
18. *Bristol-Myers Company—Special Report: The Next Century*, company publication (1987) 3–5.
19. Robert O'Brian, *Marriott: The J. Willard Marriott Story* (Salt Lake City: Deseret, 1987), 123–137.
20. "Glorified Road Stands Pay," *Business Week*, 17 February 1940; "The Howard Johnson Restaurants," *Fortune*, September 1940.
21. *Values and Visions: A Merck Century* (Rahway, NJ: Merck, 1993), 13–15.
22. Samuel Mines, *Pfizer: An Informal History* (New York: Pfizer, 1978), 1–6.
23. Harry Mark Petrakis, *The Founder's Touch* (New York: McGraw-Hill, 1965), 62–111.
24. *International Directory of Corporate Histories* (Chicago: St. James Press, 1988), 123.
25. John W. Nordstrom, *The Immigrant in 1887* (Seattle: Dogwood Press, 1950), 44–50; "Nordstrom History," company publication, 26 November 1990.
26. Francis C. Rooner, Jr., *Creative Merchandising in an Era of Change* (New York: Newcomen Society, 1970), 8–12; "Largest American Shoe Retailer," *Barron's*, 8 April 1935; *Hoover's Handbook 1991* (Emeryville, CA: The Reference Press, 1990), 372.
27. "Procter & Gamble Chronology," company publication; Oscar Schisgall, *Eyes on Tomorrow: The Evolution of Procter & Gamble* (New York: Doubleday, 1981), 1–14; Alfred Lief, *It Floats: The Story of Procter & Gamble* (New York: Rinehart, 1958), 14–32; plus over forty outside articles on the company dating back to the 1920s.
28. "Colgate Palmolive Company: Memorable Dates," company publication; "Colgate-Palmolive-Peet," *Fortune*, April 1936; William Lee Sims II, *150 Years . . . and the Future! Colgate-Palmolive (1806–1956)* (New York: Newcomen Society, 1956), 9–10.
29. *The Philip Morris History*, company publication (1988).
30. *RJ Reynolds: Our 100th Anniversary*, company publication (1975).
31. Nick Lyons, *The Sony Vision* (New York: Crown, 1976), 1–35.
32. *Japan Electronics Almanac '88*, (Tokyo, Japan: DEMPA Publications, 1988), p. 282; Kenwood annual reports.
33. Vance Trimble, *Sam Walton* (New York: Dutton, 1990), 45–72.
34. "Cornering the Market," *Forbes*, 23 May 1983, 46. Also *Hoover's Handbook 1991* (Emeryville, CA: The Reference Press, 1990), 84.
35. Richard Schickel, *The Disney Version* (New York: Simon & Schuster, 1968), 91–117
36. Clive Hirschhorn, *The Columbia Story* (New York: Crown, 1989), 7–16.

TABLES

Table A.1

Categories Tracked Across the Entire History (From Founding Date to 1991) of the Visionary and Comparison Companies in our Research Study

Category 1: Organizing Arrangements. "Hard" items, such as organization structure, policies and procedures, systems, rewards and incentives, ownership structure, and general business strategies and activities of the company (e.g., acquisitions, significant changes in strategy, going public).

Category 2: Social Factors. "Soft" items, such as the company's cultural practices, atmosphere, norms, rituals, mythology and stories, group dynamics, and management style.

Category 3: Physical Setting. Significant aspects of the way the company handled physical space, such as plant and office layout or new facilities. This included any significant decisions regarding the geographic location of key parts of the company.

Category 4: Technology. How the company used technology: information technology, state-of-the-art processes and equipment, advanced job configurations, and related items.

Category 5: Leadership. Leadership of the firm since its inception: the transition between key early shapers of the organization and later generations, leadership tenure, the length of time the leaders were with the organization before becoming CEO (Were they brought in from the outside or grown from within? When did they join?), leadership selection processes and criteria.

Category 6: Products and Services. Significant products and services in the company's history. How did the product or service ideas come about? What guided their selection and development? Did the company have any product failures, and how did it deal with them? Did the company lead with new products or follow in the marketplace?

Category 7: Vision: Core Values, Purpose, and Visionary Goals. Were these variables present? If yes, how did they come into being? Did the organization have them at certain points in its history and not others? What role did they play? If it had strong values and purpose, did they remain intact or become diluted? Why?

Category 8: Financial Analysis. Ratio and spreadsheet analysis of all income statements and balance sheets for every year going back to the date when the company became public: sales and profit growth, gross margins, return on assets, return on sales, return on equity, debt to equity ratio, cash flow and working capital, liquidity ratios, dividend payout ratio, increase in gross property plant and equipment as a percentage of sales, asset turnover. We also examined stock returns and overall stock performance relative to the market.

Category 9: Markets/Environment. Significant aspects of the company's external environment: major market shifts, dramatic national or international events, government regulations, industry structural issues, dramatic technology changes, and related items.

Table A.2

Sources of Information in Our Research Study

- Historical materials obtained directly from the companies: archive materials, historical documents (such as prospectuses from when the company went public), historical descriptions, internal publications, video footage, transcripts of interviews and speeches of alive and deceased leaders, corporate policy documents, historical and current vision (values, purpose, mission) statements, employee handbooks, training and socialization materials, and related materials.
- Books written about the industry, the company, and/or its leaders published either by the company or by outside observers. (We placed more weight on books written by outsiders). We obtained all books (old and new) available through the unified catalog of library listings at Stanford, University of California, Harvard, Yale, and Oxford.
- Articles written about the company. We did extensive literature searches from the time of the company's founding up to the present and examined *all* major articles on each company through the decades from broad sources such as *Forbes, Fortune, Business Week, Wall Street Journal, Nation's Business, New York Times, U.S. News, New Republic, Harvard Business Review, The Economist*, and selected articles from industry or topic specific sources such as *Discount Merchandiser, Marketing*, and *Hotel and Restaurant Quarterly*.
- Corporate annual reports and financial statements. In some cases, this involved nearly a hundred separate income statements and balance sheets for a single company.
- Harvard and Stanford Business School case studies and industry analyses. We obtained every available business case study on each company and each industry in our study.
- Financial databases, including the University of Chicago Center For Research in Security Prices (CRSP) Market Index Database, which gave us monthly stock returns for every company dated back to when first available.
- Interviews with key major figures, employees, ex-employees, and outside "experts" about the company or the industry (e.g., analysts and academics).
- Business and industry reference materials, such as the *Biographical Dictionary of American Business Leaders*, the *International Directory of Company Histories, Hoover's Handbook of Companies, Development of American Industries*, and *Movie Industry Almanac*.

Table A.3

Leadership* as a Distinguishing Variable During Formative Stages?

* *Leadership* is defined as top executive(s) who displayed high levels of persistence, overcame significant obstacles, attracted dedicated people, influenced groups of people toward the achievement of goals, and played key roles in guiding their companies through crucial episodes in their history. NOTE: In selecting dates, we tried to cover the period during which the executive still had significant influence over the direction of the company; in some cases, the executive held numerous titles over the course of time—for example, president, CEO, chairman, and general manager. The point of this table is to show that both the visionary and comparison companies had such people during formative stages of evolution and, therefore, *leadership* so defined does not show up as a distinguishing variable.

Pair	Visionary Company	Comparison Company	Distinguishing Variable?
3M vs. Norton	William McKnight (1914–1966)	Milton Higgins (1855–1912)	No
American Express vs. Wells Fargo	Henry Wells and William Fargo (1850–1868)	Henry Wells and William Fargo (same people) (1852–1860s)	No
Boeing vs. McDonnell Douglas	William Boeing (1916–1934)	Donald Douglas (1920–1967) James McDonnell (1939–1980)	No
Citicorp vs. Chase	James Stillman (1891–1918)	Albert Wiggin (1911–1933)	No
Ford vs. GM	Henry Ford, I (1899–1945)	Alfred P. Sloan (1923–1946)	No
GE vs. Westinghouse	Charles Coffin (1892–1922)	George Westinghouse (1866–1909)	No

Hewlett-Packard vs. Texas Instruments	Dave Packard and William Hewlett (1937–)	Eugene McDermott (1930–1948) Pat Haggarty (1958–1976)	No
IBM vs. Burroughs	Thomas J. Watson (1914–1956)	Joseph Boyer (1898–1930)	No
J & J vs. Bristol-Myers	R W Johnson (1886–1910)	William Bristol (1887–1915)	No
Marriott vs. Howard Johnson	J. Willard Marriott (1927–1964)	Howard Johnson (1925–1959)	No
Merck vs. Pfizer	George Merck (1895–1925)	Charles Pfizer (1849–1906)	No
Motorola vs. Zenith	Paul Galvin (1926–1956)	Commander Eugene F. McDonald, Jr. (1923–1958)	No
Nordstrom	John Nordstrom (1901–1928)	Frank Melville (1892–1930)	No
Procter & Gamble vs. Colgate	William Procter and James Gamble (1837–1870s)	William Colgate (1806–1857)	No
Philip Morris vs. R.J. Reynolds	None Evident	R.J. Reynolds (1875–1918)	Perhaps in favor of the comparison company
Sony vs. Kenwood	Masaru Ibuka (1945–)	Not enough information	Not enough information
Wal-Mart vs. Ames	Sam Walton (1945–1992)	Gilman Brothers (1958–1981)	No
Walt Disney vs. Columbia	Walt Disney (1923–1966)	Harry Cohn (1920–1958)	No

Table A.4

Evidence of Core Ideology

METHOD: In assessing the ideological nature of the visionary and comparison companies, we considered evidence along each of the following dimensions:

A: Statements of Ideology
B: Historical Continuity of Ideology
C: Ideology Beyond Profits
D: Consistency Between Ideology and Actions

In each category, we gave each visionary and comparison company a rating *based on the evidence we had available*. We then calculated an overall index based on a summation of the company's ratings across these dimensions, scoring each "*H*" as a 3, each "*M*" as a 2, and each "*L*" as a 1.

A: Statements of Ideology

H: Significant evidence that the company stated an ideology (core values and/or purpose as per our definitions) with the intent to use the ideology as a source of guidance. Evidence that key members of the company spoke and/or wrote about the ideology more than a few times and that the ideology was communicated widely to people throughout the organization.

M: Some evidence that the company stated an ideology (core values and/or purpose as per our definitions) with the intent to use the ideology as a source of guidance. Some evidence that key members of the company spoke and/or wrote about the ideology, but perhaps only once or a few times, and some evidence that the ideology was communicated to people in the organization, but less than those that received an "*H*" on this dimension.

L: Little or no evidence that the company made any serious attempt to clarify and declare an ideology (core values and/or purpose as per our definitions).

B: Historical Continuity of Ideology

H: Evidence that the stated ideology discussed in Part A has changed little and has been continually emphasized throughout the company's history since the time the ideology was first articulated.

M: Evidence that the stated ideology discussed in Part A has changed substantially and/or that the company has been sporadic in its references to the ideology through its history since the ideology was first articulated.

L: Little evidence of any continuity of an ideology through the history of the company.

C: Ideology Beyond Profits

H: Evidence of explicit discussions about the role of profitability or shareholder wealth as being only a part of the company's objectives, and not the primary driving objective. Explicit use of phrases like "reasonable" returns, "adequate" returns, "fair" returns, "profitability as a necessary condition to pursue other aims," rather than "maximal" or "highest" returns.

M: Evidence that profitability and shareholder returns are highly important—equal to or greater than other aims and values. Ideological concerns are also important, but noticeably less so (relative to profit motives) than the companies that receive an "*H*" on this dimension.

L: Evidence that the company is highly profit or shareholder wealth oriented with ideological concerns deeply subordinated to making money. Evidence that the company sees maximizing wealth as the reason for existence and number one goal far ahead of any other concerns.

D: Consistency Between Ideology and Actions

H: Significant evidence that the company's ideology has been more than words on paper. Significant evidence (consistently throughout the company's history) of major strategic (such as product, market, or investment) and/or organization design decisions (such as structure, incentive systems, policies) being guided by and consistent with the stated ideology.

M: Some evidence that the company's ideology has been more than words on paper. Some evidence of major strategic (product, market, investment) and/or organization design decisions (structure, incentive systems, policies) being guided by and consistent with the stated ideology or that this has been less consistent through history than for those companies that receive an "*H*" on this dimension.

L: Little evidence of any guidance by the ideology and consistency between stated ideologies and corporate actions.

Visionary Companies	"A"	"B"	"C"	"D"	Index Score	Total Delta	Index Score	"A"	"B"	"C"	"D"	Comparison Companies
3M	H	H	M	H	11.00	3.00	8.00	M	M	M	M	Norton
American Express	M	M	M	M	8.00	2.00	6.00	M	L	L	M	Wells Fargo
Boeing	H	H	M	H	11.00	5.00	6.00	M	L	L	M	McDonnell Douglas
Citicorp	M	M	M	M	8.00	0.00	8.00	M	L	H	M	Chase Manhattan
Ford	H	M	H	M	10.00	4.00	6.00	M	L	L	M	GM
General Electric	H	M	M	M	9.00	2.00	7.00	M	L	M	M	Westinghouse
Hewlett-Packard	H	H	H	H	12.00	6.00	6.00	M	L	L	M	Texas Instruments
IBM	H	H	M	M	10.00	6.00	4.00	L	L	L	L	Burroughs
Johnson & Johnson	H	H	H	H	12.00	5.00	7.00	M	L	M	M	Bristol-Myers Squibb
Marriott	H	H	H	H	12.00	6.00	6.00	M	L	M	L	Howard Johnson
Merck	H	H	H	H	12.00	5.00	7.00	M	L	M	M	Pfizer
Motorola	H	H	H	H	12.00	5.00	7.00	M	L	M	M	Zenith
Nordstrom	H	H	M	H	11.00	3.00	8.00	M	M	M	M	Melville
Philip Morris	M	L	M	H	8.00	1.00	7.00	M	L	M	M	RJR Nabisco
Procter & Gamble	H	H	M	H	11.00	3.00	8.00	H	L	M	M	Colgate
Sony	H	H	H	H	12.00	5.00	7.00	M	L	M	M	Kenwood
Wal-Mart	M	H	M	H	10.00	6.00	4.00	L	L	L	L	Ames
Walt Disney	H	H	M	H	11.00	7.00	4.00	L	L	L	L	Columbia
Frequency Counts												
No. of Hs	14	13	7	13				1	0	1	0	
No. of Ms	4	4	11	5				14	2	10	14	
No. of Ls	0	1	0	0				3	16	7	4	
Total	18	18	18	18				18	18	18	18	
VC > CC	14	17	12	14	17							
VC = CC	4	1	5	4	1							
VC < CC	0	0	1	0	0							
Total	18	18	18	18	18							

Table A.5

Evidence of BHAGs

METHOD: In assessing the use of BHAGs in the visionary and comparison companies, we considered evidence along each of the following dimensions:

A: Use of BHAGs
B: Audacity of BHAGs
C: Historical Pattern of BHAGs

In each category, we gave each visionary and comparison company a rating *based on the evidence we had available*. We then calculated an overall index based on a summation of the company's ratings across these dimensions, scoring each "*H*" as a 3, each "*M*" as a 2, and each "*L*" as a 1.

A: Use of BHAGs

H: Significant evidence that the company used BHAGs to stimulate progress.

M: Some evidence that the company used BHAGs to stimulate progress, but less clear or prominent than those that received an "*H*."

L: Little or no evidence that the company made any serious use of BHAGs in its history.

B: Audacity of BHAGs

H: Significant evidence that the BHAGs used were highly "audacious" (evidence that they were very difficult to achieve and/or highly risky).

M: Evidence that the BHAGs used were "audacious," but significantly less risky or difficult to achieve than those that received an "*H*" on this dimension.

L: Little evidence that goals were highly audacious.

C: Historical Pattern of BHAGs

H: Evidence that the company had a repetitive historical pattern of BHAGs, or set BHAGs that transcended through multiple generations of leadership.

M: Less evidence (than those that received an "*H*") of a repetitive historical pattern of BHAGs, or use of BHAGs that transcended through multiple generations of leadership.

L: Little evidence of a historical pattern of BHAGs in its history.

Visionary Companies	"A"	"B"	"C"	Index Score	Total Delta	Index Score	"A"	"B"	"C"	Comparison Companies
3M	M	M	L	5.00	0.00	5.00	M	M	L	Norton
American Express	M	M	L	5.00	1.00	4.00	M	L	L	Wells Fargo
Boeing	H	H	H	9.00	4.00	5.00	M	M	L	McDonnell Douglas
Citicorp	H	H	H	9.00	4.00	5.00	M	M	L	Chase Manhattan
Ford	H	H	M	8.00	1.00	7.00	H	H	L	GM
General Electric	H	H	M	8.00	1.00	7.00	H	H	L	Westinghouse
Hewlett-Packard	M	H	L	6.00	-2.00	8.00	H	H	M	Texas Instruments
IBM	H	H	M	8.00	5.00	3.00	L	L	L	Burroughs
Johnson & Johnson	M	M	M	6.00	0.00	6.00	M	M	M	Bristol-Myers Squibb
Marriott	H	M	M	7.00	3.00	4.00	M	L	L	Howard Johnson
Merck	H	H	M	8.00	2.00	6.00	M	M	M	Pfizer
Motorola	H	H	H	9.00	3.00	6.00	H	M	L	Zenith
Nordstrom	M	M	M	6.00	0.00	6.00	M	M	M	Melville
Philip Morris	H	H	L	7.00	1.00	6.00	M	M	M	RJR Nabisco
Procter & Gamble	H	H	M	8.00	2.00	6.00	M	M	M	Colgate
Sony	H	H	H	9.00	4.00	5.00	M	M	L	Kenwood
Wal-Mart	H	H	H	9.00	4.00	5.00	M	M	L	Ames
Walt Disney	H	H	M	8.00	3.00	5.00	M	M	L	Columbia
Frequency Counts										
No. of *H*s	13	13	5				4	3	0	
No. of *M*s	5	5	9				13	12	6	
No. of *L*s	0	0	4				1	3	12	
Total	18	18	18				18	18	18	
VC > CC	10	12	10		14					
VC = CC	7	6	6		3					
VC < CC	1	0	2		1					
Total	18	18	18		18					

Table A.6

Evidence of Cultism

METHOD: In assessing cultism in the visionary and comparison companies, we considered evidence indicating that the company seeks to create an intense sense of loyalty and dedication and to influence the behavior of those inside the company to be consistent with the company's ideology. We examined evidence along three key dimensions of cultlike environments:

A: Indoctrination
B: Tightness of Fit
C: Elitism.

In each category we gave each visionary and comparison company a rating *based on the evidence we had available.* We then calculated an overall index based on a summation of the company's ratings across these dimensions, scoring each "*H*" as a 3, each "*M*" as a 2, and each "*L*" as a 1.

A: Indoctrination

H: Significant evidence that the company has a history of formal and/or tangible employee indoctrination processes. These processes might include:

— Orientation programs that teach such things as values, behavioral norms, corporate ideology, history, and tradition
— Ongoing "training" that has ideological content
— Internal publications: books, newspapers, and periodicals that reinforce ideology
— "On-the-job" ideological socialization by peers, immediate supervisors, and others
— Members of the company becoming the primary social group for new employees; employees being encouraged to socialize primarily with other employees
— Singing corporate songs, yelling corporate cheers
— Exposure to a mythology of "heroic deeds" by exemplar employees
— Use of unique language and terminology that reinforces a frame of reference
— Making pledges or affirmations
— Hiring young, promoting from within, shaping the employee's mind-set from a young age; everyone starting at the bottom, so as to force people to "grow up" in the ideology

M: Some evidence that the company has a long history of formal and tangible employee indoctrination processes around the core ideology, but less prominent and/or less historically consistent than those that received an "*H.*"

L: Little or no evidence that the company has a long history of formal and/or tangible employee indoctrination processes around the core ideology.

B: Tightness of Fit

H: Significant evidence that the company has historically imposed "tightness of fit"—people tend to either fit well with the company or tend to not fit at all; the boundaries of "fit" are very tight (especially with respect to the company's ideology). The company uses a variety of tangible methods to enforce tightness of fit, which might include:

— Tangible recognition and rewards for those who fit and tangible negative reinforcement and penalties for those who don't fit (those who fit seem to be happy, rewarded, valued; those who don't fit seem to be unhappy, unvalued, "left behind")
— Tolerance for mistakes that do not breach the company's ideology ("non-sins"); severe penalties for those who breach the ideology ("sins")
— Tight screening processes, either during hiring or within the first few years
— Severe expectations of loyalty; penalties and/or sense of betrayal for perceived "lack of loyalty"
— Overtight behavioral norms and intrusive behavior control which tends to repel those who don't fit
— Expectations of zealousness of behavior and espousement of the ideology
— Seeking buy-in (as in financial or time investment) which will tend to repel those not willing to fully "join"

M: Some evidence that the company has historically imposed "tightness of fit," but less prominent and/or less historically consistent than those that received an "*H.*"

L: Little or no evidence that the company has historically imposed "tightness of fit."

C: Elitism

H: Significant evidence that the company has historically reinforced a sense of belonging to something special and superior. Both parts of this are important—belonging and specialness. This can be reinforced in a variety of ways, such as:

— Continual verbal and written emphasis on being part of a special group, the elites
— An obsession with secrecy and control over information, especially in regard to the outside world
— Celebrations to reinforce successes, belonging, and specialness
— Use of names ("Motorolans," "Nordies," "Proctoids," "Cast Members") and special language to reinforce being part of a special group
— Lots of emphasis on a "family feeling"—all belonging to "a big, happy family"
— Physical isolation; that is, the company has its own facilities (post offices, restaurants, health clubs, social gathering places) that minimize the need for employees to deal with the outside world

M: Less evidence (than those that received an "*H*") that the company has historically reinforced a sense of belonging to something special and superior.

L: Little or no evidence that the company has historically reinforced a sense of belonging to something special and superior.

Visionary Companies	"A"	"B"	"C"	Index Score	Total Delta	Index Score	"A"	"B"	"C"	Comparison Companies
3M	M	H	H	8.00	2.00	6.00	M	M	M	Norton
American Express	L	M	M	5.00	0.00	5.00	L	M	M	Wells Fargo
Boeing	M	M	H	7.00	2.00	5.00	M	L	M	McDonnell Douglas
Citicorp	M	M	H	7.00	0.00	7.00	M	M	H	Chase Manhattan
Ford	M	M	H	7.00	0.00	7.00	M	M	H	GM
General Electric	H	M	H	8.00	4.00	4.00	L	L	M	Westing-house
Hewlett-Packard	H	H	H	9.00	2.00	7.00	H	M	M	Texas Instruments
IBM	H	H	H	9.00	5.00	4.00	L	L	M	Burroughs
Johnson & Johnson	H	M	H	8.00	2.00	6.00	M	M	M	Bristol-Myers Squibb
Marriott	H	H	H	9.00	3.00	6.00	M	M	M	Howard Johnson
Merck	H	H	H	9.00	4.00	5.00	L	M	M	Pfizer
Motorola	H	M	M	7.00	3.00	4.00	L	L	M	Zenith
Nord-strom	H	H	H	9.00	4.00	5.00	L	M	M	Melville
Philip Morris	M	M	M	6.00	0.00	6.00	M	M	M	RJR Nabisco
Procter & Gamble	H	H	H	9.00	3.00	6.00	M	M	M	Colgate
Sony	H	M	H	8.00	3.00	5.00	M	L	M	Kenwood
Wal-Mart	H	M	H	8.00	4.00	4.00	L	L	M	Ames
Walt Disney	H	H	H	9.00	5.00	4.00	L	M	L	Columbia
Frequency Counts										
No. of Hs	12	8	15				1	0	2	
No. of Ms	5	10	3				9	12	15	
No. of Ls	1	0	0				8	6	1	
Total	18	18	18				18	18	18	
VC > CC	11	13	13		14					
VC = CC	7	5	5		4					
VC < CC	0	0	0		0					
Total	18	18	18		18					

Table A.7
Evidence of Purposeful Evolution

METHOD: In assessing the use of evolutionary progress in the visionary and comparison companies, we considered evidence collected in the course of our study that would indicate purposeful evolution to stimulate progress. We examined evidence along three dimensions:

A: Conscious Use of Evolutionary Progress
B: Operational Autonomy to Stimulate and Enable Variation
C: Other Mechanisms to Stimulate and Enable Variation and Selection

In each category we gave each visionary and comparison company a rating *based on the evidence we had available*. We then calculated an overall index based on a summation of the company's ratings across these dimensions, scoring each "*H*" as a 3, each "*M*" as a 2, and each "*L*" as a 1.

A: Conscious Use

H: Significant evidence that the company has a history of *consciously* embracing the concept of making progress by an evolutionary process of variation and selection. Although the company might also embrace other forms of progress (such as BHAGs, or self-improvement), it must also have made conscious use of evolutionary processes. Evidence that the company has, in fact, made some significant strategic shifts and moves stemming from use of this type of progress.

M: Some evidence that the company has a history of consciously embracing the concept of making progress by an evolutionary process of variation and selection, but less prominent and/or less historically consistent conscious adoption than those that received an "*H*."

L: Little or no evidence that the company has a history of consciously embracing the concept of making progress by an evolutionary process of variation and selection.

B: Operational Autonomy

H: Significant evidence that the company has made historical use of operational autonomy as a means of enabling variation. *Operational autonomy* means that employees have wide personal discretion in how to go about fulfilling their responsibilities via decentralized organization structures and job designs that enable operational freedom.

M: Some evidence that the company has made historical use of operational autonomy as a means of enabling variation, but less prominent and/or less historically consistent conscious adoption than those that received an "*H*."

L: Little or no evidence that the company has made historical use of operational autonomy as a means of enabling variation.

C: Other Mechanisms

H: Significant evidence that the company has a history of using a variety of mechanisms other than operational autonomy to stimulate and enable evolutionary progress via variation and selection. These mechanisms can be designed to stimulate creativity and new ideas, experimentation, opportunism (quick, vigorous action in response to unexpected opportunities), lack of penalties (or actual rewards) for mistakes, rewards for innovations and new directions, individual initiative, and incentives for creating new opportunities for the organization.

M: Some evidence that the company has a history of using a variety of mechanisms to stimulate and enable evolutionary progress via variation and selection, but less prominent and/or less historically consistent conscious adoption than those that received an "*H*."

L: Little or no evidence that the company has a history of using a variety of mechanisms to stimulate and enable evolutionary progress via variation and selection.

Visionary Companies	"A"	"B"	"C"	Index Score	Total Delta	Index Score	"A"	"B"	"C"	Comparison Companies
3M	H	H	H	9.00	5.00	4.00	L	M	L	Norton
American Express	H	M	M	7.00	2.00	5.00	M	M	L	Wells Fargo
Boeing	M	M	L	5.00	2.00	3.00	L	L	L	McDonnell Douglas
Citicorp	M	H	M	7.00	3.00	4.00	M	L	L	Chase Manhattan
Ford	M	M	M	6.00	0.00	6.00	M	M	M	GM
General Electric	M	M	M	6.00	1.00	5.00	M	M	L	Westinghouse
Hewlett-Packard	H	H	H	9.00	3.00	6.00	M	M	M	Texas Instruments
IBM	M	M	M	6.00	3.00	3.00	L	L	L	Burroughs
Johnson & Johnson	H	H	M	8.00	2.00	6.00	M	M	M	Bristol-Myers Squibb
Marriott	H	M	M	7.00	3.00	4.00	M	L	L	Howard Johnson
Merck	M	M	M	6.00	-2.00	8.00	H	H	M	Pfizer
Motorola	H	H	H	9.00	5.00	4.00	M	L	L	Zenith
Nordstrom	M	H	L	6.00	0.00	6.00	M	H	L	Melville
Philip Morris	M	M	L	5.00	1.00	4.00	M	L	L	RJR Nabisco
Procter & Gamble	M	M	L	5.00	1.00	4.00	M	L	L	Colgate
Sony	H	H	M	8.00	2.00	6.00	M	M	M	Kenwood
Wal-Mart	H	H	H	9.00	6.00	3.00	L	L	L	Ames
Walt Disney	M	L	M	5.00	1.00	4.00	M	L	L	Columbia
Frequency Counts										
No. of Hs	8	8	4				1	2	0	
No. of Ms	10	9	10				13	7	5	
No. of Ls	0	1	4				4	9	13	
Total	18	18	18				18	18	18	
VC > CC	10	12	10		15					
VC = CC	7	5	8		2					
VC < CC	1	1	0		1					
Total	18	18	18		18					

Table A.8
Evidence of Management Continuity

METHOD: In assessing management continuity in the visionary and comparison companies, we considered evidence along the following dimensions:

A: Internal Versus External Chief Executives
B: No "Post-Heroic-Leader Vacuum" or "Savior Syndrome"
C: Formal Management Development Programs and Mechanisms
D: Careful Succession Planning and CEO Selection Mechanisms.

In each category we gave each visionary and comparison company a rating *based on the evidence we had available*. We then calculated an overall index based on a summation of the company's ratings across these dimensions, scoring each "*H*" as a 3, each "*M*" as a 2, and each "*L*" as a 1.

A: Internal/External

H: Significant evidence that the company has a history of selecting chief executive officers only from inside.

M: Evidence that the company has a history of selecting chief executive officers primarily from inside, but one or two deviations from this rule.

L: Evidence that the company has deviated from the "inside only" rule more than two times.

B: No "Post-Heroic-Leader Vacuum" or "Savior Syndrome"

H: No evidence that the company has experienced a "Post-heroic-leader vacuum" (a dearth of highly qualified successors after the departure of a strong CEO) or the "Savior Syndrome" (looking to the outside in times of trouble to find a "savior" who will come in and revive the company).

M: Evidence that the company has experienced a "Post-heroic-leader vacuum" or the "Savior Syndrome" at least once in its history.

L: Evidence that the company has experienced a "Post-heroic-leader vacuum" or the "Savior Syndrome" at least twice in its history.

C: Management Development Mechanisms

H: Significant evidence that the company has a history of conscious attention to management development via internal management training programs, rotation programs, conscious use of on-the-job experiences to develop managers, exposure to top management issues and thinking, and so on.

M: Some evidence that the company has a history of conscious attention to management development but less prominent and/or less historically consistent conscious adoption than those that received an "*H*."

L: Little or no evidence that the company has a history of conscious attention to management development.

D: Succession Planning and CEO Selection Mechanisms

H: Significant evidence that the company has a history of careful succession planning and formal CEO selection mechanisms.

M: Some evidence that the company has a history of careful succession planning and formal CEO selection mechanisms, but less prominent and/or less historically consistent conscious adoption than those that received an "*H*."

L: Little or no evidence that the company has a history of careful succession planning and formal CEO selection mechanisms.

Visionary Companies	"A"	"B"	"C"	"D"	Index Score	Total Delta	Index Score	"A"	"B"	"C"	"D"	Comparison Companies
3M	H	H	M	H	11.00	3.00	8.00	M	H	L	M	Norton
American Express	H	M	M	M	9.00	3.00	6.00	L	M	M	L	Wells Fargo
Boeing	H	H	M	H	11.00	4.00	7.00	H	M	L	L	McDonnell Douglas
Citicorp	H	H	H	M	11.00	5.00	6.00	L	L	M	M	Chase Manhattan
Ford	H	M	M	M	9.00	0.00	9.00	M	M	H	M	GM
General Electric	H	H	H	H	12.00	5.00	7.00	L	M	M	M	Westinghouse
Hewlett-Packard	H	H	H	H	12.00	3.00	9.00	H	M	M	M	Texas Instruments
IBM	H	M	H	M	10.00	4.00	6.00	M	M	L	L	Burroughs
Johnson & Johnson	H	H	H	M	11.00	1.00	10.00	H	H	M	M	Bristol-Myers Squibb
Marriott	H	H	M	M	10.00	4.00	6.00	L	M	L	M	Howard Johnson
Merck	H	H	M	M	10.00	0.00	10.00	H	H	M	M	Pfizer
Motorola	H	H	H	H	12.00	7.00	5.00	M	L	L	L	Zenith
Nordstrom	H	H	M	H	11.00	2.00	9.00	H	M	M	M	Melville
Philip Morris	L	M	M	M	7.00	0.00	7.00	L	M	M	M	RJR Nabisco
Procter & Gamble	H	H	H	H	12.00	6.00	6.00	M	L	M	L	Colgate
Sony	H	H	M	M	10.00	2.00	8.00	M	M	M	M	Kenwood
Wal-Mart	H	H	M	M	10.00	5.00	5.00	M	L	L	L	Ames
Walt Disney	M	L	M	L	6.00	2.00	4.00	L	L	L	L	Columbia
Frequency Counts												
No. of Hs	16	13	7	7				5	3	1	0	
No. of Ms	1	4	11	10				7	10	10	11	
No. of Ls	1	1	0	1				6	5	7	7	
Total	18	18	18	18				18	18	18	18	
VC > CC	12	10	12	10		15						
VC = CC	6	8	5	8		3						
VC < CC	0	0	1	0		0						
Total	18	18	18	18		18						

Table A.8 Backup Data

CEO Statistics
1806–1992

Visionary Companies	No. of CEOs	Averge Tenure	No. of Outside CEOs	No. of Outside CEOs	Averge Tenure	No. of CEOs	Comparison Companies
3M	12	7.50	0	1	8.92	12	Norton
American Express	9	15.78	0	4	9.33	15	Wells Fargo
Boeing	8	9.63	0	0	14.40	5	McDonnell Douglas
Citicorp	20	9.00	0	4	11.50	10	Chase Manhattan
Ford	5	17.80	0	2	7.00	12	GM
General Electric	7	14.29	0	3	8.15	13	Westinghouse
Hewlett-Packard	3	18.00	0	0	7.75	8	Texas Instruments
IBM	6	13.50	0	1	10.00	10	Burroughs
Johnson & Johnson	7	15.14	0	0	21.00	5	Bristol-Myers Squibb
Marriott	2	32.50	0	3	13.40	5	Howard Johnson
Merck	5	20.20	0	0	13.00	11	Pfizer
Motorola	3	21.33	0	1	11.50	6	Zenith
Nordstrom	3	30.33	0	0	20.00	5	Melville
Philip Morris	12	12.08	3	3	8.36	14	RJR Nabisco
Procter & Gamble	9	17.22	0	1	16.91	11	Colgate
Sony	2	23.50	0	1	11.50	4	Kenwood
Wal-Mart	2	23.50	0	2	8.50	4	Ames
Walt Disney	6	11.50	1	5	9.00	8	Columbia
Averages	6.72	17.38			11.68	8.78	Averages
Totals	121		4	31		158	
No. of CEOs where we have internal versus external data	113					140	
% of Total no. external	3.54%					22.14%	

Table A.9

Performance Rankings of Chief Executive Eras
General Electric Company

Rank	GE Chief Executive Era	Average Annual Pretax Return on Equity[1]
1	Wilson, 1940–49	46.72%
2	Cordiner, 1950–63	40.49%
3	Jones, 1973–80	29.70%
4	Borch, 1964–72	27.52%
5	Welch, 1981–90[2]	26.29%
6	Coffin, 1915–1921[3]	14.52%
7	Swope/Young 1922–39[4]	12.63%

Rank	Average Annual Cumulative Stock Return Performance Relative to General Market[5]	Rank	Average Annual Cumulative Stock Return Performance Relative to Westinghouse[7]
1	Swope/Young 1929–39[6]	1	Cordiner, 1950–63
2	Welch, 1981–90[6]	2	Jones, 1973–80
3	Cordiner, 1950–63	3	Swope/Young, 1926–39
4	Borch, 1964–72	4	Wilson, 1940–49
5	Wilson, 1940–49	5	Welch, 1981–90[8]
6	Jones, 1973–80	6	Borch, 1964–72

Stock Return Raw Numbers:

Cumulative Stock Returns	No. of Years	GE at Start	GE at End	Market at Start	Market at End	Westinghouse at Start	Westinghouse at End
Swope/Young	13	$1.00	$2.93	$1.00	$1.69	$1.00	$2.83
Wilson	10	$2.93	$4.88	$1.69	$4.22	$2.83	$5.04
Cordiner	14	$4.88	$50.96	$4.22	$31.63	$5.04	$17.60
Borch	9	$50.96	$108.23	$31.63	$68.18	$17.60	$56.39
Jones	8	$108.23	$99.15	$68.18	$89.71	$56.39	$38.57
Welch	10	$99.15	$679.25	$89.71	$415.18	$38.57	$345.94

Notes to Table A.9

1. Calculated as pretax profit divided by year-end stockholder's equity.
2. Our return on equity database cuts off in 1990. However, using 1991 and 1992 annual reports, we found that the rank order does not change adding in these additional years. Welch ROE from 1980–1992 comes out at 26.83 percent. (For 1991 ROE, we excluded the change in accounting for postretirement benefits in our calculations.)
3. Return on equity database dates back only to 1915; Coffin was in office beginning in 1892.
4. Swope and Young operated as a chief executive team.
5. Calculated as the ratio of cumulative GE stock return during the CEO era divided by cumulative general market stock return during the GE CEO era.
6. Our stock return database runs from January 1926 through December 1990.
7. Calculated as the ratio of cumulative GE stock return during the CEO era divided by cumulative general market stock return or cumulative Westinghouse stock return during the GE CEO era.
8. Given Westinghouse's difficulties and GE's success in 1988–1993, we predict that GE under Welch will rise significantly on this dimension.

Table A.10
Evidence of Self-Improvement

METHOD: In assessing self-improvement in the visionary and comparison companies, we considered evidence along the following dimensions:

A: Long-Term Investments (PP&E, R&D, Earnings, Reinvestments)
B: Investment in Human Capabilities: Recruiting, Training, and Development
C: Early Adoption of New Technologies, Methods, Processes
D: Mechanisms to Stimulate Improvement.

In each category we gave each visionary and comparison company a rating *based on the evidence we had available*. We then calculated an overall index based on a summation of the company's ratings across these dimensions, scoring each "*H*" as a 3, each "*M*" as a 2, and each "*L*" as a 1.

A: Long-Term Investments

H: Significant evidence that the company has a history of reinvesting earnings for long-term growth, based on PP&E ratio as percentage of sales, R&D expenditures, and dividend payout ratios.

M: Some evidence that the company has a history of reinvesting earnings for long-term growth.

L: Evidence that the company has neglected investments for long-term growth.

B: Investment in Human Capabilities

H: Significant evidence that the company has a history of investment in employee recruiting, training, and professional development—even in downturns.

M: Some evidence that the company has a history of investment in employee recruiting, training, and professional development—even in downturns.

L: Little evidence that the company has a history of investment in employee recruiting, training, and professional development—even in downturns.

C: Early Adoption

H: Significant evidence that the company has a history of being an early adopter of, for example, new technologies, processes, or management methods.

M: Some evidence that the company has a history of being an early adopter of new technologies, processes, management methods.

L: Evidence that the company has a history of being a late adopter of new technologies, processes, management methods.

D: Mechanisms

H: Significant evidence that the company has a history of tangible "mechanisms of discomfort" that impel change and improvement from within before the external environment demands change and improvement.

M: Some evidence that the company has a history of tangible "mechanisms of discomfort" that impel change and improvement from within before the external environment demands change and improvement.

L: Little or no evidence that the company has a history of tangible "mechanisms of discomfort" that impel change and improvement from within before the external environment demands change and improvement.

Visionary Companies	"A"	"B"	"C"	"D"	Index Score	Total Delta	Index Score	"A"	"B"	"C"	"D"	Comparison Companies
3M	M	H	H	H	11.00	4.00	7.00	L	M	M	M	Norton
American Express	M	M	L	L	6.00	0.00	6.00	M	M	L	L	Wells Fargo
Boeing	M	M	H	H	10.00	3.00	7.00	M	L	M	M	McDonnell Douglas
Citicorp	M	H	H	M	10.00	4.00	6.00	M	M	L	L	Chase Manhattan
Ford	M	M	M	M	8.00	1.00	7.00	M	M	M	L	GM
General Electric	M	H	H	H	11.00	4.00	7.00	M	L	M	M	Westinghouse
Hewlett-Packard	H	H	M	H	11.00	2.00	9.00	M	M	H	M	Texas Instruments
IBM	H	H	M	L	9.00	4.00	5.00	M	L	L	L	Burroughs
Johnson & Johnson	M	M	H	M	9.00	2.00	7.00	M	L	M	M	Bristol-Myers Squibb
Marriott	H	H	M	H	11.00	4.00	7.00	M	L	M	M	Howard Johnson
Merck	H	H	M	H	11.00	3.00	8.00	M	M	M	M	Pfizer
Motorola	M	H	H	H	11.00	6.00	5.00	L	L	L	M	Zenith
Nordstrom	H	M	M	H	10.00	2.00	8.00	M	M	M	M	Melville
Philip Morris	M	M	M	M	8.00	3.00	5.00	L	M	L	L	RJR Nabisco
Procter & Gamble	M	H	H	H	11.00	5.00	6.00	L	M	M	L	Colgate
Sony	M	M	M	M	8.00	0.00	8.00	M	M	M	M	Kenwood
Wal-Mart	M	M	H	H	10.00	5.00	5.00	M	L	L	L	Ames
Walt Disney	H	H	H	L	10.00	6.00	4.00	L	L	L	L	Columbia
Frequency Counts												
No. of Hs	6	10	9	10				0	0	1	0	
No. of Ms	12	8	8	5				13	10	10	10	
No. of Ls	0	0	1	3				5	8	7	8	
Total	18	18	18	18				18	18	18	18	
VC > CC	10	13	11	13		16						
VC = CC	8	5	6	5		2						
VC < CC	0	0	1	0		0						
Total	18	18	18	18		18						

Table A.10 Backup Data

Average Annual Increase in Gross PP&E as Percentage of Sales

Pair	Visionary Company	Comparison Company	Years Compared
3M/Norton	3.50%	1.44%	1961–1986
American Express/Wells Fargo	NA	NA	NA
Boeing/McDonnell Douglas	.70%	11.84%	1967–1986
Citicorp/Chase Manhattan	NA	NA	NA
Ford/General Motors	2.19%	1.80%	1950–1986
General Electric/Westinghouse	1.23%	1.43%	1915–1987
Hewlett-Packard/Texas Instruments	4.13%	2.89%	1957–1990
IBM/Burroughs	8.03%	3.28%	1934–1988
Johnson & Johnson/Bristol-Myers	2.38%	2.23%	1943–1988
Marriott/Howard Johnson	9.29%	4.20%	1960–1978
Merck/Pfizer	3.59%	3.54%	1941–1990
Motorola/Zenith	2.66%	.72%	1942–1990
Nordstrom/Melville	5.03%	1.23%	1971–1988
Philip Morris/R.J. Reynolds	2.11%	1.13%	1937–1990
Procter & Gamble/Colgate	2.32%	1.15%	1928–1988
Sony/Kenwood	NA	NA	NA
Wal-Mart/Ames	2.53%	2.33%	1970–1989
Walt Disney/Columbia	7.00%	.34%	1939–1980

Table A.10 Backup Data
Average Annual Dividend Payout Ratio

Pair	Visionary Company	Comparison Company	Years Compared
3M/Norton	.50	.50	1961–1986
American Express/Wells Fargo	NA	NA	NA
Boeing/McDonnell Douglas	.27	.17	1967–1986
Citicorp/Chase Manhattan	.40	.47	1954–1989
Ford/General Motors	.36	.65	1950–1986
General Electric/Westinghouse	.65	.51	1915–1987
Hewlett-Packard/Texas Instruments	.10	.23	1957–1990
IBM/Burroughs	.50	.64	1934–1988
Johnson & Johnson/Bristol-Myers	.32	.52	1943–1988
Marriott/Howard Johnson	.20	.27	1960–1978
Merck/Pfizer	.55	.47	1941–1990
Motorola/Zenith	.32	.52	1942–1990
Nordstrom/Melville	.15	.34	1971–1988
Philip Morris/R.J. Reynolds	.54	.63	1937–1990
Procter & Gamble/Colgate	.79	.70	1926–1988
Sony/Kenwood	NA	NA	NA
Wal-Mart/Ames	.10	.12	1970–1989
Walt Disney/Columbia	.06	.27	1950–1980

appendix 4 | CHAPTER NOTES

CHAPTER 1

1. Author interview, November 19, 1990.
2. "The Character of Procter & Gamble," text of speech by John G. Smale, November 7, 1986.
3. We used the Center for Research in Securities Market Index Database (CRSP) as the source of our stock return data. The "general-market" portfolio consists of the weighted average (based on market value) of all stocks traded on the NYSE beginning in 1926, AMEX beginning in 1962, and NASDAQ beginning in 1972. Analysis does not include Nordstrom versus Melville and Sony versus Kenwood (data not available in CRSP), which would have improved the performance of the visionary companies. We were faced with a decision about how to handle Texas Instruments, which merged with Intercontinental Rubber Company in 1953. To maintain consistency across the data source, we elected to use the CRSP data directly—since this is what we did in all of our other companies in the analysis. However, to ensure that TI would not unduly skew the data, we also calculated the returns using TI data only after the 1953 merger. This produced a comparison total of $1,024, thus not dramatically changing the overall result; the visionary companies still outperformed the comparison companies by over six times.
4. We used descriptive statistics, histograms, confidence intervals, and t-tests. We examined:

  - Population versus returns. Expected returns based on: (number of companies headquartered in each state in the population) times (total number of returns)/(total population), as compared to actual returns.

- Population versus sample. Expected sample based on: (number of companies headquartered in each state in the population) times (total sample/total population), as compared to actual sample by state.
- Sample versus returns. Expected returns based on: (number of companies headquartered in each state) times (total number returned)/(total sample), as compared to actual returns by state.
- In all three of the preceding cases, the difference scores proved not significantly different from zero.

5. *Fortune* 500 industrial: 23 percent; *Fortune* 500 service: 23 percent; *Inc.* 500 private: 27 percent; *Inc.* 100 public: 25 percent.
6. Darwin didn't see the tortoises and *immediately* have the flash of insight that led to his theory of evolution (in fact, he left the Galapagos still a creationist). But the tortoises (and other variations in species) that didn't fit neatly into prior assumptions about species planted a tiny seed of doubt and discontent, which later germinated in his evolutionary theory of variation and natural selection. (See Stephen J. Gould's book *The Flamingo's Smile*, "Darwin at Sea," Norton, 1985.)
7. Jerry I. Porras, *Stream Analysis—A Powerful Way to Diagnose and Manage Organizational Change* (Reading, MA: Addison-Wesley, 1987).

CHAPTER 2

1. Schickel, Richard, *The Disney Version* (New York: Simon & Schuster, 1968), 44, 363.
2. Sam Walton with John Huey, *Sam Walton: Made in America* (New York: Doubleday, 1992), 234.
3. The original inspiration for this analogy came from a lecture series on intellectual history and the Newtonian Revolution entitled *The Origin of the Modern Mind*, taught by Alan Charles Kors, Professor of History, University of Pennsylvania, and captured on audiotape as part of the Superstar Teacher Series from the Teaching Company, Washington, D.C.
4. Hewlett-Packard Company Archives, "An Interview with Bill Hewlett," 1987, 4.
5. "Research Packed with Ph.Ds," *Business Week*, 22 December 1956, p. 58.
6. John McDonald, "The Men Who Made T.I.," *Fortune*, November 1961, 118.
7. Akio Morita, *Made in Japan* (New York: Dutton, 1986), 44–57.
8. Nick Lyons, *The Sony Vision* (New York: Crown, 1976), 4–5.
9. Akio Morita, *Made in Japan* (New York: Dutton, 1986), 44–57.
10. *Japan Electronics Almanac*, 1988, 282.
11. Vance Trimble, *Sam Walton* (New York: Dutton, 1990), 121.
12. Sam Walton with John Huey, *Sam Walton: Made in America* (New York: Doubleday, 1992), 35.
13. *Hoover's Handbook of Corporations*, 1991.
14. Vance Trimble, *Sam Walton* (New York: Dutton, 1990), 102–104.
15. Ibid., 121–122.

16. Robert O'Brien, *Marriott: The J Willard Marriott Story* (Salt Lake City: Deseret, 1987).

17. John W. Nordstrom, *The Immigrant in 1887* (Seattle: Dogwood Press, 1950), 44–50; "Nordstrom History," company publication, 26 November 1990.

18. *Values and Visions: A Merck Century* (Rahway, NJ: Merck, 1993), 13–15.

19. "Procter & Gamble Chronology," company publication; Oscar Schisgall, *Eyes on Tomorrow: The Evolution of Procter & Gamble* (New York: Doubleday, 1981), 1–14; Alfred Lief, *It Floats: The Story of Procter & Gamble* (New York: Rinehart, 1958), 14–32.

20. Harry Mark Petrakis, *The Founder's Touch* (New York: McGraw-Hill, 1965), 62–63.

21. *The Philip Morris History*, company publication, 1988.

22. *Our Story So Far* (St. Paul, MN: 3M Company, 1977), 51.

23. Charles W. Cheape, *Norton Company: a New England Enterprise* (Cambridge, MA: Harvard University Press, 1985), 12.

24. Robert J. Serling, *Legend and Legacy* (New York: St. Martin's Press, 1992), 2–6.

25. "Take off for the Business Jet," *Business Week*, 28 September 1963.

26. René J. Francillon, *McDonnell Douglas Aircraft Since 1920*, (Annapolis, MD: Naval Institute Press, 1988), 1–12.

27. Richard Schickel, *The Disney Version* (New York: Simon & Schuster, 1968), 106–107.

28. Clive Hirschhorn, *The Columbia Story* (New York: Crown, 1989), 7–16.

29. Grover and Lagai, *Development of American Industries*, 4th Edition, 1959, 491.

30. Robert Lacey, *Ford: The Men and the Machine* (New York: Ballantine Books, 1986), 47–110.

31. *Centennial Review*, Internal Westinghouse Document, 1986.

32. Ibid.

33. Leonard S. Reich, *The Making of American Industrial Research: Science and Business at GE and Bell, 1876–1926* (Cambridge: Cambridge University Press, 1985), 69–71. (*Author's note:* We cannot verify that GE's lab was definitely America's first, but we do know that it preceded Bell Labs, one of the other early labs, by a full twenty-five years.)

34. Bill Hewlett internal speech, 1956. Courtesy Hewlett-Packard Company Archives.

35. Dave Packard, "Industry's New Challenge: The Management of Creativity," Western Electronic Manufacturers' Association, San Diego, 23 September 1964, Courtesy Hewlett-Packard Company Archives.

36. "Hewlett-Packard Chairman Built Company by Design, Calculator by Chance," *The AMBA Executive*, September 1977, 6–7.

37. Harry Mark Petrakis, *The Founder's Touch* (New York: McGraw-Hill, 1965), x–63.

38. Oscar Schisgall, *Eyes on Tomorrow: The Evolution of Procter & Gamble* (New York: Doubleday, 1981), xii.

39. "National Business Hall of Fame Roster of Past Laureates," *Fortune*, 5 April 1993, 116.

40. *Hoover's Handbook, 1991,* 381.
41. *Our Story So Far* (St. Paul, MN: 3M Company, 1977), 59.
42. Mildred Houghton Comfort, *William L. McKnight, Industrialist* (Minneapolis: T. S. Denison, 1962), 35, 45, 182, 194, 201.
43. Akio Morita, *Made in Japan* (New York: Dutton, 1986), 147.
44. Oscar Schisgall, *Eyes on Tomorrow: The Evolution of Procter & Gamble* (New York: Doubleday, 1981), 1–15.
45. Robert J. Serling, *Legend and Legacy: The Story of Boeing and Its People* (New York: St. Martin's Press, 1992), 70.
46. *Values and Visions: A Merck Century* (Rahway, NJ: Merck, 1993), 12.
47. Camille B. Wortman and Elizabeth F. Loftus, *Psychology* (New York: McGraw-Hill, 1992), 385–418.
48. Harold van B. Cleveland and Thomas F. Huertas, *Citibank 1812–1970* (Cambridge, MA: Harvard Universtity Press, 1985), 32.
49. *Citibank, 1812–1970,* 301.
50. Harold van B. Cleveland and Thomas F. Huertas, *Citibank 1812–1970* (Cambridge, MA: Harvard Universtity Press, 1985), 41, 301; and John Donald Wilson, *The Chase* (Boston: Harvard Business School Press, 1986), 25.
51. *Citibank, 1812–1970,* 54.
52. Anna Robeson Burr, *Portrait of a Banker: James Stillman, 1850–1918* (New York: Duffield, 1927), 249.
53. "Wiggin Is the Chase Bank and the Chase Bank Is Wiggin," *Business Week,* April 30, 1930.
54. Vance Trimble, *Sam Walton* (New York: Dutton, 1990), see pp. 1–45 for a good account of Walton's early life.
55. Sam Walton with John Huey, *Sam Walton: Made in America* (New York: Doubleday, 1992), 78–79.
56. "America's Most Successful Merchant," *Fortune,* 23 September 1991.
57. Much of the detail in this section comes from: Sam Walton with John Huey, *Made in America* (New York: Doubleday, 1992), 225–232.
58. Vance H. Trimble, *Sam Walton* (New York: Dutton, 1990), 274.
59. Sam Walton with John Huey, *Made in America* (New York: Doubleday, 1992), 225.
60. Vance Trimble, *Sam Walton* (New York: Dutton, 1990), 121.
61. "Industry Overview," *Discount Merchandiser,* June 1977.
62. "Gremlins are Eating up the Profits at Ames," *Business Week,* 19 October 1987.
63. "David Glass Won't Crack Under Fire," *Fortune,* 8 February 1993, 80.
64. "Pistner discusses Ames Strategy," *Discount Merchandiser,* July 1990.
65. "James Harmon's Two Hats," *Forbes,* May 28, 1990.
66. Goals for the year 2000 from a letter we received from a Wal-Mart director in 1991. See our chapter on vision for more details.
67. Harry Mark Petrakis, *The Founder's Touch* (New York: McGraw-Hill, 1965), 49, 61.
68. Ibid., 69, 88.
69. Ibid., 114–15.

70. Ibid., p. xi.
71. Robert W. Galvin, *The Idea of Ideas* (Schaumburg, IL: Motorola University Press, 1991), 45, 65.
72. "Zenith Bucks the Trend," *Fortune*, December 1960.
73. "At the Zenith and on the Spot," *Forbes*, September 1, 1961.
74. "Zenith Bucks the Trend," *Fortune*, December 1960; "Irrepressible Gene McDonald," *Reader's Digest*, July 1944; and "Commander McDonald of Zenith," *Fortune*, June 1945.
75. *International Directory of Corporate Histories* (Chicago: St. James Press, 1988), 123.
76. Zenith Bucks the Trend," *Fortune*, December 1960.
77. Ibid.
78. Galvin died in November of 1959; McDonald died in May of 1958.
79. *International Directory of Company Histories* (Chicago: St. James Press, 1988), Volume 2, 135.
80. *International Directory of Company Histories* (Chicago: St. James Press, 1988), Volume 2, 135.
81. Clive Hirschhorn, *The Columbia Story* (New York: Crown, 1989).
82. Schickel, Richard, *The Disney Version* (New York: Simon & Schuster, 1968), 362.
83. *The Disney Studio Story* (Hollywood: Walt Disney, 1987), 18.
84. *The Disney Studio Story* (Hollywood: Walt Disney, 1987); and Schickel, Richard, *The Disney Version* (New York: Simon & Schuster, 1968), 180.
85. *The Disney Studio Story* (Hollywood: Walt Disney, 1987), 42.
86. *Personnel*, December 1989, 53.
87. John Taylor, *Storming the Magic Kingdom* (New York: Ballantine Books, 1987), 14.
88. Ibid., p. viii.
89. We have paraphrased from the lecture series "The Origin of the Modern Mind," by Alan Charles Kors, Professor of History, University of Pennsylvania, for this paragraph.
90. For the best coverage of the theory of evolution, we suggest *Biology*, by Norman K. Wessells and Janet L. Hopson (New York: Random House, 1988), chapters 9–15, 19, 41–43.
91. For an excellent description of the personalities and processes of the constitutional convention see *Miracle at Philadelphia—The Story of the Constitutional Convention: May to September, 1787*, by Catherine Drinker Bowen (Boston: Little, Brown, 1966).

INTERLUDE

1. F. Scott Fitzgerald, *The Crack-up* (1936).

CHAPTER 3

1. Author interview, 17 April 1992.
2. Merck & Company, Management Guide, Corporate Policy Statement, February 3, 1989, courtesy Merck & Company.
3. Written personally by Don Petersen atop this chapter when he reviewed our manuscript, January 1994.
4. George W. Merck, "An Essential Partnership—The Chemical Industry and Medicine," speech presented to the Division of Medicinal Chemistry, American Chemical Society, 22 April 1935.
5. Merck & Company, 1991 Annual Report, Inside Cover.
6. David Bollier and Kirk O. Hansen, *Merk & Co. (A–D)*, Business Enterprise Trust Case, No. 90-013.
7. David Bollier and Kirk O. Hansen, *Merk & Co. (A–D)*, Business Enterprise Trust Case, No. 90-013, case D, 3.
8. George W. Merck, Speech at the Medical College of Virginia at Richmond, December 1, 1950, courtesy Merck & Company historical archives.
9. "Chas Pfizer: Successful Upstart," *Forbes*, 15 December 1962.
10. Akio Morita, *Made in Japan* (New York: Dutton, 1986), 43–44.
11. There is some debate as to the exact translation of the prospectus from Japanese into English. We have relied on two sources to capture the essence of this part of the prospectus: Nick Lyons's book, *The Sony Vision* (New York: Crown, 1976), 1–18; and a translation by one of our Japanese students, Tsuneto Ikeda, to whom we are grateful for his perspective on the document.
12. Nick Lyons, *The Sony Vision* (New York: Crown, 1976), 10.
13. Akio Morita, *Made in Japan* (New York: Dutton, 1986), 147–148.
14. Ibid., 79.
15. Ranganath Nayak and John M. Ketteringham, *Break-throughs!* (New York: Rawson Associates, 1986), 130–150; and Nick Lyons, *The Sony Vision* (New York: Crown, 1976), xv–xvii.
16. Robert L. Shook, *Turnaround: The New Ford Motor Company* (New York: Prentice-Hall, 1990), 94.
17. Robert L. Shook, *Turnaround: The New Ford Motor Company* (New York: Prentice-Hall, 1990), 96.
18. Detroit News, November 14, 1916, cited in Lacey, 179.
19. Robert Lacey, *Ford—The Men and the Machine* (New York: Ballantine Books, 1986), 179.
20. Ibid., 128.
21. Ibid., 129.
22. Peter F. Drucker, *Concept of the Corporation* (New York: John Day, 1972), 305–307.
23. Peter F. Drucker, *Management: Tasks, Responsibilities, Practices* (New York: Harper & Row, 1985), 808.
24. David Packard, speech given to HP's training group on 8 March 1960, courtesy of Hewlett-Packard Company archives.

25. David Packard, "A Management Code of Ethics," speech presented to the American Management Association, San Francisco, CA, 24 January 1958, courtesy Hewlett-Packard Company archives.
26. Ibid.
27. Watt's Current, internal employee newsletter, *From Our President's Desk*, November 1961, courtesy Hewlett-Packard Company archives.
28. Dave Packard, "Objectives of the Hewlett-Packard Company," January 1957; courtesy Hewlett-Packard Company archives.
29. Author interview with John Young, 17 April 1992.
30. John McDonald, "The Men Who Made TI," *Fortune*, November 1961, 123.
31. "Running Things With a Slide Rule," *Business Week*, 27 April 1968.
32. "The Men Who Made T.I.," *Fortune*, November 1961.
33. "Running Things With a Slide Rule," *Business Week*, 27 April 1968.
34. "Texas Instruments: Pushing Hard into Consumer Markets," *Business Week*, 24 August 1974.
35. "Japanese Heat on the Watch Industry," *Business Week*, 5 May 1980.
36. Internal HP Speech by David Packard emphasizing to division managers the importance of thinking in terms of contribution, *not* in terms of market share or size, courtesy of Hewlett-Packard Company archives.
37. "How TI Beat the clock on its $20 digital watch," *Business Week*, 31 May 1976; "Japanese Heat on the Watch Industry," *Business Week*, 5 May 1980; HP internal archives speech by David Packard, February 11, 1974; Interview with John Young, April 1992.
38. Lawrence G. Foster, *A Company that Cares* (New Brunswick, NJ: Johnson & Johnson, 1986), 17.
39. Ibid., 64–67.
40. Ibid., 65.
41. R. W. Johnson, Jr., *Try Reality*, a pamphlet he wrote in 1935.
42. Lawrence G. Foster, *A Company that Cares* (New Brunswick, NJ: Johnson & Johnson, 1986), 108–109.
43. Francis J. Aguilar and Arvind Bhambri, "Johnson & Johnson (A)," Harvard Business School Case No. 384-053, 4.
44. Warren Bennis, *On Becoming a Leader* (Reading, MA: Addison-Wesley, 1989), 192.
45. Francis J. Aguilar and Arvind Bhambri, "Johnson & Johnson (A)," Harvard Business School Case No. 384-053, 3.
46. Francis J. Aguilar and Arvind Bhambri, "Johnson & Johnson (A)," Harvard Business School Case No. 384-053.
47. Ibid., 5.
48. "Bristol-Meyers Prescription for Profits," *Dun's Business Month*, December 1982.
49. See E. E. Tauber, *Boeing in Peace and War* (Enumaclaw, WA: TABA, 1991); Robert J. Serling, *Legend and Legacy: The Story of Boeing and Its People* (New York: St. Martin's Press, 1992); Harold Mansfield, *Vision* (New York: Popular Press, 1966).

50. From "Gamble in the Sky," *Time*, 19 July 1954, and "Accelerating the Jet Age," *Nation's Business*, August 1967.

51. Robert J. Serling, *Legend and Legacy: The Story of Boeing and Its People* (New York: St. Martin's Press, 1992), 285.

52. Harry Mark Petrakis, *The Founder's Touch* (New York: McGraw-Hill, 1965), 134, 153.

53. Ibid., 111.

54. Robert W. Galvin, *The Idea of Ideas* (Schaumburg, IL: Motorola University Press, 1991).

55. "For Which We Stand—A Statement of Purpose, Principles, and Ethics," Motorola Internal Publication, 1988.

56. Robert O'Brien, *Marriott: The J Willard Marriott Story* (Salt Lake City: Deseret, 1987), 324.

57. Ibid., 320.

58. "Staying Power," *Vis a Vis*, February 1981, 60.

59. Robert O'Brien, *Marriott: The J Willard Marriott Story* (Salt Lake City: Deseret, 1987), 256.

60. "Money, Talent, and the Devil by the Tail: J. Willard Marriott," *Management Review*, January 1985.

61. Ibid.

62. Marriott 1988 Annual Report, 3.

63. "Howard Johnson Tries a Little Harder," *Business Week*, 29 September 1973; "HoJos will Repaint its Roofs," *Business Week*, 13 December 1982; "How a Great American Franchise Lost its Way," *Forbes*, 30 December 1985; "The Sad Case of the Dwindling Orange Roofs," *Forbes*, 3 December 1985.

64. "HoJos will Repaint its Roofs," *Business Week*, 13 December 1982; "How a Great American Franchise Lost its Way," *Forbes*, 30 December 1985.

65. Interview with Ross Millhauser, *New York Times*, 25 January 1979, D1.

66. "Voyage into the Unknown," *Forbes*, 1 December 1971, 41.

67. *Fortune*, 8 May 1989.

68. Discussion with the authors at a conference at Stanford University, October 1991.

69. "Philip Morris: Unconventional Wisdom," *Forbes*, 1 January 1971.

70. "How Philip Morris Diversified Right," *Fortune*, 23 October 1989.

71. "Can He Keep Philip Morris Growing," *Fortune*, 6 April 1992.

72. "How Philip Morris Diversified Right," *Fortune*, 23 October 1989.

73. Prior to the early 1950s, Philip Morris appears to not have had much of a coherent ideology; this discussion relates to the mid-1950s on. Philip Morris is the only visionary company in our study in which the ideology doesn't appear until relatively late in the company's history.

74. Mildred Houghton Comfort, *William L. McKnight, Industrialist* (Minneapolis: T. S. Denison, 1962); Virginia Huck, *Brand of the Tartan—The 3M Story* (New York: Appleton-Century-Crofts, 1955); *Our Story So Far* (St. Paul, MN: 3M Company, 1977); various historical business articles; "Getting to Know Us," 3M publication.

75. Alden Hatch, *American Express 1850–1950: A Century of Service* (Garden City, NY: Country Life Press, 1950); Jon Friedman and John Meechan, *House of Cards: Inside the Troubled Empire of American Express* (New York: Putnam, 1992); "Eight Principles: Lou Gerstner Discusses the Staying Power of Corporate Philosophy," *TRS Express* (American Express Publication), December 1987; Peter Grossman, *American Express: The Unofficial History.*

76. E. E. Tauber, *Boeing in Peace and War* (Enumaclaw, WA: TABA, 1991), Robert J. Serling, *Legend and Legacy* (New York: St. Martin's Press, 1992); Harold Mansfield, *Vision* (New York: Popular Press, 1966); Boeing statement of mission and values, courtesy Boeing Corporation; "Accelerating the Jet Age," *Nation's Business*, August 1967.

77. Harold van B. Cleveland and Thomas F. Huertas, *Citibank 1812–1970* (Cambridge, MA: Harvard Universtity Press, 1985); Richard B. Miller, *Citicorp: The Story of a Bank in Crisis* (New York: McGraw-Hill, 1993); Robert B. Levering, *The 100 Best Companies to Work for in America* (New York: New American Library, 1984), 43; "Our Future" and "Ethical Choices," internal Citicorp publications.

78. Henry Ford, II, *The Human Environment and Business* (New York: Weybright & Talley, 1970); Robert L. Shook, *Turnaround: The New Ford Motor Company* (New York: Prentice-Hall, 1990); Anne Jardin, *The First Henry Ford* (Colonial Press, 1970); Robert Lacey, *Ford—The Men and the Machine* (New York: Ballantine Books, 1986); *American Legend* and *This is the Ford Motor Company*, Ford corporate publications; *Ford at Fifty* (New York: Simon & Schuster, 1953).

79. Ronald G. Greenwood, *Managerial Decentralization: A Study of the General Electric Philosophy* (Lexington, MA: Lexington Books, 1974); Robert Conot, *Thomas A. Edison—A Streak of Luck* (New York: Da Capo Press, 1979); *The General Electric Story* (Schenectady, NY: Hall of History Foundation, 1981), volumes 1 & 2; Noel M. Tichy and Stratford Sherman, *Control Your Destiny or Someone Else Will* (New York: Doubleday Currency, 1993); "1956 Statement of GE's Company Objectives," courtesy General Electric Company.

80. "Objectives of the Hewlett-Packard Company," January 1957, courtesy Hewlett-Packard Company archives; Interviews with William Hewlett and John Young; various internal publications.

81. Thomas J. Watson, Jr., *Father, Son, & Company* (New York: Bantam Books, 1990), 302; Thomas J. Watson, Jr., *A Business and Its Beliefs* (New York: McGraw-Hill, 1963); "IBM Yesterday and Today," corporate publication; Lou Mobley and Kate McKeown, "Beyond IBM; IBM 75th Anniversary," *Think*, September 1989.

82. "Our Credo," courtesy of Johnson & Johnson Company; Francis J. Aguilar and Arvind Bhambri, "Johnson & Johnson (B)," Harvard Business School Case No. 384-054; James E. Burke, letter "One Hundred Years," published in *A Company that Cares* (New Brunswick, NJ: Johnson & Johnson, 1986), 163; various articles and internal company newsletters.

83. Robert O'Brien, *Marriott: The J Willard Marriott Story* (Salt Lake City: Deseret, 1987); Marriott 1988 Annual Report; various articles.

84. Merck & Company, "Statement of Corporate Objectives," courtesy Merck & Company; Merck Century Celebration Videos, courtesy Merck & Company; *Values and Visions: A Merck Century* (Rahway, NJ: Merck, 1993); various articles and documents from Merck archives.

85. *For Which We Stand—A Statement of Purpose, Principles, and Ethics*, Motorola internal publication, 1988; Robert W. Galvin, *The Idea of Ideas* (Schaumburg, IL: Motorola University Press, 1991); Harry Mark Petrakis, *The Founder's Touch* (New York: McGraw-Hill, 1965); various articles.

86. Drawn from "Nordstrom History," company publication, talk by Bruce Nordstrom at Stanford Business School, 1991; various articles.

87. (Note: Prior to the early 1950s, Philip Morris appears not to have much of a coherent ideology; this list relates to the mid-1950s on.) *Sources:* "How Philip Morris Diversified Right," *Fortune*, 23 October 1989; "Voyage into the Unknown," *Forbes*, 1 December 1971; "Philip Morris: Unconventional Wisdom," *Forbes*, 1 January 1971; "Can He Keep; Philip Morris Growing," *Fortune*, 6 April 1992; Interview with Ross Millhauser, *New York Times*, 25 January 1979, D1; "The Two Tier Market Still Lives," *Forbes*, 1 March 1974; "A Machine That Will Sell Anything," *Business Week*, 4 March 1967.

88. "Facts about Procter & Gamble," company publication, 1988, 6; Oscar Schisgall, *Eyes on Tomorrow: The Evolution of Procter & Gamble* (New York: Doubleday, 1981); *It Floats: The Story of Procter & Gamble* (New York: Rinehart, 1958).

89. Akio Morita, *Made in Japan* (New York: Dutton, 1986), especially pages 147–48; Nick Lyons, *The Sony Vision* (New York: Crown, 1976), Chapter 1; *Genryu— Sony Challenge 1946–1968*, special collection of Sony Management Newsletters, 40th anniversary edition (Tokyo: Sony, 1986).

90. Sam Walton with John Huey, *Sam Walton: Made in America* (New York: Doubleday, 1992); Vance Trimble, *Sam Walton* (New York: Dutton, 1990); company interviews.

91. "The Wonderful Worlds of Walt Disney," company publication, 1966; Schickel, Richard, *The Disney Version* (New York: Simon & Schuster, 1968); John Taylor, *Storming the Magic Kingdom* (New York: Ballantine Books, 1987); Disney University Employee Brochure and Course Offerings; from *In Search of Excellence Video* on Disney, the Tom Peters Group, Palo Alto, CA; Joe Fowler, *Prince of the Magic Kingdom: Michael Eisner and the Re-Making of Disney* (New York: Wiley, 1991); Marc Eliot, *Walt Disney: Hollywood's Dark Prince* (New York: Birch Lane Press, 1993); author interviews.

92. Robert B. Cialdini, *Influence* (New York: Quill, 1984); Philip G. Zimbardo and Michael R. Leippe, *The Psychology of Attitude Change and Social Influence* (New York: McGraw-Hill, 1991).

93. Memo from John F. Welch to GE corporate officers, October 4, 1991.

94. "Feisty P&G Profile," *Publishers Weekly*, 2 August 1993.

95. Francis J. Aguilar and Arvind Bhambri, "Johnson & Johnson (A)," Harvard Business School Case No. 384–053, 5.

96. Thomas J. Watson, Jr., *A Business and Its Beliefs* (New York: Columbia University Press, 1963), 5–6, 72–73.

97. Sam Walton with John Huey, *Sam Walton: Made in America* (New York: Doubleday, 1992), 183, 233.
98. "Memorable Years in P&G History," company publication, 7.
99. Author interview with John Young, 17 April 1992.
100. Thomas J. Watson, Jr., *A Business and Its Beliefs* (New York: Columbia University Press, 1963), 12–13.
101. David Packard, commencement speech, Colorado College, June 1, 1964, courtesy Hewlett-Packard Company archives.
102. *Values and Visions: A Merck Century* (Rahway, NJ: Merck, 1993), 173.
103. "Disney's Philosophy," *New York Times Magazine*, 6 March 1938; Richard Schickel, *The Disney Version* (New York: Simon & Schuster, 1968); Walt Disney, speech about the opening of Disneyland, 18 July 1955; John Taylor, *Storming the Magic Kingdom* (New York: Ballantine Books, 1987); Christopher Finch, *Walt Disney's America* (New York: Abbeville Press, 1978).
104. Formal/Explicit: H-P, J&J, Merck, Motorola, Sony, Walt Disney; Implicit/Informal: 3M, Boeing, Ford, GE, Marriott, Philip Morris, Wal-Mart.
105. Lawrence G. Foster, *A Company that Cares* (New Brunswick, NJ: Johnson & Johnson, 1986), 17.

CHAPTER 4

1. Paraphrased from Robert W. Galvin, *The Idea of Ideas* (Schaumburg, IL: Motorola University Press, 1991), 16–34.
2. Oscar Schisgall, *Eyes on Tomorrow: The Evolution of Procter & Gamble* (New York: Doubleday, 1981), 269.
3. Sam Walton with John Huey, *Sam Walton: Made in America* (New York: Doubleday, 1992), 249.
4. Thomas J. Watson, Jr., *A Business and Its Beliefs* (New York: McGraw-Hill, 1963), 5–6, 72–73.
5. Robert O'Brien, *Marriott: The J Willard Marriott Story* (Salt Lake City: Deseret, 1987), 307, 326.
6. Robert W. Galvin, *The Idea of Ideas* (Schaumburg, IL: Motorola University Press, 1991), 165–166.
7. Bronze plaque on the wall of Boeing corporate headquarters.
8. Jottings in Henry Ford's notebooks. From the Ford Archives of the Edison Institute, cited in Robert Lacey, *Ford: The Men and the Machine* (New York: Ballantine Books, 1986), 141.
9. "Nordstrom Gets the Cold," *Stores*, January 1990.
10. One of the authors worked directly with this marketing manager at Hewlett-Packard.

CHAPTER 5

1. *Bartlett's Familiar Quotations*, Fifteenth Edition, 686.
2. Tsueneto Ikeda, "*Masaru Ibuka*," unpublished research paper, Stanford University Graduate School of Business, November 1992.
3. Schickel, Richard, *The Disney Version* (New York: Simon & Schuster, 1968), 171.
4. "How Boeing Bet the Company and Won," *Audacity*, Winter 1993.
5. Robert J. Serling, *Legend and Legacy: The Story of Boeing and Its People* (New York: St. Martin's Press, 1992), 72–79.
6. According to "How Boeing Bet the Company and Won" in *Audacity* and Serling (page 122), the project would cost between $15 million and $16 million. We then went back and compared the $15 million figure with Boeing's income statements and balance sheets for the period 1947–1951.
7. "How Boeing Bet the Company and Won," *Audacity*, Winter 1993.
8. H. Ingells, *The McDonnell Douglas Story*, 121.
9. "Zooming Airlines Grab for New Jets," *Business Week*, 22 May 1964.
10. Robert J. Serling, *Legend and Legacy: The Story of Boeing and its People* (New York: St. Martin's Press, 1992), 31.
11. Ibid., 180–192.
12. Ibid., 285–290.
13. Daniel J. Boorstin, *The Americans: The Democratic Experience* (New York: Vintage Books, 1974), 593–597.
14. Ibid., 596.
15. Noel M. Tichy and Stratford Sherman, *Control Your Destiny or Someone Else Will* (New York: Doubleday Currency, 1993), 245–246.
16. Robert Slater, *The New GE* (Homewood, IL: Richard D. Irwin, 1993), 77–93.
17. Ibid., 77–93.
18. Westinghouse 1989 Annual Report.
19. "Reynolds Gets a Bang out of the Cigarette Brand Explosion," *Fortune*, October 1976.
20. "Bad News Can Mean Good Growth," *Forbes*, 15 November 1968
21. Daniel J. Boorstin, *The Americans: The Democratic Experience* (New York: Vintage Books, 1974), 548.
22. Robert Lacey, *Ford: The Men and the Machine* (New York: Ballantine Books, 1986), 89–100.
23. Ibid., 89–100.
24. *Genryu—Sony Challenge 1946–1968*, special collection of Sony Management Newsletters, 40th anniversary edition (Tokyo: Sony, 1986), 131.
25. Akio Morita, *Made in Japan* (New York: Dutton, 1986), 74.
26. For good overall coverage of these events, read Akio Morita, *Made in Japan*, *Genryu—Sony Challenge 1946–1968*, and *The Sony Vision*.
27. Akio Morita, *Made in Japan* (New York: Dutton, 1986), 66–69.
28. *Genryu—Sony Challenge 1946–1968*, special collection of Sony Management Newsletters, 40th anniversary edition (Tokyo: Sony, 1986), 98.

29. Ibid., 98.
30. Ibid., 98.
31. Sam Walton & John Huey, *Sam Walton: Made in America* (New York: Doubleday, 1992), 22.
32. Ibid., 29.
33. Vance Trimble, *Sam Walton* (New York: Penguin Books, 1990).
34. Ibid., 306.
35. E. E. Bauer, *Boeing in Peace and War* (Enumclaw, WA: TABA, 1991), 288.
36. John Taylor, *Storming the Magic Kingdom* (New York: Ballantine Books, 1987), 8–12.
37. Walt Disney Company Annual Report, 1992, 1.
38. "Close Encounters at Columbia Pictures," *Fortune*, 1 December 1978.
39. T. A. Heppenheimer, "How IBM Did It," *Audacity*, Winter 1994, 59.
40. Thomas J. Watson, Jr., *Father, Son, & Company* (New York: Bantam, 1990), 346–351.
41. "Anatomy of a Turnaround," *Forbes*, 1 November 1968, 28.
42. Thomas J. Watson, Jr., *Father, Son, & Company* (New York: Bantam, 1990), 16.
43. IBM 75th Anniversary, *Think*, September 1989, 23.
44. Thomas J. Watson, Jr., *Father, Son, & Company* (New York: Bantam, 1990), 28.
45. Oscar Schisgall, *Eyes on Tomorrow: The Evolution of Procter & Gamble* (New York: Doubleday, 1981), 87–98.
46. Ibid., 98.
47. Ibid., 200.
48. "Where Management Style Sets the Strategy," *Business Week*, 23 October 1978.
49. Nick Lyons, *The Sony Vision* (New York: Crown, 1976), 150.
50. Ibid., 152.
51. Harold van B. Cleveland and Thomas F. Huertas, *Citibank 1812–1970* (Cambridge, MA: Harvard Universtity Press, 1985), 32.
52. "James Stillman," *Cosmopolitan*, July 1903, 334.
53. Richard B. Miller, *Citicorp: The Story of a Bank in Crisis* (New York: McGraw-Hill, 1993), 1.
54. Harold van B. Cleveland and Thomas F. Huertas, *Citibank 1812–1970* (Cambridge, MA: Harvard Universtity Press, 1985), 89.
55. Richard B. Miller, *Citicorp: The Story of a Bank in Crisis* (New York: McGraw-Hill, 1993), 59.
56. Ibid., 80.
57. Ibid., 4.
58. Harold van B. Cleveland and Thomas F. Huertas, *Citibank 1812–1970* (Cambridge, MA: Harvard Universtity Press, 1985), 88.
59. Richard B. Miller, *Citicorp: The Story of a Bank in Crisis* (New York: McGraw-Hill, 1993), 82.
60. Harry Mark Petrakis, *The Founder's Touch* (New York: McGraw-Hill, 1965), 170–171.
61. Robert W. Galvin, *The Idea of Ideas* (Schaumburg, IL: Motorola University Press, 1991), entire booklet.

62. Ibid., 24.

63. "Motorola Gets Closer to Orbit," *Business Week*, 6 August 1993, 36.

64. "Zenith Corporation (C)," *Harvard Business School Case Study*, No. 9-674-095, Rev. 8/77, 14.

65. Paper on the General Electric revolution; paper kept confidential at request of the author.

CHAPTER 6

1. Sam Walton with John Huey, *Sam Walton: Made in America* (New York: Double-day, 1992), 223.

2. From *In Search of Excellence Video* on IBM, Tom Peters Group, Palo Alto, CA.

3. Robert Levering, Milton Moskowitz, and Michael Katz, *The 100 Best Companies to Work for in America* (New York: New American Library, 1985), 243–245.

4. "Nordstrom's Push East Will Test its Renown For the Best Service," *Wall Street Journal*, 1 August 1979, A 1.

5. "Nordstrom," Harvard Business School Case No. 9-191-002 and 1-192-027, Rev. 9/6/91.

6. "Why Rivals as Quaking as Nordstrom Heads East," *Business Week*, 15 June 1987.

7. William Davidow and Bro Utall, *Total Customer Service* (New York: Harper & Row, 1989), 91.

8. Interview transcript from discussion with Jim Nordstrom by the staff of *The Reporter*, Stanford Graduate School of Business, 1991.

9. Author interview with a Nordstrom manager, May 1993.

10. *60 Minutes*, CBS television interview, 6 May 1990.

11. Robert Levering and Milton Moskowitz, *The 100 Best Companies to Work for in America* (New York: Doubleday Currency, 1993), 327–332.

12. "The Secrets Behind Nordstrom's Service," *San Francisco Chronicle*, 24 December 1992.

13. Nordstrom orientation packet.

14. Robert Levering and Milton Moskowitz, *The 100 Best Companies to Work for in America* (New York: Doubleday Currency, 1993), 327–332.

15. "At Nordstrom Stores, Service Comes First—But at a Big Price," *Wall Street Journal*, 20 February 1990.

16. "The Other Nordstrom," *Los Angeles Times*, 4 February 1990, Business Section.

17. Ron Zemke and Dick Schaaf, *The Service Edge* (New York: New American Library, 1989), 352–355; William Davidow and Bro Utall, *Total Customer Service* (New York: Harper & Row, 1989), 86–87.

18. "Nordstrom's Push East Will Test its Renown For the Best Service," *Wall Street Journal*, 1 August 1979, A 1; William Davidow and Bro Utall, *Total Customer Service* (New York: Harper & Row, 1989), 130.

19. Author interview with a Nordstrom manager, May 1993.

20. "Nordstrom," *Harvard Business School Case* No. 9-191-002 and 1-192-027, Rev. 9/6/91.
21. Ron Zemke and Dick Schaaf, *The Service Edge* (New York: New American Library, 1989), 352–355.
22. Robert Levering, Milton Moskowitz, and Michael Katz, *The 100 Best Companies to Work for in America* (New York: New American Library, 1985), 243–245.
23. Robert Levering, Milton Moskowitz, and Michael Katz, *The 100 Best Companies to Work for in America* (New York: New American Library, 1985), 243–245.
24. *Wall Street Journal*, 20 February 1990.
25. "Nordstrom," Harvard Business School Case No. 9-191-002 and 1-192-027, Rev. 9/6/91.
26. *Wall Street Journal*, 20 February 1990.
27. Author interview with a Nordstrom manager, May 1993.
28. *Wall Street Journal*, 20 February 1990.
29. Author interview with a Nordstrom manager, May, 1993.
30. 1990 Nordstrom Annual Report, 12.
31. *Wall Street Journal*, February 20, 1990
32. 1988 Nordstrom Annual Report, 9.
33. *Wall Street Journal*, 1 August 1989.
34. Nordstrom 1988 Annual Report, 5.
35. *Wall Street Journal*, 1 August 1989.
36. Ibid.
37. The secretive nature of Nordstrom came clear from a variety of sources, including some of the articles already cited, our discussions with a Nordstrom manager, and the fact that Nordstrom was one of the few visionary companies in our research to refuse to assist us in our research efforts on the company.
38. *Wall Street Journal*, 20 February 1990.
39. Ibid.
40. Robert Levering, Milton Moskowitz, and Michael Katz, *The 100 Best Companies to Work for in America* (New York: New American Library, 1985), 243–245.
41. Ibid., 318–322.
42. "How Disney Does It," *Newsweek*, 3 April 1989.
43. We relied on the following sources in the literature on the study of cults:

- John J. Collins, *The Cult Experience: An Overview of Cults, Their Traditions, and Why People Join Them* (Springfield, IL: Thomas Books, 1991).
- Marc Galanter, M.D., *Cults and the New Religious Movements* (Washington, DC: American Psychiatric Association, 1989).
- Marc Galanter, M.D., "Cults and Zealous Self-Help Movements: A Psychiatric Perspective," *American Journal of Psychiatry*, May 1990.
- Willa Appel, *Cults in America* (New York: Holt, Rinehart, 1983).
- Robert B. Cialdini, *Influence—The New Psychology of Modern Persuasion* (New York: Quill Press, 1984).
- Susan Landa, "Children and Cults: A Practical Guide," *Journal of Family Law*, Volume 29, 1990–91.

- Literature from the International Cult Education Program, Gracie Station, NY.
- Literature from Cult Awareness Network, Chicago.

44. Thomas J. Watson, Jr., *Father, Son & Company* (New York: Bantam Books, 1990), 82.
45. Robert Sobel, *IBM: Colossus in Transition* (New York: Truman Talley Books, 1981), 58–69.
46. Robert Sobel, *IBM: Colossus in Transition* (New York: Truman Talley Books, 1981), 58–69.
47. Thomas J. Watson, Jr., *Father, Son, & Company* (New York: Bantam Books, 1990), 68.
48. Ibid., 68–71.
49. "IBM: A Special Company," special issue of *Think*, September 1989, IBM Corporation.
50. Robert Levering, Milton Moskowitz, and Michael Katz, *The 100 Best Companies to Work for in America* (New York: New American Library, 1985), 163–168.
51. Ibid.
52. Ibid., 165.
53. F. G. "Buck" Rodgers with Robert L. Shook, *The IBM Way* (New York: Harper & Row, 1986), 48.
54. Robert Sobel, *IBM: Colossus in Transition* (New York: Truman Talley Books, 1981), 59.
55. "IBM: A Special Company," special issue of *Think*, September 1989, IBM Corporation, 78–79.
56. *Training*, August 1989, 38.
57. Disney University Employee Brochure and Course Offerings.
58. Ron Zemke and Dick Schaaf, *The Service Edge* (New York: New American Library, 1989), 526–533.
59. Schickel, Richard, *The Disney Version* (New York: Simon & Schuster, 1968), 319.
60. "How Disney Does It," *Newsweek*, 3 April 1989.
61. Marc Eliot, *Walt Disney: Hollywood's Dark Prince* (New York: Birch Lane Press, 1993), 89.
62. Schickel, Richard, *The Disney Version* (New York: Simon & Schuster, 1968), 319.
63. From *In Search of Excellence Video* on Disney, Tom Peters Group, Palo Alto, CA.
64. Ibid.
65. Schickel, Richard, *The Disney Version* (New York: Simon & Schuster, 1968), 318.
66. Ron Zemke and Dick Schaaf, *The Service Edge* (New York: New American Library, 1989), 526–533.
67. *Training*, August 1989, 38.
68. From a student paper on Walt Disney, Stanford University Graduate School of Business; author name kept anonymous at her request.
69. Interview with thirteen-year Disney imagineering veteran.
70. Walt Disney Company annual reports, 1987–1992.

71. Joe Flower, *Prince of the Magic Kingdom: Michael Eisner and the Re-Making of Disney* (New York: Wiley, 1991), 3.
72. Author observation.
73. Joe Flower, *Prince of the Magic Kingdom: Michael Eisner and the Re-Making of Disney* (New York: Wiley, 1991), 3.
74. For an excellent account of Walt's relationship to his employees, see Marc Eliot, *Walt Disney: Hollywood's Dark Prince* (New York: Birch Lane Press, 1993).
75. Marc Eliot, *Walt Disney: Hollywood's Dark Prince* (New York: Birch Lane Press, 1993), 85.
76. Ibid., 89.
77. Ibid., Chapter ten and page xviii; Schickel, chapter eight.
78. Richard Schickel, *The Disney Version* (New York: Simon & Schuster, 1968), 319.
79. Robert Levering and Milton Moskowitz, *The 100 Best Companies to Work for in America* (New York: Doubleday Currency, 1993), 372–376.
80. Robert Levering, Milton Moskowitz, and Michael Katz, *The 100 Best Companies to Work for in America* (New York: New American Library, 1985), 286–290.
81. Author interviews with P&G recruits; Oscar Schisgall, *Eyes on Tomorrow: The Evolution of Procter & Gamble* (New York: Doubleday, 1981), introduction and 165.
82. Documents furnished by the Procter & Gamble Company.
83. Oscar Schisgall, *Eyes on Tomorrow: The Evolution of Procter & Gamble* (New York: Doubleday, 1981), 116.
84. Robert Levering, Milton Moskowitz, and Michael Katz, *The 100 Best Companies to Work for in America* (New York: New American Library, 1985), 288.
85. Alecia Swasy, *Soap Opera: The Inside Story of Procter & Gamble* (New York: Times Books, 1993), 21.
86. "Memorable Years in P&G History," P&G corporate publication, 17–19; Robert Levering and Milton Moskowitz, *The 100 Best Companies to Work for in America* (New York: Doubleday Currency, 1993), 375; Alecia Swasy, *Soap Opera: The Inside Story of Procter & Gamble* (New York: Times Books, 1993), 6–7.
87. "Memorable Years in P&G History," P&G corporate publication, 17–19.
88. Ibid.
89. Author interview, October 1993.
90. "The Character of Procter & Gamble," speech by John G. Smale, 7 November 1986.
91. Alecia Swasy, *Soap Opera: The Inside Story of Procter & Gamble* (New York: Times Books, 1993), chapter 1; author interviews with P&G brand managers graduated from Stanford Business School.
92. The Character of Procter & Gamble," text of speech by John G. Smale, 7 November 1986; Oscar Schisgall, *Eyes on Tomorrow: The Evolution of Procter & Gamble* (New York: Doubleday, 1981).
93. Comment from Rick Tranquilli about the "Tide Ones Operation," captured in Smale's speech, page 7.
94. "A Policy that Guided 118 Years of Steady Growth," *System—The Magazine of Business*, December 1924, 717–720.

95. "How to Be Happy Thought # 2," *Forbes*, 15 July 1976; "The Morning After," *Forbes*, 22 January 1979.
96. Sam Walton with John Huey, *Sam Walton: Made in America* (New York: Doubleday, 1992), 157.
97. See Chapter 7.
98. Paraphrased from John Nordstrom visit to Stanford Business School.

CHAPTER 7

1. Darwin, Charles, *The Origin of Species* (Buffalo, NY: Prometheus Books, 1991), 222.
2. This is more of a motto than a quote and appears in various forms throughout materials on 3M. We paraphrased this version from *Our Story So Far* (St. Paul, MN: 3M Company, 1977), 107.
3. Lawrence G. Foster, *A Company that Cares* (New Brunswick, NJ: Johnson & Johnson, 1986), 116.
4. Ibid., 32.
5. Elyse Tanouye, "Johnson & Johnson Stays Fit by Shuffling Its Mix of Businesses," *Wall Street Journal*, 22 December 1992, A1.
6. Lawrence G. Foster, *A Company that Cares* (New Brunswick, NJ: Johnson & Johnson, 1986), 82.
7. Robert O'Brian, *Marriott: The J. Willard Marriott Story* (Salt Lake City: Deseret, 1987), 182.
8. Ibid., 180–184.
9. Alden Hatch, *American Express 1850–1950: A Century of Service* (Garden City, NY: Country Life Press, 1950), chapter 6; Jon Friedman and John Meechan, *House of Cards: Inside the Troubled Empire of American Express* (New York: Putnam, 1992), chapter 3; "About American Express," company historical publication.
10. Alden Hatch, *American Express 1850–1950: A Century of Service* (Garden City, NY: Country Life Press, 1950), 93.
11. Jon Friedman and John Meechan, *House of Cards: Inside the Troubled Empire of American Express* (New York: Putnam, 1992), 52.
12. Ibid., 106.
13. "About American Express," company historical publication; Alden Hatch, *American Express 1850–1950: A Century of Service* (Garden City: Country Life Press, 1950), 96–108.
14. Alden Hatch, *American Express 1850–1950: A Century of Service* (Garden City, NY: Country Life Press, 1950), 106.
15. Author interview.
16. "How Hewlett-Packard Entered the Computer Business," Hewlett-Packard Company archives document.
17. Author interview.

18. "Riding the Electronics Boom," *Business Week*, 27 February 1960; Harry Mark Petrakis, *The Founder's Touch* (New York: McGraw-Hill, 1965), 215–218.

19. Jon Friedman and John Meechan, *House of Cards: Inside the Troubled Empire of American Express* (New York: Putnam, 1992), 53.

20. *International Directory of Corporate Histories* (Chicago: St. James Press, 1988), 395; Alden Hatch, *American Express 1850–1950: A Century of Service* (Garden City, NY: Country Life Press, 1950), 133.

21. "About American Express," company historical publication; Alden Hatch, *American Express 1850–1950: A Century of Service* (Garden City, NY: Country Life Press, 1950), chapter 11.

22. *A Company that Cares* (New Brunswick, NJ: Johnson & Johnson, 1986), 38, 116, 119.

23. Elyse Tanyoue, "Johnson & Johnson Stays Fit by Shuffling Its Mix of Businesses," *Wall Street Journal*, 22 December 1992, A1.

24. Ibid.

25. Sam Walton with John Huey, *Made in America* (New York: Doubleday, 1992), 70.

26. Darwin quote from *Origin of Species*.

27. Author interview with Wal-Mart operations executive that attended Stanford Executive Program in Organization Change.

28. Noel M. Tichy and Stratford Sherman, *Control Your Own Destiny or Someone Else Will* (New York: Doubleday, 1993), 52.

29. Virginia Huck, *Brand of the Tartan—The 3M Story* (New York: Appleton-Century-Crofts, 1955), 23.

30. Mildred Houghton Comfort, *William L. McKnight, Industrialist* (Minneapolis: T. S. Denison, 1962), chapter 5; *Our Story So Far* (St. Paul, MN: 3M Company, 1977), 60.

31. Virginia Huck, *Brand of the Tartan—The 3M Story* (New York, Appleton Century-Crofts, 1955), chapters 3–8.

32. "Product Directory 1990," 3M Corporation, 261.

33. *Our Story So Far* (St. Paul, MN: 3M Company, 1977), 58.

34. Virginia Huck, *Brand of the Tartan—The 3M Story* (New York: Appleton-Century-Crofts, 1955), chapter 12.

35. Ibid.

36. *Our Story So Far* (St. Paul, MN: 3M Company, 1977), 56–58.

37. Mildred Houghton Comfort, *William L. McKnight, Industrialist* (Minneapolis: T. S. Denison, 1962), 127.

38. From all sources on 3M, with particular emphasis on *William L. McKnight, Industrialist*, and *Our Story So Far*.

39. *Our Story So Far* (St. Paul, MN: 3M Company, 1977), 12.

40. Virginia Huck, *Brand of the Tartan—The 3M Story* (New York, Appleton-Century-Crofts, 1955), chapter 15.

41. Ibid., 134; *Our Story So Far*, 70; Comfort, 138.

42. Virginia Huck, *Brand of the Tartan—The 3M Story* (New York, Appleton-Century Crofts, 1955), 189–190.

43. *Our Story So Far* (St. Paul, MN: 3M Company, 1977), 113–115.
44. Robert Levering and Milton Moskowitz, *The 100 Best Companies to Work for in America* (New York: Doubleday Currency, 1993), 299.
45. *Our Story So Far* (St. Paul, MN; 3M Company, 1977), 93.
46. Ibid., 112.
47. P. Ranganth Nayak and John M. Ketteringham, *Break-throughs!* (New York: Rawson Associates, 1986), 55–56.
48. "Keeping the Fire Lit Under the Innovators," *Fortune*, 28 March 1988, 45; 1992 3M Annual Report, 3.
49. "Masters of Innovation," *Business Week*, 10 April 1989, 58.
50. *Our Story So Far* (St. Paul, MN: 3M Company, 1977), 5.
51. "Masters of Innovation," *Business Week*, 10 April 1989, 62.
52. *Our Story So Far* (St. Paul, MN: 3M Company, 1977), 12.
53. Ibid., 101.
54. "Masters of Innovation," *Business Week*, 10 April 1989, 60.
55. *Getting to Know Us*, 3M corporate publication.
56. Robert Levering and Milton Moskowitz, *The 100 Best Companies to Work for in America* (New York: Doubleday Currency, 1993), 299.
57. *Our Story So Far* (St. Paul, MN: 3M Company, 1977), 4.
58. Ibid., 7.
59. 1992 3M Annual Report, 3.
60. 3M Annual Report, 1989; Robert Levering and Milton Moskowitz, *The 100 Best Companies to Work for in America* (New York: Doubleday Currency, 1993), 299.
61. Virginia Huck, *Brand of the Tartan—The 3M Story* (New York, Appleton-Century-Crofts, 1955), 115–118.
62. P. Ranganth Nayak and John M. Ketteringham, *Break-throughs!* (New York: Rawson Associates, 1986), 63.
63. Ibid., 57.
64. Ibid., 54.
65. Charles W. Cheape, *Family Firm to Modern Multinational: Norton Company, A New England Enterprise* (Boston: Harvard University Press, 1985), chapter 2.
66. A phrase Tom Peters has often used to describe 3M.
67. Charles W. Cheape, *Family Firm to Modern Multinational: Norton Company, A New England Enterprise* (Boston: Harvard University Press, 1985), chapter 2.
68. Ibid., 145.
69. Ibid., 159.
70. Ibid., 145.
71. Ibid., 235.
72. Ibid., 264.
73. Ibid., 291.
74. "It's no Longer Just Grind, Grind at Norton," *Fortune*, August 1963, 120.
75. Charles W. Cheape, *Family Firm to Modern Multinational: Norton Company, A New England Enterprise* (Boston: Harvard University Press, 1985), 264.
76. Ibid., 263.
77. Paul B. Brown, "See Spot Run," *Forbes*, 10 May 1982, 140.

78. Charles W. Cheape, *Family Firm to Modern Multinational: Norton Company, A New England Enterprise* (Boston: Harvard University Press, 1985), 313.
79. P. Ranganth Nayak and John M. Ketteringham, *Break-throughs!* (New York: Rawson Associates, 1986), 72.
80. Charles W. Cheape, *Family Firm to Modern Multinational: Norton Company, A New England Enterprise* (Boston: Harvard University Press, 1985), 307.
81. P. Ranganth Nayak and John M. Ketteringham, *Break-throughs!* (New York: Rawson Associates, 1986), 65; Paul B. Brown, "See Spot Run," *Forbes*, 10 May 1982, 140.
82. Charles W. Cheape, *Family Firm to Modern Multinational: Norton Company, A New England Enterprise* (Boston: Harvard University Press, 1985), 356.
83. *Our Story So Far* (St. Paul, MN: 3M Company, 1977), 23.
84. Nick Lyons, *The Sony Vision* (New York: Crown, 1976), 147–149.
85. "The Three Year Deadline at David's Bank," *Fortune*, July 1977; author interviews.
86. Suzanna Andrews, "Deconstructing the Mind of America's Most Powerful Businessman," *Manhattan Inc.*, 1989.
87. "Things Are Adding Up Again at Burroughs," *Business Week*, 11 March 1967; "Anatomy of a Turnaround," *Forbes*, 1 November 1968; "Burroughs's Wild Ride with Computers," *Business Week*, 1 July 1972; "How Ray McDonald's Growth Theory Created IBM's Toughest Competitor," *Fortune*, January 1977.
88. "Texas Instruments Cleans up Its Act," *Business Week*, 19 September 1983.
89. Bro Uttal, "Texas Instruments Regroups," *Fortune*, 9 August 1982.
90. Thomas J. Peters and Robert H. Waterman, *In Search of Excellence* (New York: Harper & Row, 1982), 15.
91. *Our Story So Far* (St. Paul, MN: 3M Company, 1977), 7.

CHAPTER 8

1. Robert Slater, *The New GE* (Homewood, IL: Irwin, 1993), 268.
2. Robert W. Galvin, *The Idea of Ideas* (Schaumburg, IL: Motorola University Press, 1991), 51–52.
3. "A Master Class in Radical Change," *Fortune*, 13 December 1993.
4. Welch was born on November 19, 1935 (Slater, 27). He began work at GE on October 17, 1960 (Slater, 33). The board named him CEO-elect on December 19, 1980; he took office four months later (Tichy, 58).
5. Robert Slater, *The New GE* (Homewood, IL: Irwin, 1993), 24.
6. *The General Electric Story* (Schenectady, NY: Hall of History Foundation, General Electric Company, 1981), volume 4, 81; Robert Slater, *The New GE* (Homewood, IL: Irwin, 1993), 25.
7. GE under Jones grew pretax profits at an average annual rate of 14.06 percent; GE under Welch grew pretax profits at 8.49 percent. Using a combination of return on equity, return on sales, and return on assets, Jones attained an average of 17.32 percent; Welch attained 16.03 percent.

8. *The General Electric Story* (Schenectady, NY: Hall of History Foundation, General Electric Company, 1981), volume 4, 28–31.

9. Noel M. Tichy and Stratford Sherman, *Control Your Own Destiny or Someone Else Will* (New York: Doubleday, 1993), 256.

10. *The General Electric Story* (Schenectady: Hall of History Foundation, General Electric Company, 1981), volume 4, 23.

11. Noel M. Tichy and Stratford Sherman, *Control Your Own Destiny or Someone Else Will* (New York: Doubleday, 1993), 39.

12. Calculated as pretax profit divided by year-end stockholder's equity. We constructed Excel Spreadsheets dating back to 1915 using Annual Reports and Moody's financial analysis reports.

13. Calculated as the ratio of cumulative GE stock return during the CEO era divided by cumulative general market stock return or cumulative Westinghouse stock return during the GE CEO era.

14. Noel M. Tichy and Stratford Sherman, *Control Your Own Destiny or Someone Else Will* (New York: Doubleday, 1993), 42.

15. Robert Slater, *The New GE* (Homewood, IL: Irwin, 1993), chapter 4.

16. Noel M. Tichy and Stratford Sherman, *Control Your Own Destiny or Someone Else Will* (New York: Doubleday, 1993), 56–58.

17. Robert Slater, *The New GE* (Homewood, IL: Irwin, 1993), chapter 4.

18. Noel M. Tichy and Stratford Sherman, *Control Your Own Destiny or Someone Else Will* (New York: Doubleday, 1993), 44.

19. *Centennial Review*, Internal Westinghouse document, 1986.

20. Gwilym Price had been hired two years earlier to negotiate military war contracts. Succeeded Andrew Robertson. Source: *International Directory of Company Histories* (Chicago: St. James Press, 1988).

21. "Westinghouse's New Warrior," *Business Week*, 12 July 1993, 38; Westinghouse 1992 Annual Report.

22. An "outsider" is someone who had not worked inside the company prior to becoming chief executive. Companies use different official titles at different times in history: president, general manager, chief executive officer, chairman, and others. CEO is actually a relatively new term, not used extensively in business until the 1970s. We picked the person who held the de facto role of operating chief executive, regardless of the exact title. We counted CEO transitions during and after acquisitions or mergers in our tabulations.

23. Sidney M. Colgate, "A Policy that Guided 118 Years of Steady Growth," *System: The Magazine of Business*, December 1924, 717.

24. "Colgate-Palmolive-Peet," *Fortune*, April 1936, 120–144.

25. Ibid.

26. Shields T. Hardin, *The Colgate Story* (New York: Vantage Press, 1959), 71–75.

27. We calculated an average return on sales for both companies for the first three years of Pearce's tenure (1928–1930) and compared to an average return on sales for the second three years of his tenure (1931–1933).

28. Colgate's core ideology prior to Pearce is well documented in Sidney M. Colgate's "A Policy that Guided 118 Years of Steady Growth," *System: The Magazine of Business*, December 1924, 717.

29. "Colgate-Palmolive-Peet," *Fortune*, April 1936, 120–144.

30. Ibid.

31. P&G sales grew a total of 178.58 percent and Colgate sales grew at 87.52 percent during the period 1934–1943. Cumulative profit before tax for the period 1934–1943 was $285 million at P&G and $74 million at Colgate.

32. *Business Week*, 4 May 1957, 120.

33. "Colgate vs. P&G," *Forbes*, 1 February 1966.

34. "More for Lesch?" *Forbes*, 1 March 1969.

35. Hugh D. Menzies, "The Changing of the Guard," *Fortune*, 24 September 1979.

36. Ibid.

37. Oscar Schisgall, *Eyes On Tomorrow: The Evolution of Procter & Gamble* (New York: Doubleday, 1981), 76–78, 108–109.

38. "The Character of Procter & Gamble," speech by John G. Smale, 7 November 1986.

39. P&G: 'We Grow our Own Managers,' " *Dun's Review*, December 1975, 48.

40. "Neil McElroy of Procter & Gamble," *Nation's Business*, August 1970, 61.

41. Ibid.

42. Richard Hammer, "Zenith Bucks the Trend," *Fortune*, December 1960.

43. Ibid.

44. "Zenith Radio Corporation (C)," Harvard Business School Case No. 9-674-095, Rev. 8/77, 3.

45. Bob Tamarkin, "Zenith's New Hope," *Forbes*, 31 March 1980.

46. "Underpromise, Overperform," *Forbes*, 30 January 1984.

47. "Bob Galvin's Angry Campaign Against Japan," *Business Week*, 15 April 1985.

48. Robert W. Galvin, *The Idea of Ideas* (Schaumburg, IL: Motorola University Press, 1991), 63.

49. Harry Mark Petrakis, *The Founder's Touch* (New York: McGraw-Hill, 1965), chapters 17–18.

50. Robert W. Galvin, *The Idea of Ideas* (Schaumburg, IL: Motorola University Press, 1991), 45.

51. Robert W. Galvin, *The Idea of Ideas* (Schaumburg, IL: Motorola University Press, 1991), 64–65.

52. Barnaby J. Feder, "Motorola Will Be Just Fine, Thanks," *New York Times* 31 October 1993, section 3.

53. "Melville Show," *Forbes*, 1 February 1969, 22.

54. Roger Beardwood, "Melville Draws a Bead on the $50-Billion Fashion Market," *Fortune*, December 1969.

55. Wilbur H. Morrison, *Donald Douglas—A Heart With Wings* (Ames, IA: Iowa State University Press, 1991), 252.

56. "Remarkable Revival of RJR Industries," *Business Week*, 17 January 1977.

57. "When Marketing Takes Over at R.J. Reynolds," *Business Week*, 13 November 1978.

58. "The Burroughs Syndrome," *Business Week*, 12 November 1979; "A 'tough street kid' steps in at Burroughs," *Business Week*, 29 October 1979.

59. John Taylor, *Storming the Magic Kingdom* (New York: Ballantine Books, 1987), 203.

60. Author interview.
61. Vance H. Trimble, *Sam Walton* (New York: Dutton, 1990), 118.
62. "Employee Development, 1958," Internal HP document, courtesy Hewlett-Packard Company archives.

CHAPTER 9

1. George Plimpton, *The Writer's Chapbook* (New York: Viking Penguin, 1989), 31.
2. *Business Month*, December 1987, 46.
3. Robert O'Brian, *Marriott* (Salt Lake City: Deseret, 1987), 10, 11, 315.
4. Oscar Schisgall, *Eyes on Tomorrow: The Evolution of Procter & Gamble* (New York: Doubleday, 1981), chapter 1.
5. We could not find the specific date at which Colgate introduced a competing brand management process. In culling through all articles, books, and company publications, we found no specific mention of anything resembling P&G's mechanism until the 1960s.
6. Louis Galambos and Jeffrey L. Sturchio, "The Origins of an Innovative Organization: Merck & Co., Inc., 1891–1960," seminar paper delivered at Johns Hopkins University, 5 October 1992, 34–35.
7. Itzkik Goldberger, unpublished research study on Motorola, ALZA Corporation Organization Design Project, summer 1992.
8. Jill Bettner, "Underpromise, Overperform," *Forbes*, 30 January 1984.
9. Itzkik Goldberger, unpublished research study on Motorola, ALZA Corporation Organization Design Project, summer 1992.
10. Robert Slater, *The New GE* (Homewood, IL: Irwin, 1993), chapter 13.
11. Robert J. Serling, *Legend & Legacy* (New York: St. Martin's Press, 1992), 448.
12. Sam Walton with John Huey, *Made in America* (New York: Doubleday, 1992), 240 (photograph).
13. "Nordstrom," Harvard Business School Case No. 9-191-002 and 1-192-027, Rev. 9/6/91.
14. Transcript of interview with *The Reporter*, Stanford Graduate School of Business, 1991.
15. Based on author's personal experience as an H-P employee.
16. "Human Resources at Hewlett-Packard," Harvard Business School Case No. 482-125, 5.
17. Hewlett-Packard Videotape session with Bill Hewlett and Dave Packard, August–March 1980-1981. Transcript courtesy Hewlett-Packard Company archives, part 3, 3–4.
18. Ibid., 13–14.
19. Ibid., 3–4.
20. Ibid.
21. David Packard, comments at the corporate annual meeting of stockholders, 24 February 1976.

22. "On Managing HP for the Future," David Packard, contained in 18 March 1975 memo from Dave Kirby regarding "HP Executive Seminars"; courtesy Hewlett Packard Company archives.

23. "Perspectives on HP," David Packard, general manager's meeting, 17 January 1989, courtesy Hewlett Packard Company archives.

24. "The Men Who Made TI," *Fortune*, November 1961, 121.

25. "Texas Instruments Wrestles with the Consumer Market," *Fortune*, 3 December 1979.

26. "Texas Instruments: Pushing Hard into the Consumer Markets," *Business Week*, 24 August 1974; "The Great Digital Watch Shakeout," *Business Week*, 2 May 1977; "Texas Instruments Wrestles with the Consumer Market," *Fortune*, 3 December 1979; "When Marketing Failed at Texas Instruments," *Business Week*, 22 June 1981; "Texas Instruments Regroups," *Fortune*, 9 August 1982; "TI: Shot Full of Holes and Trying to Recover," *Business Week*, 5 October 1984.

27. Four cases came directly from income statement line items: Boeing, IBM, Johnson & Johnson, and Merck. Four other cases came from a variety of published sources that led us to a convincing conclusion: H-P, 3M, Motorola, and Procter & Gamble.

28. Based on financial statement analysis and a wide variety of articles on the pharmaceutical industry.

29. Itzkik Goldberger, unpublished research study on Motorola, ALZA Corporation Organization Design Project, summer 1992.

30. Ibid.

31. *Values & Visions: A Merck Century* (Rahway, NJ: Merck, 1991), 121.

32. Nancy A. Nichols, "Scientific Management at Merck," *Harvard Business Review*, January 1994.

33. Bryan Burrough and John Helyar, *Barbarians at the Gate* (New York: Harper-Perennial, 1991), chapters 2–3.

34. Schickel, Richard, *The Disney Version* (New York: Simon & Schuster, 1968), 107.

35. Bryan Burrough and John Helyar, *Barbarians at the Gate* (New York: Harper-Perennial, 1991), chapters 2–3.

36. Ibid.

37. "Where Management Style Sets the Strategy," *Business Week*, 23 October 1978.

38. "Colgate vs. P&G," *Forbes*, 1 February 1966.

39. "More for Lesch?" *Forbes*, 1 March 1969.

40. Hugh D. Menzies, "The Changing of the Guard," *Fortune*, 24 September 1979.

41. John A. Byrne, "Becalmed," *Forbes*, 20 December 1982.

42. H. John Steinbreder, "The Man Brushing Up Colgate's Image," *Fortune*, 11 May 1987.

43. Gretchen Morgenson, "Is Efficiency Enough?" *Forbes*, 18 March 1991.

44. *Business Week*, 2 July 1966, 46.

45. John Merwin, "The Sad Case of the Dwindling Orange Roofs," *Forbes*, 30 December 1985, 76.

46. "The Individual Star Performer is in Trouble," *Forbes*, 15 May 1975.

47. John Merwin, "The Sad Case of the Dwindling Orange Roofs," *Forbes*, 30 December 1985, 79.
48. Ibid., 75.
49. "HoJo's Will Repaint Its Roofs," *Business Week*, 13 December 1982, 109.
50. John Merwin, "The Sad Case of the Dwindling Orange Roofs," *Forbes*, 30 December 1985, 75.
51. "Howard Johnson Tries a Little Harder," *Business Week*, 29 September 1973, 82.
52. John Merwin, "The Sad Case of the Dwindling Orange Roofs," *Forbes*, 30 December 1985, 79.
53. S. M. Sullivan, "Money, Talent, and the Devil by the Tail," *Management Review*, January 1985, 21.
54. Ron Zemke and Dick Schaaf, *The Service Edge*, (New York: New American Library, 1989), 117–120.
55. S. M. Sullivan, "Money, Talent, and the Devil by the Tail: J. Willard Marriott," *Management Review*, January 1985.
56. "The Marriott Story," *Forbes*, 1 February 1971, 22.
57. Ibid.
58. Ron Zemke and Dick Schaaf, *The Service Edge*, (New York: New American Library, 1989), 117–120; company documents.
59. In the February 1971 *Forbes* article, Marriott claimed to be spending $1 million per year on management development. 1970 pretax profits were just under $20 million.
60. "The Marriott Story," *Forbes*, 1 February 1971, 23.
61. *Success*, October, 1989, 10.
62. "Ames Has a Plan," *Discount Merchandiser*, July 1991, 10
63. Harvard Business School Case No. 9-384-024, 12.

CHAPTER 10

1. Speech given November 10, 1942.
2. Robert L. Shook, *Turnaround: The New Ford Motor Company* (New York: Prentice-Hall, 1990), 131.
3. Ibid., 99–100
4. Ibid., 90, 193.
5. Ibid., 207.
6. Ibid., 123.
7. Ibid. 136.
8. Ibid., chapter 6.
9. Ibid., chapter 7.
10. Welcoming address by George W. Merck at dedication of the Merck Research Laboratory, 25 April 1933, courtesy Merck & Co. archives.
11. Goal clearly evident in early 1930s. The quote comes from George Merck speech, 22 April 1935, courtesy Merck & Co. archives.

12. Laboratories created in the 1930s. Quote from George W. Merck talk at the Medical College of Virginia, 1 December 1950, courtesy Merck & Co. archives.

13. *Values and Visions: A Merck Century* (Rahway, NJ: Merck, 1991), 23.

14. Louis Galambos and Jeffrey L. Sturchio, "The Origins of an Innovative Organization: Merck & Co., Inc., 1891–1960," 19, 27.

15. Many references to this throughout internal and external documents. Although we could not confirm the actual date of this practice, we believe it dates back at least to the 1960s, perhaps earlier.

16. "Profiles: Scientists in Basic Biology and Chemistry, Merck Sharp & Dohme Research Laboratories," courtesy Merck & Co. archives.

17. Welcoming address by George W. Merck at dedication of the Merck Research Laboratory, 25 April 1933, courtesy Merck & Co., archives; *Values & Visions: A Merck Century* (Rahway, NJ: Merck, 1991); Louis Galambos and Jeffrey L. Sturchio, "The Origins of an Innovative Organization: Merck & Co., Inc., 1891–1960.

18. Welcoming address by George W. Merck at dedication of the Merck Research Laboratory, 25 April 1933, courtesy Merck & Co., archives.

19. Quote from Vagelos, *MIT Management*, Fall 1988; almost identical to a comment he made during a visit to Stanford Business School faculty in 1990.

20. We're not exactly sure when this practice began. It might have been much earlier than the 1970s. Quote from "The Miracle Company," *Business Week*, 19 October 1987.

21. "Merck Has Made Biotech Work," *Fortune* reprint from 1987 article.

22. *Business Week*, 19 October 1987, 87.

23. Goal clearly evident in early 1930s. The quote comes from George Merck speech, 22 April 1935, courtesy Merck & Co. archives.

24. *Values & Visions: A Merck Century* (Rahway, NJ: Merck, 1991), 29.

25. *Forbes*, 26 November 1979.

26. *Wall Street Journal*, 23 June 1989.

27. Nancy A. Nichols, "Scientific Management at Merck," *Harvard Business Review*, January 1994, 90–91.

28. *Values & Visions: A Merck Century* (Rahway, NJ: Merck, 1991), 51.

29. Ibid., 41.

30. Ibid., 51.

31. Ibid.

32. Nancy A. Nichols, "Scientific Management at Merck," *Harvard Business Review*, January 1994, 89.

33. David Bollier and Kirk O. Hansen, Merck & Co. (A–D), Business Enterprise Trust Case No. 90-013.

34. Ibid.

35. *Values & Visions: A Merck Century* (Rahway, NJ: Merck, 1991), 168.

36. Again, not clear when the practice began exactly. We, as faculty at Stanford, have had to write some of these recommendations; they are unlike any other we've found in industry.

37. Many references to this throughout internal and external documents. The turnover rate comes from *Merck World*, July 1989.

38. Author interview.

39. David Packard memo to employees from "Watt's Current," November 1961, courtesy Hewlett-Packard Company archives.

40. Letter to IEEE Awards Board, 23 May 1972, courtesy Hewlett-Packard Company archives.

41. Courtesy Hewlett-Packard Company archives.

42. Documents courtesy Hewlett-Packard Company archives; quote from Packard on 22 March 1982.

43. Memo to HP employees that went with HP prospectus in 1957.

44. Speech by David Packard on 25 March 1982. Confirmed by other documents, courtesy Hewlett-Packard Company archives.

45. Began as a outgrowth of the 1945 layoffs at the end of World War II.

46. First articulated during the transfer of the Oscilloscope Division from Palo Alto to Colorado Springs in 1964, courtesy Hewlett-Packard Company archives.

47. HP implemented this with the recession in the early 1970s.

48. Packard speech, 25 March 1982, courtesy Hewlett-Packard Company archives.

49. Based on author interview with Bill Hewlett, 1991.

50. Letter to IEEE Awards Board, 23 May 1972, courtesy Hewlett-Packard Company archives.

51. Speech by Bill Hewlett, 1956, courtesy Hewlett-Packard Company archives.

52. Personal author experience.

53. Speech by David Packard, 23 September 1964, courtesy Hewlett-Packard Company archives; "Turning R&D Into Real Products," *Fortune*, 2 July 1990.

54. Runs throughout H-P's history. Quote from Bill Hewlett, 20 April 1977, courtesy Hewlett-Packard Company archives.

55. Direct author experience.

56. Runs throughout HP's history. Quote from Bill Hewlett, 20 April 1977, courtesy Hewlett Packard Company archives.

57. Speech by David Packard, 23 September 1964, courtesy Hewlett-Packard Company archives.

58. Courtesy Hewlett-Packard Company archives.

59. Ibid.

60. Speech by David Packard, 8 October 1959, and description by David Packard on 19 September 1963, courtesy Hewlett-Packard Company archives.

61. Runs throughout HP's history. Quote from Bill Hewlett, 20 April 1977, courtesy Hewlett-Packard Company archives.

62. Bill Hewlett, 20 April 1977, courtesy Hewlett-Packard Company archives.

63. "Human Resources at Hewlett-Packard," Harvard Business School Case No. 482-125, 5.

64. Karl Schwarz, HP general manager, "HP Grenoble, a Case Study in Technology Transfer," May 1988, courtesy Hewlett-Packard Company archives.

65. From HP video transcripts of Bill Hewlett and David Packard, 1980–1981, courtesy Hewlett-Packard Company archives.

66. Based on David Packard's remarks at the beginning of new management training program on 17 March 1985, courtesy Hewlett-Packard Company archives.
67. Author interview with John Young, 1992.
68. Speech by Dave Packard, 1974, courtesy Hewlett-Packard Company archives.
69. First published versions appear around 1958. Quote from Packard on 25 March 1982, courtesy Hewlett-Packard Company archives.
70. Quote from interview with David Packard, 20 August 1981. Other sources indicate that the program began in the early 1960s, courtesy Hewlett-Packard Company archives.
71. Author interview with Bill Hewlett, 1990.
72. Letter to IEEE Awards Board, 23 May 1972, courtesy Hewlett-Packard Company archives.

INDEX